AND YOU
WELCOMED ME

AND YOU WELCOMED ME

*A Sourcebook on Hospitality
in Early Christianity*

Amy G. Oden
Editor

ABINGDON PRESS
Nashville

AND YOU WELCOMED ME:
A Sourcebook on Hospitality in Early Christianity

Copyright © 2001 by Abingdon Press

This book is printed on recycled, acid-free, elemental-chlorine–free paper.

Library of Congress Cataloging in Publication Data

And you welcomed me : a sourcebook on hospitality in early Christianity / Amy G. Oden, editor.
    p. cm.
    Includes bibliographical references.
    ISBN 0-687-09671-5 (alk. paper)
    1. Hospitality—Religious aspects—Christianity—History—Sources. I. Oden, Amy, 1958-

    BV4647.H67 A53 2001
    241'.671—dc21

                                                                    2001041244

All Scripture quotations, unless otherwise noted, are taken from the *New Revised Standard Version of the Bible*, copyright 1989, Division of Christian Education of the National Council of the Churches of Christ in the United States of America. Used by permission. All rights reserved.

Scriptures marked (RSV) are from the *Revised Standard Version of the Bible*, copyright 1946, 1952, 1971 by the Division of Christian Education of the National Council of the Churches of Christ in the United States of America. Used by permission. All rights reserved.

The Appendix, pp. 298-303, may be reproduced for educational purposes.

(Credits continued on page 6)

01 02 03 04 05 06 07 08 09 10 — 10 9 8 7 6 5 4 3 2 1

MANUFACTURED IN THE UNITED STATES OF AMERICA

To Tal and Jane Oden
Altus, Oklahoma
and
Oasis: Maggie Ball, Kathy Leithner,
Kathy McCallie, Susan Ross, and Helen Taylor

CONTENTS

ACKNOWLEDGMENTS

The research for this book has been conducted in a context of hospitality. I am grateful to Oklahoma City University for granting a sabbatical year to read and research ancient writings. Particular thanks go to my colleagues in the Wimberly School of Religion, Linda Herndon, Donna Dykes, John Starkey, A. W. Martin, Jr., Don Emler and our work-study student, Kyle Kiner. In addition, the Dulaney Browne Library provided extensive support, especially through the efforts of Christine Chen and Joyce Peterson in the Inter-Library Loan Office.

I am deeply grateful to those whose conversations have clarified my thoughts on ancient texts and hospitality, who have read drafts of this work, and who have lived hospitality with me: Kathy Leithner, Susan Ross, Helen Taylor, Kathy McCallie, Maggie Ball, Jim Brandt, Heidi Peterson, Bob Gardenhire III, Perry Williams, David Wiggs, Jeni Markham Clewell, Jerry Thompson, Rick Kyte, Beth Newman, Scott Moore, Carol Cook, Susan S. Vogel and Thomas C. Oden.

For their help and support during the demands of a sabbatical year I thank my parents, Tal and Jane Oden, and my husband's parents, Jesse and Jackie Lindley. Their thoughtful care made it considerably more manageable.

My husband, Steve Lindley, and son, Walker Oden Lindley, have been joyful companions on this journey, tolerant of its twists and turns. Their love and care made it possible for me to conduct this research at home. Thank you.

PREFACE

This book presents a collection of early Christian texts regarding hospitality and its practice. The range of excerpts both in time and space shows just how central a role hospitality played in Christian life throughout the early centuries. One encounters it at every turn, under every rock, around every corner. Still, the reader should be warned that this book is not a set of instructions for hospitality. This book will not give do's and don'ts nor will it offer a blueprint of how to be hospitable. While the word "hospitality" will not even be found in many of the excerpts, hospitality is nonetheless powerfully present in these words. It is often the subtext, the context, the background that allows a story to be told. There is not so much explicit reflection by these early Christians on the idea of hospitality as there is tacit expectation and practice of hospitality. Hospitality is not an object to be had. Rather, we breathe it in deeply when we partake of these early Christian stories. As we fill our lungs with it, we come to know hospitality in early Christian communities.

The riches these texts yield are deep and wide and are offered to all. This book is intended primarily for a wide audience of students and practitioners within the Christian community. Among students, I hope it will be useful to undergraduates and graduates alike. But it is intended also for laity and clergy, particularly those interested in spirituality or the common life, and secondarily for scholars of religion. It delights me to introduce these ancient voices to such a broad audience and to encourage our conversations with them.

I have kept endnotes to a minimum in order to keep the focus on the primary literature. The short bibliography will give some pointers on how to pursue the subject of hospitality, and the appendix encourages reflection on the practice of it in our own communities.

The reader will note a decidedly communal tone to the writing in this book. "We" and "us" may be found more frequently than is customary in academic publishing. It is important to acknowledge, perhaps especially in a book on hospitality, that I speak from within the Christian tradition. Even as I listen to these voices, I dwell with them in the Christian tradition. As one with an abiding appreciation for the Christian tradition, I call other Christians to engage it critically and substantively. I am convinced that current conversations among Christians about hospitality can be furthered and more deeply rooted by listening to our own tradition.

We have much to learn. Welcome to the table.

Amy G. Oden
Feast of Cosman and Damianos
Oklahoma City

CHAPTER ONE

HOSPITALITY AND THE EARLY CHRISTIAN WORLD

They had come to listen. Time had gotten on, and the people were hungry. Rather than sending them away, five fish and two loaves were passed around. Everyone ate. All were filled. There was food left over to fill twelve baskets.

In the oft retold story of the feeding of the five thousand, there is no mention of the term hospitality, but it is amply evident. Jesus and his disciples become hosts to the thousands crowding around for a look or a touch or a word. As makeshift hosts they offer hospitality to these strangers with whatever they have on hand, and, in the end, receive more food in the twelve baskets of leftovers than they started out with.

The Christian tradition has much to say about hospitality, and among Christians today there is renewed interest in hospitality as a virtue and a practice within the Christian life. Conversations, scholarship, and conferences on hospitality in the last few years have brought attention to the ways a developed notion of hospitality might contribute to Christian community and identity, as well as to mission, spiritual growth, and even contemporary worship.[1]

As the conversation broadens, it is important to bring historical voices to the table, listening to how our ancestors learned and lived hospitality. Like grandparents, aunts, and uncles at a family reunion, these voices remind us of who we are as the Christian family, what we have lived, and how God has moved among us. This collection contributes to the conversation, garnering the wealth and wisdom of early Christian voices on hospitality.

What Is Hospitality?[2]

At the very least, hospitality is the welcoming of the stranger (*hospes*).[3] While hospitality can include acts of welcoming family

and friends, its meaning within the Christian biblical and historical traditions has focused on receiving the alien and extending
one's resources to them. Hospitality responds to the physical,
social, and spiritual needs of the stranger, though, as we shall see,
those of the host are addressed as well. Early Christian texts pay
attention to each of these areas.

On the face of it, hospitality begins with basic physical needs of
food and shelter, most powerfully symbolized in table fellowship,
sharing food and drink at a common table. Sharing food together
enables more than getting nourishment. Eating together is symbolic of partaking of life itself.[4] Jesus' own table fellowship with
sinners and socially marginal people witnesses to the power of the
hospitality of the realm of God.

Hospitality might entail meeting physical needs beyond food,
such as a foot washing or bath, medical treatment, shelter, clothing, supplies for the journey, and even care of animals. Jesus' final
meal with the disciples (Matthew 26:17-30; Luke 22:14-28; Mark
14:12-25) illustrates several of the material features of hospitality,
namely, washing feet, a servant host, food and drink.

Hospitality includes meeting social as well as physical needs.
An important component of hospitality is helping the outsider or
the poor feel welcome, which at times requires more than food and
drink—a recasting of social relations. Including the other in one's
circle of friends or business associates, sponsoring an outsider,
welcoming a servant, or mentoring an apprentice can be acts of
social hospitality. Acts of inclusion and respect, however small, can
powerfully reframe social relations and engender welcome.

Finally, hospitality encompasses spiritual needs. Prayer features
in early Christian texts about hospitality as an acknowledgment of
common dependence of both host and guest on God for everything. Prayers of healing and safe travel are frequent, as are
prayers of gratitude. Sometimes hospitality means including the
stranger in worship, Eucharist, or other liturgical acts. Hosts also
attend to the spiritual needs of guests through listening to their
stories or receiving them into the larger community.

Taken as a feature of Christian life, hospitality is not so much a
singular act of welcome as it is a way, an orientation that attends
to otherness, listening and learning, valuing and honoring. The

hospitable one looks for God's redemptive presence in the other, confident it is there, if one only has eyes to see and ears to hear. Hospitality, then, is always a spiritual discipline of opening one's own life to God's life and revelation.

Hospitality as a Moral Category

For all this, the word "hospitality" has lost its moral punch over recent centuries. Reduced to connoting refreshments at meetings or magazine covers of gracious living,[5] the moral landscape in which it resides has all but faded into the background. Yet it is this moral and spiritual landscape that early Christian voices can help us recover.[6]

Hospitality is characterized by a particular moral stance in the world that can best be described as readiness. Early Christian voices tell us again and again that whether we are guest or host we must be ready, ready to welcome, ready to enter another's world, ready to be vulnerable. This readiness is expectant. It may be akin to moral nerve. It exudes trust, not so much that one will succeed in some measurable way, but that participation in hospitality is participation in the life of God. Such readiness takes courage, gratitude, and radical openness. This moral orientation to life relinquishes to God both the practice of hospitality and its consequences. At the same time, the readiness that opens into hospitality also leads to repentance.

For those who participate in hospitality, a "de-centering of perspective" occurs.[7] In the experience of hospitality both the host and the guest encounter something new, approaching the edge of the unfamiliar and crossing it. Hospitality shifts the frame of reference from self to other to relationship. This shift invariably leads to repentance, for one sees the degree to which one's own view has become the only view. The sense one has of being at home and of familiarity with the way things are is shaken up by the reframing of reference to the other, and then to relationship. One can then not be "at home" in quite the same way. When we realize how we have inflated our own frame of reference and imposed it on all of reality, we know we have committed the sin of idolatry, of taking our own particular part and making it the whole.

This de-centering and reframing that accompanies hospitality is the very movement the New Testament calls *metanoia*, or turning, usually translated "repentance." This turning and repentance occurs not only in the interior landscape of the individual, but also in the exterior landscape of the community. As communities become more hospitable they experience a de-centering of perspective, too: they become more aware of the structural inequalities that exist in and around them and repent.[8]

While we may look at hospitable practices of early Christians and see them as nothing more than good deeds, hospitality was not simply a matter of private virtue. It was embedded in community and a sign of God's presence in that community, and so was an embodiment of a biblical ethic. Both the Old and New Testaments identify a duty of hospitality (Genesis 18:4, 19:7, Judges 19:20, Matthew 10:40-41, Romans 12:13). Abraham in particular is identified as embodying hospitality when he receives the strangers under the oaks of Mamre (Genesis 18:1-15), the benefits of which extend far beyond himself. Through "entertaining angels unawares" the creation of God's people begins as the birth of Isaac is promised to Sarah. The New Testament continues this theme through the frequent references to the breaking of the bread which symbolizes the presence of sacred community.[9] While texts usually focus on a particular host and a particular guest, there is almost always a larger communal context for hospitality that orients and undergirds it.

One wonders whether early Christians would have offered hospitality to the vulnerable without these injunctions to reach out to these groups. Turning attentions to vulnerable populations entails risk. It exposes one to the possibility of illness, injury, theft, or disgrace. What incentive would anyone have to extend hospitality when little reward could be expected and danger was likely? It is precisely this circumstance that makes a population vulnerable. But we shall see that it is not the requirement to do good that moves early Christians to practice hospitality, though that must surely play a part. Rather, it is the location of hospitality within a larger spiritual economy, the *oikos* or household of God, that provides the rationale for hospitality.

Precedents for Hospitality in the Ancient World

Christians were not unique in the ancient world either in the practice of or the value they placed on hospitality. Hospitality was valued to varying degrees across most cultures. The ancient cultures from which Christianity drew most heavily, Hebrew, Greek, and Roman, all valued hospitality highly. These cultural precedents should briefly be noted.

Hebrew Precedents

Ancient Hebrews understood themselves to be outsiders in Pharaoh's Egypt, wanderers in the wilderness, and settlers in the Promised Land. Their corporate identity was deeply rooted in a sense of being strangers, even though they also understood themselves to be God's chosen people.[10] It is no surprise, then, that Mosaic law speaks to the proper attitude to "strangers and sojourners among us," providing inclusion in the community and specific protections as well. For example, the requirement to rest on the Sabbath specifically includes slaves and resident aliens (Exodus 20:10; 23:12; Deuteronomy 5:14-15). Further, the Torah prohibits the abuse or exploitation of aliens, the poor, widows and orphans (Exodus 22:21; 23:9; Deuteronomy 24:14-15).

This awareness in Hebrew culture of the vulnerability of strangers has precedents in Egyptian culture and law. The teachings of Amen-em-ope, an Egyptian who taught between 1250 and 1000 B.C.E., includes the following:

> Do not steal from the poor,
>   Do not cheat the cripple.
> Do not abuse the elderly,
>   Do not refuse to let the aged speak.[11]

The Hebrew prophets follow suit, listing the poor, the sick, the aged, and the widow together as protected classes.

Hospitality in Hebrew culture, however, is more than negative commands to avoid harming certain groups. Hospitality is positively expressed through stories of welcome told in the Old Testament. Abraham and Sarah welcome the strangers under the oaks of Mamre (Genesis 18:19). Rahab welcomes and protects the stranger spies from Joshua's army (Joshua 2). The widow of Zarephath gives her all to the stranger prophet, Elijah (1 Kings 17:8-24). In all of these stories, hospitality centers in the household and the sharing of its resources with strangers. All of these acts of hospitality play a role in furthering God's movement in creating and redeeming God's people.

Greek and Roman Precedents

Ancient Greek culture had a well-developed notion of hospitality and its obligations.[12] Because wayfarers were considered helpless and therefore under the special protection of Zeus, ancient Greeks considered hospitality a basic feature of a civilized people which distinguished them from more primitive cultures that succumbed to xenophobia, or fear of strangers.[13] The sense that strangers warranted protection is found frequently in the most ancient Greek literature. Not only do humans seek and receive welcome, but often gods in disguise do, as well. This theme of divine visitation, or *theoxenia,* can be found throughout Greek literature.[14]

So also in Roman culture, hospitality is prized as a virtue of civilization and a privilege of patrons. Early in Roman society, perhaps as soon as 399 B.C.E., hospitality to strangers was simply obedience to divine will. Both Cicero and Ovid cite the sacred duty of hospitality. The *jus hospitii,* or law of hospitality, regulated seven different categories of relationship and the hospitality properly accorded in each case.[15]

New Testament Passages

The Christian New Testament, written in Greek, reflects all of these influences with regard to hospitality. First-century Judaism incorporated hospitality especially into the institutions of the Sabbath and the synagogue.[16] The Gospels portray Jesus' notion of hospitality most vividly in Matthew 25 and Luke 14. In Matthew 25, Jesus tells of the great day of reckoning, in which those who have been hospitable to the least are welcomed into the Kingdom. Jesus identifies hospitality to these with hospitality to himself:

> "Come, you that are blessed by my Father, inherit the Kingdom prepared for you from the foundation of the world; for I was hungry and you gave me food, I was thirsty and you gave me something to drink,

I was a stranger and you welcomed me, I was naked and you gave me clothing, I was sick and you took care of me, I was in prison and you visited me." Then the righteous will answer him, "Lord, when was it that we saw you hungry and gave you food, or thirsty and gave you something to drink? And when was it that we saw you a stranger and welcomed you, or naked and gave you clothing? And when was it that we saw you sick or in prison and visited you?" And the king will answer them, "Truly I tell you, just as you did it to one of the least of these who are members of my family, you did it to me."[17]

We shall see that receiving the "least of these" is a recurrent theme throughout early Christian literature on hospitality.

Similarly, in Luke, Jesus recasts the conventional notions of hospitality in his instructions about who is to be welcomed when one gives a banquet.[18] God's household does not rest on the usual family and social ties that reinforced status and brought mutual benefit. Instead, God's household extends much further:

When you give a dinner or a banquet, do not invite your friends or your brothers or your kinsmen or rich neighbors, lest they also invite you in return, and you be repaid. But when you give a feast, invite the poor, the maimed, the lame, the blind, and you will be blessed, because they cannot repay you. You will be repaid at the resurrection of the just.[19]

It is significant that, in the last days of his life, Jesus proclaims the new covenant while gathered together with friends to share the Passover meal. In fact, the food and drink are themselves the signs of the new covenant (Matthew 26:28, Mark 14:24; Luke 22:20; John 6:51). Jesus' presence in the bread and the wine signals the hospitality of Christ himself welcoming all who would come into the table fellowship of the Kingdom. This correlation of incarnated presence with hospitality will be made explicitly in early Christian texts.

Warrants for Hospitality

The Vulnerable

If hospitality is welcoming the stranger, this begs the question: who is the stranger? In this collection of early Christian texts, descriptions of hospitality and its constituents cover quite a scope. Early Christians talk about hospitality to the sick and injured, to the widow and orphan, to the sojourner and stranger, to the aged, to the slave and imprisoned, to the poor and hungry. At times it seems there is no class of people not included within the scope of hospitality. Perhaps that is as it should be, for there are many ways to construe otherness, in terms of health, economic class, family relations, nationality, age, or social status.

If we look closely at the specific categories of people who warrant hospitality in these texts, we will see that they have one thing in common: they are all vulnerable populations. They exist on the margins, both socially and economically. They can easily be ignored and seldom bring status or financial gain to those who reach out to them.

Early Christians, along with many other ancient cultures, often group these different vulnerable populations together when enumerating their moral obligations. Jesus himself proclaims his mission to bring good news to the poor, the captives, the blind, and the oppressed, appealing to Isaiah (Isaiah 61:1-2; Luke 4:18-19). Similar lists occur in writings from early Christian communities trying to determine how to live out the gospel. For example, a letter attributed to Clement of Rome commands Christians to visit the sick, the orphans and widows, the poor, the hungry, and those harassed by evil spirits. Similarly, a text reminding Christians to honor the image of God in every person lists the hungry, thirsty, naked, the stranger, and the prisoner, groups of people whose *imago dei* might not typically be presumed.[20] Their mutual vulnerability is recognized following Christ's pattern in Matthew 25:37-40 where the same list of groups constitutes the "least of these who are members of my family."

What follows is a brief look at the vulnerability of each of these populations in the ancient world, roughly the first five centuries of Christianity, with occasional excerpts that provide the warrant for hospitality.

The Sick

There were many sources of illness in the ancient world, particularly in places where clean water and sanitary living conditions were minimal. Contagion could spread quickly and mysteriously. Chronic conditions and disability could weaken health and make one more vulnerable to disease.

While home remedies were practiced widely, only the well-off had access to professional medical care. Even if one could afford it, such medical care might not have been available. For example, the second-century Roman emperor Antoninus Pius ruled that major cities could have no more than ten physicians, while provincial cities could have seven.[21] Outlying areas were not likely to have any. Serious illness could easily become chronic for workers who could not afford time off for rest or recovery.

Injury could also lead to lifelong illness or disability. Broken bones not set or fully healed could leave the injured with permanent deformities that prevented gainful employment. Moreover, sickness or disability could connote evil spirits or moral perversity that estranged one from the community that might otherwise offer resources.

To be sick in the ancient world was a dangerous and oftentimes stigmatizing state. The sick, maimed, or disabled were at a decided disadvantage in cultures that found such conditions mysterious at best and divine punishment at worst. This Egyptian teaching from the thirteenth century B.C.E. recognizes the vulnerability of these groups to exploitation and ridicule:

> Do not make fun of the blind,
>> Do not tease the dwarf,
>> Do not trip the lame.
> Do not tease the insane,
>> Do not lose patience with them when they are wrong.[22]

These injunctions attempt to protect the sick or disabled.

The Poor

The poor were extremely vulnerable in an economy based on social and familial relations.[23] One could expect to remain in the socioeconomic class to which one was born, as social mobility was extremely rare and limited. Any movement up the ladder depended entirely on the goodwill of someone higher up. The poor seldom enjoyed such relationships. A pervasive presence in early Christian texts, the poor were often without refuge of any kind, living on the mercies of those with resources.[24] The chronically and terminally ill and the permanently disabled made up many of the ranks of the poor. While we cannot know the numbers of poor, early Christian texts assure us that there were those who were destitute, such as beggars and those living on the streets of cities.[25] Gregory of Nyssa describes the destitute in his sermon, *As You Did It To One of These*:

> Why do you not allow yourself to be moved to show mercy? You see men wandering about as swine in search of food with torn rags for clothing; they have staffs in hand, one for a weapon and another for a support which they do not grasp by the fingers but bind to their hands with a rod. Their pouches are ripped and the lump of bread they possess is thoroughly rotten. Their hearth, home, mattress, bed, possessions, table and all their other belongings are inadequate. Should you not, then, take their plight into consideration? [26]

Besides the destitute, this category might also include the working poor. Chronic hunger was a fact of life in much of the ancient world.[27] Those who worked the land or practiced a trade were vulnerable to the fortunes of weather and politics. A drought, an infestation of pests, disease, or a conquering enemy could push the working poor over the edge of poverty to hunger. Malnourishment, in turn, led to illness which prohibited employment and the spiral continued downward.

Interestingly, almsgiving and hospitality are frequently associated in early Christianity as these excerpts will show.[28] The state of being poor and vulnerable intersects with the Christian duty to show hospitality. While we usually think of giving alms as an act of mercy, early Christians often rank it among the acts of hospitality.

Travelers and Pilgrims

The vulnerability of strangers traveling far from home can hardly be overestimated.[29] Without social, ethnic or familial ties to protect them, travelers were easy targets for exploitation and violence. Xenophobia put them under a veil of suspicion. Someone traveling far from home must have left for a reason and is presumed guilty of something, whether debt, murder, or dishonor. Sojourners might not know the local customs, currency, language, or dialect, making it difficult to find accommodations, establish fair prices for goods and services, or even get a fair rate of exchange. Away from the protection of family, who would miss them if they disappeared or who would speak up for them if they were victims of injustice?

Travelers were prey to natural calamities, as well. The author of *The Lives of the Desert Fathers,* a chronicle of visits with several desert fathers, warns that travel in the desert is particularly dangerous.

> This place is a waste land lying at a distance of a day's and a night's journey from Nitria through the desert. It is a very perilous journey for travelers. For if one makes even a small error, one can get lost in the desert and find one's life in danger.[30]

At the end of the chronicle, there is an explanation of why these sojourners did not visit even more desert holy men. The hardships of the travelers are listed as attacks by brigands, hunger and thirst, marshy ground, lacerated feet, sinking in a swamp, wading through a rising river, being chased by robbers, a capsized boat, running aground, exposure to rain and hail, and, last, but not least, crocodiles.[31]

Pilgrims were a special group of travelers that warranted hospitality. This tradition extends back at least to ancient Greek pilgrimage to oracles and healing shrines. Pilgrims in ancient Greece were understood to be sacred and inviolable.[32] While Christians were seeking out holy places as early as the third century, Christian pilgrimage emerges as a widespread pattern in the late fourth and fifth centuries. Pilgrims were sometimes less vulnerable than other travelers if they were recognized as being on a holy errand. Their pilgrimage gave them a certain status in the world of the late Roman Empire. Still, embarking on a pilgrimage entailed the risk of traveling far from home and being at the mercy of strangers along the way.[33] At the Council of Chalcedon in 451, canon 11 set out the use of letters to authorize hospitality to travelers. A commendatory or canonical letter, usually shown by presbyters and other clergy, verified that one was doctrinally orthodox and under no suspicion. A pacifical letter, or letter of peace, showed that the traveler was of good reputation and that the journey was legitimately authorized. Therefore, one deserved hospitality, especially if one was poor. The canon read as follows:

> We have decreed that the poor and those needing assistance shall travel, after examination, with letters merely pacifical from the church, and not with letters commendatory, inasmuch as letters commendatory ought to be given only to persons who are open to suspicion.[34]

Widows and Orphans

Without a clear place within patriarchal family structure as the wife or child of a man within the community, a person could lose all consideration. Vulnerable not only to exposure and starvation but also to sexual predation, widows and orphans were to be hospitably taken in and cared for. Further, they were to be taken seriously in the law courts and in other civil and financial matters, for they had no one to press their case for them. Even before Mosaic law required special care for them, ancient Mesopotamian and Egyptian texts enjoined such attention. From Egypt, the story of "A Farmer and the Courts During the Middle Kingdom," which takes place in the period 2258–2052 B.C.E., shows the farmer extolling the justice of the judge:

> When you sail the Lake of Justice
> Fairness fills your sail.
> You father the orphan,
> You husband the widow.
> You brother the divorced,
> You mother the motherless.
> I will extol your name throughout the land,
> I will proclaim you a just judge.[35]

Of course, Hebrew writings continue this injunction through both the Law and the Prophets. Deuteronomy 10:17-18 explicitly states God's concern for this special class:

> For the Lord your God is God of gods and Lord of lords, the great God, mighty and awesome, who is not partial and takes no bribe,

who executes justice for the orphan and the widow, and who loves the strangers, providing them food and clothing.[36]

Similarly, the prophet Isaiah (1:17) lifts up the widow and orphan for special protection and care.

> Cease to do evil,
>   learn to do good;
> seek justice,
>   rescue the oppressed,
> defend the orphan,
>   plead for the widow.[37]

In the Roman Empire, widows under the age of fifty were required by law to remarry within a year or face penalties. However, Christianity promoted widowhood as a model life of chastity. By the fourth century, Christian rulers abolished laws that required widows to remarry. Instead, the widow was praised as an *univira*, a woman who only married once. However, such women had to be maintained by some head of household, or by the charity of others.[38]

Slaves and Prisoners

Early Christians refer to "the captive," "those in bonds," "prisoners," and "slaves" as vulnerable people in need of hospitality. While in modern culture "prisoners" usually refers to the incarcerated, in the ancient world the category included several groups. First, prisoners were people, both military and civilian, who had been conquered in war and taken prisoner by the victorious army. They were then considered property of the state and could be sold, enslaved, or held for ransom, a solid source of revenue for a state treasury depleted from war. Such prisoners' lives were forfeit as they no longer had possession even of their own persons. Several texts tell of efforts to ransom Christians taken in war.[39]

Second, prisoners could refer to criminals taken into state custody awaiting punishment. Most ancient cultures did not warehouse criminals in prisons for years at a time. Criminals were either executed, sentenced to slave labor for the state or, less frequently, fined, and returned to public life. Members of society who violate the law are, in a sense, strangers to the law and those who abide by it. Prisoners were often physically marked in some way, so that they carried their criminal records on their bodies and would be prevented from ever fully enjoying the benefits of society.

"Captive" can also refer to slaves, a clearly defined class of people in the ancient world, whose place in society was highly circumscribed. Slaves were very often slaves from birth, although one could also put oneself in bondage in order to pay a debt. There can be no doubt that slaves were the economic base of society throughout most of the empire. They ran households, the mines, all aspects of farming and production, and made up a significant portion of civil servants in the government. None of these texts promotes abolishing slavery or reforming the place of slavery as an institution in the early Christian world.

Hosts

Just as we must ask who the stranger is, we must also ask who the host is. On the face of it, we might think of the host as the moral agent here, the one who acts for, or on behalf of, the other.[40] There is no doubt that hosts have resources, whether it is food, shelter or connections. By definition, a host makes those resources available to the stranger/guest. However, the host also receives by participating in the economy of hospitality whereby God's grace gifts both host and guest. On the one hand, the host has resources. On the other hand, the host identifies with the stranger/guest and chooses not to live out of any privilege those resources offer, but rather to understand himself or herself as a recipient, too.

In addition, the identification of host and guest with one another creates a dynamic tension among having, giving, and receiving. The inevitable asymmetry of relationship between host and guest does not prevent due honor and respect. Hospitality requires that the host recognize both the need and the full humanity of the stranger. There is a respectful balance in successful hospitality that neither denigrates the guest's neediness nor denies it. The other is fully honored as a child of God, while at the same time, genuine needs are addressed.

It is common for readers to identify almost automatically with the host, but seldom with the stranger. This may be partly due to belief that the position of host carries greater power. But it may also be due to the greater clarity often given to the host's identity. We read of the monk who offers loaves of bread or the Christian who opens a room for travelers. In these narratives, the host is frequently identified by name or position, and so, has a concrete identity. The "other" in these stories, however, is faceless and nameless, merely the unidentified stranger or the sick. It is easy to fall into the pattern of thinking that "we" are the host and "they" are the guests.

The astounding range and depth of the evidence tells us that hospitality as a practice and as a virtue held a central place in early Christian life. Indeed, there is hardly a place we can look where we will not see traces of it. One encounters it at every turn. Paradoxically, however, hospitality is rarely addressed directly as a topic, but more commonly is touched upon in the context of discussing something else. When describing a young man settling down to start a new life, or chastising the infighting of church leaders, or complaining of the burdens put on a wife by a nonbelieving husband, brief references to the importance of hospitality occur. The pervasive character of hospitality in early Christian writing demonstrates a lack of self-consciousness, a matter-of-factness, that suggests it is simply a given part of life, not the stuff of esoteric treatise.

The Excerpts

All of the texts below are portions or excerpts from larger texts. Examples of and references to hospitality tend to be sprinkled throughout early Christian writings rather than concentrated in a few places. It is not unusual to find an anecdote here or a sentence there addressing hospitality in the middle of a letter or sermon on another topic. Excerpts in this collection are generally taken out of context and are only a fraction of the original source. Because hospitality was an ongoing part of the Christian life, the excerpts often convey the sense of having stepped in midstream. The excerpts themselves seldom tell the whole story, but only a part.

Further, the texts are only one kind of evidence about early Christian faith and life. Reading and writing were not even a part of many Christians' lives. We cannot assume that written descriptions or claims represent early Christianity in any normative sense. Each excerpt tells about particular individuals and particular communities, just as a single window allows a view only into one room, a glimpse of one particular Christian practice. The full interior of the house cannot be seen from any one window, so the best we can do is to look through as many windows as we can.

Christians of many stripes are quoted here. Some are church leaders, some are preachers, some are monastics, and some are seekers. Subsequently, some have been declared heretics while others have been deemed saints. The Christian tradition has not judged all these voices of equal merit.

Genres

Glimpses of hospitality in early Christianity come through many different literary genres. From ecclesiastical life we look at sermons, prayers, accounts of saints' lives (hagiography), monastic rules, church histories, and canon law. From intellectual life excerpts are taken from theological treatises, philosophical arguments or expositions, and scholarly treatment of Scripture. From private life we include letters, diaries, and autobiography.

In the texts we will explore, hospitality is addressed both descriptively and prescriptively. Early Christians directly describe their own and others' practices of hospitality as a witness of faith. They also reflect theologically on that witness of faith, discussing hospitality as a concept or virtue, often prescribing what they think it should be. The various genres included in these excerpts include both kinds of reference, descriptive and prescriptive. Not surprisingly, hospitality is a virtue lived out in daily life, the discussion of which occurs most frequently within the context of its practice. We get thick description from early Christian life of its place and practice.

Times and Places

Geographically the excerpts presented come from as far west as the British Isles and as far east as Azerbaijan near the Caspian Sea. The range includes North Africa, Egypt, Palestine, and Syria, in addition to Europe, covering virtually all of the early Christian world.

Moreover, these texts are taken from a historical sweep that covers the first through the eighth centuries. While the bulk of the excerpts come from the fourth and fifth centuries, the earliest Christians sources outside of the New Testament used here come from around 100 C. E.

During these centuries Christianity's social location shifts significantly from a fledgling, almost invisible religious minority, to a spreading movement largely hostile to the dominant culture, to a powerful institution wedded to the civil state, to a cadre of elites ruling a financial and ecclesiastical bureaucracy. Even this description oversimplifies the stages and nuances of the social history of Christianity.

The historical and local context, then, of each source must be taken into account at least to some degree. Hospitality carries a different power within an outlawed community than within a privileged one. Similarly, hospitality can have different shadings when practiced in the context of internal church fighting than in the context of monastic life on the edges of the empire.

Scope

My study is motivated by an interest in both the conceptual and practical aspects of hospitality. What did Christians say about hospitality, that is, how did they conceive of it? Why did they practice it? How did they practice it?

Because this study intends to cast a wide net in order to understand early Christian notions of hospitality, these excerpts come from a great variety of sources, times, and places. They do not all say the same thing nor speak with one voice. They offer a broad view of early Christian life and practice from several vantage points both within and around the edges of the Christian community. I have made no attempt to screen out some notions of hospitality in favor of others. While patterns will emerge here and there, these voices cannot be neatly forced into categories or conceptual frameworks that dilute or ignore some significant differences. Rather than try to determine an official position on hospitality, we can listen to the many stories the mothers and fathers in the faith have to tell about the many ways hospitality has been enacted within the Christian community. The riches from the tradition are so great we must simply step back and let them have the floor. They not only tell us stories about hospitality and its embodiment, they also articulate a well-developed spiritual and moral economy in which hospitality thrives.

To be sure, this study is neither exhaustive nor systematic in its treatment of hospitality in early Christianity. This is not so much a presentation of *the* early Christian view of hospitality as it is an ingathering of the resources the tradition has to offer.

Organization

Excerpts are organized into thematic chapters. The chapters move through the spiritual dynamics of hospitality starting with *Christian identity* (chapter 2). Early Christian texts make clear that Christians must first understand who they are in God's life. Identification with the other, the stranger, the sojourner, the poor, is central to Christian identity and is the ground of hospitality.

The next movement of hospitality is *recognizing the stranger before us* (chapter 3). The notion of Christian identity illustrated in chapter 2 gives us eyes to see so that we can truly recognize who the stranger is. Without eyes to see, we will fail to recognize the stranger as Christ, and thereby miss the opportunity to participate in hospitality. When we do see Christ in the other, then the full power of hospitality blossoms for both host and guest.

Once the identity of host and guest has been laid bare, the groundwork is in place to *explore the spiritual dynamics of hospitality* (chapter 4). These early texts draw our eye not to the acts of host and guest, but to the presence of God and the grace that imbues all of life. The larger spiritual context of God's movement in the world provides the landscape in which all kinds of things can happen. Early Christians describe with amazement the possibilities of transformation of host, of guest, of community, even of creation, when hospitality is shared. No one is left unchanged. Further, God's gracious movement gives an orientation of spirit that accompanies hospitality so that all participants know themselves to be operating within and for God's life. This orientation of spirit focuses the Christian life on the crucial role of presence, both ours and God's, in hospitality. At its heart, the spiritual power of hospitality rests in simple presence. Hospitality, then, is a spiritual discipline that directs our attention to God's life, opens our hearts to participating in that life through presence and humility, and transforms our lives toward holiness and abundance. Seen this way, hospitality is the opportunity to give our life away in order to gain it, to lose it in order to find it.[41]

Having set out the understandings of early Christians about the nature and dynamics of hospitality, chapter 5 turns to the evidence of *specific practices of hospitality*. These excerpts reveal a wide range of behaviors including welcoming, foot washing, feeding, and lodging. Practices of hospitality are as varied as the people participating in it. Still, these specific practices can be organized into stages of hospitality identified as welcome, restoration, dwelling, and sending forth. Finally, early Christians understood that a spirit of hospitality had to be cultivated in most communities. There is ancient wisdom in the knowledge that communal habits and disciplines can help foster hospitality. Tending to those features of common life enables us to recognize ourselves (chapter 2) and others (chapter 3) and to experience God's gracious movement in the world through hospitality (chapter 4) so that we can practice it (chapter 5).

Extending specific practices of hospitality to institutional settings is an important development in the early Christian centuries. We can learn much from *the record of institutions* designated to offer hospitality, their officers, and rules (chapter 6).

Early Christians praised *biblical and historical figures* for their devotion to and expressions of hospitality. Those testimonies make up the excerpts in chapter 7.

There is an appendix for communities interested in reflecting on their own understanding and practice of hospitality. Discussion questions for each chapter are intended to prompt conversation about hospitality in our own communities, homes, and hearts based on insights and questions gleaned from the ancient sources.

Keys to Understanding

Reading and writing in the ancient world bore different cultural signals than today. For example, while we read and write within a contemporary context of literacy that views reading as primarily a private act, usually pursued for entertainment or education, this was not so in the ancient world. Written documents were almost always to be read aloud, almost never privately. So a communal context can usually be assumed when reading these excerpts.

Each excerpt is preceded by a brief introduction that tells when and by whom the text was written. The most comprehensive information on an author or text will be given in the first use of an excerpt from that author or text. Subsequent introductions will be more abbreviated.

Abbreviations used in excerpt introductions are as follows:

ca. = circa, literally, around	ANF = Ante-Nicene Fathers Series
fl. = flourished	NPNF = Nicene and Post-Nicene
d. = died	Fathers Series
b. = born	

Excerpts have been translated into English and are used with permission. In some cases, previous English translations have been changed for easier reading in modern English. These are identified with an asterisk (*).

Notes

1. In 1983 in *Social Aspects of Early Christianity* (Philadelphia: Fortress Press) Abraham J. Mahlerbe wrote, "The practice of early Christian hospitality has received some attention in the last decade, but its theological implications as perceived by the early church still await serious attention" (p. 67). That can no longer be said. The most recent book by Christine Pohl reflects this trend, *Making Room: Recovering Hospitality as a Christian Tradition* (Grand Rapids: Eerdmans, 1999).

2. Many contemporary writers have offered extended discussion on the nature of hospitality, its definition and characteristics. For more developed reflection see: Thomas W. Ogletree, *Hospitality to the Stranger: Dimensions of Moral Understanding* (Philadelphia: Fortress Press, 1985); Christine D. Pohl, *Making Room: Recovering Hospitality as a Christian Tradition* (Grand Rapids, Michigan: William B. Eerdmans, 1999); Henri Nouwen, *Reaching Out: The Three Movements of the Spiritual Life* (New York: Image Books, 1975); Parker Palmer, *The Company of Strangers: Christians and the Renewal of America's Public Life* (New York: Crossroad, 1981); John Koenig, *New Testament Hospitality: Partnership with Strangers as Mission and Promise* (Philadelphia: Fortress Press, 1985).

3. Interestingly, language itself provides the strong connection between host and guest. In Latin *hospes* can refer to either host or guest. The Greek *xenos* carries the same double meaning, as does *hôte* (French) and *ospite* (Italian).

4. Koenig argues that Paul uses feast as the image for new life in Christ, so that everyday meals become signs of life in Christ as feast. See pp. 52-57.

5. For a thoughtful discussion of the trivialization of the notion of hospitality, see Pohl, pp. 3-8, and 36-39; Nouwen, pp. 46-7.

6. For discussion of hospitality as a moral category in early Christianity, see Ogletree; Rowan A. Greer, "Hospitality," chapter 5 in *Broken Lights and Mended Lives: Theology and*

Common Life in the Early Church (University Park, Pennsylvania: The Pennsylvania State University Press, 1986), pp. 119-40.

7. Paul Ricoeur, *Freedom and Nature: The Voluntary and the Involuntary,* trans. Erazim V. Kohak (Evanston, Ill.: Northwestern University Press, 1966), p. 126.

8. Thomas Ogletree offers an insightful discussion of the way hospitality reveals the moral bankruptcy of the community's/one's frame of reference and leads to repentance. See pp. 1-10.

9. For a case study on the notion of hospitality in the New Testament see G. C. Nicholson, "Houses for Hospitality: 1 Corinthians 11:17-34," *Colloquium* 19, no. 1 (1986), pp. 1-6. Greek and Roman cultures both had highly developed concepts of hospitality as well. See Ladislaus J. Bolchazy, *Hospitality in Early Rome: Livy's Concept of Its Humanizing Force* (Chicago: Ares Publishers, 1977), particularly pp. 1-34.

10. Pohl, *Making Room,* pp. 27-29.

11. Victor H. Matthews and Don C. Benjamin, *Old Testament Parallels: Laws and Stories from the Ancient Near East* rev. ed. (New York: Paulist Press, 1991, 1997), p. 275. Also see Robert E. Meagher, "Strangers at the Gate: Ancient Rites of Hospitality," *Parabola* 2, no. 4 (1977), pp. 10-15.

12. Lexigraphical work regarding the semantic domain of hospitality is very useful. See Johannes P. Louw, *Greek-English Lexicon of the Greek New Testament Based on Semantic Domains,* vol. 1 (New York: American Bible Society, 1994), pp. 121-33.

13. Ladislaus J. Bolchazy, *Hospitality in Early Rome: Livy's Concept of Its Humanizing Force* (Chicago: Ares Publishers, 1977), p. 1.

14. See Adelbert Denaux, "The Theme of Divine Visits and Human Hospitality in Luke-Acts: Its Old Testament and Graeco-Roman Antecedents," in *The Unity of Luke-Acts,* ed. J. Verheyden (Leuven: Leuven University Press, 1999) pp. 263-68. Also, "Hospitality," *Encyclopedia of Religion and Ethics,* pp. 808-12.

15. Ladislaus J. Bolchazy, *Hospitality in Early Rome: Livy's Concept of Its Humanizing Force* (Chicago: Ares Publishers, 1977), pp. 17-34.

16. John Koenig, *New Testament Hospitality: Partnership with Strangers in Mission and Promise* (Philadelphia: Fortress Press, 1985), pp. 15-20.

17. Matthew 25:34-40 (NRSV).

18. More recent scholarship has gone so far as to suggest that hospitality is an organizing theme for Luke. See Adelbert Denaux, "The Theme of Divine Visits and Human Hospitality in Luke-Acts: Its Old Testament and Graeco-Roman Antecedents," in *The Unity of Luke-Acts,* ed. J. Verheyden (Leuven: Leuven University Press, 1999), pp. 255-79; John Koenig, "Guest and Hosts Together in Mission (Luke)," *New Testament Hospitality: Partnership with Strangers in Mission and Promise* (Philadelphia: Fortress Press, 1985), pp. 85-123.

19. Luke 14:12-14. This construal of hospitality could certainly be seen as excessive within the context of first century Judaism. See Koenig, pp. 20-26.

20. Pseudo-Clementine, *First Epistle Concerning Virginity,* ANF, 8:59-60. See also, *Recognitions,* 5.23, ANF 8:148-9; Ignatius of Antioch, *Letter to Smyrnaeans* 8.

21. For a discussion of the development of public physicians or *archiatroi* in the ancient world, see Nigel Allan, "Hospice to Hospital in the Near East: An Instance of Continuity and Change in Late Antiquity," *Bulletin of Medical History* 64, no. 3 (1990), pp. 446-62. Also see, Peregrine Horden, "Saint and Doctors in the Early Byzantine Empire: The Case of Theodore of Sykeon," *The Church and Healing,* ed. W. J. Sheils (Oxford, Basil Blackwell, 1982), pp. 1-13; Ralph Jackson, *Doctors and Diseases in the Roman Empire* (Norman: University of Oklahoma Press, 1988).

22. Matthews and Benjamin, p. 281.

23. For a brief treatment of social stratification in the Roman Empire see Wayne A. Meeks, *The Moral World of the First Christians* (Philadelphia: Westminster Press, 1986), pp. 32-39.

24. In many ancient societies a clear distinction was made between the poor and beggars. See Julian Pitt-Rivers, "The Stranger, The Guest and The Hostile Host: Introduction to the Study of the Laws of Hospitality," in *Contributions to Mediterranean Sociology: Mediterranean*

Rural Communities and Social Change, ed. J.-G. Peristiany, Acts of the Mediterranean Sociological Conference, Athens, July 1963 (Paris: Mouton & Co: 1968), p. 21.

25. For a treatment of wealth in the early church, see L. William Countryman, *The Rich Christian in the Church of the Early Empire: Contradictions and Accommodations* (New York: Edwin Mellen Press, 1980).

26. Gregory of Nyssa. "Homily: As You Did It To One of These, You Did It To Me" in *The Collected Works of Gregory of Nyssa*, trans. Richard McCambly. Gregory of Nyssa Homepage. Bhse.edu/dsalomon/nyssa/home.html. Greenwich, Conn.: Great American Publishing Society, 1999.

27. When early Christian texts include the hungry among the list of the needy, this is no symbolic category. Feeding the poor was a logistic and material challenge for early Christianity both in its infancy and in its imperial glory. For a discussion of public distribution of grain and the office of *diaconia*, see Francis Niederer, "Early Medieval Charity," *Church History* 21 (1952), pp. 285-95.

28. See Greer, p. 121.

29. General information on travel and mobility in the ancient world can be explored in Lionel Casson, *Travel in the Ancient World* (London: George Allen & Unwin, 1974); Lionel Casson, *Ships and Seamanship in the Ancient World* (Baltimore: Johns Hopkins University Press, 1995); Edith Cohen, "Roads and Pilgrimage: A Study in Economic Interaction," *Studi Medievali*, 3rd *Series*, 21 (1980), pp. 321-41; K. J. Conant, *Carolingian and Romanesque Architecture* [800-1200] (Baltimore: Penguin Books, 1959); L. de Ligt, *Fairs and Markets in the Roman Empire*, Dutch Monographs on Ancient History and Archaeology, vol. XI (Amsterdam, 1993); Debra Birch, *Pilgrimage to Rome in the Middle Ages: Continuity and Change* (Woodbridge, UK: Boydell Press, 1998); Gary Vikan, "Guided by Land and Sea: Pilgrim Art and Pilgrim Travel in Early Byzantium," *Tesserae: Festschrift fûr Josef Engemann, Jahrbuch Fûr Antike und Christentum Ergânzungsband* 18 (Munster: Aschendorffsche Verlagsbuchhandlung, 1991), pp. 74-92; Georgia Frank, "The Historia Monarchorum in Aegypto and Ancient Travel Writing," *Studia Patristica*, ed. Elizabeth A. Livingstone, vol. XXX (Leuven: Peeters, 1997). For particular treatment of the mobility of women in the empire see Ramsay MacMullen, "Women in Public in the Roman Empire," *Historia*, Ban XXIX/2 (1980), pp. 209-18.

30. *The Lives of the Desert Fathers*, trans. Norman Russell (Kalamazoo, Mich.: Cistercian, 1981), p. 113.

31. Ibid., 118.

32. For survey of pilgrims in ancient Greece, see Matthew Dillon, *Pilgrims and Pilgrimage in Ancient Greece* (London: Routledge, 1997).

33. There is a vast and important body of literature on Christian pilgrims and pilgrimage in the late Roman and Byzantine periods. See E. D. Hunt, *Holy Land Pilgrimage in the Later Roman Empire AD 312–460* (Oxford: Clarendon Press, 1982); Joan E. Taylor, *Christians and the Holy Places: The Myth of Jewish-Christian Origins* (Oxford: Clarendon Press, 1993); Jan Willem Drijvers, *Helena Augusta: The Mother of Constantine the Great and the Legend of Her Finding of the True Cross* (Leiden: E. J. Brill, 1992); Robert L. Wilken, *The Land Called Holy: Palestine in Christian History and Thought* (New Haven: Yale University Press, 1992); John Wilkinson, "Jewish Holy Places and the Origins of Christian Pilgrimage," in *The Blessings of Pilgrimage*, ed. Richard Ousterhout (Chicago: University of Illinois Press, 1990), pp. 41-53; John Wilkinson, "Christian Pilgrims in Jerusalem During the Byzantine Period," *Palestine Exploration Quarterly* 108 (1976), pp. 75-101; Victor Turner and Edith Turner, *Image and Pilgrimage in Christian Culture: Anthropological Perspectives* (Oxford: Basil Blackwell, 1978); Matthew Dillon, *Pilgrims and Pilgrimage in Ancient Greece* (London: Routledge, 1997). For a treatment of Jewish pilgrimage see *The Jews Among Pagans and Christians in the Roman Empire*, ed. Judith Lieu, John North, and Tessa Rajak (London: Routledge, 1992).

34. *Canons of Chalcedon*, NPNF, ser. 2, Vol. 14.

35. Victor H. Matthews and Don C. Benjamin, *Old Testament Parallels: Laws and Stories from the Ancient Near East* rev. ed. (New York: Paulist Press, 1991, 1997), pp. 217, 81. See many other examples throughout this collection, such as this Ugaritic text from Syria from the fourteenth century B. C. E. The speaker chides an unjust ruler for not caring for the widow and orphan:

> Your illness made you derelict.
>> You did not hear the case of the widow.
> You did not hear the case of the poor.
>> You did not sentence the oppressor.
> You did not feed the orphan in the city.
>> You did not feed the widow in the country.

36. Also in the Torah, see Exod. 22:22, Deuteronomy 14:29, 24:19-21, 26:12-13, 27:19.

37. Also in the prophets, see Isaiah 1:23; Jeremiah 7:6, 22:3; Ezekiel 22:7, Zechariah 7:10, Malachi 3:5.

38. For an extensive treatment of the place of widows in the ancient world and the rise of the order of widows in the early church, see Bonnie Bowman Thurston, *The Widows: A Women's Ministry in the Early Church* (Minneapolis: Fortress Press, 1989).

39. For example, Sulpitius Severus in his *Dialogues* tells of St Martin of Tour receiving a reward from a man whose family he had cured. St. Martin uses the money to ransom captives. See Sulpitius Severus, *Dialogue III*, NPNF, ser. 2, 11:52. St. Patrick praises the Gallo-Romans who ransom Christian captives at great cost from the invading Franks and other tribes, "Letters to the Soldiers of Coroticus," *The Works of St. Patrick*, trans. Ludwig Bieler, Ancient Christian Writers, no. 17 (New York: Newman Press, 1953), p. 45.

40. Henri Nouwen offers a contemporary discussion of the poverty of mind and heart that makes for a good host. See "Hospitality and the Host," in *Reaching Out: The Three Movements of the Spiritual Life* (Garden City, New York: Doubleday & Co., 1975), pp. 72-78.

41. See Matthew 10:39, 16:25-26; Mark 8:34-39; Luke 9:23-27.

CHAPTER TWO

FOR YOU WERE STRANGERS IN EGYPT: REMEMBERING WHO WE ARE

You shall not oppress a stranger; you know the heart of a stranger, for you were strangers in the land of Egypt. (Exodus 23:9 RSV)

Many early Christian texts deliberately confuse the roles of host and guest. Particularly in stories about hospitality offered, it is sometimes hard to tell who is giving and who is receiving. For example, Palladius tells the story of Elias, a solitary ascetic who lived near a road.[1] When a large group of visitors stopped by looking for refreshment, Elias was eager to offer hospitality but only had three loaves of bread to feed them all. Miraculously two loaves were plenty to fill all twenty guests, and the loaf that was left fed Elias for twenty-five days. Elias the host became the recipient of abundance as a result of his visitors. This reversal of roles is a common theme in early Christian stories of hospitality.

Another common theme relates to the question of identity. Contested or displaced identity marked much of Christian life in the Roman Empire. Early Christians talk about Christian identity in terms of the stranger, the sojourner, or the foreigner.[2] Christians of the first three centuries certainly understood themselves to be aliens, pilgrims in this world with citizenship in another.[3] Given their political location in the Roman Empire, it is not surprising that stranger status would be a primary way Christians understood themselves and their place in the world. These Christians frequently remind one another that their true allegiance is not with the powers of this world and they must hold a sort of double-consciousness, seeking to be good citizens in their communities yet never fully at home in the world. Christians under arrest often identify themselves not by referring to their nationality or province or even their family of origin, but by reference to Jerusalem or God as authoritative sources of identity, virtually unintelligible in the early empire. Eusebius tells the story in *The Martyrs of Palestine* of Pamphilius, martyred along with others. When brought before the judge Firmilianus, the martyrs express this sense of displaced identity, giving the names of prophets as their own. Pamphilius even claims his homeland as Jerusalem.

> He [Firmilianus] heard in reply the name of some prophet instead of his proper name. For it was their [Christians'] custom, in place of the names of idols given them by their parents, if they had such a name, to take other names; so that you would hear them calling themselves Elijah or Jeremiah or Isaiah or Samuel or Daniel. This way they themselves were inwardly true Jews, and the genuine Israel of God, not only in deeds, but in the names which they bore. When Firmilianus had heard some such name from the martyr, and did not understand the force of what he was saying, he asked next the name of his country. But he gave a second answer similar to the former, saying that Jerusalem was his country, meaning that of which Paul says, "Jerusalem which is above is free, which is our mother," and, "You have come to Mount Sion, to the city of the living God, the heavenly Jerusalem." This was what he meant. But the judge, thinking only of the earth, sought diligently to discover what that city was, and in what part of the world it was situated. He applied tortures to find out the truth. But the man, with his hands twisted behind his back, and his feet crushed by strange devices, asserted firmly that he had spoken the truth. And being questioned repeatedly what and where the city was of which he spoke, he said that it was the country of the pious alone, for no others should have a place in it, and that it lay toward the far East and the rising sun . . . . But the judge being perplexed, was impatient, thinking that the Christians were about to establish a city somewhere, inimical and hostile to the Romans. So he inquired much about this, and investigated where that country toward the East was located. But when he had lacerated the young man with scourgings for a long time, and punished him with all sorts of torments, he realized that his persistence in what he had said could not be changed, and passed against him the death sentence. This was what was done to this man. And having inflicted similar tortures on the others, he sent them away in the same manner.[4]

The reigning powers, in this case, the judge Firmilianus, can only imagine cities located geographically, not spiritually. So he completely misunderstands the identity these Christians profess. In his frustration, he punishes them. This disconnection between Christian identity and earthly, pagan powers is similarly expressed in Tertullian's now famous question, "What has Athens to do with Jerusalem?"[5]

Moreover, Christians' sense of cultural alienation was often expressed through identification with exiles and refugees. Because Christians were at times under threat from civil authorities, the act of harboring refugees who were brothers and sisters in Christ became imperative. Sheltering strangers was essential to the survival of Christianity in a hostile empire. Christians became well known within the larger culture for their practices of hospitality and were often cited as examples of morality on this account. When Julian the Apostate came to power in the middle of the fourth century, his attempts to revitalize pagan traditions drew heavily on the positive press Christian practices of hospitality had received, what he called the "humanity evinced by Christians towards strangers."[6] It is not so far a step from understanding oneself to be a stranger in the world to identifying with other political, economic, and social strangers, nor vice versa.

The stranger status at the heart of Christian identity has biblical roots as well as cultural and political ones. Remembering that "we were strangers in Egypt" is central to Christian identity because it is central to the salvation history told in the Hebrew Bible.[7] God saved the people from their alien, slave status in Egypt. In delivering them, God reminds them of who they truly are, divinely chosen people far from home. Salvation history reinforces a central aspect of identity as alien, foreigner enslaved in a strange land, or sojourner wandering in a foreign desert.

This theme continues through the New Testament writings. The letter to the Hebrews emphasizes the faithfulness of the Hebrew patriarchs in their status as "strangers and foreigners on the earth, for people who speak in this way make it clear that they are seeking a homeland" (11:13-14). They sought a true home, remaining strangers on earth all their lives.[8]

After the reign of Constantine, as Christianity became an accepted religion and eventually the official state religion,

Christianity enjoyed a new location of privilege and power within the culture. Still, Christians continued to use the language of stranger status to describe Christian identity, though with different shadings and nuances. One way some Christians expressed this status was through identification with the poor and outcast. It is not uncommon in Christian literature of the fourth and fifth centuries for Christians to enact their alien status most powerfully in economic terms. In hagiography, poverty is a standard-bearer of Christian identity, signaling to the reader that one is dealing here with a *real* Christian (see Aldegund, Gertrude). This identification with the poor or the stranger can also be cast as an identification with Christ, who became poor and outcast on behalf of all.

Some Christians, though no longer under political threat, continued to identify themselves as citizens of another realm, as pilgrims on their way to the Holy City. John Chrysostom (ca. 347-407), the great preacher at Constantinople, calls his listeners to embrace their identity as sojourners here:

> Don't you know that we live in a foreign land, as though strangers and sojourners? Don't you know that it is the lot of sojourners to be ejected when they don't think they will be, when they least expect it? This is also our lot . . . but seeing we are by nature sojourners, let us also be so by choice; that we be not there [with God] sojourners and dishonored and cast out. For if we are set upon being citizens here, we shall be so neither here nor there; but if we continue to be sojourners, and live in such wise as sojourners ought to live in, we shall enjoy the freedom of citizens both here and there.[9]

The early Christian voices below reflect the profound conviction that Christian identity is rooted in otherness. Before one can truly offer hospitality, one must understand one's own marginal position.[10] Some will express this notion of Christian identity through a call to stranger status. More often, they will lift up one whose life exemplifies identification with the stranger. Excerpts are in approximate chronological order.

Epistle to Diognetus

Neither Diognetus, the author, nor the date of this letter from the second century is known. Written as a defense of Christians in the face of pagan misunderstanding, the letter describes the paradox of Christian identity. Christians are at once citizens and foreigners. They appear to follow the norms of the culture, yet they seem to have their origins elsewhere.

> But, inhabiting Greek as well as barbarian cities, according as the lot of each of them has determined, and following the customs of the locals in respect to clothing, food, and the rest of their regular daily life, they [Christians] display to us their wonderful and admittedly striking way of life. They dwell in their own countries, but simply as sojourners. As citizens, they share in all things with others, and yet endure all things as if foreigners. Every foreign land is to them as their native country, and every land of their birth as a land of strangers.

Basil, *Letter 2 to Gregory*

In this letter, Basil (ca. 330–379) writes to his friend, Gregory of Nazianzus (329–389) and complains that his own place in the world is like a ship tossed at sea, frenzied and burdened. He advises a Christian identity that is separate from the world, an interior sense of estrangement from the cultural expectations of his day.[11] He claims that only by becoming estranged from the world can one's heart become a smooth, waxen tablet, ready to receive "the impress of divine doctrine."

> What I do myself, day and night, in this remote spot, I am ashamed to write. I have abandoned my life in town, as one sure to lead to countless ills. But I cannot escape myself. I am like travelers at sea, who have never gone on a voyage before, and are upset and seasick. They quarrel with the ship because it is so big and makes such a tossing, but when they get out of it into a smaller boat or rowboat, are everywhere and always seasick and distressed. Wherever they go their nausea and misery go with them. My state is something like that. I carry my own troubles with me, and so everywhere I am in the midst of similar discomforts. So in the end my solitude hasn't done me much good. What I should have done, what would have enabled me to keep close to the footprints of Him who has led the way to salvation (for He says, "If any one will come after me, let him deny himself and take up his cross, and follow me") is this.
>
> We must strive after a quiet mind. It's just as likely that the eye could pick out an object right in front of it while it is wandering restlessly up and down and sideways without ever fixing a steady gaze

on it, as that the mind, distracted by a thousand worldly cares, could clearly apprehend the truth. A person who is not yet bound in marriage is harassed by frenzied cravings, and rebellious impulses, and hopeless attachments. A person who has found a mate is encompassed with another tumult of cares. If the person is childless, there is desire for children. Or for those with children, there is anxiety about their education, attention to their mate, care of the house, oversight of servants, misfortunes in trade, quarrels with neighbors, lawsuits, the risks of the merchant, the toil of the farmer. Each day, as it comes, burdens the soul in its own way; and night after night takes up the day's anxieties, and cheats the mind with illusions. Now one way of escaping all this is separation from the whole world, that is, not physical withdrawal, but the separation of the soul's sympathy toward the body. This would mean to become cityless, homeless, possessionless, friendless, jobless, without business transactions, human fellowship or human learning, that the heart may readily receive every impress of divine doctrine. Preparation of heart means unlearning the prejudices of evil converse. It means smoothing the waxen tablet before attempting to write on it.

Paula, *Letter to Marcella*

Paula (347–404) represents an early model of Christian life that many Roman matrons were to emulate. They eschewed the privileges of their rank and family status, renounced Rome and took on the identity of strangers in a foreign land. Paula went on the arduous journey to Palestine and, after visiting various holy sites, settled at Bethlehem to join Jerome in the wilderness. In this letter to her friend still in Rome, Marcella, Paula is eager to distance herself from the cultural mores that confer status, instead claiming to be no longer "persons of importance." The lack of social distinction among Christians there demonstrates stranger status.

To these places we have come, not as persons of importance, but as strangers, that we might see in them the foremost men of all nations. Among all this will be found what is, perhaps, the greatest virtue among Christians—no arrogance, no overweening pride in their chastity; all of them vie with one another in humility. Whoever is last is reckoned as first. In their dress there is no distinction, no ostentation. The order in which they walk in procession neither implies disgrace nor confers honor.

John Chrysostom, *Homily 16 on 2nd Corinthians*

John Chrysostom (ca. 347–407), bishop of Constantinople and theologian of the early church, preached in the late fourth century to a Christian world that had quickly become accustomed to worldly powers and its advantages. In these sermons he reminds his listeners of their true allegiance and their alien status in this world.

Don't you know that we live in a foreign land, as though strangers and sojourners? Don't you know that it is the lot of sojourners to be ejected when they don't think they will be, when they least expect it? This is also our lot . . . but seeing we are by nature sojourners, let us also be so by choice; so that we are not there [with God] sojourners and dishonored and cast out. For if we just focus on being citizens here, we shall be so neither here nor there. But if we continue to be sojourners, and live in the way that sojourners should live, we will enjoy the freedom of citizens both here and there. For the just, although having nothing, will both dwell here amidst all worldly possessions as though they were their own and also, when they depart to heaven, will be eternally at home there. And they won't be uncomfortable here, for no one can make a stranger out of one who counts every land as home. When they have been restored to their own country, they shall receive the true riches. In order that we may gain both the things of this life and of that, let us use aright the things we have. For then will we be citizens of the heavens, and shall enjoy much boldness. These things may we all attain, through the grace and love towards all of our Lord Jesus Christ, with Whom to the Father with the Holy Spirit, be glory and power for ever. Amen.

John Chrysostom, *Homily 24 on Hebrews*

Chrysostom draws upon Paul and Abraham as examples of the stranger status for those who know themselves to be sojourning here.

The first virtue, indeed, the whole of virtue, is to be a stranger to this world, and a sojourner, to have nothing in common with things here and let go of them, as we would from anything strange to us. This is just like those blessed disciples did, of whom he says, "They wandered about in sheepskins, and in goat-skins, being destitute, afflicted, tormented, of whom the world was not worthy" (11:37, 38).

So they called themselves "strangers," but Paul went beyond this. For he did not merely call himself a stranger, but said that he was dead to the world, and that the world was dead to him. "For the world," he says, "has been crucified to me and I to the world" (Galatians 6:14). But we, being both citizens and very much alive, busy ourselves about everything here as citizens do. What the righteous were to the world, namely, "strangers" and "dead," that we are to Heaven. And what they were to Heaven, alive and acting as citizens, that we are to the world. On this account, we are dead, because we have refused that which is truly life, and have chosen this which is but fleeting. On this account, we have provoked God to wrath, because when the blessings of Heaven have been set before us, we are not willing to be separated from things on earth. Instead we act like worms, we turn about from the earth to the earth, and again from this to that. In short, we are not willing to look up even for a little while, nor to withdraw ourselves from human affairs, but as if drowned in stupor and sleep and drunkenness, we are stupefied with delusions. . . .

The saints were "strangers and sojourners." How and in what way? And where does Abraham confess himself "a stranger and a sojourner?" Probably indeed even he himself confessed it, but David both confessed "I am a stranger" and "As all my fathers were" (Psalm 39:12). For those who dwell in tents and who have to buy even their own burial places, evidently were in some sense strangers, as they didn't even have a place to bury their dead.

What then? Did they mean that they were "strangers" from the land that is in Palestine? Of course not. But they were strangers in respect to the whole world and with good reason, because they saw therein none of the things they truly longed for, but everything foreign and strange. They certainly wished to practice virtue but here there was so much wickedness, and things were quite alien to them. They had no friend, no familiar acquaintance, save only some few.

But how were they "strangers?" They had no concern for things here. And this they showed not by words, but by deeds. In what way?

He said to Abraham, "Leave what seems to be your country and come to one that is foreign." He [Abraham] did not cleave to his relatives, but let go as unconcernedly as if he were about to leave a foreign land. He said to him, "Offer up your son," and he offered him up as if he had no son, as if he had divested himself of his nature, so he offered him up. The wealth he had acquired was common to all passers-by, and this he accounted as nothing. He yielded the first places to others. He threw himself into dangers. He suffered troubles innumerable. He built no splendid houses, he enjoyed no luxuries, he had no care about dress, which all are things of this world, but lived in all respects as belonging to the city yonder. He showed hospitality, brotherly love, mercifulness, forbearance, contempt for wealth and for present glory, and for all else.

Paulinus of Nola, *Letter 24*

Paulinus (353–431) was bishop of Nola where he and his wife founded a home for monks and cared for the poor. His vast correspondence with well-known figures of his day paints a picture of popular Christianity. Writing around 400 C.E. to his friend Sulpitius Severus, Paulinus here praises Severus' witness to an understanding of Christian identity as involving social displacement. Paulinus explicitly cites Severus' living as an exile in this world by identifying with the poor. We get a glimpse here of an interesting pattern in late antique Christianity. Severus no longer owns land, but retains its use for travelers and beggars. From Paulinus' point of view, this is the best of both worlds. Severus has divested himself of worldly status to fulfill his Christian identity as stranger, yet accesses resources on behalf of others.

As I have said, you have undertaken two saintly roles, by refusing to own the land you have retained, and by achieving perfection through that which you have sold. So in your apparent role of owner you are perfect, because your mind is free from the ties of possessions; mindful of how short the time is, you fulfill Paul's injunction by possessing without possessing, for you keep possessions not for yourself but for those with nothing. You play host in your house so that your house may be a hospice. You are a traveler from your native land and an exile in this world that you may dwell in Paradise and be a citizen of your former country. You do not crowd your houses with dining tables, or cram them with masses of furniture or wealth. You measure off a corner for yourself and fill the house with travelers and beggars. You live as a fellow servant with your own slaves. The temporary lodging which is your dwelling you do not possess like the father of a household, but you lodge there like a mercenary or a lodger, paying the Lord a regular rent for the favor of the lodging by serving your neighbors with body and mind.

Paulinus of Nola, *Letter 29*

Also written around 400 C.E. to Severus, this letter reports to his friend about a visit from the well-known Melania at Nola. In describing

Melania's renunciation of aristocratic ways in favor of a spiritual service at Jerusalem, Paulinus employs the language of Christian identity as stranger.

Abandoning worldly life and her own country, she chose to bestow her spiritual gift at Jerusalem, and to dwell there in pilgrimage from her body. She became an exile from her fellow citizens, but a citizen amongst the saints. With wisdom and sanctity she chose to be a servant in this world of thrall so as to be able to reign in the world of freedom.

Augustine, Sermon 61

Augustine (354–430) grew up and was educated in Roman North Africa. He became a Christian at age 33 and went on to become bishop of Hippo, on the north coast of Africa. In this sermon on the gospel of Luke, Augustine discusses the kingdom of God and the residence of Christians. Augustine claims that Christians are strangers here and that is the ground of hospitality.

Acknowledge the duty of hospitality, for by this some have attained unto God. You take in some stranger, whose companion in the way you yourself also are, for we are all strangers. This person is a Christian who, even in his own house and in his own country, acknowledges himself to be a stranger. For our country is above, there we shall not be strangers. For every one here below, even in his own house, is a stranger. If he is not a stranger, let him not pass on from here. If pass on he must, he is a stranger. Let him not deceive himself, he is indeed a stranger. Whether he wills it or not, he is a stranger. If he leaves that house to his children, he leaves it one stranger to other strangers. Why? If you were at an inn, wouldn't you leave when another comes? You do the same thing even in your own house. Your father left a place to you, you will some day leave it to your children. You don't live here as one who will live forever, nor will those to whom you leave it live forever. If we are all passing away, let us do something which cannot pass away, so that when we shall have passed away, and we come to that place where we no longer pass away, we may find our good works there. Remember, Christ is the keeper, so why do you fear you might lose what you spend on the poor?

John Cassian, *Institutes of the Cenobia*

In his instructions to monastic communities John Cassian (ca. 360–435) is concerned that no matter how materially successful they are, they remember their identity as merely sojourners, not residents, in this world. Success and achievement can be the enemies of Christian identity based on alien status. Cassian ties Christian identity to preserving a state of poverty and dependence.

And although each one of them may bring in by his work and labor every day so great a return to the monastery that he could not only satisfy his own moderate demands but could also abundantly supply the wants of many out of it, yet he is no way puffed up. Neither does he flatter himself on account of his work and this large gain from his labor, but, except for two biscuits, which are sold there for scarcely a few pennies, no one thinks that he has a right to anything further. And among them there is nothing (and I am ashamed to say this, and heartily wish it was unknown in our own monasteries) which is claimed by any of them as his special property, either in the way they act or even in thought. Moreover, even though he believes that the whole granary of the monastery forms his substance, and, as Lord of all, devotes his whole life and energy to it all, yet nevertheless, in order to maintain that excellent state of want and poverty which he has secured and which he strives to preserve to the very end in unbroken perfection, he thinks of himself as a foreigner and an alien to them all. He conducts himself as a stranger and a sojourner in this world, and considers himself a pupil of the monastery and a servant instead of imagining that he is Lord and master of anything.

Gerontius, *Life of Melania the Younger*

Melania's life (383–438) is a model of the wealthy Roman matron who leaves her privilege behind, choosing poverty and service. This vita, composed around 452, highlights her dislocation from worldly prestige to stranger status. Notice the vocabulary of reciprocity whereby Melania's poverty can only be understood in the context of Christ's.

Thus being much encouraged and praising God even more, they set sail for Jerusalem and hastened on to their destination. They stayed in the Church of the Holy Sepulcher. Since they themselves did not want to distribute with their own hands the gold left to them, they gave it to those who were entrusted with administering charity for the poor. They did not wish for people to see them doing good deeds. They were in such a state of poverty that the holy woman Melania assured us of this: "When we first arrived here, we thought of inscribing ourselves on the church's register and of being fed with the poor from alms." Thus they became extremely poor for the sake of the Lord, who himself became poor for our sakes and who took the form of a servant.

Bede, *Ecclesiastical History of the English People*

In his historic work on the history of the English people Bede (ca. 673–735) chronicles many saints' lives. He tells the story of a woman who found her Christian identity by leaving the familiar. In this excerpt from his account of Hild, abbess of the monastery at Whitby, Bede notes her desire to leave her home and become "a stranger for the Lord's sake."

When she had decided to give up the secular habit and serve the Lord alone, she withdrew to the kingdom of the East Angles, for she was a relation of a king of that land. It was her wish, if possible, to cross over to Gaul, leaving her home and all that she had, to live as a stranger for the Lord's sake in the monastery of Chelles, so that she might the more easily attain to her eternal home in heaven.

Aldegund, *Life*

The higher one's social status, the more one attempts to make explicit this identification with the stranger or the poor. In several lives of women saints from the Middle Ages, stress is given to their intentional lowliness and adoption of servant's roles. In this excerpt from the life of Aldegund (d. ca. 684), the author has just established her noble lineage so the riches of her status can be contrasted with her chosen poverty.

Their human state was wonderful but God's power is more wonderful. So one of such high birth was made poor for the love of Christ and from that poverty we are all made rich, as the witness says: "Blessed are the poor in spirit for theirs is the kingdom of heaven."

Later in the account, Aldegund and her sister nun, Waldetrude, share in this divestiture of goods and seek a life of poverty and service. Just as both women refuse to move to larger living quarters, "fearing to lose the security of [their] poverty," the story is told of their miraculous powers to open barred gates. This story links Christian identity with the poor and divine intervention.

Then her sister, the most holy virgin Aldegund, whom we mentioned above, used to come from her own monastery to visit her on certain days. They transfused one another with the sweet life-giving words and the soft bread of the heavenly homeland. For as yet they were unable to rejoice perfectly, but they tasted it in hope. Once Aldegund noticed the smallness of the place, seeing that as yet but a few nuns belonged to her sister's service. Pulsating with human love, she urged compassionately that, because of her poverty, she should leave the place that they might hasten together to her monastery. But almighty God's servant, loving to weary herself in his service more than to gather the honors of transitory human life, would in no way consent, for she feared to lose the security of her poverty like a miser guards perishable wealth. Nor must we pass over the miracle which almighty God deigned to show his maidservants. When they met as usual one day for fruitful discussion of eternal life, a reason for the monastery's good arose for them to go a little way outside the walls. Having disposed of the business for which they went out, they returned to the monastery to find the gatekeeper absent. All the gates were closed and tightly barred. But soon something wonderful happened. For as the servants of Christ came to the basilica entrance, immediately the gates were divinely shaken and sprung open as if horrified to impede their prayers.

Notes

1. Palladius, *The Lausiac History* 51, trans. Robert T. Meyer, Ancient Christian Writers, no. 34 (New York: Newman Press, 1964), p. 133. See chapter 4 above for the full account.

2. For a useful discussion of this phenomenon in early Christian writing, see Rowan A. Greer, *Broken Lights and Mended Lives: Theology and Common Life in the Early Church* (University Park, Penn.: The Pennsylvania State University Press, 1986), Chapter 6: "Alien Citizens: A Marvelous Paradox," pp. 141-61. Also see W. H. C. Frend, *Martyrdom and Persecution in the Early Church: A Study of a Conflict from the Maccabees to Donatus* (Oxford: Basil Blackwell & Mott, 1965); Robert L. Wilken, *The Christians as the Roman Saw Them* (New Haven: Yale University Press, 1984). For a case study, see Richard Valantasis, "The Stranger Within, The Stranger Without: Ascetical Withdrawal and the Second Letter of Basil the Great," *Christianity and the Stranger: Historical Essays*, ed. Francis W. Nichols (Atlanta: Scholars Press, 1995), pp. 65-81.

3. For a discussion of the eschatological dimensions of hospitality see Thomas W. Ogletree, *Hospitality to the Stranger: Dimensions of Moral Understanding* (Philadelphia: Fortress Press, 1985), p. 7.

4. Eusebius, *The Martyrs of Palestine* 11, NPNF, ser. 2, vol. 1.

5. Tertullian, *Prescription Against Heretics* 7, ANF 3, p. 443.

6. Sozomen, *Ecclesiastical History* 15.16, NPNF, ser. 2, vol. 2

7. For other references in the Hebrew Bible to stranger status see Genesis 23:4, 47:4, 9; Leviticus 19:34, 25:23; 1 Chronicles 29:15; Psalm 39:12.

8. For other references in the New Testament to stranger status see Ephesians 2:19; Hebrews 13:1; 1 Peter 1:1, 2:11.

9. John Chrysostom, *Homily 16 on 2nd Corinthians*, NPNF, ser. 1, vol. 12, p. 359. Cf. *Homily 12 on Matthew* (NPNF, ser. 1, vol. 10, 78); *Homily 23 on Ephesians* (NPNF, ser. 1, vol. 13, p. 166).

10. For a contemporary discussion, see Christine D. Pohl, "Hospitality From the Edge: The Significance of Marginality in the Practice of Welcome," *The Annual of the Society of Christian Ethics*, ed. Harlan Beckley (Boston, Massachusetts: The Society of Christian Ethics, 1995), pp. 121-136. Also see Christine D. Pohl, *Making Room: Recovering Hospitality as a Christian Tradition* (Grand Rapids, Mich.: William B. Eerdmans, 1999).

11. For a helpful study of the interior dynamics of being a stranger in Basil's letter, see Richard Valantasis, "The Stranger Within, The Stranger Without: Ascetical Withdrawal and the Second Letter of Basil the Great," in *Christianity and the Stranger*, ed. Francis W. Nichols (Atlanta, Georgia: Scholars Press, 1995), pp. 64-81.

Bibliography

"Aldegund, Abbess of Maubeuge." In *Sainted Women of the Dark Ages,* translated and edited by JoAnn McNamara and John Halborg. Durham: Duke University Press, 1992, 238, 261.

Augustine. "Sermon 61." In *Homilies on the Gospels,* translated by the Rev. R. G. MacMullen. *Nicene and Post-Nicene Fathers of the Christian Church.* Edited by Philip Schaff. 1st ser. New York: The Christian Literature Company, 1887, VI:446.

Basil. "Letter 2 to Gregory." In *Letters and Select Works,* translated by the Rev. Blomfield Jackson. *Nicene and Post-Nicene Fathers of the Christian Church.* Edited by Philip Schaff and Henry Wace. 2nd ser. New York: The Christian Literature Company, 1895, VIII:110.

Bede. *Ecclesiastical History.* Edited by Bertram Colgrave and R. A. B. Mynors. Oxford: Oxford University Press, 1969, 407.

Epistle to Diognetus. Translated by Alexander Roberts and James Donaldson. *Ante-Nicene Fathers: The Writings of the Fathers Down to A.D. 325.* Edited by Alexander Roberts and James Donaldson. New York: The Christian Literature Company, 1884, I:26.

Gerontius. *Life of Melania the Younger.* Translated by Elizabeth A. Clark. Studies in Women and Religion, vol. 14. New York: The Edwin Mellen Press, 1984, 51.

John Cassian. *Institutes of the Coenobia.* Translated by the Rev. Edgar C. S. Gibson. *Nicene and Post-Nicene Fathers of the Christian Church.* Edited by Philip Schaff and Henry Wace. 2nd ser. New York: The Christian Literature Company, 1894, XI:222-23.

John Chrysostom. "Homily 16 on 2nd Corinthians." In *Homilies on 1st and 2nd Corinthians,* translated by the Rev. Hubert Kestell Cornish, the Rev. John Medley and the Rev. J. Ashworth. *Nicene and Post-Nicene Fathers of the Christian Church.* 1st ser. New York: The Christian Literature Company, 1889, XII:359.

_____."Homily 24 on Hebrews." In *Homilies on John and Hebrews,* translated by the Rev. G. T. Stupart, *Nicene and Post-Nicene Fathers of the Christian Church.* 1st ser. New York: The Christian Literature Company, 1890, XIV:473-74.

Paula. *Letter of Paula and Eustochium to Marcella About the Holy Places.* Translated by Aubrey Stewart. Palestine Pilgrims' Text Society. London: Adam Street, 1889, 10.

Paulinus of Nola. "Letter 24." Translated by P. G. Walsh. Ancient Christian Writers, no. 36. New York: Newman Press, 1967, 53.

_____."Letter 29." Translated by P. G. Walsh. *Ancient Christian Writers,* no. 36. New York: Newman Press, 1967, 112.

CHAPTER THREE

HAVING EYES TO SEE: RECOGNIZING THE STRANGER

If the first step of living in hospitality is remembering who we are as Christians, the second step is recognizing who the stranger is, standing before us.[1] On first glance, the poor at the gate or the stranger at the door may seem to be just that, the supplicant wanting something. The stranger may seem suspicious or even dangerous. The very presence of the stranger can be disorienting.[2] But if we look a little closer, we will see our initial reading of the situation is wrong. Over and over again, early Christian voices remind us to be prepared for surprises. The apparent stranger is not simply the poor, the stranger, the widow, the sick who knock, but Christ himself. For those with eyes to see, hospitality offered to another is always hospitality offered to Christ. In receiving others, we receive Christ. In rejecting them, we reject Christ.[3]

Early Christians turn to the Gospel of Matthew to ground the recognition of the stranger:

> "Lord, when was it that we saw you hungry and gave you food, or thirsty and gave you something to drink? And when was it that we saw you a stranger and welcomed you, or naked and gave you clothing? And when was it that we saw you sick or in prison and visited you?" And the king will answer them, "Truly I tell you, just as you did it to one of the least of these who are members of my family, you did it to me."[4]

In order to recognize Christ, one must have eyes to see. To recognize Christ in the guest at the door is not easy. It is rarely the Christ we expect or the Christ of our imaginings. The Matthew passage emphasizes that the Christ who comes will be needy, hungry, thirsty, a Christ known by "the least of these." In some of these early Christians texts, the visitor will not even be human, but an animal seeking refuge or help. Eyes that can only see Christ in the triumphant or powerful will fail to recognize Christ present in the stranger or the poor. This recognition changes everything, for now it is Christ with whom we are dealing. Only proper recognition makes union with Christ possible. Jesus' followers on the road to Emmaus (Luke 24:13-35) powerfully portray this experience of recognition and surprise when they unexpectedly encounter Christ as traveler and guest.

Because the guest is actually more than just a guest, but is Christ, then there is another surprise as well. Christ becomes the host and the host becomes the guest. When we attend to the guest, we are not left unchanged. We become the guest of God, who, acting as host, receives us into God's life. Again, however, this depends on our having eyes to see. Only when we recognize the guest as Christ can we, in turn, be received. The Greek of the New Testament that is used to express hospitality carries within it the reality of shared identity and partnership. The same word, *xenos*, can mean guest, host, or stranger. The semantic fluidity conveys the blurred identities of guest and host, heightened by the recognition of Christ. Chapter 4 will discuss the transformative character of the encounter with Christ in the stranger.

Early Christians use several different vocabularies and sets of images for this act of recognition. It is not unusual for combinations of these vocabularies to be used at the same time. The first vocabulary is scriptural. Many texts call upon Matthew 25, "just as you did it to one of the least of these who are members of my family, you did it to me." The "least of these" vocabulary appeals to the identification of the least, the lost, the poor, with Christ. It reminds the listener that Christ is to be found among the least likely and in the most out of the way places, like a manger or a cross. One can, therefore, never make the mistake of reducing the other to anything less than Christ.[5]

Another set of biblical images comes from Genesis 18. Abraham receives the strangers under the oaks of Mamre, offering them hospitality and refreshment even though they are unknown to him. He thereby entertains angels unawares (Hebrews 13:2). The vocabulary of "entertaining angels" reminds the listener of the holiness of visitors and the possibility that, at the very least, they are messengers of God.

Finally, another vocabulary of recognition in these texts involves seeing a common humanity in the other. While those with disabilities or contagious sicknesses may seem of a different species and the slave may seem to be of a different nature, proper recognition proves otherwise. Those with eyes to see will know that these are brothers and sisters created by the same God and living as mutual guests in the same house provided by the same divine host. Eyes of recognition will see the common humanity shared by the other and thereby truly recognize him or her.[6]

In the Gospels Jesus talks about having eyes to see and ears to hear as necessary to recognizing the kingdom of God. Hospitality may be a mark of God's new reign, and strangers may be its bearers. These early Christian voices express a profound appreciation for this insight. Excerpts are in approximate chronological order.

Clement of Alexandria, *The Instructor (Pedagogue)**

Clement of Alexandria (ca. 150–ca. 215) was a student and then head of the catechetical school at Alexandria where he pursued philosophical and theological studies. The Instructor gives guidance on matters of Christian practice and life. Addressing the relationship of masters to servants and slaves, important in the ancient world, Clement appeals to Matthew 25:40 as well as to God's invitation to both free and bond.

Domestics, too, are to be treated like ourselves, for they are human beings, as we are. For God is the same to free and bond, if you consider it. . . . Respecting liberality He said: "Come, you that are blessed by my Father, inherit the kingdom prepared for you from the foundation of the world. For I was a hungry, and you gave me food. I was thirsty, and you gave me something to drink. I was a stranger, and you welcomed me. I was naked, and you gave me clothing. I was sick and you took care of me, I was in prison and you visited me." And when have we done any of these things to the Lord? The Instructor Himself will say again, loving to show that the kindness of the kindred refers to Himself, "Just as you did it to one of the least of these who are members of my family, you did it to me. And these shall go away into everlasting life."

Clement of Alexandria, *Who Is the Rich Person that Shall Be Saved?**

Clement addresses the question the Gospel raises in this exposition of Matthew 10:17-31. Love of God and love of neighbor cannot be separated, for the neighbor is Christ.

In both the commandments, then, He introduces love; but in order distinguishes it. And in the one He assigns to God the first part of love, and allots the second to our neighbor. Who else can it be but the Savior Himself? . . .

He then is first who loves Christ; and second, he who loves and cares for those who have believed on Him. For whatever is done to a disciple, the Lord accepts as done to Himself, and reckons the whole as His. "Come, you that are blessed by my Father, inherit the kingdom prepared for you from the foundation of the world. For I was hungry, and you gave me food. I was thirsty, and you gave me something to drink. I was a stranger, and you welcomed me. I was naked, and you gave me clothing. I was sick and you took care of me, I was in prison and you visited me." . . . "Whoever receives you, receives me, and whoever doesn't receive you, rejects me."

Pseudo-Clementine, *First Epistle Concerning Virginity**

Clement of Rome (fl. ca. 96) was bishop of Rome at the turn of the first century. This letter, however, was likely written around 200 to 250. Though wrongly attributed to him, it is a very early Christian voice that calls for serving God by serving the stranger and the poor. He enjoins Christians to visit them in order to obey "the least of these" commandment. However, he also calls for the recognition that our well-being is bound to the well-being of others. Loving strangers requires recognition of our common lot as well as of God's presence with them.

Moreover, also, this is desirable and useful, that one "visit orphans and widows," and especially those poor people who have many children. These things are, without question, required of the servants of God, and desirable and appropriate for them . . . . For such persons as these a nice reward is laid up by God, because they serve their kindred with the gifts which have been given them by the Lord. This is also desirable and appropriate to the servants of God, because they act according to the injunctions of our Lord, who said: "I was sick, and you visited me," and so on. And this is good and right and just, that we visit our neighbors for the sake of God with totally appropriate manners and purity of behavior. As the Apostle said: "Who is sick, and I am not sick? Who is offended, and I am not offended?" But all these things are spoken with a focus on the love with which one should love neighbors. And these are the things we should focus our attention on, without giving offense. We should not do anything with partiality or for the shaming of others, but love the poor as the servants of God, and especially visit them. For this is desirable before God and before people, that we should remember the poor, and be lovers of the kindred and of strangers, for the sake of God and for the sake of those who believe in God, because we have learned from the law and from the prophets, and from our Lord Jesus Christ, about loving the kindred and loving strangers. For you know the words which have been spoken concerning the love of the kindred and the love of strangers. Powerfully are the words spoken to all those who do them.

Pseudo-Clementine, *Recognitions of Clement**

Part of the Pseudo-Clementine literature, the Recognitions *was likely written in the early 200s and has some gnostic elements. Still, it offers philosophical musings on the image of God. In this passage, a powerful argument is made for recognizing the stranger, the hungry, the naked as beings in the image of God. Hospitality to the image of God is just a logical extension of worship of the invisible God.*

For if you really wished to worship the image of God, you would do good to humans, and so worship the true image of God in them. For the image of God is in every one, though His likeness is not in all, but where the soul is benign and the mind pure. If, therefore, you wish truly to honor the image of God, we declare to you what is true, that you should do good to and pay honor and reverence to everyone, who is made in the image of God. You should minister food to the hungry, drink to the thirsty, clothing to the naked, hospitality to the stranger, and necessary things to the prisoner. That is what will be regarded as truly bestowed upon God. And so much do these things honor God's image, that the one who doesn't do them is regarded as insulting the divine image. In fact, be assured, that whoever commits murder or adultery, or anything that causes suffering or injury to anyone, in all these the image of God is violated. For to injure someone is a great impiety towards God. Whenever, therefore, you do to another what you would not have another do to you, you defile the image of God with undeserved distresses.

Pseudo-Clementine, Homily 11*

Homily 11 repeats the sentiments above almost verbatim. The connection between worshiping God and doing good to humans made in God's image is repeated. Also wrongly attributed to Clement of Rome, the Clementine Homilies are purportedly an account of Clement's travels with the apostle Peter and share much of the material of Recognitions.

You are the image of the invisible God. So don't let those who would be pious say that idols are images of God, and therefore that it is right to worship them. For the image of God is a human being. Whoever wishes to be pious towards God does good to humans, because the body of a person bears the image of God. But all do not as yet bear His likeness, but the pure mind of the good soul does. However, as we know that humans were made after the image and after the likeness of God, we tell you to be pious towards them, that the favor may be counted as done to God, whose image each one is. Therefore it behooves you to give honor to the image of God, which is humanity—in these ways: food to the hungry, drink to the thirsty, clothing to the naked, care to the sick, shelter to the stranger, and visiting one who is in prison, to help each as you can. In other words, whatever good things any one wishes for oneself, so give to another in need, and then a good reward can be reckoned to one as being pious towards the image of God. And by like reason, whoever will not undertake to do these things, shall be punished as neglecting the image.

Cyprian, Treatise 8: On Works and Alms

Cyprian (d. 258) was bishop of Carthage during the Decian persecution in which many Christians lapsed, that is, they gave in to the authorities and denounced their faith. Preaching during difficult times for the Christian Church in the Roman Empire, he makes the case for the opportunity to cleanse one's sins through almsgiving and good works. This was not an uncommon argument in the early church, linking benevolence to forgiveness for post-baptismal sin. In this passage Cyprian suggests that some need Christ to anoint their eyes with special salve so their eyes may be open to the plight of the poor and recognize that it is always God one serves.

And you who are a wealthy and rich matron in Christ's Church, anoint your eyes, not with the eye ointment of the devil, but with Christ's eye salve, that you may be able to attain to see God, by deserving well of God, both by good works and character.

But you who are such as this, cannot be productive in the Church. For your eyes, overcast with the gloom of blackness, and shadowed in night, do not see the needy and poor. You are wealthy and rich. Do you think you celebrate the Lord's Supper, not at all thinking about the offering, coming to the Lord's Supper without a sacrifice, and yet take part of the sacrifice which the poor person has offered? . . . And in order that we may understand that their labors are given to God, and that whoever performs them deserves well of the Lord, Christ calls this "the offerings of God," suggesting that the widow has cast in two farthings into the offerings of God, so that it may be absolutely clear that whoever has pity on the poor lends to God.

Commodianus, Instructions in Favor of Christian Discipline

Commodianus (fl. ca. 250) was an African Christian who made his mark through poetry. In this poem he instructs Christians to open their tables to those who cannot return the favor. By feeding those in need, Christians are attending to God.

To the Pastors

Those of you who seek to feed others, and have prepared what you could by assiduously feeding, have done the right thing. But still look after the poor person, who cannot feed you in turn, then will your table be approved by the one God. The Almighty has commanded those especially to be fed. Think about it—when you feed the sick, you are also lending to the High One. In that thing the Lord has wished that you should stand before Him approved.

Lactantius, The Divine Institutes

Lactantius (ca. 240–ca. 320) was an early Christian apologist who wrote The Divine Institutes *as a systematic explanation of Christianity to educated pagans. In an interesting twist on having eyes to see, Lactantius chastises the pagans who cannot see their sacred duty to provide hospitality for the dead because they only have eyes to see what they think is useful. What utility or gain is there in caring for the dead?*

Lactantius argues for eyes to see that the dead, too, are the workmanship of God and are made in God's image.

On the Kinds of Beneficence and Works of Mercy

The last and greatest duty of piety is the burying of strangers and the poor, a subject which those [pagan] teachers of virtue and justice have not touched upon at all. For they were unable to see this who measured all their duties by utility . . . but they abandoned this because they were unable to see any advantage in it.

Moreover, there have not been lacking those who esteemed burial as unnecessary, and said that it was no evil to lie unburied and neglected. But their unholy wisdom is rejected alike by the whole human race, and by the divine commands to perform the rite. But they do not go so far as to say that it shouldn't be done, but only that, if it happens to be overlooked, no harm is done. They perform their duty, not so much by holding principles as by trying to give consolation, in case this happens to some wise person, so that person will not consider himself or herself any the less on this account. But we're not talking about what ought to be endured by someone wise, but of what that wise person should do. We're not asking whether the whole system of burial is practical or not. It must be practiced, even if only because it seems among people to be done rightly and kindly, whether they imagine it useless or not. For it is the feeling which is inquired into, and it is the purpose which is weighed. Therefore we will not tolerate the image and workmanship of God to lie exposed as a prey to beasts and birds. Instead, we will restore it to the earth, from which it had its origin. If it happens to be a case of someone we don't know, we will stand in the place of relatives, letting kindness fill their empty place. Wherever humanity is called for, there we will think that our duty is required. What is more consistent with the heart of justice than our affording to strangers through kindness, the things we freely give to our own relatives through affection? And this kindness is much more sure and just when it is now afforded, not to one who is dead and unaware, but to God alone, to whom a just work is a most acceptable sacrifice.

Gregory of Nazianzus, Panegyric on Basil

Thanks to this eulogy for his friend, Gregory of Nazianzus (329–389) has given us a wealth of information about Basil of Caesarea and his hospice for lepers. Gregory's panegyric testifies to Basil's hospitality especially to the lepers, "that terrible and piteous spectacle of men who are living corpses." Gregory identifies the gift of recognition necessary in order for Basil to offer hospitality in his treatment of lepers as though offering it to Christ.

> He [Basil] . . . who took the lead in pressing upon those who had humanity, that they shouldn't despise their fellow human beings, nor dishonor Christ, the one Head of all, by their inhuman treatment of them. Rather, they should use the misfortunes of others as an opportunity of firmly establishing their own lot, and to lend to God that mercy of which they stand in need at His hands. He did not disdain to honor with his lips this disease, even though he had a brilliant reputation and was of noble ancestry himself. He saluted them as kindred, not, as some might assume, from self-righteousness (for who was so far removed from this feeling?). No, he took the lead in going to tend them on account of his beliefs, and so he gave instruction not only by his words but also by his actions. The effect produced is to be seen not only in the city, but in the country and beyond, and even the leaders of society have vied with one another in their philanthropy and magnanimity towards them.

Gregory of Nyssa, Homily: As You Did It To One of These, You Did It To Me

Gregory of Nyssa (330–395) was a monk, theologian and bishop who wrote extensively. He is one of the Cappadocian Fathers whose formative work on the doctrine of the Trinity prevailed at the Council of Constantinople in 381. Gregory preaches a powerful sermon on "the least of these" that appeals to the vocabulary of shared humanity as the basis for extending hospitality. In this portion, he cites the sick and asks the healthy Christian to identify with the sick by imagining that person is, in fact, a member of his or her body. Eyes to see will recognize the stranger and hungry as ones sent by Christ. Mercy shown to them unites the host with Christ.

> Do you not see that in addition to persons in good health, there are other sound persons who often suffer affliction, boils or who are inflamed by these illnesses which develop into festering, redness and infirmities? What should we do? Do we not combat illness which afflicts a bodily member? On the other hand, we turn our attention to cure a diseased member by using the health of the entire

body. If we believe that the promise [of Christ] is true, one must observe the commandments without which a person cannot have hope. The stranger, those who are naked, without food, infirm and imprisoned are the ones the Gospel intends for you. The wanderer and naked, and ill person without necessities stand in need by reason of their hardships. A homeless person or one with no work lacks life's necessities; they are nevertheless imprisoned by illness. You have the fullness of the commandments with regard to these persons (Rom 13.10), so lend the Lord everything you have by showing mercy (Prov 19.17). Why are you then so obstinate concerning your own life? He who does not wish to have the God of all as a friend possesses nothing except stubbornness towards himself. Just as a person appropriates the commandment, another separates himself from it by not showing generosity. "Take my yoke upon yourself" (Mt 11.29). Here the text speaks of observing the commandments in terms of a yoke. Let us pay attention to Him who summons us and be united to Christ by putting on the yoke of love.

Ambrose, *On Duties of the Clergy**

Ambrose (ca. 339–397) was a Roman lawyer who became bishop of Milan in 374. He promoted the independence of the church in the face of civil power and was best known for his preaching. This treatise, patterned after Cicero's De Officiis, *addresses Christian ethics. Discussing hospitality, Ambrose seems to suggest that we owe greater hospitality to the upright. In an interesting twist, however, he goes on to cite Abraham and Lot who received guests not knowing whether they were upright. By this example, even the stranger may be the upright guest, perhaps Christ himself.*

A person ought to be hospitable, kind, upright, not desirous of what belongs to another, willing to give up some of his own rights if attacked, rather than to take away another's. He ought to avoid disputes, to hate quarrels. He ought to restore unity and the grace of quietness. When a good person gives up any of his own rights, it is not only a sign of liberality, but is also accompanied by great advantages. To start with, it is no small gain to be free from the cost of a lawsuit. Then it also brings in good results, by an increase of friendship, from which many advantages rise. These become afterwards most useful to the person that can despise a little something at the time.

In all the duties of hospitality kindly feeling must be shown to all, but greater respect must be given to the upright. For "Whoever receives a righteous person, in the name of a righteous person, shall receive a righteous person's reward," as the Lord has said. So much does hospitality stand in favor with God, that not even the glass of cold water shall fail of getting a reward. You see that Abraham, in looking for guests, received God Himself to entertain. You see that Lot received the angels. And how do you know that when you receive someone, you do not receive Christ? Christ may be in the stranger that comes, for Christ is there in the person of the poor, as He Himself says: "I was in prison and you came to me, I was naked and you clothed me."

Ambrose, *Epistle 63*

In this letter Ambrose makes explicit the identification of Christ with the guest.

Love hospitality, whereby holy Abraham found favor, and received Christ as his guest, and Sarah already worn with age gained a son. Lot also escaped the fire of the destruction of Sodom. You too can receive Angels if you offer hospitality to strangers. What shall I say of Rahab who by this means found safety?

John Chrysostom, *Homily 26 on Matthew**

John (ca. 347–407) named Chrysostom, or "golden-mouthed," on account of his eloquent preaching, delivered the following sermons while still a priest at Antioch. He would later become bishop of Constantinople and a controversial figure as he sought reforms both in the church and the government. In his sermon on Matthew, Chrysostom comments on the centurion's receiving Christ under his roof (Matthew 8:5). Christ's presence is not a historical event of the past, but a possibility for the present, if we have eyes to see.

What then said the centurion? "I am not worthy that you should come under my roof." Let us pay attention, as many as are to receive Christ, for it is possible to receive Him even now. Let us pay attention, and emulate, and receive Him with as great zeal. For indeed, when you receive a poor person who is hungry and naked, you have received and cherished Him.

John Chrysostom, *Homily 45 on the Acts of the Apostles**

John Chrysostom wrote many sermons on Acts. He pursues an extensive discussion here of lodging visitors based on Acts 21:16-17. Many people may make excuses by claiming that if Paul were to show up at the door, hospitality would be eagerly extended. Chrysostom warns them that, indeed, Paul's Master knocks at their doors. Further, it is Christ himself who is either honored or insulted, depending on the host's powers of recognition. Hospitality to the least of these is hospitality to Christ.

So it seems to me that this writer in the Acts epitomizes the events of many years, relating only the matters of chief importance. So unwilling were they to burden the Church, when there was another to lodge them, and so little did they stand upon their dignity. "The kindred," it says, "received us gladly." Affairs among the Jews were now full of peace. There was not much warfare among them. "Bringing us," it says, "to one with whom we should lodge." Paul was the guest he entertained. Perchance some one of you says, Sure, if it were given me to entertain Paul as a guest, I readily and with much eagerness would do this. Pay attention! It is in your power to entertain Paul's Master for your guest, and you refuse. For "he that receives one of these least," he said, "receives me." By how much the kindred may be least, so much the more does Christ come to you through him. For whoever receives the great, often does it from vainglory also, but the one who receives the small, does it purely for Christ's sake. It is in your power to entertain even the Father of Christ as your guest, and you refuse! For, "I was a stranger," He says, "and you took me in," and again, "To one of the least of these of my family, you have done it to me." Though it may not be Paul, yet if it is a believer and kindred, although the least, Christ comes to you through that one. Open your house, take him in. "Whoever receives a prophet," He says, "shall receive a prophet's reward." Therefore too the one that receives Christ, shall receive the reward of whoever has Christ for a guest. Do not disbelieve His words, but be believing. Christ has said, "Through them I come to you." So that you may not disbelieve, He lays down both punishments for those who do not receive, and honors for those who do receive, since He would not have done this, unless both the person honored and the person insulted were Himself. "You received Me," He said, "into your lodging, I will receive you into the Kingdom of My Father. You took away My hunger, I take away your sins. You saw Me bound, I see you loosed. You saw Me a stranger, I make you a citizen of heaven. You gave Me bread, I give you an entire Kingdom, that you may inherit and possess it."

Later in the same sermon, he returns to the theme of recognizing Christ in the stranger. One's house can be Christ's resting place. He ends this portion with an exasperated note—Christ isn't asking that we kill our best calf. He's only asking for the minimum: feed the hungry, give clothes to the naked, shelter the stranger.

Do you want to put us to shame? Then do this. Surpass us in generosity. Have a room, to which Christ may come. Say, "This is Christ's space. This building is set apart for Him." Even if it is just a basement and tiny. He won't refuse it. Christ goes about "naked and a stranger." It is only a shelter He wants. Abraham received the strangers in the place where he himself lived. His wife stood in the place of a servant, the guests in the place of masters. He didn't know that he was receiving Christ, didn't know that he was receiving Angels. Had he known it, he would have lavished his whole substance. But we, who know that we receive Christ, don't show even so much enthusiasm as he did who thought that he was receiving humans. "But many of them are impostors and ungrateful," you will say. And for this the greater your reward when you receive for the sake of Christ's name. For if you know indeed that they are impostors, don't receive them into your house. But if you don't know this, why do you accuse them lightly? "Therefore I tell them to go to the receiving house." But what kind of excuse is there for us, when we do not even receive those whom we know, but shut our doors against all? Let our house be Christ's general receiving place. Let us demand of them as a reward, not money, but that they make our house the receiving place for Christ. Let us run about everywhere, let us drag them in, let us seize our prize. Greater are the benefits we receive than what we confer. He does not require you to kill a calf, but only to give bread to the hungry, raiment to the naked, shelter to the stranger.

John Chrysostom, *Homily 21 on Romans**

It is tempting when offering hospitality to judge the worthiness of the receiver. Does this person deserve my hospitality? Is this person truly in need? Chrysostom reminds Christians that they can never know another's need. If we tried to first judge another's need or worthiness, we would never offer mercy or hospitality. Instead, says Chrysostom, recog-

nize that it is Christ we are attempting to judge. This sermon on Paul's powerful image of the members in one body of Christ (Romans 12:4-13) calls upon the many members of Christ's body to identify with one another. In this passage, Chrysostom compares the hospitality of his contemporaries to that of Lot and Abraham with scorching words.

"Given to hospitality." He does not say doing it, but "given" to it, so to instruct us not to wait for those that shall ask it, and see when they will come to us, but to run to them, and be given to finding them. Thus did Lot, thus Abraham. . . . Not as we do, if we happen to see a stranger or someone poor, knitting our brows, and not deigning even to speak to them. And if after thousands of entreaties we are softened, and tell our servant to give them a little something, we think we have quite done our duty. But he [Abraham] didn't do that. He assumed the role of a supplicant and a servant, though he did not know who he was going to take under his roof. But we, who have clear information that it is Christ Whom we take in, do not grow gentle even for this. But he both beseeches, and entreats, and falls on his knees to them, yet we insult those that come to us. . . . As did Abraham also. Besides his generosity and ready mind we especially admire him on the grounds that when he had no knowledge who his guests were, yet he so acted. Don't be curious then, either, since for Christ you receive him. And if you are always so scrupulous about the character of your guests, many a time you will pass by a person of esteem, and lose your reward. Yet whoever receives someone not of high status has no fault found with him, but is even rewarded. For "he that receives a prophet in the name of a prophet, shall receive a prophet's reward." Rather, the one who, because of their own inordinate pickiness, passes one that should be admired, will even suffer punishment. So don't busy yourself with people's lives and doings. For this is the very extreme of stinginess, to nit pick about a person's entire life to avoid giving them one loaf of bread. For if this person is a murderer, if a robber, or what not, does he therefore seem to you not to deserve a loaf and a few coins? And yet your Master causes even the sun to rise upon him! And do you judge him unworthy of food even for a day?

John Chrysostom, *Homily 30 on Romans**

When we recognize one another as Christ coming to stay we will see our homes and lives in a new light as well. Chrysostom describes the new abode that results from welcoming Christ.

Knowing all this then, let us receive the Saints, that the house may shine, that it may be freed from choking weeds, that the bed-chamber may become a haven. And let us receive them, and wash their feet. . . .

And don't focus on the fact that in appearance the Saints that lodge with you are but poor, and as beggars, and in rags many times, but be mindful of that voice which says, "Inasmuch as you have done it to the least of these, you have done it unto me" (Matthew 25:40). And, "Despise not one of these little ones, because their angels do always behold the face of My Father which is in heaven" (Matthew 18:10). Receive them then with readiness of mind, bringing as they do ten thousand blessings to you, through the greeting of peace.

*John Chrysostom, Homily 14 on 1 Timothy**

Chrysostom lifts up widows as a model of hospitality throughout this sermon. He concludes that if one cannot receive the stranger as Christ, one should not receive the stranger at all.

Observe, the hospitality here spoken of is not merely a friendly reception, but one given with zeal and full of life, with readiness, and going about it as if one were receiving Christ Himself. The widows should perform these services themselves, not commit them to their handmaids. For Christ said, "If I your Master and Lord have washed your feet, you ought also to wash one another's feet" (John 13:14). And though a woman may be very rich, and of the highest rank, vain of her birth and noble family, there is not the same distance between her and others, as between God and the disciples. If you receive the stranger as Christ, be not ashamed, but rather glory. But if you receive him not as Christ, receive him not at all. "He that receives you," He said, "receives Me" (Matthew 10:40). If you give to the poor, don't disdain to give it yourself, for it is not to the poor that it is given, but to Christ, and who is so wretched, as to disdain to stretch out his own hand to Christ?

*John Chrysostom, Homily 11 on Hebrews**

Chrysostom praises those who can offer hospitality with open hands in this portion of his sermon on Hebrews. *Those who try to judge others' lives first are doomed to closed hearts and closed hands, for they cannot see the true need in another's life. They look at the surface rather than the depths and thereby miss the deep need for Christ in their own lives as well. Recognition that the apparent unworthy ones may be angels elicits generosity. Chrysostom does not mince words here, and we can hear the preacher's voice rising in the rhetorical questions he hammers out.*

Then we are heard, when we ourselves also hear the poor who come to us. "Whoever," it is said, "stops his ears that he may not hear the poor," his prayer our God will not pay attention to. "Blessed is the one who considers the poor and needy. The Lord will deliver him in the evil day." But what day is evil except that one which is evil to sinners?

What is meant by "one who considers"? Whoever understands what it is to be poor, who has thoroughly learned the affliction of the poor. For the one who has learned such affliction, will certainly and immediately have compassion on the poor. When you see someone poor, do not hurry by, but immediately reflect what you would have been, had you been that person. What would you not have wished that all should do for you? "One that considers," he says. Reflect that this person is a free person like yourself, and shares the same noble birth with you, and possesses all things in common with you. Yet oftentimes such a one is not on a level even with your dogs. On the contrary, while they are satiated, the poor person oftentimes lies, sleeps, hungry, and the free person has become less honorable than your slaves. . . .

If only it stopped here, but immediately accusations are brought against the needful person. For why doesn't he work, you ask? And why is he to be maintained in idleness? But, tell me, is it by working that you have what you have? Did you not receive it as an inheritance from your parents? And even if you do work, is this a reason why you should reproach another? Don't you listen to what Paul said? For after saying, "Whoever does not work, does not eat," next he says, "But don't be weary in well doing." But what do they say? He is an impostor. What do you have to say? Do you call him an impostor, for the sake of a single loaf or some clothing? But, you say, he will sell it immediately. And do you manage all your affairs well? But what? Are all poor through idleness? Is no one so from shipwreck? None from lawsuits? None from being robbed? None from dangers? None from illness? None from any other difficulties? If, however, we hear anyone bewailing such evils, and crying out aloud, and looking up naked toward heaven, and with long hair, and clad in rags, at once we call him, The fake! The deceiver! The swindler! Aren't you ashamed? Whom do you call impostor? Give nothing, and do not accuse the poor person. But, you say, he has means, and pretends. This is a charge against yourself, not against him. . . . "Give to every one that asks of you, and from anyone who would borrow of you don't turn away." (Matthew 5:42) Stretch out your hand. Let it not be closed up. We have not been made judges into other's lives, because then we would have compassion on no one. . . . Stop this unhealthy fondness for meddling, which is Satanic, which is destructive. . . . Inquire, if you will, how Abraham showed hospitality towards all who came to him. If he had been over-curious about those who fled to him for refuge, he would not have "entertained angels." For perhaps not thinking them to be angels, he would have thrust them too away with the rest. But since he received all, he received even angels.

John Chrysostom, *Homily 41 on Genesis*

Chrysostom preaches extensively on Genesis and on Abraham's hospitality to the strangers in Genesis 18. He connects that story to the "least of these" passages from the Gospels in this sermon on Genesis. We can always be as lucky as Abraham, "the just man," and get "a good catch" if we only have eyes to see.

Let us discover and emulate the just man's virtue. If, in fact, we do so, it is likely that we, too, will have the good luck of such a wonderful catch. Rather, we could always have that good luck if we wanted to. The loving Lord's intention, you see, was that we should not be indifferent about such friendship nor be too picky about our visitors—hence his words, "Whoever receives one of the least of these in my name receives me." So don't pay attention to the status of the visitor nor despise the person on the basis of what you can see, but consider that in the visitor you are welcoming your Lord.

Jerome, *Letter 52**

Jerome (ca. 342–420) was an early Latin scholar of the church to whom we owe the first translation of the Bible into Latin. Most of his adult life was spent in study and monastic discipline in Palestine. In his letter to Nepotian in 394 Jerome details the duties of clergy. This was important because Nepotian and others had come to the priesthood from military service so Jerome took pains to instruct them on their new respons-

ibilities. This letter was widely read in his day. He charges clergy with serving not the wealthy but the poor so that they may host Christ. Shifting from military service where their eyes were always upon the powerful, they must now learn to recognize Christ in the lowly.

Anyone who possesses the Lord, and who says with the prophet, "The Lord is my portion," can commit themselves to nothing besides the Lord. For if someone holds to something besides the Lord, the Lord will not be that one's portion. Suppose, for instance, that a person holds to gold or silver, or possessions or inlaid furniture; with such portions as these the Lord will not deign to be that person's portion. . . . I warn you, therefore, and again and yet again admonish you, don't look to your military experience for a standard of clerical obligation. Under Christ's banner seek for no worldly gain, lest having more than when you first became a clergyman, you hear people say, to your shame, "Their portion shall not profit them." Welcome the poor and strangers to your homely board, that with them Christ may be your guest. Avoid as you would the plague any clergyman who engages in business, and who rises from poverty to wealth, and from obscurity to a high position.

Jerome, Letter 77

In several letters Jerome praises Fabiola (d. 399), a Roman matron who left her life of privilege in Rome to follow a life of study and service in Palestine. Jerome calls her "the praise of the Christians, the marvel of the Gentiles, the sorrow of the poor, and the consolation of the monks." After detailing the repulsive symptoms of the sick she gathered into her hospital, Jerome reminds the reader that Fabiola's acts of hospitality and mercy rest on a recognition of shared humanity. If we have eyes to see, we, too, will know that these outcasts' suffering is our own.

In the day of prosperity she was not forgetful of affliction. . . . She broke up and sold all her property she could lay hands on (it was large and suitable to her rank), and turning it into money she laid it out for the benefit of the poor. She was the first person to found a hospital, into which she might gather sufferers out of the streets, and where she might nurse the unfortunate victims of sickness and poverty. Do I need to recount the various ailments of human beings? Need I speak of noses slit, eyes put out, feet half burnt, hands covered with sores? Or of limbs dropsical and atrophied?

Or of diseased flesh alive with worms? Often did she carry on her own shoulders persons infected with jaundice or with filth. Often too did she wash away the matter discharged from wounds which others, even though men, could not bear to look at. She gave food to her patients with her own hand, and moistened the scarcely breathing lips of the dying with sips of liquid. I know of many wealthy and devout persons who, unable to overcome their natural repugnance to such sights, perform this work of mercy by the agency of others, giving money instead of personal aid. I do not blame them and am far from construing their weakness of resolution into a lack of faith. While however I pardon such squeamishness, I extol to the skies the enthusiastic zeal of a mind that is above it. A great faith makes little of such trifles. But I know how terrible was the retribution which fell upon the proud mind of the rich man clothed in purple for not having helped Lazarus. The poor wretch whom we despise, whom we cannot so much as look at, and the very sight of whom turns our stomachs, is human like ourselves, is made of the same clay as we are, is formed out of the same elements. All that he suffers we too may suffer. Let us then regard his wounds as though they were our own, and then all our insensibility to another's suffering will give way before our pity for ourselves.

Jerome, Letter 108

Jerome wrote an extensive and famous letter to the nun Eustochium as a eulogy of her mother, Paula, who had been Jerome's fellow worker in Bethlehem. Paula's virtue of hospitality is glimpsed here in his reference to the guest house she built in the desert so that Mary and Joseph would not be turned away again.

In each of His saints she believed that she saw Christ Himself; and whatever she bestowed upon them she rejoiced to feel that she had bestowed it upon the Lord. . . . Not long afterwards, making up her mind to dwell permanently in holy Bethlehem, she took up her abode for three years in a miserable hostelry until she could build the requisite cells and monastic buildings, to say nothing of a guest house for passing travelers where they might find the welcome which Mary and Joseph had missed.

Jerome, Apology in Answer to Rufinus

Throughout his ecclesiastical career Jerome weighed in on several important controversies. Rufinus was an adversary in several of those and their correspondence is extensive. In this response to Rufinus concerning a dispute over the treatment of some monks who had been exiled by their bishop, Jerome points out the duties of monks to offer impartial hospitality. One might actually welcome Joseph and Mary, or Christ himself, in the guests if one has eyes to see.

Our duties in our monastery are those of hospitality. We welcome all who come to us with the smile of human friendliness. We must take care lest it should again happen that Mary and Joseph do not find room in the inn, and that Jesus should be shut out and say to us, "I was a stranger and you did not take me in." . . . Bring to your memory, my brother, how he whom we speak of had confessed Christ, think of that breast which was gashed by the scourges, recall to mind the imprisonment he had endured, the darkness, the exile, the work in the mines, and you will not be surprised that we welcomed him as a passing guest. Are we to be thought rebels by you because we give a cup of cold water to the thirsty in the name of Christ?

Paulinus of Nola, Letter 1

Paulinus (353–431), from a wealthy family in Bordeaux, gave his fortune to the poor and, with his Spanish wife, settled at Nola, where he became bishop in 409. This letter was written in early 395 C.E. to Paulinus' friend Sulpitius Severus. He praises Severus for recognizing Christ in the needy and the poor.

You revealed the increase of your inheritance amongst the saints. This you did by your wholesome disposal of the burdens of this world, for you have purchased heaven and Christ at the price of brittle worldly goods. You have true understanding concerning the needy and the poor, for you came to believe that they reside in Christ, and that Christ, as He Himself taught us, is clothed and fed and lent money when they are.

Paulinus of Nola, Letter 13

Paulinus makes explicit the identification of the stranger with Christ and his angels in this letter to Pammachius in 396.

Let us also, then, open our homes to our brothers, whether after the fashion of the fathers just mentioned we fear the danger of rejecting an angel when we repulse men, or whether we hope to deserve to have angels as our guests as we assist the passage of every stranger with ready kindness. For when our father Abraham entertained strangers, he received Christ the Lord and his angels; in his hospitable tent he saw that day which in the Gospel the Savior reveals in Abraham's presence.

Therefore, glory in the Lord, for flesh and blood have not revealed to you the wisdom of this foresight, but Christ Himself who is the true light and the wisdom of God. By this wisdom you are aware that Christ is given food, drink, covering, and visitation in the person of every man in need and poverty.

Sulpitius Severus, Dialogues*

Sulpitius Severus (ca. 360–420) converted to a life of asceticism after the death of his wife around 394 and became a historian of the early church. In a remarkable series of stories told by his friend Postumianus about his travels and recorded by Severus, the theme of identification of the lowly with Christ is extended to include animals. In the first story, a wolf transgresses the hospitality offered it by a desert monk. But it repents and seeks forgiveness, thereby evidencing Christ's power in it and proving itself a servant of Christ at the gate.

We found another equally remarkable man living in a small hut, capable only of containing a single person. Concerning him we were told that a she-wolf was accustomed to stand near him at dinner; and that the beast could by no means be easily fooled so as to fail to be with him at the regular time he ate. It was also said that the wolf waited at the door until he offered her the bread leftover from his own humble dinner; that she was accustomed to lick his hand, and then, her duty being, as it were, fulfilled, and her respects paid to him, she took her departure. But it so happened that that holy man, while he escorted a brother who had paid him a visit, on his way home, was a pretty long time away, and only returned under night. In the meanwhile, the beast made its appearance at the usual dinner time. Having entered the vacant cell and perceived that its benefactor was absent, it began to search round the hut with some curiosity to discover, if possible, the inhabitant. Now it so happened that a basket of palm-twigs was hanging close at hand with five loaves of bread in it. Taking one of these, the beast devoured it, and then, having committed this evil deed, went its way. The recluse on his return found the basket in a state of disorder, and the number of loaves less than it should have been. He was aware of the loss of his household goods, and observed near the threshold some fragments of the loaf which had been stolen. Considering all this, he had little doubt as to the author of the theft. Accordingly, when on the following days the beast did not, as usual, make its appearance (undoubtedly hesitating from a consciousness of its audacious deed to come to him on whom it had inflicted injury), the recluse was deeply grieved at being deprived of the happiness he had enjoyed in its company. At last, being brought back through his prayers, it appeared to him as usual at dinner time, after the lapse of seven days. But to make clear to every one the shame it felt, through regret for what had been done, it did not dare to draw very near, and with its eyes cast upon the earth from profound shame, it was plain to every one that it seemed to beg, in a sort of way, for pardon. The recluse, pitying its confusion, bade it come close to him, and then, with a kindly hand, stroked its head. Then, by giving it two loaves instead of the usual one, he restored the guilty creature to its former position. So it laid aside its misery upon being forgiven, and returned anew to its former habits. Behold, I beg of you, even in this case, the power of Christ, to whom all is wise that is irrational, and to whom all is mild that is by nature savage. A wolf does its duty. A wolf acknowledges the crime of theft. A wolf is confounded with a sense of shame and, when called for, it presents itself. It offers its head to be stroked; and it has a perception of the pardon granted to it, just as if it had a feeling of shame on account of its misconduct—this is your power, O Christ—these, O Christ, are your marvelous works. For in truth, whatever things your servants do in your name are your doings. The only cause we find for deep grief here is that, while wild beasts acknowledge your majesty, intelligent beings fail to do you reverence.

The second story describes a lioness who reciprocates the hospitality and healing offered her by bringing to her host, a desert monk, a rare animal skin for his use as a cloak. The story makes clear that, while the lioness is a supplicant, she must also be recognized as an agent of Another.

He was said already to have dwelt in these solitudes for twelve years. But although he shunned interaction with people, yet he did not shrink from meeting these friends. On the contrary, he yielded himself to their affection for a period of three days. On the fourth day, when he had gone some distance escorting them in their return journey, they beheld a lioness of remarkable size coming towards them. The animal, although meeting with three persons, showed no uncertainty as to the one she went for, but threw herself down at the feet of the anchorite. Lying there with a kind of weeping and lamentation, she manifested mingled feelings of sorrow and supplication. The sight affected all, and especially him who perceived that he was sought for. He therefore set out, and the others followed him. For the beast stopping from time to time, and, from time to time looking back, clearly wished it to be understood that the anchorite should follow wherever she led. What need is there of many words? We arrived at the den of the animal, where she, the unfortunate mother, was nourishing five whelps already grown up. But as they had come forth with closed eyes from the womb of their mother, so they had continued in persistent blindness. Bringing them out one by one from the hollow of the rock, she laid them down at the feet of the anchorite. Then at length the holy man figured out what the creature wanted. He called upon the name of God, then touched with his hand the closed eyes of the whelps; and immediately their blindness ceased, while light, so long denied them, streamed upon the open eyes of the animals. So those brothers, having visited the anchorite whom they had wanted to see, returned with a very precious reward for their labor, inasmuch as, having been permitted to be eye-witnesses of such power, they had beheld the faith of the saint, and the glory of Christ, to which they will in future bear testimony. But I have still more marvels to tell: the lioness, after five days, returned to the man who had done her so great a kindness, and brought him, as a gift, the skin of an uncommon animal. Frequently clad in this, as if it were a cloak, that holy man did not hesitate to receive that gift through the instrumentality of the beast. All the time, he rather regarded Another as being the giver.

Maximus of Turin, *Sermon 36**

Maximus (d. 408–423) was bishop at Turin whose many sermons show an able and thoughtful preacher. This sermon paints a wretched picture of master-slave relations in some households. Like charity, hospitality begins at home. Maximus points out that Christian slaves are "brothers by grace" and warrant mercy and consideration. He calls for masters to recognize slaves as family members if they ever hope to offer hospitality beyond the household.

Some people, however, who are heedless of the divine precepts, exercise such an absolute power over their slaves and those subject to them that they do not hesitate these days to cut them to pieces with scourges, to fasten them with fetters and, if perchance the waiter is a little bit late when mealtime has come, to lacerate him at once with blows and to satiate themselves with the slave's blood before doing so with the pleasures of the table. . . . And, what is still more tragic, these days a Christian master does not spare his Christian slave and does not consider that, even though he is a slave by condition, nonetheless he is a brother by grace, for he has also put on Christ, participates in the sacraments and, just as you do, has God for his Father. Why would he not have you as his brother? For there are many who, on returning from the hunt, pay more attention to their hounds than to their slaves. Not caring if their slaves die of hunger, they have their hounds recline or sleep next to them while they themselves feed them a daily portion. And, what is worse, if the food has not been well prepared for them, a slave is slain for the sake of a dog. In some homes you may see sleek and fat dogs running around, but human beings going about wan and faltering. Will such persons ever take pity on the poor when they are without mercy for their own households?

Macarius, *Fifty Spiritual Homilies*

The Fifty Spiritual Homilies *have traditionally been attributed to Macarius of Egypt, though current scholarship has proved this incorrect. However, we can determine that Macarius, or "Blessed One," who wrote these homilies was a deeply spiritual teacher and writer in the context of fourth-century desert monasticism. He is often described as intoxicated with the love of God because of his enthusiasm. In* Homily 15 *he exhorts Christians to see beyond the exterior appearance of illness, disability, or paralysis. Macarius argues that because we "have been made participators of divine grace" we can put on eyes to see the wholeness in each person.*

Christians, therefore, should strive in all things and ought not to pass judgment of any kind on anyone, not on the prostitute nor on sinners nor on disorderly persons. But they should look upon all persons

73

with a single mind and a pure eye so that it may be for such a person almost a natural and fixed attitude never to despise or judge or abhor anyone or to divide people and place them into boxes.

If you see a man with one eye, do not make any judgment in your heart but regard him as though he were whole. If someone has a maimed hand, see him not as maimed. See the crippled as straight, the paralytic as healthy. For this is purity of heart, that, when you see the sinners and the weak, you have compassion and show mercy toward them. For it can happen that the holy ones of the Lord suit as though they were in the theater, watching the follies of the world but in the interior they are conversing with God. According to their exterior they seem to be looking with their eyes at the things of the world.

The Lives of the Desert Fathers

All we know of the authorship of this text (ca. 400) is that it claims to be written by a monk from the Jerusalem monastery on the Mount of Olives. It is the account of the journey he and six other monks undertook in Egypt in the late 300's and is organized around their encounters with each desert father. Several passages reflect a concern to properly recognize strangers. The first comes from an experience of welcome in the city of Oxyrhynchus. There watchmen are posted to keep an eye out for strangers in need and welcome them as angels.

The chief officials and magistrates of the city, who distributed largesse to the common people, had watchmen posted at the gates and entrances, so that if some needy stranger should appear, he would be taken to them and receive victuals for his sustenance. And what can one say about the piety of the common people, who when they saw us strangers crossing the agora approached as if we were angels? . . . It is beyond my power to describe their hospitality and their love for us. In fact each of us had our cloaks rent apart by people pulling us to make us go and stay with them.

In the stories about their encounter with Saint Apollo in Thebaid, they report this story of angelic visitors who act not as guests in need but represent God's providence with the small group of Apollo and his followers.

38. Some time before this, Saint Apollo was living in a cave in the mountain with five brothers. He had recently come from the desert

and these were his first disciples. Easter came, and when they had finished giving worship to God they ate whatever they happened to have. There were a few dry loaves and some pickled vegetables. 39. Then Apollo said to them, "If we have faith, my children, and are true sons of Christ, let each of us ask of God what he desires to eat." 40. But they entrusted the whole matter to him, considering themselves unworthy of such a grace. He therefore prayed with a radiant face and they all said, "Amen." And at once in the night a number of men arrived at the cave, complete strangers to them, who said that they had traveled a long distance. They were carrying things which the brothers had never even heard of before, things which do not grow in Egypt: fruits of paradise of every kind, and grapes and pomegranates and figs and walnuts, all procured out of season, and honeycombs, and a pitcher of fresh milk, and giant dates, and white loaves still warm although brought to them from a foreign country. 41. The men who brought these things delivered them simply with the message that they had been sent by a rich magnate, and immediately they departed in a hurry. The brothers partook of these provisions until Pentecost and satisfied their hunger with them, so that they wondered and said, "Truly these were sent by God."

This same Apollo advised the visiting monks to pay attention to hospitality to visitors so that they would recognize "it is not them but God you venerate."

55. When we were alone with him he taught us much about ascesis and how to regulate our lives. And he frequently spoke about the reception of visitors, saying, "You must prostrate yourselves before brothers who come to visit you, for it is not them but God you venerate. Have you seen your brother? Says Scripture; you have seen the Lord your God" 56. "This," he said, "has come down to us from Abraham (Genesis 18:2). And that we must press the brothers to refresh themselves we have learned from Lot, who pressed the angels in this way" (Genesis 19:1-30).

John Cassian, Institutes of the Coenobia*

John Cassian (360–435) was a monk who studied asceticism in Egypt then traveled west to establish monasteries in Marseilles. His Institutes, *setting forth basic rules for monastic life, have widely influenced other monastic rules in the west. In Book 5 on the spirit of gluttony, Cassian argues that even the fasting rule of the community should be suspended when Christ enters. Recognizing Christ in his guests, an elder places hospitality above piety, knowing that fasting can be pursued again once the guests are on their way.*

We had come from the region of Syria and had sought the province of Egypt, in our desire to learn the rules of the Elders. We were astonished at the eagerness of heart with which we were received there so that no rule forbidding refreshment until the exact time the fast was over was observed, such as we had been brought up to observe in the monasteries of Palestine. Except in the case of the regular days, Wednesdays and Fridays, wherever we went the daily fast was broken. When we asked why the daily fast was thus ignored by them without scruple one of the elders replied, "The opportunity for fasting is always with me. But as I am going to conduct you on your way, I cannot always keep you with me. And a fast, although it is useful and advisable, is yet a free-will offering. But the exigencies of a command require the fulfillment of a work of charity. And so receiving Christ in you I ought to refresh Him, but when I have sent you on your way I shall be able to balance the hospitality offered for His sake by a stricter fast on my own account. For 'the children of the bridegroom cannot fast while the bridegroom is with them' but when he has departed, then they will rightly fast."

Fulgentius, *To the Abbot Euggippius*

Fulgentius (468–533) was bishop at Ruspe and a fierce defender of the Catholic faith against the Arian Vandals that occupied North Africa. He, too, ties love of God with love of neighbor, charging the abbot Euggippius to recognize God in the neighbor.

So, the love of God and neighbor, which is the fullness of the law and the purpose of the commandment, in God, loves the charity which God is and, in the neighbor, loves charity which is from God; thus God and neighbor are rightly loved, if love itself is loved both in God and in the neighbor. Thus it comes about that without a doubt we love both God himself in God and God in the neighbor. Nor is it in vain that after the love of God, no other love has been commanded us except only the love of neighbor, viz., that we recognize that we must love that creature where we can find charity itself. For every irrational animal, just as it does not have reason, so it does not have charity; nor does there appear to me to be special reason other than that fitting and ordered love which is owed by a human being only to God and neighbor.

Benedict, *Rule*

Benedict (480–550) drafted this rule of life for his community of monks at Monte Cassino around 540. In several chapters he addresses hospitality, making clear in 53 that it always requires recognition of who is really at the door.

Chapter 53. On the Reception of Guests.

Let all guests who arrive be received like Christ, for He is going to say, "I came as a guest, and you received Me." And to all let due honor be shown, especially to the domestics of the faith and to pilgrims.

As soon as a guest is announced, therefore, let the Superior or the brethren meet him with all charitable service. And first of all let them pray together, and then exchange the kiss of peace. For the kiss of peace should not be offered until after the prayers have been said, on account of the devil's deceptions.

In the salutation of all guests, whether arriving or departing, let all humility be shown. Let the head be bowed or the whole body prostrated on the ground in adoration of Christ, who indeed is received in their persons. . . . In the reception of the poor and of pilgrims the greatest care and solicitude should be shown, because it is especially in them that Christ is received.

The chapter on the sick reiterates the theme of recognition.

Chapter 36. On the Sick Brethren.

Before all things and above all things, care must be taken of the sick, so that they will be served as if they were Christ in person; for He Himself said, "I was sick, and you visited Me," and, "What you did for one of these least ones, you did for Me." But let the sick on their part consider that they are being served for the honor of God, and let them not annoy their brethren who are serving them by their unnecessary demands. Yet they should be patiently borne with, because from such as these is gained a more abundant reward. Therefore the abbot shall take the greatest care that they suffer no neglect.

Cyril of Scythopolis, *Lives of the Monks of Palestine*

Cyril of Scythopolis (500s) wrote this account of the desert fathers as an inspiration to Christians seeking a disciplined life. Cyril's own parents ran a hostel for traveling monks and it was likely that through those connections he came to know St. Sabas, a well-known figure among eastern monastics. This pericope shows the interplay of recognizing and receiving strangers. St. Sabas first builds a hospice, then buys cells to host foreign monks. He extends hospitality on behalf of strangers, and God, through a stranger, provides the rest.

31. After occupying the throne of Jerusalem for eight years and three months, Archbishop Sallustius died in Christ on 23 July of the second indiction, and Elias, often mentioned in my account of the holy Euthymius, succeeded to the patriarchate, in the fifty-sixth year of the life of blessed Sabas. Patriarch Elias built a monastery near the episcopal palace and brought together in it those ascetics of the holy church of the Resurrection who had been scattered in the district around the Tower of David, assigning to each of them a cell with every bodily comfort. When they had been gathered together, as has been said, our father Sabas purchased various cells from them and made them into a hospice for the laura. To the north of the cells he purchased were other cells, which he wished to purchase on behalf of foreign monks. He tried to find a sufficient quantity of money, but had only one half solidus. Relying on faith in God, he gave the half solidus as a deposit, with the words, "If I do not pay you in full tomorrow, I forfeit the deposit." On the same day, before sunrise, as he was thinking about this and praying mentally, a completely unknown stranger came up to him, gave him one hundred and seventy solidi, and immediately withdrew, not even giving his name. Astonished at the prompt assistance of God, the blessed one gave the price of the cells and founded a second hospice for the relief of monks coming from abroad. He also acquired two hospices for Castellium, one in the holy city not far from the Tower of David and the other in Jericho in one of the gardens he had bought.

Radegund, *Life*

This passage from the life story of St. Radegund (525–587), a queen to Clothar in western Europe, is typical of many accounts of saints' lives. Radegund is valorized for her purity and service to others. She is able to recognize that the very bodies of the poor belong to Christ. She built a hospice for needy women at Athies, where one is dedicated to her today.

Whenever she received part of the tribute, she gave away a tithe of all that came to her before accepting any for herself. She dispensed what was left to monasteries, sending the gifts to those she could not reach on foot. There was no hermit who could hide from her munificence. So she paid out what she received lest the burden weigh her down. The voice of the needy was not raised in vain for she never turned a deaf ear. Often she gave clothes, believing that the limbs of Christ concealed themselves under the garments of the poor and that whatever she did not give to paupers was truly lost.

Leontius, *Life of St. John the Almsgiver*

Leontius wrote this simple and inspirational biography of John the Almsgiver (fl. ca. 611) some time after 641. We are told in this extraordinary account that John's first act upon being elected Patriarch of Alexandria was to challenge the identification of authority with power. John had a different set of eyes with which to recognize who were his masters. He summons those who administer the church's finances, including funds for the poor, and tells them to hit the streets looking for his true masters.

After John had been elected and was to be enthroned in the Christ-loving capital of Alexandria most certainly by the will of God and not "from men neither through man" this was the first glorious deed and victory which he showed forth to all men—he immediately summoned the treasurers and the official who is styled "the guardian of the peace," and said to them in the hearing of all in the Patriarch's council-chamber, "It is not right, brethren, that we should consider anyone in preference to Christ." The whole assembly which had gathered together was deeply moved at his words, and agreed thereto, and then the holy man continued, "Go therefore through the whole city, please, and make a list of all my masters down to the last." But his hearers could not imagine who these could be, and besought him to tell them, as they were astonished that any could possibly be masters of the Patriarch; and he opened his angelic mouth again and said: "Those whom you call poor and beggars, these I proclaim my masters and helpers. For they, and they only, are really able to help us bestow upon us the kingdom of heaven."

Later, when John's generosity was notorious, a false beggar tries to trick John into giving him alms. Again John claims that the key to generosity and hospitality is recognition. Even the false beggar may be Christ.

Whilst this same crowd of people was still in the city, one of the strangers, noticing John's remarkable sympathy, determined to try the blessed man; so he put on old clothes and approached him as he was on his way to visit the sick in the hospitals (for he did this two or three times a week) and said to him: "Have mercy upon me for I am a prisoner of war."

John said to his purse-bearer, "Give him six nomismata." After the man had received these he went off, changed his clothes, met John again in another street, and falling at his feet said, "Have pity upon me for I am in want." The Patriarch again said to his purse-bearer, "Give him six nomismata." As he went away the purse-bearer whispered in the Patriarch's ear, "By your prayers, master, this same man has had alms from you twice over!" But the Patriarch pretended not to understand. Soon the man came again for the third time to ask for money and the attendant, carrying the gold, nudged the Patriarch to let him know that it was the same man; whereupon the truly merciful and beloved of God said, "Give him twelve nomismata, for perchance it is my Christ and He is making trial of me."

Antony of Choziba, *The Life of George of Choziba*

In telling the stories of the life of George of Choziba (ca. 570), Antony of Choziba wrote around 630 of the unfortunate superior of the monastery who did not recognize the Mother of God in the poor woman at the gate. Preoccupied with another, apparently rich, visitor whom he considers more important, the superior twice asks the doorkeeper to offer counsel or food to the woman, insisting that he himself cannot leave his first visitor to speak with her as she request.

Before her arrival, a monk had asked the superior for money to buy grain for the monastery. Lacking the necessary resources, the superior had suggested that they ask for help from communities in Jericho or Jerusalem the following day. Perhaps he even thought his rich visitor would help if entertained suitably. In any case, he again vehemently denies the woman her request for an audience, and she responds:

"Why do you care for the wealthy and disregard the poor? For this reason you justly lack money. But take this gift of alms and give it to him." And she handed to him a money-pouch with sixty pieces of gold in it. The doorkeeper ran and gave it to the superior and also told him what the woman had said. The superior took the pouch and said to him, "Go, see to her needs and apologize, and I will make arrangements for these people and come out to see her." The doorkeeper left, and he went around the whole outside of the door-keeper's lodge but he did not find her. And he ran around to all the roads, but he did not see her. It was our blessed Lady setting right their work, for this holy place is a shelter for the poor and for visitors [*xenous*], and not a shelter only for the rich.

Bede, *Life of St. Cuthbert*

We find among early Christians an important genre of stories about saints who extended hospitality and their experiences. It is not uncommon for the story to end with a surprising twist, wherein the saint recognizes the traveler for the angel he really is. Bede, the English church historian, wrote this Life of Cuthbert around 720.

Chapter II. How He Ministered to an Angel

Now this was another miracle in which Cuthbert the holy man of God was first glorified by the Lord, after he had by the Lord's help taken upon him the yoke of bondservice to Christ and the Petrine tonsure after the shape of the crown of thorns that bound the head of Christ, in the monastery which is called Ripon. This miracle our most trustworthy witnesses who are still alive have testified to. For while a neophyte, he was at once elected by the community to minister to guests on their arrival. Among these, on the morning of a certain day when the weather was wintry and snowy, an angel of the Lord appeared to him in the form of a well-built man in the flower of his age, just as angels appeared to the patriarch Abraham in the valley of Mamre in the form of men. Then having received him kindly in accordance with his wont, still thinking him to be a man and not an angel, he washed his hands and feet and wiped them with towels, and, having in his humility rubbed his guest's feet with his own hands to warm them on account of the cold, he invited him most urgently to wait until the third hour of the day to take food; but he was unwilling and refused on account of his journey. Finally Cuthbert adjured him in the name of our Lord Jesus Christ and so won his consent. When the signal was given at the third hour of the day and prayer was over, he at once set out a table and spread thereon such food as he had. Now by some chance there was no bread in the guesthouse, save that he had placed some crumbs on the table as a blessed gift of bread. Thereupon the man of God went back to the monastery to seek a loaf; but failing to get any (for they were still baking in the oven) he returned to the guest whom he had left eating alone; but he did not find him nor even his footprints although there was snow over the surface of the ground. He was amazed and removed the table to the storehouse, realizing that it was an angel of God. And immediately at the entrance, his nostrils were filled with the odor of the choicest bread and, finding three warm loaves, he gave thanks to God, because in him was fulfilled the saying of the Lord: "He that receives you receives me, and he that receives me receives him that sent me," and again, "He that receives a prophet in the name of a prophet shall receive a prophet's reward; and he that receives a righteous man in the name of a righteous man shall receive a righteous man's reward." And frequently from that day, when he was hungry, the Lord fed him, as he used to declare to faithful brethren, not boastfully, but for the edification of many, just as Paul told many things about himself.

Notes

1. The presence and identity of the stranger has been addressed with insightful reflections by several recent writers. See Christine D. Pohl, "Hospitality, Dignity and the Power of Recognition," chapter 4 in *Making Room: Recovering Hospitality as a Christian Tradition* (Grand Rapids, Michigan: William B. Eerdmans, 1999), pp. 61-84. Also see Thomas W. Ogletree, *Hospitality to the Stranger: Dimensions of Moral Understanding* (Philadelphia: Fortress Press, 1985); Parker Palmer, *The Company of Strangers: Christians and the Renewal of America's Public Life* (New York: Crossroad, 1981); Henri Nouwen, *Reaching Out: The Three Movements of the Spiritual Life* (New York: Doubleday & Co., 1975); John Koenig, "Hospitality, Strangers, and the Love of God," *New Testament Hospitality: Partnership with Strangers as Mission and Promise* (Philadelphia: Fortress Press, 1985), pp. 1-14; *Christianity and the Stranger: Historical Essays*, ed. Francis W. Nichols (Atlanta: Scholars Press, 1995).

2. Ogletree reminds us not to romanticize the stranger for that trivializes the genuine risk of hospitality. See pp. 41-43.

3. The identification of the stranger with the divine is commonplace in classical literature. Visitation of gods disguised as humans, or *theoxenia*, is a frequent motif in Greek literature. See J.H. Rose, "Divine Disguisings," *Harvard Theological Review* 49 (1956), pp. 63-72; S. Murnaghan, *Disguise and Recognition in the Odyssey* (Princeton, NJ: Princeton University Press, 1987); "The Theme of Divine Visits and Human Hospitality in Luke-Acts: Its Old Testament and Graeco-Roman Antecedents," in *The Unity of Luke-Acts*, ed. J. Verheyden (Leuven: Leuven University Press, 1999), pp. 263-268; Julian Pitt-Rivers, "The Stranger, The Guest and The Hostile Host: Introduction to the Study of the Laws of Hospitality," in *Contributions to Mediterranean Sociology: Mediterranean Rural Communities and Social Change*, ed. J.-G. Peristiany, Acts of the Mediterranean Sociological Conference, Athens, July 1963

(Paris: Mouton & Co: 1968). For treatment of this theme in an eastern religious tradition, see Teigo Yoshida, "The Stranger as God: The Place of the Outsider in Japanese Folk Religion," *Ethnology* 20 (1981), p. 87.

4. Matthew 25:37-40 (NRSV).

5. For a discussion of the moral appeal of the "other," see Thomas W. Ogletree, "Hospitality to the Stranger: The Role of the 'Other' in Moral Experience," in *Hospitality to the Stranger: Dimensions of Moral Understanding* (Philadelphia: Fortress Press, 1985), pp. 35-63.

6. Describing the patterns of welcome and hospitality in the New Testament with regard to mutuality and shared mission Koenig argues for the category, "partnership with strangers."

Bibliography

Ambrose. "On Duties of the Clergy." In *Selected Works and Letters,* translated by the Rev. H. De Romestin, the Rev. E. De Romestin and the Rev. H. T. F. Duckworth. *Nicene and Post-Nicene Fathers of the Christian Church.* Edited by Philip Schaff and Henry Wace. 2nd ser. New York: Christian Literature Company, 1893, X:59-60.

_____. "Epistle 63." In *Selected Works and Letters,* translated by the Rev. H. De Romestin, the Rev. E. De Romestin and the Rev. H. T. F. Duckworth. *Nicene and Post-Nicene Fathers of the Christian Church.* Edited by Philip Schaff and Henry Wace. 2nd ser. New York: Christian Literature Company, 1893, X:472.

Antony of Choziba. *The Life of Saint George of Choziba and the Miracles of the Most Holy Mother of God at Choziba.* Translated by Tim Vivan and Apostolos N. Athanassakis. San Francisco: International Scholars Publications, 1994, 58-59.

Bede. "The Life of St. Cuthbert." In *Two Lives of Saint Cuthbert: A Life by an Anonymous Monk of Lindisfarne and Bede's Prose Life,* translated by Bertram Colgrave. New York: Greenwood Press, 1969, 77-79.

Benedict of Nursia. *The Rule of Saint Benedict.* Translated by Leonard J. Doyle. Collegeville, Minn: Liturgical Press, 1948, 54, 72-73.

Clement of Alexandria. *The Instructor. Ante-Nicene Fathers: The Writings of the Fathers Down to A.D. 325.* Edited by Alexander Roberts and James Donaldson. New York: The Christian Literature Company, 1885, II:293.

_____. *Who Is the Rich Person that Shall Be Saved?* Translated by the Rev. William Wilson. *Ante-Nicene Fathers: The Writings of the Fathers Down to A.D. 325.* Edited by Alexander Roberts and James Donaldson. New York: The Christian Literature Company, 1885, II:599-600.

Commodianus. *The Instructions of Commodianus in Favor of Christian Discipline, Against the God of the Heathens.* Translated by the Rev. Robert Ernest Wallis. *Ante-Nicene Fathers: The Writings of the Fathers Down to A.D. 325.* Edited by Alexander Roberts and James Donaldson. New York: The Christian Literature Company, 1885, IV:218.

Cyprian. *Treatise 8: On Works and Alms.* Translated by the Rev. Ernest Wallis. *Ante-Nicene Fathers: The Writings of the Fathers Down to A.D. 325.* Edited by Alexander Roberts and James Donaldson. New York: The Christian Literature Company, 1884, V:480.

Cyril of Scythopolis. *Lives of the Monks of Palestine.* Translated by R. M. Price. Kalamazoo, Michigan: Cistercian Publications, 1991, 125-26.

Fulgentius. "To the Abbott Euggippius." *Fulgentius: Selected Works.* Translated by Robert B. Eno. *The Fathers of the Church: A New Translation.* Vol. 95. Washington, D.C.: The Catholic University of America Press, 1997, 346.

Gregory of Nazianzus. "Orations 43: Panegyric on Basil." *Select Orations.* Translated by Charles Gordon Browne and James Edward Swallow. *Nicene and Post-Nicene Fathers of the Christian Church.* Edited by Philip Schaff and Henry Wace. 2nd ser. New York: The Christian Literature Company, 1894, VII:416.

Gregory of Nyssa. "Homily: As You Did It To One of These, You Did It To Me" in *The Collected Works of Gregory of Nyssa,* trans. Richard McCambly. *Gregory of Nyssa Homepage.*

bhsu.edu/dsalomon/nyssa/home.html. Greenwich, CT.: Great American Publishing Society, 1999.

Jerome. "Letter 52." In "Principal Works," translated by W. H. Fremantle. *Nicene and Post-Nicene Fathers of the Christian Church.* Edited by Philip Schaff and Henry Wace. 2nd ser. New York: The Christian Literature Company, 1893, VI:91.

_____. "Letter 77." In "Principal Works," translated by W. H. Fremantle. *Nicene and Post-Nicene Fathers of the Christian Church.* Edited by Philip Schaff and Henry Wace. 2nd ser. New York: The Christian Literature Company, 1893, VI:160.

_____. "Letter 108." In "Principal Works," translated by W. H. Fremantle. *Nicene and Post-Nicene Fathers of the Christian Church.* Edited by Philip Schaff and Henry Wace. 2nd ser. New York: The Christian Literature Company, 1893, VI:202.

_____. "Apology in Answer to Rufinus." Translated by Ernest Cushman Richardson. *Nicene and Post-Nicene Fathers of the Christian Church.* Edited by Philip Schaff and Henry Wace. 2nd ser. New York: The Christian Literature Company, 1893, III:528.

John Cassian. *Institutes of the Coenobia.* Translated by Rev. Edgar C. S. Gibson. *Nicene and Post-Nicene Fathers of the Christian Church.* Edited by Philip Schaff and Henry Wace. 2nd ser. New York: The Christian Literature Company, 1894, XI:242-43.

John Chrysostom. "Homily 11 on Hebrews." In *Homilies on John and Hebrews,* translated by the Rev. G. T. Stupart. *Nicene and Post-Nicene Fathers of the Christian Church.* 1st ser. New York: The Christian Literature Company, 1890, XIV:420-22.

_____. "Homily 14 on 1 Timothy." In *Homilies on Galatians, Ephesians, Philippians, Colossians, Thessalonians, Timothy, Titus and Philemon,* translated by the Rev. James Tweed. *Nicene and Post-Nicene Fathers of the Christian Church.* 1st ser. New York: The Christian Literature Company, 1889, XIII:454-55.

_____. "Homily 21 on Romans." In *Homilies on Acts of the Apostles,* translated by the Rev. J. Walker and the Rev. J. Sheppard. *Nicene and Post-Nicene Fathers of the Christian Church.* 1st ser. New York: The Christian Literature Company, 1889, XI:504-5.

_____."Homily 26 on Matthew." In *Homilies on Matthew,* translated by the Rev. George Provost. *Nicene and Post-Nicene Fathers of the Christian Church.* 1st ser. New York: The Christian Literature Company, 1888, X:176-77.

_____. "Homily 30 on Romans." In *Homilies on Acts of the Apostles,* translated by the Rev. J. Walker and the Rev. J. Sheppard. *Nicene and Post-Nicene Fathers of the Christian Church.* 1st ser. New York: The Christian Literature Company, 1889, XI:552.

_____. "Homily 41." In *Homilies on Genesis: Saint John Chrysostom.* Volume 2: 18-45, translated by Robert C. Hill. The Fathers of the Church: A New Translation, vol. 82. Washington, D.C.: The Catholic University of America Press, 1988, 408.

_____. "Homily 45 on the Acts of the Apostles." In *Homilies on Acts of the Apostles,* translated by the Rev. J. Walker and the Rev. J. Sheppard. *Nicene and Post-Nicene Fathers of the Christian Church.* 1st ser. New York: The Christian Literature Company, 1889, XI:275-77.

Lactantius. "The Divine Institutes." Translated by the Rev. William Fletcher. *Ante-Nicene Fathers: The Writings of the Fathers Down to A.D. 325.* Edited by Alexander Roberts and James Donaldson. New York: The Christian Literature Company, 1889, VII:177.

Leontius. *St. John the Almsgiver.* In *Three Byzantine Saints: Contemporary Biographies Translated from the Greek,* translated and edited by Elizabeth Dawes and Norman H. Baynes. Oxford: Blackwell, 1948, 210-11, 216.

The Lives of the Desert Fathers: The Historia Monachorum in Aegypto. Translated by Norman Russell. Kalamazoo, Michigan: Cistercian Publications, 1980, 76, 78.

Macarius. "Homily 15." In *Intoxicated with God: The Fifty Spiritual Homilies of Macarius,* translated by George A. Maloney, S.J. Denville, N.J.: Dimension Books, 1978, 96.

Maximus of Turin. "Sermon 36." In *The Sermons of St. Maximus of Turin,* translated by Boniface Ramsey. *Ancient Christian Writers: The Works of the Fathers in Translation.* Edited by Walter J. Burghardt and Thomas Comerford Lawler, no. 50. New York: Newman Press, 1989, 88.

Paulinus of Nola. "Letter 1." In *Letters of St. Paulinus of Nola,* translated by P. G. Walsh. *Ancient Christian Writers: The Works of the Fathers in Translation.* Edited by Johannes

Quasten, Walter J. Burghardt and Thomas Comerford Lawler, no. 35. New York: Newman Press, 1966, 29.

———. "Letter 13." In "Letters of St. Paulinus of Nola," translated by P. G. Walsh. *Ancient Christian Writers: The Works of the Fathers in Translation*. Edited by Johannes Quasten, Walter J. Burghardt and Thomas Comerford Lawler, no. 35. New York: Newman Press, 1966, 137-39.

Pseudo-Clementine. "First Epistle Concerning Virginity." In "Epistles and Writings," translated by the Rev. B. P. Pratten. *Ante-Nicene Fathers: The Writings of the Fathers Down to A.D. 325*. Edited by Alexander Roberts and James Donaldson. New York: The Christian Literature Company, 1885, VIII:59-60.

———. "Recognitions of Clement." In "Epistles and Writings," translated by the Rev. B. P. Pratten. *Ante-Nicene Fathers: The Writings of the Fathers Down to A.D. 325*. Edited by Alexander Roberts and James Donaldson. New York: The Christian Literature Company, 1885, VIII:148-49.

———. "Homily 11." In "Epistles and Writings," translated by the Rev. B. P. Pratten. *Ante-Nicene Fathers: The Writings of the Fathers Down to A.D. 325*. Edited by Alexander Roberts and James Donaldson. New York: The Christian Literature Company, 1885, VIII:285.

"Radegund, Queen of the Franks and Abbess of Poitiers (ca. 525-587)." In *Sainted Women of the Dark Ages*, translated by JoAnn McNamara and John Halborg. Durham: Duke University Press, 1992, 72.

Sulpitius Severus. "Dialogues of Sulpitius Severus." Translated by the Rev. Alexander Roberts. *Nicene and Post-Nicene Fathers of the Christian Church*. Edited by Philip Schaff and Henry Wace. 2nd ser. New York: The Christian Literature Company, 1894, XI:30-32.

CHAPTER FOUR

AND WE SHALL ALL BE CHANGED: THE SPIRITUAL DYNAMICS OF HOSPITALITY

Acts of hospitality are not isolated, but are construed within a larger, spiritual framework. The spiritual dynamics of hospitality anchor these practices clearly within the life of God. This chapter organizes excerpts into five sections, identifying these dynamics present in early Christian texts.

Motivations for Hospitality

Why would early Christians, or anyone, take the risks often required for the practices of hospitality? Why bother? When demands on one's life and resources are great, when communities have their own internal needs and problems, when social struggles seem insurmountable and beyond the scope of individual acts, what calls people to the practice of hospitality? Another way to put it might be to ask, what are the motivations for hospitality?

There is the predictable amount of exhortation by preachers in the early church for Christians to practice hospitality simply because the gospel demands it; it is the right thing to do. Jesus says to Peter, "Feed my sheep" (John 21:15). Further, Jesus' description of the judgment separating the sheep and the goats in Matthew 25 puts a claim on Christians to care for "the least of these."[1] Early Christian preachers appeal to these biblical warrants for feeding the hungry, giving drink to the thirsty, welcoming the stranger, clothing the naked, caring for the sick and visiting the prisoner.

Beyond scriptural exhortation, however, early Christian texts also offer a well-developed spiritual economy, God's household, which places hospitality within the larger movement of God in the world, not a heroic act of an individual seeking merit. The larger spiritual context in which hospitality is practiced always begins with God. These early texts draw the reader's attention first to what God is doing and only secondarily to what oneself or one's community is doing. God offers hospitality to all humanity, first by establishing a home (*oikos*) for all. God provides creation and its glories for the habitation and enjoyment of all creatures. Second, God offers an abundant grace that pulls us into God's presence and life. Through God's hospitality we can participate in the divine life and be saved therein.

For early Christians, then, the practice of hospitality has a divine analogy, whereby our practice of hospitality is always in response to God's gracious offering of hospitality. While our hospitality is not proportional to God's, nevertheless it is characterized by reciprocity and gratitude. Why bother with the practice of hospitality and particularly its attendant risks? Because we are overwhelmed by the power of God's hospitable grace in our lives and cannot do otherwise.

Early Christians also talk about the larger spiritual dynamics at work that call forth the practice of hospitality in terms of the *imago dei*, or image of God, in which all humanity is created. Here, too, attention is drawn first to God and God's initiating action. God first created all of humanity in God's image, offering the opportunity for humans to share in the divine life. Though that image is tarnished and no longer whole, nevertheless God graciously offers healing and restoration of the *imago dei* so that we can find our dwelling place in God. Because all have been created with this image, all humans warrant our attention and care. We share a common humanity, however different our social and cultural locations may be. God has set the stage for all humans to share in the economy of salvation so we are all in this together. Lactantius reminds his audience that even the dead share in this *imago dei* and need the hospitality of the living.[2] The motivation for participating in the practices of hospitality rests in that divine initiative. Because God has brought us into God's life and because God has brought us *all* into God's life, we are responsible for one another. These excerpts express the conviction that the practice of hospitality flows from this larger spiritual context of the life of God.

Pseudo-Clementine, *Homily 11**

Though wrongly attributed to Clement of Rome (fl. ca. 96), the Clementine Homilies are a part of the Pseudo-Clementine literature (200–250). Homily 11 argues for acts of mercy and hospitality on two grounds. First, because all humans bear the image of God they warrant our attention on that count alone. Second, we are to be imitators of God whose love is not contingent upon the moral status of the recipient.

However, as we know that humans were made after the image and after the likeness of God, we tell you to be pious towards them, that the favor may be counted as done to God, whose image each one is. Therefore it behooves you to give honor to the image of God, which is humanity—in these ways: food to the hungry, drink to the thirsty, clothing to the naked, care to the sick, shelter to the stranger, and visiting one who is in prison, to help each as you can. In other words, whatever good things any one wishes for oneself, so give to another in need, and then a good reward can be reckoned to one as being pious towards the image of God. And by like reason, whoever will not undertake to do these things, shall be punished as neglecting the image.

Lactantius, *The Divine Institutes**

Lactantius (ca. 240–ca. 320) points out the connection between hospitality and justice. In a long discourse on justice, mercy and the virtue of hospitality, he has argued that hospitality is justly practiced where no self-interest is involved. Perhaps hospitality for the dead is one of the most profound expressions of disinterested hospitality. Lactantius reminds his audience that because the dead bear the imago dei, *they deserve the same kindness as relatives. In any case, hospitality in burying the dead is done for God alone.*

The last and greatest duty of piety is the burying of strangers and the poor, a subject which those [pagan] teachers of virtue and justice have not touched upon at all. For they were unable to see this who measured all their duties by utility . . . but they abandoned this because they were unable to see any advantage in it. We're not asking whether the whole system of burial is practical or not. It must be practiced, even if only because it seems among people to be done rightly and kindly, whether they imagine it useless or not. For it is the feeling which is inquired into, and it is the purpose which is weighed. Therefore we will not tolerate the image and workmanship of God to lie exposed as a prey to beasts and birds. Instead, we will restore it to the earth, from which it had its origin. If it happens to be a case of someone we don't know, we will stand in the place of relatives, letting kindness fill their empty place. Wherever humanity is called for, there we will think that our duty is required. What is more consistent with the heart of justice than our affording to strangers through kindness, the things we freely give to our own relatives through affection? And this kindness is much more sure and just when it is now afforded, not to one who is dead and unaware, but to God alone, to whom a just work is a most acceptable sacrifice.

*Lactantius, Epitome**

Again Lactantius argues for the shared nature of all human beings through their creation in the image of God as the ground of hospitality. The common good that derives from this shared nature warrants acts of mercy and hospitality, which, while performed for other people, are offered to God.

For since human nature is more feeble than that of the other animals, which God has provided with means of inflicting violence, and with defenses for repelling it, He has given to us the feeling of compassion, that we might place the whole protection of our life in helping each other. For if we are created by one God, and descended from one human, and are thus connected by blood relationship, we ought on this account to love every person. Therefore, we are bound not only to abstain from the infliction of injury, but not even to avenge it when inflicted on us, that there may be in us complete harmlessness. And on this account God commands us to pray always even for our enemies. Therefore we ought to be an animal fitted for companionship and society, that we may mutually protect ourselves by giving and receiving assistance. For our frailty is subject to many accidents and inconveniences. Expect that what you see has happened to another may also happen to you. Thus you will at length be motivated to render aid, if you shall assume the mind of one who, being placed in evils, implores your aid. If any one is in need of food, let us bestow it. If any one meets us who is naked, let us clothe him. If any one suffers injury from one who is more powerful than himself, let us rescue him. Let our house be open to strangers, or to those who are in need of shelter. Let our defense not be wanting to wards, or our protection to the defenseless. To ransom captives is a great work of compassion, and also to visit and comfort the sick who are in poverty. If the helpless or strangers die, we should not permit them to lie unburied. These are the works, these the duties, of compassion. If anyone undertakes these, he will offer to God a true and acceptable sacrifice.

Gregory of Nyssa, Homily: *As You Did It To One of These, You Did It To Me*

Gregory of Nyssa (ca. 330–395), one of the Cappadocian fathers, was younger brother to the great Basil of Caesarea and the learned Macrina. Involved in doctrinal controversy much of his life, he was an important thinker for the early church. In the closing arguments of this sermon on Jesus' gospel command, Gregory reminds his audience of the reason for extending mercy. The demands of hospitality are placed upon us because all humanity shares a common human nature. Ours is a common lot, so we should not be fooled by apparent differences in current fortunes. Our common humanity is owed to a common Creator, who is the ultimate warrant for hospitality.

If there is anything further to be added, we should show sympathy towards misfortunate persons deprived of good health. It is a fine idea to be first in extending mercy to those beset by afflictions. Since all mankind shares one human nature and since no one can remain constant in doing good, we should always be mindful of the Gospel's precept to carry out whatever is demanded of us. Although we may be well equipped for a voyage, we should extend a hand to shipwrecked persons. We all share the sea, waves and surging billows along with the deep, rocks, promontories, and anything else which fills our life's voyage with fear. While you remain healthy and ply the sea of life in safety, do not pass by without showing mercy to those who have suffered shipwreck before you. Who is near you to always provide a successful voyage? You have not yet attained the harbor of rest, have exited the billowing waves, nor have you attained firm ground. You still travel through life on the sea. You experience similar experiences with persons in distress and assist those on a similar voyage. But we escort everyone through the Holy Spirit on the voyage of life into the harbor of rest. Let the performance of the commandments and love be our rudder. With those who are guided aright, let us attain the land of the Gospel which contains the great city whose architect and builder is our God (Heb 11:20), to whom be glory and power forever (Rom 16:27). Amen.

John Chrysostom, Homily 21 on Romans*

Chrysostom (ca. 347–407) addresses in several sermons the spiritual dynamics of the Christian life, particularly in turning one's life toward the other in hospitality and service. In this sermon he exhorts his listeners to see the larger spiritual context for offering hospitality. If a Christian gets caught up in questions of whether someone else is worthy or whether one's act will bear fruit, the point is lost. God's own life has set the pattern of healing even enemies.

Don't be curious then, either, since for Christ you receive him. And if you are always so scrupulous about the character of your guests, many a time you will pass by a person of esteem, and lose your reward. Yet whoever receives someone not of high status has no fault found with him, but is even rewarded. For "whoever that receives a prophet in the name of a prophet, shall receive a prophet's reward." Rather, the one who, because of inordinate pickiness, passes one that should be admired, will even suffer punishment. So don't busy yourself with people's lives and doings. For this is the very extreme of stinginess, to nit pick about a person's entire life just to avoid giving them one loaf of bread. For if this person is a murderer, if a robber, or what not, does he therefore seem to you not to deserve a loaf and a few coins? And yet your Master causes even the sun to rise upon him! And do you judge him unworthy of food even for a day? I will put another case to you besides. Now even if you were positively certain that this person were laden with countless crimes, not even then would you have an excuse for depriving him of daily bread. For you are the servant of Him Who said, "You know not what spirit you are of" (Luke 9:55). You are servant to Him Who healed those that stoned Him, or rather Who was crucified for them. And do not tell me that he killed another, for even if he were going to kill you yourself, even then you should not neglect him when starving. For you are a disciple of Him Who desired the salvation even of them that crucified Him. The One Who said upon the Cross itself, "Father, forgive them, for they know not what they do" (Luke 23:34). You are the servant of Him Who healed the one who hurt

Him, Who upon the Cross itself crowned the man who had scorned Him. And what can equal this?

John Chrysostom, *Homily 20 on 1st Corinthians**

Hospitality can never be driven by hope of personal gain. Chrysostom says that's why the gospel instructs us to offer our table with a truly open spirit to those who cannot reciprocate. It is for God's sake that hospitality is offered.

Why did God command us call to our suppers and our feasts the lame, and the maimed, and those who cannot repay us? Because these are most of all properly called good deeds which are done for God's sake. Whereas if you entertain some great and distinguished person, it is not such pure mercy, because some credit many times is assigned to yourself also, both by vain-glory, and by the return of the favor, and by your rising in many people's estimation on account of your guest. At any rate, I think I could point out many who with this view pay attention to the more distinguished among the saints, namely, that by their means they may enjoy a closer relationship with rulers, and that they may find them in the future more useful in their own affairs and to their families. And many such favors do they ask in return from those saints, a thing which mars the repayment of their hospitality, they seeking it with such a mind.

Paulinus of Nola, *Letter 13*

Paulinus (353–431) wrote this letter to Pammachius in 396 to console him after his wife, Paulina, had died. Paulinus praises his friend for the charitable acts Pammachius had performed in honor of his deceased wife. Paulinus paints a vivid picture of a scene in the basilica at Rome in which food is distributed to the poor, drawing an analogy between Christ's abundant feeding of Pammachius and Pammachius's feeding others. Christ initiates hospitality, Pammachius follows.

In the basilica of the apostle you gathered together a crowd of poor people, the patrons of our souls, those from the whole of Rome deserving of alms. I myself feast on the splendid scene of this great work of yours. For I seem to behold all those pious swarms of the wretched populace, the nurslings of God's affection, thronging in great lines deep into the huge basilica of the renowned Peter, through that venerable colonnade smiling afar with azure front, so that all the precincts are thronged—inside the basilica, before the gates of the atrium, and on the whole level area before the steps. I see the gathering being divided amongst separate tables, and all the people being filled with abundance of food, so that before their eyes there appears the plenty bestowed by the Gospel's blessing and the picture of those crowds whom Christ, the true Bread and the Fish of living water, filled with five loaves and two fishes.

Indeed the Lord Himself was and is in you, because no man performs Christ's works without His aid. By His gift and blessing you received from Him blessed bread to distribute, you apportioned it to the countless mouths of the poor. They ate and were filled, and all filled their baskets from the abundant bread remaining. With what pleasure did you delight the apostle himself when you packed the whole of his basilica with dense crowds of the needy!

Later in the letter Paulinus again draws the analogy between divine hospitality and human hospitality. He pictures the world as God's home for all people to share. If God offers such expansive hospitality, how can anyone refuse to do the same with an individual household?

It will be easy for you to realize that it is a murderous crime to despise the poor on our own judgment, for no act of God has set them apart from us. How, then, can we shut out from our small dwellings those whom God has enclosed with us in the single house of this world? How can we disdain to make them associates in the enjoyment of earthly possessions, when however unwillingly we have them as partners in the unity of our divine origin? It was by clinging to this truth that Abraham became dear to God. By observing it, Lot escaped from Sodom. By following it, Job triumphed over the devil.

Let us also, then, open our homes to our brothers, whether after the fashion of the fathers just mentioned we fear the danger of rejecting an angel when we repulse men, or whether we hope to deserve to have angels as our guests as we assist the passage of every stranger with ready kindness. For when our father Abraham entertained strangers, he received Christ the Lord and his angels; in his hospitable tent he saw that day which in the Gospel the Savior reveals in Abraham's presence.

Maximus of Turin, Sermon 21 On Hospitality

In this sermon written around 398 Maximus (d. 408–423) has several interesting things to say about hospitality. Among them is the notion that the practice of hospitality is based on the analogy of divine hospitality. God has given to "people of different races" one world, one home to share, so how can we not do the same?

But perhaps someone might say: "In those three men who came to Abraham the Lord also came." This in fact is true, for so Scripture tells us. But I say that even now Christ comes to us in his bishops. Let us, then, brethren, imitate our father Abraham. But why do I say Abraham? Let us imitate God our Father! For if God wished people of different races to dwell in the one hospice of heaven, why do not we, who are brothers, stay with one another in one hospice? And if he desired our diversity to be contained within the one home of this world, why is not our concord maintained by the holy dwelling of His tabernacles?

Maximus of Turin, Sermon 34 On Hospitality in the Gospel

Maximus draws the analogy of divine hospitality again when preaching on Matthew 10:11: "In whatever city you enter, ask in it who is worthy and remain there until you leave." Again, God initiates hospitality as shown here in the images of Christ and Church as host and hostess respectively.

For it does not seem to me to have ordered us to inquire diligently about a host or a house in this world so much as about Him who, as an unoffended and unhurt host, can safeguard us until the day of our departure. Now we quickly hurt and quickly offend a host of this world, and sometimes we also displease him after three days. It was ordered that a faithful house and worthy host be sought after. What house is more faithful than the Church, what host more worthy than the Savior? He takes in strangers as sons, while she refreshes those who have been taken in as infants; He longs to wash the feet of His guests, as we have experienced, while she hastens to set the table. The ones the Savior refreshes with living water, while the others the Church restores with heavenly foods.

Leo the Great, *Sermon 12 On the Fast**

Leo the Great's (d. 461) sermons give voice to Christian worship and practice in the fifth century. Several sermons focus on fasting and its purpose in deepening the Christian life. He explains the spiritual dynamics by which God restores the original imago dei. *God loves first and humans imitate that love, not only for God, but for those whom God loves. Practices of mercy and hospitality are expressions of that love whereby God restores the divine image. Later in the sermon, Leo says that if the common nature all human beings share is not warrant enough for extending love to neighbor, grace is.*

Restoration to the divine image in which we were made is only possible by our imitation of God's will. If, dearly beloved, we comprehend faithfully and wisely the beginning of our creation, we shall find that humanity was made in God's image, to the end that we might imitate our Creator, and that our race attains its highest natural dignity, by the form of the divine goodness being reflected in us, as in a mirror. And surely each day the Savior's grace is restoring us to this image. . . . And the cause of our restoration is nothing else but the mercy of God, Whom we could not have loved, unless He had first loved us, and dispelled the darkness of our ignorance by the light of His truth. . . . Thus it is that God, by loving us, restores us to His image, and, in order that He may find in us the form of His goodness, He gives us that whereby we ourselves too may do the work that He does, kindling the lamps of our minds, and inflaming us with the fire of His love, that we may love not only Himself, but also whatever He loves. . . .

We must love both God and our neighbor, and "our neighbor" must be interpreted in its widest sense. And so, when the Lord says, "You shall love the Lord your God, from all your heart and from all your mind, and you shall love your neighbor as yourself," let the faithful soul put on the unfading love of its Author and Ruler. . . . But this godly love cannot be perfect unless you love your neighbor also. Under which name must be included not only those who are connected with us by friendship or neighborhood, but absolutely all people, with whom we have a common nature, whether they be foes or allies, slaves or free. For the One Maker fashioned us, the One Creator breathed life into us. We all enjoy the same sky and air, the same days and nights, and, though some are good, others bad, some righteous, others unrighteous, yet God is bountiful to all, kind to all, as Paul and Barnabas said to the Lycaonians concerning God's Providence, "who in generations gone by suffered all the nations to walk in their own ways. And yet He left Himself not without witness, doing them good, giving rain from heaven and fruitful seasons, and filling our hearts with food and gladness." But the wide extent of Christian grace has given us yet greater reasons for loving our neighbor, which, reaching to all parts of the whole world, looks down on no one, and teaches that no one is to be neglected.

Leo the Great, *Sermon 16 On the Fast**

In another sermon on fasting, Leo says that hospitality to the poor and stranger are motivated by the gratitude one feels to God who has provided everything one has. Even human agricultural practices are not sufficient to produce a good crop without God's providence.

Whatever therefore the cornfields, the vineyards and the olive groves have borne for human purposes, all this God in His bounteous goodness has produced. For under the varying condition of the elements He has mercifully aided the uncertain toils of the farmers so that wind, and rain, cold and heat, day and night might serve our needs. For human methods would not have sufficed to give effect to their works, had not God given the increase to their customary planting and watering. So it is but godly and just that we, too, should help others with that which the Heavenly Father has mercifully bestowed on us. For there are many people who have no fields, no vineyards, no olive-groves, whose wants we must provide out of the store which God has given. Then they, too, along with us may bless God for the richness of the earth and rejoice at its possessors having received things which they have shared also with the poor and the stranger. That storage barn is blessed and most worthy that all fruits should increase manifold in it, from which the hunger of the needy and the weak is satisfied, from which the wants of the stranger are relieved, from which the desire of the sick is gratified.

Dorotheos of Gaza, *On Building Up Virtues*

In this lesson, Dorotheos of Gaza, a great spiritual teacher of the sixth century, lays out the various motives one may have in alms-giving. He lifts up the noble way, acting from the compassion we have experienced from God. When people are motivated by gratitude, they can act as children of the merciful one through simple acts of hospitality.

If you want to know the special good and grace attached to alms-giving and how great it is, consider that it is able to take away sins. As the Prophet says: "The ransom of a man is his own riches," and in another place it says, "By almsgiving redeem your sins." Our Lord himself says, "Be merciful as your heavenly Father is merciful." He does not say, "Practice fasting as your heavenly Father fasts," nor does he say, "Be without possessions as your heavenly Father is without possessions." What does he say? "Be merciful as your heavenly Father is merciful." This is the virtue which emulates God in a special way; it is characteristic of him. It is, therefore, necessary to pursue this aim always and to act with knowledge. . . .

In doing good we have to pass through three different states, as St. Gregory says. Of these we have spoken to you elsewhere: Either we do good because we are afraid of punishment, and we are in the state of servility; or to earn a reward, then we are in the state of hirelings; or for the sake of the good itself, then we are in the state of sonship. A son does not do his father's will out of fear, or because he wants to earn a reward, but because he wants to be of service, to honor his father and to make him happy. And, therefore, we ought to give alms in this way because it is a noble thing to have compassion on one another as if caring for our own affairs; and on treating another as we are treated by Him; giving to others as we receive. This is to give alms with knowledge and in this way we are found to be in the state of sonship, as we said. No one can say, "I am poor and hence I have no means of giving alms." For even if you cannot give as the rich gave their gifts into the temple treasury, give two farthings as the poor widow did, and from you God will consider it a greater gift than the gifts of the rich. And if you do not have as much as two farthings? You still have power to give alms, you can take pity on the sick and give alms by ministering to them. And if you cannot do even this? You can comfort your brother by your words. Express your pity for him in words and take heed of the one who said, "A good word is better than the best of gifts." Suppose you cannot even help him by words; you can still, even when he is incensed against you, take pity on him and bear with him in the time of his fury, seeing that he is being dealt with spitefully by the common enemy and, instead of making a sharp remark and adding to his fury, keep silent and so have pity on him and his soul, thus dragging him away from the enemy. Even if he offends against you, you can have mercy on him and forgive his offence against you, so that you may receive forgiveness from God. For it says, "Forgive and it shall be forgiven you." And you shall be found to have mercy on your brother's soul by pardoning him his offence against you. God made us a gift of power, if we wish to use it, of forgiving one another the sins committed against us, so that if we do not have the means of coming to the aid of their bodies, we may come to the aid of their souls. And what act of mercy is as great as having mercy on a soul? As the soul is more honorable than the body, so doing a work of mercy for the soul is greater than a corporal work of mercy. So, you see, no one can say he does not have the power to do works of mercy. Everyone according to his ability and the condition of his soul has the power to be merciful. . . . May God, who is a lover of men, grant you may hear, and what you hear, do, that these words do not become your condemnation on the day of judgment, so that to him be glory for all ages. Amen.

Leontius, Life of St. John the Almsgiver

Much beloved, John, the Patriarch of Alexandria in the early 600s, earned the appellation Almsgiver for his generous heart. Always a champion of those in need John encouraged his leaders to give with an open hand to the refugees from Syria that poured into Alexandria. John argues that it is God's generosity at work, not theirs, and so they have no choice as agents of God but to distribute alms to whoever asks.

He [John] accordingly gave immediate orders that the wounded and sick should be put to bed in hostels and hospitals which he himself founded, and that they should receive care and medical treatment without payment and that then they should be free to leave as each of them should choose. To those who were well but destitute and came to the daily distribution he gave sixpence apiece to the men and one shilling apiece to the women and children as being weaker members. Now some of the women, who came begging for alms, wore ornaments and bracelets, and those who were entrusted with the distribution reported this to the Patriarch. Then he, who was really gentle and of a cheerful countenance, put on a grim look and a harsh voice and said: "If you wish to be distributors for humble John, or rather for Christ, obey unquestioningly the divine command which says: 'Give to every man that asks of you.' But, if you vex by your inquiries those who come to receive alms, God has no need of mischievous servants nor has humble John. If indeed the money given were mine and had come into existence with me I might do well to be niggardly with my own possessions. But if the money given happens to be God's, where His property is in question He wishes His commands to be followed absolutely."

"But if, perhaps, because you have no faith or are of little faith, you fear that the amount given away may exceed the moneys which we receive, I myself refuse to share in your little faith. For if it is by God's good will that I, an unworthy servant, am the dispenser of His gifts, then were the whole world to be brought together in Alexandria and ask for alms they would not straiten the holy Church nor the inexhaustible treasures of God."

Later his biographer tells of John's concern for slaves, perhaps the most vulnerable group in society. In this excerpt, John reminds his followers that because they share the imago dei *slaves warrant fair, even equal, relationship. This determined bishop even claims that all of creation exists for the slave as well as the free. He goes so far as to suggest that they should treat their slaves as they might treat him, the bishop. He was known to buy and free slaves. The upshot for our purposes is that extending mercy to "the least of these" is based on simple, shared humanity. John says they should honor slaves because God does.*

If by chance the blessed man heard of anybody being harsh and cruel to his slaves and given to striking them he would first send for him and then admonish him very gently, saying: "Son, it has come to my sinful ears that by the prompting of our enemy you behave somewhat too harshly towards your household slaves. Now, I beseech you, do not give place to anger, for God has not given them to us to strike, but to be our servants, and perhaps not even for that, but rather for them to be supported by us from the riches God has bestowed on us. What price, tell me, must a man pay to purchase one who has been honored by creation in the likeness and similitude of God? Or do you, the slave's master, possess anything more in your own body than he does? Say, a hand, or foot, or hearing, or a soul? Is he not in all things like unto you? Listen to what the great light, Paul, says: 'For as many of you as were baptized into Christ did put on Christ. There can be neither Jew nor Greek, there can be neither bond nor free, for you are all one in Christ Jesus.' If then we are equal before Christ, let us become equal in our relations one with another; for Christ took upon himself the form of a servant thereby teaching us not to treat our fellow-servants with disdain. For there is one Master of all Who dwells in heaven and yet regards the things of low degree; it does not say 'the rich things' but 'things of low degree.' We give so much gold in order to make a slave for ourselves of a man honored and together with us bought by the blood of our God and Master. For him is the heaven, for him the earth, for him the stars, for him the sun, for him the sea and all that is in it; at times the angels serve him. For him Christ washed the feet of slaves, for him He was crucified and for him endured all His other sufferings. Yet you dishonor him who is honored of God and you beat him mercilessly as if he were not of the same nature as yourself."

"Tell me, is this all you care for humble John? Would you like it if each time you sinned, God were immediately to punish you and take vengeance on your sin? Assuredly not. Tell me how in your daily prayers you say 'Forgive us our debts as we forgive our debtors?' "

With such and similar arguments from the store within him would the blessed one admonish the man and then dismiss him. Unless he heard that the master had reformed his ways, he would arrange that the ill-treated slave should reach in secrecy a place of refuge; then he would ask that he might buy him, and directly the just man had purchased him he would immediately set him free.

The Spirit That Accompanies Hospitality

Participation in hospitality calls upon a particular spirit, a spirit that animates hospitality and gives it life. This animation is one of the spiritual dynamics of hospitality. The virtue of hospitality does not reside in acts alone, but in the integration of the practices of hospitality with a particular spirit.

The spirit that gives life to hospitality is described as encompassing humility and gratitude, arising as a response to God's initiating grace. These texts also describe the spirit accompanying hospitality as one of mercy, compassion, eagerness, liberality, and willingness to risk. Further, this spirit sees beyond the surface to the spiritual dynamics at work through a sense of blessedness, lack of concern for personal gain, and an understanding that God is at work in both host and guest. For some early Christians, attitude was everything, so much so, that even when one's acts were limited, one's intentions were counted virtuous. For others, calling for a godly spirit to accompany hospitable practices was just another way of reminding Christians what they already knew about the

Christian life, namely, that to live in Christ is to do what Christ would do, but it is also to cultivate the mind, or, in this case, the spirit, that was in Christ.

Conversely, the wrong spirit can undermine hospitality. Imagine offering one's table with grumbling and resentment or with pride and arrogance. Or imagine extending care to the sick with condescension or revulsion. These are all understandable human affections, but they violate the spirit of hospitality. Empty of the right spirit, such behaviors become hollow actions that do not serve God or neighbor and ultimately serve to impoverish the possibilities for transformation that hospitality holds.

One danger identified by early Christians is a spirit of indifference. It may be the most deadly to the practice of hospitality, for indifference makes one immune to the knock on the door. Also destructive is an instrumentalist spirit by which acts of hospitality become not ends in themselves, but instruments toward some other end, often personal gain in prestige or wealth, or the satisfaction of controlling another's life and its exigencies. Too easily others become merely instruments for one's own plotting. Instead, say these early Christian voices, be clear that what one does, one does for God's sake, not for one's own sake or even another's.

Best of all, say early Christians in the texts below, is the congruence of spirit and action in hospitality. It is in the integration of spirit and practice that the spiritual dynamics of hospitality can most fully be made manifest.

Hermas, *The Shepherd*

This very early and popular text from the second century offers a series of visions, many concerning penance and forgiveness, followed by a series of commandments. In this commandment Hermas is concerned with almsgiving and the spirit which accompanies it. He calls for the spirit of simplicity to characterize all service. There is to be no calculating, mixed motives or prima facie *judgments of the recipients of service.*

Put on a holiness in which there is no wicked cause of offense, but all deeds that are equable and joyful. Practice goodness and from the rewards of your labors, which God gives you, give to all the needy in simplicity, not hesitating as to whom you are to give or not to give. Give to all, for God wishes His gifts to be shared among all. They who receive, will render an account to God why and for what they have received. For the afflicted who receive will not be condemned, but they who receive on false pretenses will suffer punishment. Whoever gives is guiltless. For as he received from the Lord, so has he accomplished his service in simplicity, not hesitating as to whom he should give and to whom he should not give. This service, then, if accomplished in simplicity, is glorious with God. He, therefore, who thus ministers in simplicity, will live to God.

Clement of Alexandria, *Stromata*

Clement of Alexandria (150–215), an early Christian teacher in Alexandria, knew very well the dangers and risks involved in offering hospitality, especially to other Christians in an empire hostile to the faith. He fled persecution in 202. Clement here writes that willingness to risk oneself for another is as virtuous as the ability to do so. One's spirit, in this case, a brave heart, carries weight with Clement.

And He means by the merciful, not only those who do acts of mercy, but those who wish to do them though they are not able, those who do as far as purpose is concerned. For sometimes we wish by the gift of money or by personal effort to do mercy, to help someone in need, or help one who is sick, or stand by one who is in any emergency, yet we are not able either from poverty, or disease, or old age (for this also is natural disease), to carry out our purpose, in reference to the things to which we are compelled, not being able to carry them out the way we wished. Those who have entertained the desire and whose purpose is equal, share in the same honor with those who have the ability, although others have the advantage of resources. And since there are two paths of reaching the perfection of salvation, works and knowledge, He called the "pure in heart blessed, for they shall see God."

Pseudo-Clementine, *First Epistle Concerning Virginity*

This treatise likely dates from around 200 to 250. Earlier in the letter, Christians are reminded not to visit the sick and hungry with ostentation, loud prayers, or long speeches to show off. Rather, a humble spirit is called for that witnesses to the glory of God. No guile or ulterior motives are brought to the offer of God's love.

Let them with holiness ask and beg of God, with cheerfulness and all circumspection and purity, without hatred and without malice. In this way let us approach a brother or a sister who is sick, and visit them in a way that is right, without guile, and without covetousness, and without noise, and without talkativeness, and without such behavior as is alien to the fear of God, and without haughtiness, but with the meek and lowly spirit of Christ. Let them, therefore, with fasting and with prayer make their entreaties. They should do this not with the elegant and well-arranged and fitly-ordered words of learning, but as people who have received the gift of healing from God, confidently, to the glory of God.

Ambrose, *On the Duties of the Clergy**

Ambrose (339–397) was a great preacher in Milan in the middle of the fourth century. Ambrose set forth the offices of the clergy in this treatise. In the middle of a discussion on hospitality to widows, orphans and strangers, Ambrose reminds his audience that liberality or generosity requires a concert of goodwill and action. Neither alone is adequate. Goodwill, the right spirit, is a light that shows the way of hospitality.

Now we can go on to speak of kindness, which breaks up into two parts, goodwill and liberality. For kindness to be perfected, it must consist of these two qualities. It is not enough just to wish well, we must also do well. Nor, again, is it enough to do well, unless this springs from a good source, even from a good will. . . .

Remove good will out of human reach, and it is as though one had withdrawn the sun from the world. For without it people would no longer care to show the way to the stranger, to recall the wanderer, to show hospitality (this latter is no small virtue, for on this point Job praised himself, when he said: "At my doors the stranger dwelt not, my gate was open to every one who came"), nor even to give water from the water that flows at their door, or to light another's candle at their own. Thus good will exists in all these, like a fount of waters refreshing the thirsty, and like a light, which, shining forth to others, doesn't fail those who have given a light to others from their own light.

John Chrysostom, *Homily 45 on the Acts of the Apostles**

Here Chrysostom (ca. 347–407) lifts up Abraham as a model of the attitude or spirit a host should bring to the practice of hospitality. He notes that Abraham's attitude was marked by liberality, humility, readiness and cheerfulness. The spirit in which guests are received, says Chrysostom, is perhaps even more important than the acts of hospitality themselves. For if the spirit is not charitable, it would be better to not receive them at all.

I tell you, he was sitting in mid-day, being in a foreign land, where he had no inheritance, "not so much as to set his foot on." He was a stranger, and the stranger entertained strangers, for he was a citizen of heaven. Therefore, not even while he was on earth was he a stranger (to Him). We are the true strangers more than that stranger, if we don't receive strangers. He had no home, and his tent was his place of reception. And mark his liberality—he killed a calf, and kneaded fine meal. Note his ready mind—both his and his wife's. Note the unassuming manner—he worships and beseeches them. For all these qualities ought to be in the one who entertains strangers—readiness, cheerfulness, liberality. For the soul of the stranger is ill at ease, and feels self-conscious. Unless the host shows excessive joy, the stranger can easily feel slighted, and goes away, and that is worse than not to have received him, his being received in this way. Therefore, he worships them, therefore he welcomes them with speech, therefore with a seat. For who would have hesitated, knowing that this work was done unto Him?

John Chrysostom, *Homily 21 on Romans**

Chrysostom, commenting on the book of Romans where Paul describes the characteristics of a Christian (12:13), again claims that hospitality is an attitude, a way of life more than particular acts. One does not wait for someone to ask for hospitality, rather, one is always on the lookout for an opportunity to be hospitable.

"Sharing with the necessity of the saints." He does not say, "Bestow upon," but "share with the necessity of the saints," to show that they receive more than they give, that it is a matter of exchange, because it is a community. Do you bring in money? They bring you in boldness toward God. "Given to hospitality." He does not say doing it, but "given" to it, so to instruct us not to wait for those that shall ask it, and see when they will come to us, but to run to them, and be given to finding them.

John Chrysostom, *Homily 14 on 1 Timothy**

As he preaches on the role of widows and hospitality, Chrysostom pauses to remind his audience of the spirit of reciprocity which characterizes hospitality. It is not exercised with pride or arrogance over what one has to offer. That only puts a guest at a disadvantage. Rather, a spirit of appreciation by the host for the opportunity the guest affords marks hospitality.

This is hospitality, this is truly to do it for God's sake. But if you give orders with pride, though you ask him take the first place, it is not hospitality, it is not done for God's sake. The stranger requires much attendance, much encouragement, and even with all that, it is difficult for him not to feel ill at ease. For so sensitive is his position, that while he receives the favor, he is ashamed. So we should remove that shame by the most attentive service, and show by words and actions that we do not think we are conferring a favor, but receiving one, that we are obliging less than we are obliged. Good will can multiply kindness by alot. For, just as one who considers himself a loser, and thinks that he is doing a favor, destroys all the merit of it, so the one who looks upon himself as receiving a kindness, increases the reward. "For God loves a cheerful giver." So really you are indebted to the poor for receiving your kindness. For if there were no poor, the greater part of your sins would not be removed. They are the healers of your wounds, their hands are medicinal to you. The physician, extending his hand to apply a remedy, does not exercise the healing art more than the poor person, who stretches out a hand to receive your alms, and thus becomes a cure for your ills. Thus you receive more than you give, you are benefitted more than you benefit. You lend to God, not to people.

John Chrysostom, *Homily 33 on Hebrews**

Preaching on Hebrews, Chrysostom comments on hospitality as a way of life.

"Let brotherly love continue. Be not forgetful of hospitality, for hereby some have entertained angels unawares." See how he enjoins them to preserve what they had? He does not add other things. He did not say, "Be loving as brethren," but, "Let brotherly love continue." And again, he did not say, "Be hospitable," as if they were not, but, "Be not forgetful of hospitality," for this was likely to happen owing to their afflictions. Therefore, "some have entertained angels unawares."

And he did not say, "Be not forgetful" of the entertaining of strangers, but "of hospitality," that is, do not merely entertain strangers, but do it with love for the strangers. Moreover he did not speak of the recompense that is future, and in store for us, lest he should make them more sluggish, but of that already given. For "thereby some," he says, "have entertained angels unawares."

Paulinus of Nola, *Letter 34*

Written near 400 this letter is actually a sermon, "On the Alms Table." In it Paulinus (353–431) calls for mercy and a generosity of spirit that reflects table hospitality. The collection of alms for the poor could be a storeroom, a chest or, as in this case, a table. The Lord's table offers hospitality and respite to the poor. One's attitude at seeing the table and walking by the table has everything to do with one's spiritual health and relation to God. The spirit behind the action is what counts.

Let this afford us an example, dearest brethren. We, too, ought to ensure that we do not run the risk of expending our souls and losing our salvation by ignoring the table which the Lord has placed in church for the poor, by gazing at it with haughty eyes and passing it with empty hands. I pray that this disease may not afflict your minds. For cancerous greed readily creeps into a heart not fortified by the bowels of mercy, and having gained access to the soul binds it with viperous coils, if the hostile serpent finds it naked of good works and full of the substance of captivity, which is barren wealth. So let us not allow the Lord's table to be left empty behind us without provision for the needy, standing there visible but without resource, lest the groans which our indifference has wrung from the poor rebound upon us. For Scripture says: "He that despises the poor provokes his Maker"—in other words, the common Creator of all, whose joy at the refreshment of the poor is matched by His sorrow at their need.

John Cassian, *The Institutes of the Cenobia**

This interesting story is told by John (360–435) in an effort to highlight the spirit of hospitality more than the utility of hospitality. The spirit of hospitality is open-handed so that one does not look to what one will receive in return. John offers a pointed example of this spirit. The purposeful work given to this guest was actually of no use, yet it offered a foreigner a meaningful place in the community and allowed him to use his gifts.

When a brother who was very dear to us, Simeon by name, a man utterly ignorant of Greek, had come from the region of Italy, one of the elders, anxious to perform for him a work of charity with some pretense of mutual benefit, as he was a stranger, asked him why he sat doing nothing in his cell. The elder had guessed from this that he would not be able to stay much longer in it both because of the roving thoughts which idleness produces and because of his lack of the necessities of life, well knowing that no one can endure such an assault except one who is happy to procure food for himself by the labor of his hands. The other replied that he could not do or manage any of the things which were usually done by the brethren there, except write a good hand, if any one in Egypt wanted a Latin book for his use. When he heard that, the elder at length seized the opportunity to secure the long wished for work of charity, under pretense of its being a mutual benefit. He said, "From God this opportunity comes, for I was just looking for someone to write out for me the Epistles in Latin, for I have a brother who is bound in the chains of military service, and is a good Latin scholar, to whom I want to send something from Scripture for him to read for his edification." And so when Simeon gratefully took this as an opportunity offered to him by God, the old man also gladly seized the pretext, under color of which he could freely carry out his work of charity. At once he not only brought him as a matter of business everything he could want for a whole year, but also gave him parchment and everything requisite for writing, and received afterwards the manuscript, which was not of the slightest use (since in those parts they were all utterly ignorant of this language), and did no good to anybody except that which resulted from this device and large outlay. For one, without shame or confusion, was able to procure necessary food and sustenance by the reward of his work and labor, and the other carried out his kindness and bounty, as it were, by the compulsion of a debt, securing for himself a more abundant reward proportioned to the zeal he had in procuring for his foreign brother not only his necessary food, but materials for writing, and an opportunity of work.

*Jerome, Letter 125**

Jerome (342–420) was a Roman ascetic who lived and taught in Bethlehem for most of his life, seeking a desert home for the study of Scripture and holiness. In this letter to Rusticus, a young monk, in 411 Jerome argues that an intense spirit accompanies the pursuit of virtue. There is a focus of energy which drives the orientation of the human heart toward love. When it comes to hospitality, we must know how precious our guests are and what we have to lose.

14. The world's philosophers drive out an old passion by instilling a new one. They hammer out one nail by hammering in another. . . . we must overcome our faults by learning to love the opposite virtues. "Depart from evil," says the psalmist, "and do good, seek peace and pursue it." For if we do not hate evil we cannot love good. Moreover, we must do good if we are to depart from evil. We must seek peace if we are to avoid war. And it is not enough merely to seek it. When we have found it and when it flees before us we must pursue it with all our energies. For "it passes all understanding." It is the habitation of God. As the psalmist says, "in peace also is his habitation." The pursuing of peace is a fine metaphor and may be compared with the apostle's words, "pursuing hospitality." It is not enough, he means, for us to invite guests with our lips. We should be as eager to detain them as though they were robbers carrying off our savings.

Hospitality as Presence

The spirit in which hospitality is offered figures centrally in much of what early Christians have to say about hospitality. But we should not mistake the language of spirit for an ethereal view of hospitality where right attitudes or affections are sufficient. The humble and gracious spirit that accompanies hospitality is only made known as it is incarnated and embodied.

Again the spiritual dynamic at work here begins with God's hospitable activity. The divine indwelling in the world sets the pattern for hospitality as presence. God expresses hospitality by being present, by being with humanity and all creation. Ancient Israelites acknowledged the reality and constancy of God's presence through the instructions for the table for the bread of the Presence in the tabernacle (Exodus 25:23-30). God's presence and provision was made manifest in the bread continually set before them on the table. Jesus' proclamation of his presence in the bread and wine continues this claim of divine presence, God with us. This holy presence by which God both draws the world to himself and gives himself to the world, offers the model for hospitality of presence, of being with, of dwelling together.

Hospitality does not entail feeling sorry for someone and trying to help. We cannot write out a check, drop off some groceries, or pay a heating bill and consider ourselves hospitable. The feeling of pity and the desire to better the lives of others is a good thing, often inspired by God in one's heart. But it is seductive, even dangerous, for the host to view herself as the helper. The would-be act of hospitality becomes an act of condescension and failure to see, either one's own need or the true identity of the stranger as Christ. One can easily stay at arm's length and offer advice or solutions without actually entering the world of the other. Ego, self-satisfaction, a need to feel off the hook, demonstrating competence and righteousness, all too easily enter the equation, with the host as hero and the guest as victim.

Instead, early Christians teach us that hospitality is more akin to compassion, to suffer *with*. The sense of solidarity with the stranger, the widow, the sick, in early Christian texts is palpable. Hospitality does not entail helping another so much as immersing oneself in a new reality, entering into a new relationship with one who before was unknown or unappreciated. The notion of "being with the other" values presence more than outcome. It may or may not be possible to alleviate another's suffering or improve another's situation. The success of hospitality, however, does not depend on end results. Rather, the success of hospitality is measured by the degree to which one offers one's genuine presence with another, to fully enter another's world and dwell with another.[3]

Equally problematic in the helping model is the concern many have about determining who is deserving of hospitality. Early Christian preachers speak to this phenomenon over and over.[4] When a stranger knocks on the door, or when the sick seek aid, Christians often go through extensive mental calculations to determine whether this person is a worthwhile investment, whether their needs are legitimate, whether he or she will use the resources offered wisely. Fear of fraud can easily override the impulse to hospitality. This sort of risk assessment and outcome-based decision making misses the mark of hospitality. It keeps the focus on worthiness rather than on simple presence, being with. Does God go through such evaluations before offering Himself? Does God determine risk, legitimate need, likely outcome, when deciding whether to become Incarnate in Christ, or offer Her grace to people? No. God offers hospitality through Christ as He seeks to dwell with us, risky though it may be. John Chrysostom puts it this way,

> "Such a one is an impostor," you say. Did I already tell you that if we give to all indiscriminately, we shall always be compassionate? But if we begin to make over-curious inquiries, we shall never be compassionate? What do you mean? Is someone an impostor just to get a loaf of bread? If indeed he asks for talents of gold and silver, or costly clothes, or slaves, or anything else of this sort, one might with good reason call him a swindler. But if he asks none of these things, but only food and shelter, things which are suited to a spiritual life, tell me, is this the part of a swindler? We must cease from this inappropriate fondness for meddling, which is Satanic, which is destructive.[5]

Early Christians were sensitive to this understandable distortion of hospitality. They refer again and again to the quality of physical presence in hospitality. The models of hospitality they lift up are those who have performed acts of hospitality themselves, not through their servants or agents. As God seeks to be fully, physically present in the Incarnation, so our own physical and spiritual presence with others makes the strongest witness of hospitality. Chrysostom warns his flock not to give resources to church leaders for them to distribute. Get your hands dirty, use your own hands to offer hospitality to those in need. Texts are in approximate chronological order.

Gregory of Nazianzus, Oration 43: Panegyric on St. Basil*

Gregory's (329–389) well-known panegyric details the "new city" Basil had created for lepers and the diseased, a place for the most despised and rejected in their society. Gregory praises Basil's leadership, not in word, but in deed, noting how Basil took the lead in tending to the sick.

He [Basil] did not disdain to honor with his lips this disease, even though he had a brilliant reputation and was of noble ancestry himself. He saluted them as kindred, not, as some might assume, from self-righteousness (for who was so far removed from this feeling?). No, he took the lead in going to tend them on account of his beliefs, and so he gave instruction not only by his words but also by his actions. The effect produced is to be seen not only in the city, but in the country and beyond, and even the leaders of society have vied with one another in their philanthropy and magnanimity towards them. Others have had their cooks, and splendid tables, and the devices and dainties of confectioners, and exquisite carriages, and soft, flowing robes. Basil's care was for the sick, and the relief of their wounds, and the imitation of Christ, by cleansing leprosy, not by a word, but in deed.

Gregory of Nyssa, Homily: As You Did It to One of These, You Did It to Me

Gregory of Nyssa (330–395) sets his appeal to Jesus' command to care for the "least of these" within the context of a final judgment. In this sermon he has already offered negative and positive examples of those who obeyed the command. He claims that it is not enough to send food to far away places or utter pretty words. Rather, Christians must get their hands dirty and get involved in people's lives.

What can we gather from all these examples? Is the law of nature sinful? Can we recite a tragedy about human afflictions, extol them, and speak passionately of their memory? Should we show sympathy and concern? Words are united to deeds with regard to what is true, and the Lord does not say that salvation consists in words but in deeds which effect salvation (Mt 7.21). Thus we are responsible to follow his command. Let no one say that it is sufficient to send food to people not involved in our lives. This does not reveal mercy but an outward show in order to remove such persons from our presence. Do not their lives put us to shame and make us like dogs? A hunter does not avoid the lairs of young animals and the farmer knows how to care for calves; many such examples may be offered. Even the traveler washes the feet of his ass, takes care of its wounds, and cleanses its stable of dung. Will we refuse to neglect human beings and their beasts? No, my brothers, no. Let us not have this attitude towards our fellow men.

Jerome, Letter 66

Pammachius was a Roman senator who had left his privileged life behind in order to become a monk upon the death of his wife, Paulina, a daughter of the early church mother, Paula. Jerome (ca. 342–420) wrote this letter in 397 to commend him on his newly chosen life. Jerome praises both Abraham and Sarah as models for their personal involvement in acts of hospitality. While they could have easily asked their servants to perform the duties of washing feet or serving food, they chose instead to participate themselves. Thereby they entertained God.

I hear that you have erected a hospice for strangers at Portus and that you have planted a twig from the tree of Abraham upon the Ausonian shore. . . . Abraham was rich in gold and silver and cattle, in resources and clothing. His household was so large that in an emergency he could bring a select body of young men into the field, and could pursue as far as Dan and then slay four kings who had already put five kings to flight. Frequently exercising hospitality and never turning anyone away from his door, he was accounted worthy at last to entertain God himself. He was not satisfied with giving orders to his servants and hand-maids to attend to his guests, nor did he lessen the favor he conferred by leaving others to care for them. But as though he had found a prize, he and Sarah, his wife, gave themselves to the duties of hospitality. With his own hands he washed the feet of his guests, upon his own shoulders he brought home a fat calf from the herd. While the strangers dined he stood by to serve them, and set before them the dishes cooked by Sarah's hands—though meaning to fast himself.

Jerome, Letter 77*

In a letter to Oceanus, Jerome praises the work of Fabiola in founding a hospital and caring for the sick with her own hands. His details of afflictions to which she attended highlights the tangible character of her hospitality. While he understands some may be squeamish, nevertheless she is the model of virtue. The letter functions as a eulogy of Fabiola, written not long after her death in 399.

Today you give me as my theme Fabiola, the praise of the Christians, the marvel of the gentiles, the sorrow of the poor, and the consolation of the monks. Whatever point in her character I choose to treat of first, pales into insignificance compared with those which follow after. Shall I praise her fasts? Her alms are greater still. Shall I commend her humility? The glow of her faith is yet brighter. Shall I mention her studied plainness in dress, her voluntary choice of plebeian costume and the garb of a slave that she might put to shame silken robes? To change one's disposition is a greater achievement than to change one's dress. It is harder for us to part with arrogance than with gold and gems. . . .

Restored to communion before the eyes of the whole church, what did she do? In the day of prosperity she was not forgetful of affliction. Having once suffered shipwreck she was unwilling again to face the risks of the sea. Instead therefore of re-embarking on her old life, she broke up and sold all that she could lay hands on of her property (it was large and suitable to her rank), and turning it into money she laid out this for the benefit of the poor. She was the first person to found a hospital, into which she might gather sufferers out of the streets, and where she might nurse the unfortunate victims of sickness and starvation. Need I now recount the various ailments of human beings? Need I speak of noses slit, eyes put out, feet half burnt, hands covered with sores? Or of limbs useless and atrophied? Or of diseased flesh alive with worms? Often did she carry on her own shoulders persons infected with jaundice or with filth. Often too did she wash away the matter discharged from wounds which others, even though men, could not bear to look at. She gave food to her patients with her own hand, and moistened the scarce breathing lips of the dying with sips of liquid. I know of many wealthy and devout persons who, unable to overcome their natural repugnance to such sights, perform this work of mercy by the agency of others, giving money instead of personal aid. I do not blame them and am far from construing their weakness of resolution into a lack of faith. While however I pardon such squeamishness, I extol to the skies the enthusiastic zeal of a mind that is above it. A great faith makes little of such trifles.

Jerome, *Preface to Commentary on Ezekiel**

Jerome pursued the study of Scripture perhaps above all else. This was his calling and his passion. Yet, he tells us in this preface, even this love had to be put aside in the face of human suffering that required him and his community to open their doors to refugees from Rome. The ministry of hospitality through physical presence took precedence over biblical study. He says it is time not to say holy things, but to do them.

Who would believe that Rome, built up by the conquest of the whole world, had collapsed? That the mother of nations had become also their tomb? That the shores of the whole East, of Egypt, of Africa, which once belonged to the imperial city, were filled with crowds of her men-servants and maid-servants? That we should every day be receiving in this holy Bethlehem men and women who once were noble and abounding in every kind of wealth but are now reduced to poverty? We cannot relieve these sufferers. All we can do is to sympathize with them, and unite our tears with theirs. The burden of this holy work was as much as we could carry. The sight of the wanderers coming in crowds, caused us deep pain. So we abandoned the exposition of Ezekiel, and almost all study, and were filled with a longing to turn the words of Scripture into action, and not to say holy things, but to do them.

There is not a single hour, nor a single moment, in which we are not relieving crowds of brothers, and the quiet of the monastery has been changed into the bustle of a guest house. And so much is this the case that we must either close our doors, or abandon the study of the Scriptures on which we depend for keeping the doors open. And so, turning to profit, or rather stealing the hours of the nights, which, now that winter is approaching, begin to lengthen somewhat, I am endeavoring by the light of the lamp to dictate these comments, whatever they may be worth, and am trying to mitigate with exposition the weariness of a mind which is a stranger to rest. I am not boasting, as some perhaps suspect, of the welcome given to the brothers, but I am simply confessing the causes of the delay. Who could boast when the flight of the people from the West, and the holy places, crowded as they are with penniless fugitives, naked and wounded, plainly reveal the ravages of the Barbarians? We cannot see what has occurred without tears and moans. Who would have believed that mighty Rome, with its careless security of wealth, would be reduced to such extremities as to need shelter, food, and clothing? And yet, some are so hard-hearted and cruel that, instead of showing compassion, they break up the rags and bundles of the captives, and expect to find gold about those who are nothing more than prisoners . . . .

*John Chrysostom, Homily 45 on Acts of the Apostles**

John Chrysostom (ca. 347–407) wrote many sermons on Acts. He pursues an extensive discussion here of lodging visitors based on Acts 21:16-17. Chrysostom appeals to the example of Abraham who received visitors not in the road or in a hostel, but in his own dwelling place. Sarah, not her servants, served them. This physical presence in hospitality is emphasized at several points in the sermon.

Make for yourself a guest-chamber in your own house. Set up a bed there, set up a table there and a candlestick. For isn't it absurd, that if soldiers happen to come, you have rooms set apart for them, and show much care for them, and furnish them with everything, because they protect you from the visible war of this world? Yet strangers have no place where they might abide? Gain a victory over the Church. Do you want to put us to shame? Then do this. Surpass us in generosity. Have a room, to which Christ may come. Say, "This is Christ's space. This building is set apart for Him." Even if it is just a basement and tiny. He won't refuse it. Christ goes about "naked and a stranger." It is only a shelter He wants. . . . Abraham received the strangers in the place where he himself lived. His wife stood in the place of a servant, the guests in the place of masters. He didn't know that he was receiving Christ, didn't know that he was receiving Angels. Had he known it, he would have lavished his whole substance. But we, who know that we receive Christ, don't show even so much enthusiasm as he did who thought that he was receiving humans. "But many of them are impostors and ungrateful," you will say. And for this the greater your reward when you receive for the sake of Christ's name. For if you know indeed that they are impostors, don't receive them into your house. But if you don't know this, why do you accuse them lightly? "Therefore I tell them to go to the receiving house." But what kind of excuse is there for us, when we do not even receive those whom we know, but shut our doors against all? Let our house be Christ's general receiving place. Let us demand of them as a reward, not money, but that they make our house the receiving place for Christ. Let us run about everywhere, let us drag them in, let us seize our prize. Greater are the benefits we receive than what we confer. He does not require you to kill a calf, but only to give bread to the hungry, raiment to the naked, shelter to the stranger.

John Chrysostom, *Homily 14 on 1 Timothy**

The context for Chrysostom's discussion here is the role of widows in the community. He has spent most of the sermon praising the hospitality widows offer to others and exhorting Christians to follow their pattern. He points out that widows practice hospitality with their own hands, not through their handmaids. Likewise, Abraham and Sarah, who had many servants, chose to perform acts of hospitality themselves. One's presence is essential to hospitality.

Look, the hospitality we're talking about is not merely a friendly reception, but one given with zeal and full of life, with readiness, and going about it as if one were receiving Christ Himself. The widows should perform these services themselves, not commit them to their handmaids. For Christ said, "If I your Master and Lord have washed your feet, you ought also to wash one another's feet" (John 13:14). And though a woman may be very rich, and of the highest rank, vain of her birth and noble family, there is not the same distance between her and others, as between God and the disciples. If you receive the stranger as Christ, be not ashamed, but rather glory. But if you receive him not as Christ, receive him not at all. "He that receives you," He said, "receives Me" (Matthew 10:40). If you do not so receive him, you have no reward. Abraham was receiving people that passed as travelers, or so he thought, and he did not leave to his servants to make the preparations for their entertainment. Instead he took the greater part of the service upon himself, and commanded his wife to mix the flour, though he had three hundred and eighteen servants born in his house, of whom there must have been many maidservants. Still, he wished that himself and his wife should have the reward, not of the cost only, but of the service. Just in this way we should exercise hospitality by our own personal exertions, so that we may be made holy, and our hands be blessed. If you give to the poor, don't disdain to give it yourself, for it is not to the poor that it is given, but to Christ, and who is so wretched, as to disdain to stretch out his own hand to Christ?

Don't give your alms to those who preside in the Church to distribute. Bestow it yourself, that you may have the reward not of giving merely, but of kind service. Give with your own hands. Cast into the furrow yourself.

John Chrysostom, *Homily 41 on Genesis*

In this sermon on Genesis 18, again Chrysostom appeals to Abraham, "the just man," and his hospitality of presence, tending to guests himself.

This, then, was the reason why he [God] appeared to him again, Scripture says, because he was obedient. So on this account blessed

Moses began in this way, in the words, "Now, God appeared to him at to the Oak of Mamre as he was sitting at the door of his house at midday." Notice, I ask you, in this instance the just man's virtue: "As he was sitting," the text says, "at his tent." He was putting hospitality into practice to such a degree as to be unwilling to entrust to anyone else in the household the task of attending to guests; instead, although he had three hundred and eighteen servants, and was himself an old man, having attained advanced years (after all, he was a hundred years old), he took his seat at the door. In his case he was practicing this virtue; old age was no problem for him, he was not concerned for his own repose, nor was he reclining inside on his bed but was seated at the door. Other people, by contrast, in many cases not only do not show such concern but just the opposite, trying to avoid meeting visitors as if they were forced to receive them against their will.

Sozomen, Ecclesiastical History*

Sozomen (fl. ca. 440), the church historian, tells the history of the monks of Nitria with admiration and praise. Among them is Melas, a priest at Rhinocorura who, Sozomen tells us, was orthodox and opposed to Arianism. When his enemies come to arrest him, Melas behaves as a servant, receiving them and serving them at the table himself. They are so impressed with his personal and humble service they offer lenience, which he refuses.

It is said that when the decree for the ejection of all priests opposed to Arianism was issued, the officers appointed to apprehend Melas found him engaged as the lowest servant, in trimming the lights of the church, with an apron soiled with oil on his cloak, and carrying the wicks. When they asked him for the bishop, he replied that he was within, and that he would conduct them to him. As they were fatigued with their journey, he led them to the episcopal dwelling, made them sit down at table, and gave them whatever he had to eat. After the repast, he supplied them with water to wash their hands, for he served the guests, and then told them who he was. Amazed at his conduct, they confessed the mission on which they had arrived. Out of respect for him, they gave him full liberty to go wherever he would. He, however, replied that he would not shrink from the sufferings to which the other bishops who maintained the same sentiments as himself were exposed, and that he was willing to go into exile. Having practiced spirituality from his youth, he had exercised himself in all the monastic virtues.

*Theodoret of Cyrrhus, Ecclesiastical History**

Theodoret (ca. 393–ca. 466), bishop of Cyrrhus, composed this church history using Eusebius's work and continuing it into his own time to 428. He adds many hagiographies as well as some documentation of the doctrinal disputes of the fourth and early fifth centuries in which his own career had become embroiled. In this account Theodoret praises the hospitality of the empress Placilia, particularly emphasizing the acts she performed by her own hands, not through those of a servant.

Yet other opportunities of improvement lay within the emperor's reach, for his wife [Placilia] used constantly to remind him of the divine laws in which she had first carefully educated herself. In no way exalted by her imperial rank she was rather fired by it with greater longing for divine things. The greatness of the good gift given her made her love for Him who gave it all the greater, so she bestowed every kind of attention on the maimed and the mutilated, declining all aid from her household and her guards, herself visiting the houses where the sufferers lodged, and providing every one with what he required. She also went about the guest chambers [*xenodochia*] of the churches and ministered to the wants of the sick, herself handling pots and pans, and tasting broth, now bringing in a dish and breaking bread and offering morsels, and washing out a cup and going through all the other duties which are supposed to be proper to servants and maids. To those who tried to stop her from doing these things with her own hands she would say, "It befits a sovereign to distribute gold. I, for the sovereign power that has been given me, am giving my own service to the Giver."

Radegund, Life

The account of the life of Radegund (525–587), the Frankish queen, points out her hands-on involvement with those to whom she offered hospitality. She washed and cared for the sick herself, and fed them at her table, perhaps unusual for aristocratic women who could pay servants to do charitable work.

Turning her mind to further works of mercy, she built a house at Athies where beds were elegantly made up for needy women gathered there. She would wash them herself in warm baths, tending to the putrescence of their diseases. She washed the heads of men, acting like a servant. And before she washed them, she would mix a potion with her own hands to revive those who were weak from sweating. . . .

How much did she spend daily on relief? Only she who bore it to the beggars ever knew. For beyond the daily meal which she fed to her enrolled paupers, twice a week, on Thursday and Saturday, she prepared a bath. Girding herself with a cloth, she washed the heads of the needy, scrubbing away whatever she found there. Not shrinking from scurf, scabs, lice or pus, she plucked off the worms and scrubbed away the putrid flesh. Then she herself combed the hair on every head she had washed. As in the gospel, she applied oil to their ulcerous sores that had opened when the skin softened or that scratching had irritated, reducing the spread of infection. When women descended into the tub, she washed their limbs with soap from head to foot. When they came out, if she noticed that anyone's clothes were shoddy with age, she would take them away and give them new ones. Thus she spruced up all who came to the feast in rags. When they were gathered around the table and the dinner service laid out, she brought water and napkins for each of them and cleaned the mouth and hands of the invalids herself. Then three trays laden with delicacies would be carried in. Standing like a good hostess before the diners, she cut up the bread and meat and served everyone while fasting herself. Moreover, she never ceased to offer food to the blind and weak with a spoon. In this, two women aided her but she alone served them, busy as a new Martha until the "brothers" were drunk and happily satisfied with their meal.

Miraculous Abundance

Early Christian texts witness to the transformative power of hospitality through miracles of abundance that occur. Host and guest are transformed, guest becomes host, the stranger is revealed as Christ, the holy Mary and Joseph are received as guests. When one participates in God's graciousness through hospitality, one is changed. When hospitality is extended or received, strange and amazing things can happen. Sometimes the miracle of abundance is directly performed by God. Other times, it is through an agent of God, a holy person, an unexpected visitor, or even an animal.

Both the Old and New Testaments give examples of miraculous

abundance. When the Israelites were wandering in the wilderness, God made it hospitable for them by providing bread from heaven (Exodus 16) and water (Exodus 17). The prophet Elisha fed a hundred people with only twenty loaves of barley and had some left over (2 Kings 4:42-44). Jesus and his disciples fed a crowd of five thousand with only five loaves and two fish, with twelve baskets of bread pieces left over (Luke 9:10-17). These stories convey the sense that when gifts are shared, there is plenty for everyone.

The literature of hospitality is full of examples of scarcity miraculously transformed into abundance. An empty granary fills to overflowing. An empty table receives loaves of bread from visitors. It is as though the very practice of hospitality invokes an experience of fullness and plenty. Many of these stories are fantastical, often with outrageous proportions. We might take this to reflect something of the dynamics early Christians saw at work in hospitality. God's graciousness is outrageous. Crazy things can happen. The profound experience of plenty changes lives so that things are never the same again. These stories all testify to the miraculous abundance that accompanies hospitality.

There seems to be in early Christian literature a sub-genre of stories of miraculous abundance that features animals. The accounts below from Sulpitius Severus, Peter the Iberian and Jerome reflect this tradition. In these stories animals welcome humans into the natural world, their domain. They play the host and are often the conduits of abundance, offering desperately needed food or water. Early Christian conviction that hospitality and miraculous abundance are fundamentally connected is expressed in these animal stories. Texts are in approximate chronological order.

Jerome, *The Life of Paul the First Hermit**

Jerome (ca. 342–420) wrote this account of Paul, a desert ascetic, in 374 while residing in the desert of Syria. He tells of Antony, the great spiritual father of monasticism, wandering in the desert and coming upon the cell of Paul. After a warm greeting and prayer, they are miraculously served a meal only to fall into an argument about who will be host and who will be guest. The amusing story ends in peace, however.

Thus with smiles Paul gave him access, and, the door being opened, they threw themselves into each other's arms, greeted one another by name, and joined in thanksgiving to God.

After the sacred kiss Paul sat down and thus began to address Antony. "Behold the man whom you have sought with so much toil, his limbs decayed with age, his gray hairs unkempt. You see before you a man who before long will be dust. But love endures all things. Tell me therefore, I pray you, how fares the human race? Are new homes springing up in the ancient cities? What government directs the world? Are there still some remaining for the demons to carry away by their delusions?" Thus conversing they noticed with wonder a raven which had settled on the bough of a tree, and was then flying gently down till it came and laid a whole loaf of bread before them. They were astonished, and when it had gone, "See," said Paul, "the Lord truly loving, truly merciful, has sent us a meal. For the last sixty years I have always received half a loaf. But at your coming Christ has doubled his soldier's rations."

Accordingly, having returned thanks to the Lord, they sat down together on the brink of the glassy spring. At this point a dispute arose as to who should break the bread, and nearly the whole day until eventide was spent in the discussion. Paul urged in support of his view the rites of hospitality, Antony pleaded age. At length it was arranged that each should seize the loaf on the side nearest to himself, pull towards him, and keep for his own the part left in his hands. Then on hands and knees they drank a little water from the spring, and offering to God the sacrifice of praise passed the night in vigil.

Sulpitius Severus, Dialogues

Sulpitius Severus (ca. 360–420), through the dialogues with Postumianus, a Christian telling of his travels, recounts many fascinating stories of travel and hospitality. In some of them animals figure as agents of hospitality, often in miraculous ways. Here a desert ascetic finds what he needs to survive through the miraculous intervention of an ibex who offers hospitality for human habitation by identifying which plants are dangerous and which can be eaten.

There was also an illustrious name of another anchorite in those regions, a man who dwelt in that part of the desert which is about Syene. This man, when first he took himself to the wilderness, intended to live on the roots of plants which the sand here and there produces, of a very sweet and delicious flavor. But being ignorant of the nature of the herbs, he often gathered those which were of a deadly character. And, indeed, it was not easy to discriminate between the kind of the roots by the mere taste, since all were equally sweet, but many of them, less well known, contained inside a deadly poison. So when the poison within tormented him on eating these, and all his vitals were tortured with terrific pains, and frequent vomiting, along with excruciating agonies, were all shattering the very citadel of life, his stomach became completely exhausted, and he was in utter terror of all that had to be eaten for sustaining existence. Having thus fasted for seven days, he was almost at the point of death when a wild animal called an ibex came up to him. To this creature standing by him, he offered a bundle of plants which he had collected on the previous day, yet had not ventured to touch. The beast, casting aside with its mouth those which were poisonous, picked out such as it knew to be harmless. In this way, that holy man, taught by its conduct what he should eat, and what to reject, both escaped the danger of dying of hunger and of being poisoned by the plants.

Palladius, *The Lausiac History*

Palladius (ca. 363–425) tells the story of Elias who, receiving travelers hospitably, miraculously fed twenty visitors with only three loaves of bread, and still had some left over.

Elias

There was Elias, too, who lived as a solitary in a cave in this vicinity. He led a most holy life of self-control. One day a good many brethren visited him, for the place was along the road, and he ran out of bread. And he assured us: "At my wit's end I entered the cell and found three loaves. There were twenty of them [visitors]. When they had eaten enough, one loaf remained. This furnished me food for twenty-five days."

Lives of the Desert Fathers

This text from about 400 also recounts stories of the desert fathers and their practices of welcome. The confidence in God's graciousness that hospitality expresses often issues in miraculous abundance, in this case, food to feed a whole village for four months.

VIII.44. For example, not long ago, when there was a famine in the Thebaid, the people who lived in the neighboring district, on hearing that Apollo's community of monks was often fed in a miraculous way, came to him as a body with their wives and children to ask him to bless them and give them food. The father, never fearing that there would be any shortage, gave to each of those who came sufficient food for one day. 45. When only three baskets of bread were left and the famine still continued, he ordered the baskets which the brethren intended to eat that day to be brought out, and in the hearing of all the monks and the people he said, "Is the hand of the Lord not strong enough to multiply these loaves? For the Holy Spirit says, 'The bread from these baskets shall not be consumed until we have all been satisfied with new wheat.'" 46. And all those who were present confirmed that the bread was sufficient for everybody for four months. And he did the same with oil and with wheat.

Abba Helle was known among desert monks for his hospitality and care of others. In this story, he extends hospitality to brother monks with confidence in God's providence and is not disappointed.

14. Once when they had almost exhausted their stock of loaves, an angel appeared in the cave in the form of a brother and brought them something to eat. Another time ten brothers who were searching for him wandered in the desert for seven days without any food. On finding them himself, he invited them to rest in his cave. 15. When they mentioned that they had not eaten, the father, having nothing to set before them, said to them, "God is able to furnish a table in the wilderness." At that moment a servant appeared at the door, a handsome young man, and persisted in knocking while the brethren were at prayer. When they opened the door, they saw that the youth was carrying a large basket full of bread and olives. They received them from him and partook of them, after giving thanks to the Lord, the servant having at once disappeared.

John Rufus, *The Life of Holy Peter the Iberian*

Peter the Iberian (ca. 409-488) lived for a good part of his life as an ascetic in the Holy Land, though he was born the son of the Christian king of Georgia. In Palestine his life intersected with many of the great figures of the day and he became a leader of the Georgian Church in the Monophysite cause at the Council of Chalcedon in 451. His biography was written soon after his death by one of his disciples, John Rufus. In this story from ca. 485, Peter invites people from all around to celebrate the life of John, his friend. But when the sea cannot supply fish for the feast, a miraculous downpour provides more than enough. Peter's biographer claims that all the fish came to commemorate the holy man. When resources are shared and hospitality is offered, plenty abounds.

When we were here, there came round the commemoration day of John the Eunuch, who had been the cell-mate of Father Peter, and had passed away on the 4th of December. According to his custom, Peter invited many people to this festival, especially from the mountain regions round about, and gave orders to buy quantities of fish from the sea nearby. Now it happened that winter came on so suddenly that sea-fishing had to be completely abandoned. We were troubled because we could not entertain the brethren as the saint had instructed. But suddenly shortage turned to plenty. During the night so much rain fell that the river which flowed near us flooded its banks and inundated the vineyards round about. In the morning such shoals of fish were picked up that the local people said they could never remember such a prodigy, and we could not cope with all the fish who had come to attend the commemoration feast of that holy man.

Cyril of Scythopolis, *Lives of the Monks of Palestine*

These stories from Cyril's (500s) account of the desert fathers clearly draw the connection between open-handed hospitality and God's abundance. In this first story, Euthymius expects plenty, even though the storehouse is virtually empty. His expectations are fulfilled as the storehouse overflows with loaves so that they have to take the door off its hinges. This miraculous abundance is God's response to the community's warm reception of strangers, according to Euthymius.

17. His Hospitality and Blessing
   When our father Euthymius had begun to make his place a laura and the twelve brethren with him were in great straits as regards the necessities of life, and Domitian had been appointed steward for the first year, it happened that a crowd of Armenians, around four hundred in number, on their way from the holy city to the Jordan, deviated off the road to the right and arrived at the laura, as if by pre-arrangement—an occurrence, in my opinion, contrived by

Providence to reveal his virtue and God-given grace. On seeing them, the elder summoned Domitian and said, "Serve these people with something to eat." He replied, "The cellar, venerable father, does not contain enough to feed ten persons. How, then, can I give bread to such a multitude?" The godly Euthymius, filled with prophetic grace, said, "Proceed as I have told you, for the words of the Holy Spirit are, 'They shall eat and have something left over.' Going accordingly to the small cell called by some the pantry, where a few loaves were lying, Domitian was unable to open the door, for God's blessing had filled the cell right to the top. So calling some of the men, he took the door off its hinges, and out poured the loaves from the cell. The same blessing occurred likewise with the wine and the oil. All ate and were satisfied, and for three months they were unable to reattach the door of the cell. Just as God through the prophet's voice made the jar of meal and the cruse of oil well up for the hospitable widow, so in the same way he granted to this godly elder a supply of blessings equal to his zeal for hospitality. Domitian in his amazement threw himself at his teacher's feet, begging to receive forgiveness for having felt something natural to human beings. The elder made him rise and said, "My child, 'he who sows with blessings will also reap with blessings.' Let us 'not neglect to show hospitality, for there (as the Apostle says) some have entertained angels unawares.' Be confident that if you and those after you receive with faith and treat worthily all the strangers and brethren who visit you, the Lord will never fail this place from now on till eternity. For God is well-pleased with such an offering."

In another story, Cyril tells of St. Sabas buying land so that foreign monks will have a monastery. Once St. Sabas extends his own generosity on behalf of strangers, God, through a stranger, miraculously provides the rest.

31. To the north of the cells he purchased were other cells, which he wished to purchase on behalf of foreign monks. He tried to find a sufficient quantity of money, but had only one half solidus. Relying on faith in God, he gave the half solidus as a deposit, with the words, "If I do not pay you in full tomorrow, I forfeit the deposit." On the same day, before sunrise, as he was thinking about this and praying mentally, a completely unknown stranger came up to him, gave him one hundred and seventy solidi, and immediately withdrew, not even giving his name. Astonished at the prompt assistance

of God, the blessed one gave the price of the cells and founded a second hospice for the relief of monks coming from abroad. He also acquired two hospices for Castellium, one in the holy city not far from the Tower of David and the other in Jericho in one of the gardens he had bought.

In a third story, Cyril tells of the miraculous abundance that occurs in the midst of enthusiastic hospitality.

46. The Miracle of the Wine
    After a long time had elapsed, the son of this Gerontius, named Thomas, on a visit to the Great Laura's guest-house at Jericho, it being late evening and in a time of famine, found Saint Sabas there and also Theodore and Paul, the administrators of the monasteries of Castellion and of the Cave. The blessed Sabas was overjoyed at seeing him and said to the guest-master, "Make us dinner." As they were dining, the guest-master, asked if he had wine, replied that he had none at all, but said that he had a gourd of vinegar for dressing pulses. The saint said, "Bring the gourd to me here. Blessed be the Lord that we are able because of him to make merry, for Christ our God, who himself turned water into wine, is able to turn vinegar also into wine." At these words of the saint the gourd was brought in and the vinegar was found to have changed into excellent wine. Thomas was overwhelmed at this extraordinary miracle, and blessed Sabas said to the guest-master, "Bring hot coals immediately and throw on incense, for God has visited us in this hour." The wine of the gourd was so blessed that for three days all drank freely from it. Thomas was amazed at the miracle and begged the elder for permission to take the gourd to his own house; the saint gave the gourd and Thomas took it with him when he departed. He continued drinking the abundant wine, both himself and his companions, all the way to Medaba.

John Moschos, The Spiritual Meadow

John Moschos (ca. 550–619), who lived during the reign of Justinian I in the 500s, collected stories and accounts from the spiritual greats of his day. The result is a meadow of spiritual flowers of Christian life. Here he reports a story told by Cyril, a man who traveled with his father and brother to Abba Julian for healing and ended up staying as part of the community. Cyril tells the story of miraculous abundance when Julian offers hospitality in feeding the community even when the granary is empty.

The elder appointed my father to be in charge of the grain. One day my father came to Abba Julian and said: "We have no grain." The elder replied: "Go, gather together whatever you can find and grind it up. God will take care of tomorrow for us." My father was troubled by this command for he knew there was nothing left in the granary; he withdrew to his cell. When need became very pressing, the elder indicated that he was to come to him and as soon as he entered, he said to him: "Brother Conon, go and prepare whatever you find for the brethren." Almost in anger he took the keys of the granary and went off, intending to bring back some earth. Having released the lock he wanted to open the doors, but he could not do so because the granary was completely filled with grain. When he saw this he humbly prostrated himself before the elder, glorifying God.

Moschos tells another story of miraculous abundance, this time about a reluctant gentile who "lends" his money to the poor on the porches of the church. The God of the Christians is generous to this reluctant giver.

On the island of Samos, Mary, the friend of both God and the poor, the mother of Master Paul, the military official attached to the court, told us that there was a Christian woman in Nisbis whose husband was a pagan. They possessed fifty *miliarisia*. One day, the husband said to his wife: "Let us lend out that money and get some advantage from it, for in drawing on it a little at a time, we are going to spend it all." The wife answered: "If you insist on lending this money, come, lend it to the God of the Christians." He said to her: "Well, where is this God of the Christians, so we can lend it to him?" She said: "I will show you. Not only shall you not lose your money, but it shall even earn interest for you and the capital shall be doubled." He said to her: "Come on, then; show me him and we will lend to him." She took her husband and led him to the most holy church. Now the church at Nisbis has five large doorways. As she brought him to the entrance, there where the great porches are, she showed him the poor and said: "If you give to these persons, the God of the Christians receives it, for these are all his." Immediately, and with gladness, he gave the fifty *miliarisia* to the poor, and went back to his house. Three months later, their expenses exceeded their ability to pay. The man said to his wife: "Sister, the God of the Christians is not going to pay us back anything of that debt and, here we are, in need." In reply, the woman said: "Yes, he will repay. Go to where you handed over the money and he will return it to you right away." He went off to the holy church at a run. When he came to the spot where he had given the *miliarisia* to the poor, he went all around the church, expecting to find somebody who would give back to him what was owing to him. But all he found was the poor, still sitting there. While he was trying to decide to which of them to speak or whom he should ask, he saw at his feet, on the marble floor, one large *miliarision* lying there, one of those which he himself had distributed to his brothers the poor. Bending down, he picked it up and went to his house. Then he said to his spouse: "Look, I just went to your church and, believe me, woman, I did not see God of the Christians as you said I would. And he certainly did not give me anything, except that I found this *miliarision* lying there where I gave fifty of them away." Then that wondrous woman said to him: "It is he who invisibly provided that *miliarision*, for he is invisible and he operates the universe with invisible power and an unseen hand. Now, go, sir; buy us something so we can eat today, and he will provide you with something else." Off he went and bought bread, wine and fish for them. He came back and gave his purchases to his wife. She took the fish and began to clean it. When she cut it open, she found within a stone so magnificent that she was struck with wonder at it. She had no idea what it was, but she kept it nevertheless. When her husband came, she showed him whilst they were eating the stone she had found and said: "Look, I found this stone inside the fish." When he saw it, he too was amazed at its beauty, but he did not know what it really was. When they had finished eating, he said to her: "Give it to me; I will go and sell it, if I can find a way of getting anything for it." As I said, he did not know what it was, for he was a simple man. He took the stone and went to the money-changer; he was also a silver-smith. It was time for the smith to go home (for it was evening) but the man said to him: "Would you like to buy this stone?" When the money-changer saw it, he said: "How much do you want for it?" The man said: "Give me what you will." The other replied: "Take five *miliarisia* for it then." Thinking that the merchant was making fun of him, the man said: "Would you give that much for it?" The merchant thought the man was being sarcastic, so he said: "Well, take ten *miliarisia* for it then." Still thinking that the merchant was making fun of him, the man remained silent, at which the other said: "Then take twenty *miliarisia* for it." As the man still kept silent and made no response, the merchant raised his offer to thirty, and then to fifty *miliarisia*, swearing that he would indeed pay that much. The seller of the stone realized that it must be very valuable if the merchant were prepared to pay fifty *miliarisia* for it. Little by little the merchant raised his offer until it reached three hundred large *miliarisia*. This sum the man accepted. He handed over the stone and went home to his wife with a glad heart. When she saw him, she asked him how much he had sold it for, expecting him to say five or ten *pholleis*. He took out the three-hundred *miliarisia* and handed them to her, saying that for so much he had sold the stone. Filled with wonder at the goodness of God, she said to him: "Oh husband, see how good and generous and affluent is the God of the Christians! Look how he has not merely returned to you the fifty *miliarisia* you lent him together with interest, but in only a few days has given you the capital multiplied by six! Know therefore that there is no other God, neither on earth nor in heaven, but him alone." Convinced by this miracle and learning the truth by experience, he immediately became a Christian and glorified our God and Savior, Jesus Christ, with the Father and the Holy Spirit, gratefully acknowledging the intelligence of his wife by which it had been granted to him to know God in very truth.

Sadalberga, Life

Sadalberga (605–670) was a Frankish, aristocratic woman who founded two convents in the seventh century. This account of her life includes a story of scarcity, in which she must offer hospitality to a visiting abbot. The beer they make for his arrival almost spoils. Still, hospitality rooted in confidence in God is proved through a miracle of abundance.

One time, when a visit from blessed Waldebert was expected and there was not enough wine, she ordered a drink called beer to be made from wheat or barley meal which, brewed by human skill, is much in the nations of the west. When it was poured into one of those vessels which the vulgar call a tun, the strong liquor did not fill it to the brim. That handmaid of Christ who was in charge of the cellar that year according to the requirements of the rule, came most humbly to the venerable mother and said, "Lady, mother, what can we do? The brew didn't fill the vessel and it is fermenting in the air. If the holy abbot's arrival is delayed, I fear the drink will sour to bitter vinegar."

And she said to her, "Go and pour what was left when the liquor was prepared into the vessel." Never doubting that she could fulfill the holy mother's orders, she ran quickly back and found the vessel full so that the air space slowly disappeared. Such is the mercy of the omnipotent God! The mother was strong in her disciple. For divine power reached out to make the short draft grow larger. Returning speedily, God's handmaid humbly told the holy mother of the miracle and she gave thanks to the highest Creator of all things, Jesus Christ, Who is always with His servants in the way of truth.

Aldegund, Life

In this story from the life of Aldegund (d. ca. 684), a Frankish woman of rank of the seventh century, her generosity in providing clothes for the poor results in money left over. Miraculously, seemingly in response to her hospitality to the poor, the coins on the scales increase in weight.

And when she was still a little girl in her parental home, she grew in love for the celestial life and care of alms for Christ's poor . . . . And then God's chosen received her own offering which she distributed for love of Christ to the poor. But when she was mother of the community and before she was perfect in good works and filled with examples by divine grace, she sent a servant to buy garments for the poor from that money. And he went and did as he was told and what remained was returned to God's servant. The moment she placed the remainder of the purchase price on the scales she found the same weight and even as she and her sister stood wondering, the weight grew. And immediately they recalled the place in Scripture where it says: "Whoever has, to him shall be given." That is, the fruit of what you give as alms for the needs of Christ's littlest brothers, you will gain many times over in eternal coin.

Alcuin, The Life of St. Willibrord

Willibrord (600s) was a native of Northumbria whose mission to Frisia was part of the larger evangelization of northern Europe in the late seventh century. Alcuin, a teacher who was a relative of Willibrord, was asked to write an edifying account of his life to be used in worship. Again the connection between hospitality and abundance is made when Willibrord's company shares water with twelve beggars on the road. Note that they only had water in the first place because of God's gracious hospitality to them on their journey.

Whilst the divinely inspired man in his urgent desire to preach the Gospel was traveling through the coastal regions where the people were suffering from the lack of fresh water he noticed that his companions could hardly bear the pangs of thirst. So he called one of them and bade him dig a small trench inside his tent. There, upon his knees, he secretly prayed to God that He, who had brought forth water from the rock for his people whilst they were in the desert, would with like compassion bring forth water for his servants from the sandy soil. At once his prayer was heard and a spring of sweet water straightway filled the trench. His followers on seeing this gave thanks to God, who in this manner had glorified His saint and condescended to hear his prayer. And when they had drunk their fill they took with them as much water as they thought would satisfy their needs on the journey that lay before them.

Again, when the holy priest of God was pursuing his way in a certain place, he saw twelve poor beggars asking alms from the passers-by. Being extremely kind-hearted, he gazed on them with compassion and bade one of his companions take his own flask and give a drink to Christ's poor. All the twelve drank from it as much as they would, and the remarkable fact was that as the company went on their way they found that the flask from which so many had drunk was just as full as it was before of the most excellent wine. When they discovered this they all blessed the Lord, saying: "Indeed, the saying of Christ in the Gospels 'Give and it shall be given unto you' has been fulfilled."

Bede, *Life of St. Cuthbert*

This life of Cuthbert was written around 720 to offer the faithful an example of Christian discipline and charity. In this story, Cuthbert extends hospitality to the man that appears at his door, washing and warming his feet, and inviting him to eat. However, when there is no bread in the midst of such hospitality, the Lord provides abundantly.

Chapter II. How He Ministered to an Angel

Now this was another miracle in which Cuthbert the holy man of God was first glorified by the Lord, after he had by the Lord's help taken upon him the yoke of bondservice to Christ and the Petrine tonsure after the shape of the crown of thorns that bound the head of Christ, in the monastery which is called Ripon. This miracle our most trustworthy witnesses who are still alive have testified to. For while a neophyte, he was at once elected by the community to minister to guests on their arrival. Among these, on the morning of a certain day when the weather was wintry and snowy, an angel of the Lord appeared to him in the form of a well-built man in the flower of his age, just as angels appeared to the patriarch Abraham in the valley of Mamre in the form of men. Then having received him kindly in accordance with his wont, still thinking him to be a man and not an angel, he washed his hands and feet and wiped them with towels, and, having in his humility rubbed his guest's feet with his own hands to warm them on account of the cold, he invited him most urgently to wait until the third hour of the day to take food; but he was unwilling and refused on account of his journey. Finally Cuthbert adjured him in the name of our Lord Jesus Christ and so won his consent. When the signal was given at the third hour of the day and prayer was over, he at once set out a table and spread thereon such food as he had. Now by some chance there was no bread in the guesthouse, save that he had placed some crumbs on the table as a blessed gift of bread. Thereupon the man of God went back to the monastery to seek a loaf; but failing to get any (for they were still baking in the oven) he returned to the guest whom he had left eating alone; but he did not find him nor even his footprints although there was snow over the surface of the ground. He was amazed and removed the table to the storehouse, realizing that it was an angel of God. And immediately at the entrance, his nostrils were filled with the odor of the choicest bread and, finding three warm loaves, he gave thanks to God, because in him was fulfilled the saying of the Lord: "He that receives you receives me, and he that receives me receives him that sent me," and again, "He that receives a prophet in the name of a prophet shall receive a prophet's reward; and he that receives a righteous man in the name of a righteous man shall receive a righteous man's reward." And frequently from that day, when he was hungry, the Lord fed him, as he used to declare to faithful brethren, not boastfully, but for the edification of many, just as Paul told many things about himself.

Giving Away Life to Gain It

Early Christian texts witness again and again to the power of hospitality not only to issue in miracles of abundance but also to transform lives. Hospitality often involves risk, risk to one's health, one's property, even one's social standing. It involves great risk for the recipient as well. Hospitality requires both host and guest to open doors to the unknown, to the unexpected. For the host, it can mean opening one's door to those who can not always reciprocate, at least not in ways one can easily understand. For the guest, it requires putting one's life in another's hands without assurance that the host will either help or not harm. Hospitality, for both host and guest, involves loss, giving away one's life and its security.

Yet, in giving away one's life, one gains new life as well. Early Christians describe the transformative power of the practice of hospitality in biblical terms, "Those who want to save their life will lose it, and those who lose their life for my sake will find it" (Matthew 16:25; cf. Mark 8:34–9:1, Luke 9:23–27). This inverse equation of losing and finding one's life particularly resonates in the context of hospitality. The more tightly one holds on to oneself and one's world, the less one is able to receive the guest or host as Christ. Conversely, the more one risks losing oneself and one's world, the more one can enter the world of the other and dwell therein, finding Christ.

In some of these excerpts the transformative character of hospitality is expressed in the theme of exchange. One gives, yet receives. The one who receives, actually gives. The host finds herself or himself blessed, receiving so much more than giving. The guest or stranger becomes the source of blessing, giving so much more than receiving.

The language of sanctification, the experience of being transformed in the image of God, also emerges within this theme of transformation. Sanctification through participation in hospitality will be expressed in a variety of ways in these texts. Writers may talk about one being made holy, being perfected in the love of God through participation in acts of mercy and hospitality. Through these acts, one is more open and malleable to the work of the Holy Spirit in renewing one's spirit. The vocabulary of restoring the *imago dei* is used as well. Some writers refer explicitly to the restoration of the *imago dei* effected by the Holy Spirit as God illumines hearts through participation in hospitality.

Some texts describe the transformation that occurs as one practices generosity and hospitality in terms of renewal. As one lives out these practices, one cannot help being changed and formed by them. Participating in hospitality leads to new and renewed life.

In all these sets of languages, early Christians point to the reality that hospitality is not only a fruit of the Spirit, but a means of grace by which God is at work in us, transforming our very lives. It is not only something we do, but something God does in us. Again, the notion of hospitality holds a surprise, for while one may think another person benefits by one's hospitality, these writers claim the true beneficiary is the one who gives life away and truly gains it. Excerpts below are in approximate chronological order.

Dionysius, *Epistle 12 to the Alexandrians*

Dionysius (d. ca. 264) was bishop in Alexandria in the third century. He faced persecution, exile and civil war in his lifetime. During this remarkable time of plague and famine in Alexandria ca. 263, the Christian community's witness in caring for the starving and dying was a powerful one. He reports many Christians who risked their own lives, out of brotherly love, to care for the sick. Giving away one's life in order to truly gain life marks this story from Dionysius.

And after we [Christians] and they [pagans] together had enjoyed a very brief season of rest, this pestilence next assailed us,—a calamity truly more dreadful to them than anything else they dread, and more intolerable than any other kind of trouble whatsoever. This was a misfortune which, as a certain writer of their own declares, alone destroys all hope. To us however, it was not so. No less than other ills, it proved an instrument for our training and probation. For it by no means stayed away from us, although it spread with greatest violence among the heathen.

To these statements he [Dionysius] in due succession makes this addition: Certainly very many of our brothers and sisters in their exceeding love and family feeling, did not spare themselves, but kept by each other, and visited the sick without thought of risk to themselves, and ministered to them continually, serving them in Christ. So they died with the others, though most joyfully, carrying others' pains, taking upon themselves their neighbors' diseases, and willingly taking over to their own bodies the burden of the sufferings of those around them. And many who had already cured others of their sicknesses, and restored them to strength, died themselves, having transferred to their own bodies the death that lay upon these. That common saying, which used to be just a polite form of address, they expressed in actual fact then, as they departed this life, like the "off-scourings" of all. Truly the very best of our own have departed this life this way, including some presbyters and some deacons, and among the people those who were highest in reputation. So this very form of death, in virtue of the distinguished piety and the steadfast faith which were exhibited in it, appeared to be no less than martyrdom itself.

Gregory of Nyssa, *Homily Concerning Almsgiving*

Gregory (330–395) preached two very meaty sermons on "the least of these." This sermon points to the transformative character of imitating God's generosity by giving life away. Gregory points to the divine source of all skill and production. God has been generous in providing natural resources and blessings so that we, too, will be generous with others. The outcome of such imitation of divine virtue is that mercy and kindness so inhabit a person as to restore the original imago dei. *The result of such transformation is joy.*

If you wish to understand how [God] cures the person afflicted by evil, then pay heed to our following words. Who has taught the bee to labor with wax and make honey? Who has distilled oil from the pine, terebinth and mastic trees? Who has made dry, aromatic fruit imported from India? Who has created oil by strenuous bodily labor? Who has discerned roots and herbs and knows their qualities? Who has creatively invented remedies for healing? Who has opened springs of warm water from the earth and has made cold and warm water gush out for us to dissipate dryness or burning? At this point we may borrow the timely words of Baruch: "He [God] found the whole way of knowledge and has given it to Jacob his servant and to Israel his beloved" (Bar. 3:6). Therefore, skills both related and not pertaining to fire, as well as those concerning water and a myriad of other techniques, are intended to serve us in many ways. God is thus the source of generosity and rich provider for our necessities.

Scripture teaches us to zealously imitate the Lord and Creator insofar as mortal beings can emulate his blessedness and immortality. However, we show contempt towards everything by appropriating them for our own enjoyment; we choose them for our own end and selfishly store them up. We have no concern for the misfortunate nor care for the poor. What a miserable attitude! A man sees someone else without food and lacks incentive for giving him nourishment. Such a person does not provide for others nor is he concerned about his security; rather, he allows this tender plant to pitifully dry up from lack of water. Instead, he is well off and does not give to the needy. Just as the season of one spring waters a great many fields, the wealth of one household suffices to sustain the poor. A sparing, grudging mind thus resembles a single stone which checks the flow of the course of water.

Corporeal concerns should not trouble us, for we should live for God. Food offers pleasure by entering through one small part of the body, the throat. It enters the stomach, decays and evacuates the body (Mt 15.17). On the other hand, mercy and kindness are beloved qualities belonging to God. They inhabit a person, divinize him and stamp him with imitation of the good in order to bring to life our original, immortal image which transcends conception. What are we striving after? It is a wonderful, hopeful, anticipation of joy. Having taken off this flesh which abounds with corruption, we put on immortality (1 Cor 15.53) or that unending, incorruptible blessed life whose joys and pleasures we cannot now comprehend.

*Gregory of Nyssa, On the Baptism of Christ, A Sermon for the Day of the Lights**

Preaching on the baptism of Christ, Gregory argues that fruits will be evident in the life of one reborn. The life given away is replaced by a new life that shines forth in the virtues of sobriety, tranquility, generosity and care for the poor.

But there is certainly need of some clear proof, by which we may recognize the newborn person, discerning by clear tokens the new person from the old. And these I think are to be found in the intentional motions of the soul, whereby it separates itself from its old way of life, and enters on a newer way of conversation. It will clearly teach those acquainted with it that it has become something different from its former self, no longer bearing the things by which the old self was recognized. This, if you are persuaded by me, and keep my words as a law, is the mode of the transformation. The person before baptism was undisciplined, greedy, grasping at the goods of others, contemptuous, a liar, a slanderer, and all characteristics like that and resulting from them. Let the person now become orderly, sober, content with his own possessions, and generous with what they have to those in poverty, truthful, courteous, affable—in a word, following every admirable course of conduct. For as darkness is dispelled by light, and black disappears as whiteness is spread over it, so the old person disappears when adorned with the works of righteousness.

John Chrysostom, *Homily 41 on Genesis*

Chrysostom (ca. 347–407) is much taken with Abraham's humility in addressing his guests with respect and even honor, even though they may have appeared to the aged patriarch as mere youths. Abraham's address and bowing to the guests reveal something of the transformative character of hospitality, according to Chrysostom. Because he has welcomed them, he is changed, formed by humility.

"On seeing them," the text says, "he ran forward from the door to his tent to meet them." Very appropriately is the word "ran forward" used, so that you may learn that they arrived unknowing and did not come to the tent for a set purpose. Hence in case this spiritual advantage should escape him, this old man, this greybeard, this centenarian ran forward and by his running revealed his enthusiasm. "Spying them he bowed to the ground and said, 'Sir, if I have really found favor with you, do no pass by your servant.'" This is really the reason why Sacred Scripture reveals the just man's virtue beyond telling in the words, "He bowed to the ground," thus giving evidence by his posture and his words of his great ardor, his great humility, his intense spirit of hospitality, his ineffable care.

"Bowing to the ground," the text goes on, he said, "'Sir, if I have really found favor with you, do not pass by your servant.'" Who could do justice in words to this just man? How could anyone praise him even with countless lips? I mean, while the term "sir" is a customary one, on the other hand saying "if I have really found favor with you" is unusual. You are giving a favor, he says, not receiving one. You see, this is what hospitality really involves: the person exemplifying it with enthusiasm receives something rather than gives it.

Maximus of Turin, *Sermon 21 On Hospitality*

Maximus of Turin (d. 408–423) may have written this sermon upon the occasion of a church council in Turin in 398, a time when bishops and other ecclesiastical leaders would have sought the hospitality of the Christian community there. We should note several important points here regarding hospitality and its powers to transform. First, Maximus says that hospitality works in such a way that the guest makes the host like himself. The mysterious grace of hospitality reverses the commonly held notion that the guest conforms to the host. Second, it is not only one's dwelling, but one's heart that is the guest house. Because the heart welcomes Christ, and receives every guest as Christ, the heart is the welcoming place for all. Third, because hospitality is seated in the heart, there is opportunity for transformation towards holiness and righteousness. Just as Sarah was transformed from barren to bearing, the hospitable one is transformed by joy and mercy from sinful to righteous.

We have read in the book of Genesis that Abraham hastened to meet three men who were approaching him, fell on his face, and begged them to turn aside to his tent so that, for his hospitality to the saints, he would receive the reward of a blessing. For he knew that this was the command of the Lord who said: "Whoever welcomes a prophet will receive a prophet's reward, and whoever welcomes a righteous person in the name of a righteous person will receive a righteous person's reward," and so forth. For this reason, then, Abraham hastened to welcome the holy men so that by joining himself to them in hospitality he would merit to be joined to them in holiness, and while performing a service of kindness he might receive a share of justification. For this is the law of hospitality—that the person who is welcomed makes the one who welcomes him like himself. This is what John the Evangelist indicated most clearly with respect to those who welcomed the Son of God when he said: "But however many welcomed Him, to them He gave the power to become sons of God." You see, then, how great the grace of hospitality is, that it even makes a son of God out of one who welcomes the Son of God in the guest house of his heart. If, therefore, whoever welcomes the Son of God becomes a son of God, how much more will the one who welcomes a righteous person merit the grace of a righteous person! For this is, as I have said, the good characteristic of hospitality—that when a holy man comes, by the association that results from a friendly welcome he makes his host to be what he himself is. Under such a condition who would not wish to welcome a holy person hospitably into his home, so that, by sharing a dwelling place with him, he might share his holiness? And even if he had been a sinner up until that moment, who would not wish to be righteous himself by welcoming a righteous person, as the prophet David says: "With the holy you will be holy, and with the innocent you will be innocent?"

Let us welcome the saints, I say, so that our sins against nature might be forgiven us. For on account of his hospitality the righteous Abraham, because he had no sin, was given a son, Isaac, contrary to nature. He was given, as I have said, so contrary to nature that frigid old age despaired that he could be born and his mother Sarah laughed. Sarah laughed, I say, because she begot a son not through nature but through grace. Blessed the offspring, then, whose birth has been preceded by mirth and not by tears! She should surely have laughed who conceived with the help of God. Such, then, is the hospitality of the blessed that it always bestows joy on the hosts. Sarah laughs because she is no longer sterile, I laugh because I put down my sins; she is freed from a bodily defect, I am washed clean of the sins of my soul; she rejoices because by her hospitality she has begotten a son, Isaac, and I am glad because I have acquired mercy with righteousness.

Maximus of Turin, Sermon 43 on Healing

Maximus of Turin also preached on the account of Jesus' healing on the Sabbath. He reminds his audience that the practice of mercy and hospitality—"Stretch out your hand!"—prepares one to receive healing and health from the Lord as well. The hand that stretches out in hospitality to the widow and the traveler is the same hand that stretches out to be healed by God. This sermon identifies the dynamic of reciprocity between hospitality and healing.

He [Savior] is eager to cure the sickness of the whole human race, and so this medicine is universal. For He says to him: "Stretch out your hand!"—he who clenched it by sacrificing to idols. He says to him: "Stretch out your hand!"—whose hand dried up by accepting usury. He says to him: "Stretch out your hand!"—he who used it to seize the goods of orphans and widows. But you who think that you have a healthy hand, beware lest avarice close it tight. Rather, stretch it out frequently to the poor for mercy's sake, more frequently to the traveler for hospitality, and always to the Lord because of sin. Be merciful, be generous, and observe what the prophet says: "Let not your hand be extended when it is time to receive and clenched when it is time to give." For thus your hand will be able to be healthy if it is held back from evil deeds but stretched out for good works.

John Moschos, *The Spiritual Meadow*

Moschos (ca. 550–619) offers in this survey of the pastures of spirituality the most spectacular blossoms of his day. The dynamic of exchange that occurs in hospitality, whereby one gives only to find that one receives, is literally played out in this story of a holy man.

At the same Laura of the Towers there was an elder who practiced poverty to an exceptional degree and yet his particular spiritual gift was that of almsgiving. One day a beggar came to his little tower asking for alms. The elder had nothing but a single loaf of bread which he brought out and gave to the beggar. "It is not bread I want" said the beggar; "I need clothing." Wishing to minister to the man's needs, the elder took him by the hand and led him into his tower. When the beggar found that there was nothing there at all other than what the elder stood up in, he was so impressed by his virtue that he opened his bag and emptied out all its contents in the middle of the cell. "Take this, good elder," he said, "I will satisfy my needs elsewhere."

Maximus Confessor, *The Ascetic Life*

A theologian and monk, Maximus (ca. 580–662) fled his monastery at Chrysopolis in 626 in the face of the Persian invasion. He suffered several exiles due to his refusal to agree to doctrinal compromises, eventually even losing his tongue and right hand. Still Maximus was convinced that the path of salvation was the path of transformation of human lives to restore the image of God in which humanity was originally created. Virtue, in this case, hospitality, is a fruit of that transformation which illumines and frees.

Let us cast from us negligence and sloth and stand manfully in strife against the spirits of wickedness. And so again Isaiah: "Loose every band of wickedness, undo the knots of forced contracts, dismiss the broken with pardon, and tear up every wicked paper. Break thy bread to the hungry and bring the poor without shelter into thy house. When thou shalt see one naked, cover him, and despise not the fellows of thy seed. Then shall thy light break forth as the morning, and thy remedies shall speedily arise, and thy justice shall go before thy face, and the glory of the Lord shall surround thee." You see how in loosing every band of wickedness from our hearts and in undoing every knot of contracts forced for grudges, and in hastening to do good for our neighbor with our whole soul—you see how we are illumined with the light of knowledge, and freed from the disgrace of passions, and filled with every virtue; and are illumined by God's glory and freed from every ignorance.

Notes

1. See Matthew 25:31.
2. Lactanitius, *The Divine Institutes*, Book 6: On True Worship, Chapter 12: On the Kinds of Beneficence and Works of Mercy, in ANF, vol. 7.
3. For a helpful discussion of this distinction between helping and compassion in a contemporary context, see Parker Palmer, *The Active Life: A Spirituality of Work, Creativity, and Caring* (San Francisco: Harper & Row, 1990) pp. 79-86.
4. Chrysostom as well as Basil and others unmask this eerily contemporary practice. See John Chrysostom, *Homily 45 on the Acts of the Apostles*, NPNF, ser. 1, vol. 11, *Homily 11 on Hebrews*, NPNF, ser. 1, vol. 14, chapters 8-10; *Homily 21 on Paul's Letter to the Romans*, NPNF, ser. 1, vol. 11, verse 13; Gregory of Nyssa, *As You Did It to One of These, You Did It to Me*.
5. John Chrysostom, *Homily 11 on Hebrews*, NPNF, ser. 1, vol. 14, p. 423.

Bibliography

Alcuin. *The Life of St. Willibrord*. In *The Anglo-Saxon Missionaries in Germany*, edited and translated by C.H. Talbot. New York: Sheed and Ward, 1954, 13-15.

"Aldegund, Abbess of Maubeuge (d. 684) and Waldetrude, Abbess of Mons (d. ca. 688)." In *Sainted Women of the Dark Ages*, translated by JoAnn McNamara and John Halborg. Durham: Duke University Press, 1992, 249.

Ambrose. "On the Duties of the Clergy." In *Selected Works and Letters*, translated by the Rev. H. De Romestin, the Rev. E. De Romestin and the Rev. H. T. F. Duckworth. *Nicene and Post-Nicene Fathers of the Christian Church*. Edited by Philip Schaff and Henry Wace. 2nd ser. New York: Christian Literature Company, 1893, X:24-5, 28-29.

Bede. "The Life of St. Cuthbert. " In *Two Lives of Saint Cuthbert: A Life by an Anonymous Monk of Lindisfarne and Bede's Prose Life,* translated by Bertram Colgrave. New York: Greenwood Press, 1969, 77-79.

Clement of Alexandria. *Stromata. Ante-Nicene Fathers: The Writings of the Fathers Down to A.D. 325*. Edited by Alexander Roberts and James Donaldson. New York: The Christian Literature Company, 1885, II:416.

Cyril of Scythopolis. *Lives of the Monks of Palestine*. Translated by R. M. Price. Kalamazoo, Michigan: Cistercian Publications, 1991, 22-23, 125-26, 146.

Dionysius. "Epistle 12." In *Epistles*, translated by the Rev. S. D. F. Salmond. *Ante-Nicene Fathers: The Writings of the Fathers Down to A.D. 325*. Edited by Alexander Roberts and James Donaldson. New York: The Christian Literature Company, 1885, VI:108-9.

Dorotheos of Gaza. *Discourses and Sayings*. Translated by Eric P. Wheeler. Kalamazoo, Michigan: Cistercian Publications, 1977, 208-210.

Gregory of Nazianzus. "Oration 43: Panegyric on Basil." In *Select Orations*, translated by Charles Gordon Browne and James Edward Swallow. *Nicene and Post-Nicene Fathers of the Christian Church*. Edited by Philip Schaff and Henry Wace. 2nd ser. New York: The Christian Literature Company, 1894, VII:416.

Gregory of Nyssa. "Homily: As You Did It to One of These, You Did It to Me." In *The Collected Works of Gregory of Nyssa*, translated by Richard McCambly. *Gregory of Nyssa Homepage*. bhsu.edu/dsalomon/nyssa/home.html. Greenwich, Conn.: Great American Publishing Society, 1999.

_____ "On the Baptism of Christ, A Sermon for the Day of the Lights." In *Select Writings and Letters*, translated by William Moore and Henry Austin Wilson. *Nicene and Post-Nicene Fathers of the Christian Church*. Edited by Philip Schaff and Henry Wace. 2nd ser. New York: The Christian Literature Company, 1893, V:523.

Hermas. *Shepherd*. Translated by the Rev. F. Crombie. *Ante-Nicene Fathers: The Writings of the Fathers Down to A.D. 325*. Edited by Alexander Roberts and James Donaldson. New York: The Christian Literature Company, 1885, II:20.

Jerome. "Letter 66." In *Principal Works*, translated by W. H. Fremantle. *Nicene and Post-Nicene Fathers of the Christian Church*. Edited by Philip Schaff and Henry Wace. 2nd ser. New York: The Christian Literature Company, 1893, VI:138-40.

_____. "Letter 77." In *Principal Works*, translated by W. H. Fremantle. *Nicene and Post-Nicene Fathers of the Christian Church*. Edited by Philip Schaff and Henry Wace. 2nd ser. New York: The Christian Literature Company, 1893, VI:158-60.

_____. "Letter 125." In *Principal Works*, translated by W. H. Fremantle. *Nicene and Post-Nicene Fathers of the Christian Church*. Edited by Philip Schaff and Henry Wace. 2nd ser. New York: The Christian Literature Company, 1893, VI:248-49.

_____. "Life of Paul the First Hermit." In *Principal Works*, translated by W. H. Fremantle. *Nicene and Post-Nicene Fathers of the Christian Church*. Edited by Philip Schaff and Henry Wace. 2nd ser. New York: The Christian Literature Company, 1893, VI:301.

_____. "Preface to the Commentary on Ezekiel." In *Principal Works*, translated by W. H. Fremantle. *Nicene and Post-Nicene Fathers of the Christian Church*. Edited by Philip Schaff and Henry Wace. 2nd ser. New York: The Christian Literature Company, 1893, VI:500.

John Cassian. *Institutes of the Coenobia*. Translated by the Rev. Edgar C. S. Gibson. *Nicene and Post-Nicene Fathers of the Christian Church*. Edited by Philip Schaff and Henry Wace. 2nd ser. New York: The Christian Literature Company, 1894, XI:247.

John Chrysostom. "Homily 14 on 1 Timothy." In *Homilies on Galatians, Ephesians, Philippians, Colossians, Thessalonians, Timothy, Titus and Philemon*, translated by the Rev. James Tweed. *Nicene and Post-Nicene Fathers of the Christian Church*. 1st ser. New York: The Christian Literature Company, 1889, XIII:454-5.

_____. "Homily 20 on 1st Corinthians." In *Homilies on 1st and 2nd Corinthians*, translated by the Rev. Hubert Kestell Cornish, the Rev. John Medley and the Rev. J. Ashworth. *Nicene and Post-Nicene Fathers of the Christian Church*. 1st ser. New York: The Christian Literature Company, 1889, XII:117.

_____. "Homily 21 on Romans." In *Homilies on Acts of the Apostles and the Epistle to the Romans*, translated by the Rev. J. Walker and the Rev. J. Sheppard. *Nicene and Post-Nicene Fathers of the Christian Church*. 1st ser. New York: The Christian Literature Company, 1889, XI:504-5.

_____. "Homily 33 on Hebrews." In *Homilies on John and Hebrews*. Translated by the Rev. G. T. Stupart. *Nicene and Post-Nicene Fathers of the Christian Church*. 1st ser. New York: The Christian Literature Company, 1890, XIV:514, 516.

_____. "Homily 41 on Genesis." In *Homilies on Genesis: Saint John Chrysostom*, Volume 2:18-45, translated by Robert C. Hill. *The Fathers of the Church: A New Translation*. Vol. 82. Washington, D.C.: The Catholic University of America Press, 1988, 406, 408-9.

_____. "Homily 45 on the Acts of the Apostles." In *Homilies on Acts of the Apostles and the Epistle to the Romans*, translated by the Rev. J. Walker and the Rev. J. Sheppard. *Nicene and Post-Nicene Fathers of the Christian Church*. 1st ser. New York: The Christian Literature Company, 1889, XI:276-7.

John Moschos. *Spiritual Meadow*. Translated by John Wortley. Kalamazoo, Michigan: Cistercian Publications, 1992, 9, 20, 155-58.

Lactantius. *The Divine Institutes*. Translated by the Rev. William Fletcher. *Ante-Nicene Fathers: The Writings of the Fathers Down to A.D. 325*. Edited by Alexander Roberts and James Donaldson. New York: The Christian Literature Company, 1889, VII:177.

_____. "Epitome 65." In *The Divine Institutes*, translated by the Rev. William Fletcher. *Ante-Nicene Fathers: The Writings of the Fathers Down to A.D. 325*. Edited by Alexander Roberts and James Donaldson. New York: The Christian Literature Company, 1889, VII:250.

Leo the Great. "Sermon 12 On the Fast." In *Leo the Great, Letters and Sermons*, translated with Introduction, Notes and Indices by the Rev. Charles Lett Feltoe, M.A. *Nicene and Post-Nicene Fathers of the Christian Church*. Edited by Philip Schaff and Henry Wace. 2nd ser. New York: The Christian Literature Company, 1894. XII:121-22.

_____. "Sermon 16 On the Fast." In *Leo the Great, Letters and Sermons*, translated with Introduction, Notes and Indices by the Rev. Charles Lett Feltoe, M.A. *Nicene and Post-Nicene Fathers of the Christian Church*. Edited by Philip Schaff and Henry Wace. 2nd ser. New York: The Christian Literature Company, 1894, XII:123-24.

Leontius. *St. John the Almsgiver*. In *Three Byzantine Saints*, edited by Elizabeth Dawes and Norman H. Baynes. Oxford: Blackwell, 1948, 214, 243-44.

The Lives of the Desert Fathers: The Historia Monachorum in Aegypto. Translated by Norman Russell. Kalamazoo, Michigan: Cistercian Publications, 1980, 76-77, 91-92.

Maximus the Confessor. *The Ascetic Life and The Four Centuries on Charity*. Translated and annotated by Polycarp Sherwood. *Ancient Christian Writers: The Works of the Fathers in Translation*. Edited by Johannes Quasten and Joseph C. Plumpe, no. 21. New York: Newman Press, 1955, 132-33.

Maximus of Turin. "Sermon 21 on Hospitality." In *The Sermons of St. Maximus of Turin*, translated by Boniface Ramsey. *Ancient Christian Writers: The Works of the Fathers in Translation*. Edited by Walter J. Burghardt and Thomas Comerford Lawler, no. 50. New York: Newman Press, 1989, 51-53, 109.

_____. "Sermon 34 on Hospitality in the Gospel." In *The Sermons of St. Maximus of Turin*, translated by Boniface Ramsey. *Ancient Christian Writers: The Works of the Fathers in Translation*. Edited by Walter J. Burghardt and Thomas Comerford Lawler, no. 50. New York: Newman Press, 1989, 82-83.

Palladius. *Palladius: The Lausiac History*. Translated by Robert T. Meyer. *Ancient Christian Writers: The Works of the Fathers in Translation*. Edited by Johannes Quasten, Walter J. Burghardt and Thomas Comerford Lawler, no. 34. New York: Newman Press, 1964, 133.

Paulinus of Nola. "Letter 13." In *Letters of St. Paulinus of Nola*, translated by P. G. Walsh. *Ancient Christian Writers: The Works of the Fathers in Translation*. Edited by Johannes Quasten, Walter J. Burghardt, and Thomas Comerford Lawler, no. 35. New York: Newman Press, 1966, 127-28, 136-37.

_____. "Letter 34." In *Letters of St. Paulinus of Nola*, translated by P. G. Walsh. *Ancient Christian Writers: The Works of the Fathers in Translation*. Edited by Johannes Quasten, Walter J. Burghardt, and Thomas Comerford Lawler, no. 36. New York: Newman Press, 1966, 162-63.

Pseudo-Clementine. "First Epistle Concerning Virginity." In *Epistles and Writings*, translated by the Rev. B. P. Pratten. *Ante-Nicene Fathers: The Writings of the Fathers Down to A.D. 325*. Edited by Alexander Roberts and James Donaldson. New York: The Christian Literature Company, 1885, VIII:59-60.

_____. "Homily 11." In *Epistles and Writings*, translated by the Rev. B. P. Pratten. *Ante-Nicene Fathers: The Writings of the Fathers Down to A.D. 325*. Edited by Alexander Roberts and James Donaldson. New York: The Christian Literature Company, 1885, VIII:285.

"Radegund, Queen of the Franks and Abbess of Poitiers (ca. 525-587)." In *Sainted Women of the Dark Ages*, translated by JoAnn McNamara and John Halborg. Durham: Duke University Press, 1992, 72, 77.

Rufus, John. *The Life of the Holy Peter the Iberian*, translated by David Marshall Lang. In *Lives and Legends of the Georgian Saints*. 2d ed. London: Mowbrays, 1976, 77-78.

"Sadalberga, Abbess of Laon (ca. 605-670)." In *Sainted Women of the Dark Ages*, translated by JoAnn McNamara and John Halborg. Durham: Duke University Press, 1992, 189-90.

Sozomen. *Ecclesiastical History*. Translated by Chester D. Hartranft. *Nicene and Post-Nicene Fathers of the Christian Church*. Edited by Philip Schaff and Henry Wace. 2nd ser. New York: The Christian Literature Company, 1890, II:369.

Sulpitius Severus. "Dialogue 1." In *Dialogues of Sulpitius Severus*, translated by the Rev.

Alexander Roberts. *Nicene and Post-Nicene Fathers of the Christian Church*. Edited by Philip Schaff and Henry Wace. 2nd ser. New York: The Christian Literature Company, 1894, XI:32.

Theodoret, *Ecclesiastical History*. Translated by the Rev. Blomfield Jackson. *Nicene and Post-Nicene Fathers of the Christian Church*. Edited by Philip Schaff and Henry Wace. 2nd ser. New York: The Christian Literature Company, 1893, III:145.

CHAPTER FIVE

UNBENDING ONESELF: THE PRACTICES OF HOSPITALITY

Specific Practices: What Is to Be Done?

In his instruction on the contemplative life and its demanding disciplines, Julianus Pomerius (fl. ca. 500) offers a caution to Christians who are seeking the most strenuous forms of witness. He tells them not to forget to relax and let go now and then, especially when guests arrive and hospitality calls for it. His actual words are, "my spiritual brethren . . . derive enjoyment from my unbending myself."[1] Practices of hospitality take precedence at times over strict disciplines. Here he refers to the regular observance of fasting which must be broken in order to "unbend oneself" and share one's table with guests. Hospitality, as an expression of love, is a higher virtue even than piety.

As we try to imagine early Christian hospitality, what practices constituted unbending oneself? When early Christians talk about hospitality, what do they have in mind? As we listen to these texts we want to get an idea of what concrete acts hospitality entails. Few of these texts prescribe specific practices. They more often describe them. Taken together, a wide range of practices is presented.

No one standard model prevails, but several practices occur frequently in these texts. Most behaviors fall into the following list: a warm greeting or welcome, visiting, foot washing or bathing, praying, feeding or feasting, lodging, protection, medical care, almsgiving, and sending forth with supplies and/or escort for the journey. We can see in these practices a pattern. Hospitality moves through several stages. It frequently begins with welcome, then turns to restoration of the guest, followed by being with or dwelling with the other, and ends in the sending forth.

The first stage encompasses a set of practices that welcome the guest. This involves a warm greeting, words of welcome or an embrace, even going out to greet the guest. In some cases, this is an act full of enthusiasm or emotion. In other cases, welcome may be more subdued or matter of fact, depending on the situation. In any case, some gesture of welcome initiates hospitality. The offer of sanctuary to an exile or fugitive also falls within the first stage of welcome. In such a case, simply receiving the stranger or allowing one to stay is an act of welcome.[2] However, the first movement of hospitality that initiates contact is not always an act of receiving. It may be expressed in the practice of visiting another, such as the sick or the hungry. In this case, hospitality is initiated by going to the other and, in a sense, receiving them, though it may be in their own homes or place of refuge, even the street. There is nearly always an offer to serve, whether implicit or explicit, in the stage of welcome.

The second movement includes practices that restore the guest, usually by addressing the most immediate needs whether physical or spiritual or both. Hospitable acts in the second stage include foot washing, bathing, feeding, clothing, and prayer. The host washes the traveler's feet or bathes the sick. A cloak is offered to a traveler whose own is threadbare or who is without one altogether. These acts help to restore the well-being of the stranger. Sharing food is perhaps the most basic act of restoration. Feeding not only serves the immediate needs for nourishment, but also represents the deeper reality of the Christian whose life is lived in Christ, that is, one always feasts at the table of the kingdom.[3] Sometimes food is shared at table, other times alms may be offered in the street so the hungry can buy bread. In either case, these practices pursue restoration. Prayer is an element that can accompany any of these acts of restoration and often does. Prayer can restore one's sense of spiritual equilibrium as well as one's sense of belonging to community.

From restoration hospitality moves to dwelling together, a stage characterized by the tasks of common life together. Particularly important in this set of practices is the willingness to share one's life with the other, to be present to the mundane and ongoing realities of one another's lives. Practices in this stage include sharing lodging or shelter of some kind, providing protection or sanctuary, and sharing resources such as food, clothing, medical care, and alms. This stage of hospitality can also include practices that reframe social relations away from exploitation and toward dwelling together. For example, the relationship of master to slave may be reoriented toward living in the awareness of a shared *imago dei*, or a wealthy person may divest themselves, reframing their social location so that they no longer help the poor but are the poor, dwelling together. These reorientations of social relations fall within this stage of hospitality to the degree that they seek life together, a hospitality of presence. Finally, early Christians identify burying the dead as an hospitable practice that can be categorized in this stage of hospitality as an act of dwelling together, being willing to be with the dead. Burial can also fall within the last movement of hospitality, sending forth.

Sending forth entails release, letting go of the stranger or guest with whom one has dwelt. This stage suggests that hospitality does not create systems of dependence, but empowers the other to move on. Just as hospitality is offered with open hands, so one does not hang on to the other in order to justify one's continued hospitality. It includes acts such as blessing, giving food or other supplies for the journey, or giving companions for escort. The notion of sending forth as a movement of hospitality has another meaning as well. The act of release includes letting go of the outcome of the practices of hospitality. More than one early writer says that the practices of hospitality are independent of their outcomes. One lives hospitably without any guarantee of a payoff. The sick person may die, the stranger may misuse the resources shared, the hospitality offered may not be honored. Desire for a particular consequence of hospitality must be released.

Usually texts include two or more of these stages in any one description of hospitality. Few texts will offer description of the practices at every stage of hospitality. Most texts pick up at some point in the movement and stop at another without exhausting the whole pattern. Some texts offer descriptions of these practices and behaviors through narrative accounts, others offer prescriptions, for example, through rules or standards. It is helpful to keep in mind this pattern that flows from welcome to restoration to dwelling together to sending forth as these voices offer particular incidents of hospitality. While we cannot tell to what extent early Christians on the whole observed these practices, we can get clues from specific communities and settings about what they regarded as hospitality. The excerpts are in approximate chronological order.

Didache

The Didache, *also called* The Teaching of the Twelve Apostles, *is a very early Christian document dating from the second century. It contains instructions to Christians on baptism, the Lord's Supper, ecclesiastical offices and moral discipline. It addresses hospitality in at least two places, with particular attention to traveling preachers and healers. Instructions are very specific regarding how many days such visitors may stay and whether to give them money.*

Now about the apostles and prophets: Act in line with the gospel precept. Welcome every apostle on arriving, as if he were the Lord. But he must not stay beyond one day. In case of necessity, however, the next day too. If he stays three days, he is a false prophet. On departing, an apostle must not accept anything save sufficient food to carry him till his next lodging. If he asks for money, he is a false prophet.

Everyone "who comes" to you "in the name of the Lord" must be welcomed. Afterward, when you have tested him, you will find out about him, for you have insight into right and wrong. If it is a traveler who arrives, help him all you can. But he must not stay with you more than two days, or, if necessary, three. If he wants to settle with you and is an artisan, he must work for his living. If, however, he has no trade, use your judgment in taking steps for him to live with you as a Christian without being idle. If he refuses to do this, he is trading on Christ. You must be on your guard against such people.

Tertullian, *To His Wife**

In this treatise Tertullian (ca. 160–ca. 225) praises his wife and reflects on the responsibilities of wives in general. Acknowledging the difficulties faced by women who marry nonbelievers, Tertullian complains of the limits such husbands put upon their Christian wives. In particular, acts of devotion, such as prayer and fasting, may be curbed. Tertullian here iden-

tifies acts of hospitality as visiting the poor and imprisoned, hosting pilgrims, and distributing food, all of which a nonbelieving husband may resent.

But let her pay attention to the issue of how she discharges her duties to her husband. For the Lord, at all events, she is unable to do what discipline requires because she has at her side a servant of the devil, his lord's agent for hindering the pursuits and duties of believers. So that if a station is to be kept, the husband at daybreak makes an appointment with his wife to meet him at the baths. If there are fasts to be observed, the husband that same day holds a friendly banquet. If a charitable visitation has to be made, never is family business more urgent. For who would tolerate his wife, for the sake of visiting the faithful, to go around from street to street to other men's homes, and indeed to all the poorer cottages? Who will willingly bear her being taken from his side by nighttime gatherings, if need so be? Who, finally, will without anxiety, endure her absence all night long at the Easter services? Who will, without some suspicion of his own, dismiss her to attend that Lord's Supper which they slander? Who will allow her to creep into prison to kiss a martyr's bonds? No, truly, or even to meet any one of the faithful to exchange the kiss? Or to offer water for the saints' feet? Or to sneak food or drink for them? Or to long for them? Or to have them on her mind? If a pilgrim brother arrives, what hospitality for him in an alien home? If bounty is to be distributed to any, the granaries, the storehouses, are foreclosed.

On the other hand, says Tertullian, a marriage of believers allows for a more faithful exercise of Christian virtue, very specifically embodied by hospitality as follows.

Together they pray, together prostrate themselves, together perform their fasts, mutually teaching, mutually exhorting, mutually sustaining. Equally they are both found in the Church of God, equally at the banquet of God, equally in straits, in persecutions, in refreshments. Neither hides anything from the other, neither shuns the other, neither is troublesome to the other. The sick are visited and the indigent relieved with openness. Alms are given without danger of retaliation, sacrifices attended without scruple, daily diligence performed without impediment, that is, there is no stealthy signing, no trembling greeting, no mute benediction.

Pseudo-Clementine, First Epistle Concerning Virginity*

Clement (fl. ca. 96), bishop of Rome at the end of the first century, is credited with this epistle though scholars conclude it likely comes from sometime between 200 and 250. Its value here is as an early document describing particular acts of hospitality that Christians were to perform. It describes Christian duty to visit orphans and widows, the sick and those bothered by evil spirits. Visiting is an act of welcoming that initiates hospitality. One's behavior when visiting, more than one's words, demonstrates hospitality so that such visits should not involve long-winded speeches or high-handedness, but genuine prayers. The letter specifically prohibits attempts at shaming or showing partiality when visiting the poor or sick.

Moreover, also, this is desirable and useful, that one "visit orphans and widows," and especially those poor persons who have many children. These things are, without question, required of the servants of God, and desirable and appropriate for them. This also, again, is suitable and right and desirable for those who are brothers and sisters in Christ, that they should visit those who are harassed by evil spirits, and pray in earnest appeal over them, intelligently, offering such prayer as is acceptable before God. Do not do this with a multitude of fine words, well prepared and arranged, so that they may appear to others eloquent and memorable. Such are "like a sounding pipe, or a tinkling cymbal." They bring no help to those over whom they make their appeals, but they speak with terrible words, and scare people. They do not act with true faith, consistent with the teaching of our Lord, who has said, "This kind doesn't act without fasting and prayer," offered unceasingly and with earnest mind. Let them with holiness ask and beg of God, with cheerfulness and all circumspection and purity, without hatred and without malice. In this way let us approach a brother or a sister who is sick, and visit them in a way that is right, without guile, and without covetousness, and without noise, and without talkativeness, and without such behavior as is alien from the fear of God, and without haughtiness, but with the meek and lowly spirit of Christ . . . because they act according to the injunctions of our Lord, who said: "I was sick, and you visited me, and so on." And this is good and right and just, that we visit our neighbors for the sake of God with totally appropriate manners and purity of behavior. As the Apostle said: "Who is sick, and I am not sick? Who is offended, and I am not offended?" But all these things are spoken with a focus on the love with which one should love neighbors. And these are the things we should focus our attention on, without giving offense. We should not do anything with partiality or for the shaming of others, but love the poor as the servants of God, and especially visit them. For this is desirable before God and before people, that we should remember the poor, and be lovers of the kindred and of strangers, for the sake of God and for the sake of those who believe in God, because we have learned from the law and from the prophets, and from our Lord Jesus Christ, about loving the kindred and loving strangers. For you know the words which have been spoken concerning the love of the kindred and the love of strangers. Powerfully are the words spoken to all those who do them.

Commodianus, *The Instructions of Commodianus in Favor of Christian Discipline, Against the God of the Heathens**

Little is known of Commodianus (fl. ca. 250) other than that he was an African who converted to Christianity during the middle 200s. This instruction on Christian discipline is very specific regarding what one is to do when visiting the hungry and sick. Don't bother with bringing words, bring food and drink. Offer material relief. God requires that you share what you have, or, at the very least, send money.

If your brother should be weak—I speak of the poor person—do not visit empty-handed such a one who lies ill. Do good under God. Pay your obedience by your money. Then the person shall be restored. Or, if he should perish, let a poor person be refreshed, who has nothing wherewith to pay you, but the Founder and Author of the world on his behalf. Or if you don't want to go to the poor because you are disdainful, send money, and something he can use to recover himself. And, similarly, if your poor sister lies upon a sickbed, let your matrons take her food. God Himself cries out, Break your bread to the needy. There is no need to visit with words, but with benefits. It is wicked that your brother should be sick through lack of food. Satisfy him not with words. He needs meat and drink. Look upon such assuredly weakened, who are not able to act for themselves. Give to them right now! I pledge my word that fourfold shall be given you by God.

Cyprian, *Letter 7*

Cyprian (d. 258), bishop of Carthage, writes this letter around 250 to his flock while he is in hiding. Due to widespread persecution by Decius of Christians, Cyprian has left Carthage, a Roman colony with a strong Christian community. He is concerned that the practices of ministry continue in his absence. He sends them money to ensure their work and specifies that, even in circumstances of persecution, acts of hospitality for the sick, the poor, widows, and for any strangers must continue. Cyprian took very seriously the bishop's role to provide hospitality to strangers and to see that they were provided for.

I urge that you be scrupulous in your care for the widows, the sick, and all the poor, and further, that you meet the financial needs of any strangers who are in want out of my own personal funds which I have left in the care of our fellow presbyter Rogatianus. In case these funds have already been completely expended, I am sending to Rogatianus by the acolyte Naricus a further sum, to ensure that the work of charity amongst those in difficulties may be carried out the more generously and readily.

I wish that you, my dearest brothers, may fare well.

Dionysius, *Epistle 12 to the Alexandrians**

This remarkable letter written ca. 263 chronicles the difficulties faced by Christians during the third century. Our source is Eusebius's Church History *where he reports this letter from Dionysius (d. ca. 264), bishop of Alexandria. Dionysius describes a situation of widespread famine and sickness and the heroic efforts made by Christians to minister to the needs of the sick, the infected and the dying as well as to care for the dead. The population noted these acts of mercy by the Christians which set them apart from non-Christians, who, according to Dionysius, cast out the sick and left the dead unburied for fear of catching disease. These behaviors of caring for the sick and dying fall within the stage of dwelling together as Christians host the most vulnerable and needy abandoned by society.*

To others, indeed, the present state of matters would not appear to offer a fit season for a celebration. This certainly is no festive time to them, nor, in truth, is any other time festive to them. And I say this not only about occasions that are obviously sorrowful, but even about occasions which people might consider to be most joyous. And now certainly all things are turned to mourning, and everyone is in grief, and lamentations sound throughout the city, due to the multitude of the dead and of those who are dying day by day. For just as it is written in the case of the first-born of the Egyptians, so now too a great cry has arisen. "For there is not a house in which there is not one dead." And if only this were all! . . .

To these statements he [Dionysius] in due succession makes this addition:

> Certainly very many of our brothers and sisters in their exceeding love and family feeling, did not spare themselves, but kept by each other, and visited the sick without thought of risk to themselves, and ministered to them continually, serving them in Christ. So they died with the others, though most joyfully, carrying others' pains, taking upon themselves their neighbors' diseases, and willingly taking over to their own bodies the burden of the sufferings of those around them. And many who had already cured others of their sicknesses, and restored them to strength, died themselves, having transferred to their own bodies the death that lay upon these. That common saying, which used to be just a polite form of address, they expressed in actual fact then, as they departed this life, like the "off-scourings" of all. Truly the very best of our own have departed this life this way, including some presbyters and some deacons, and among the people those who were highest in reputation. So this very form of death, in virtue of the distinguished piety and the steadfast faith which were exhibited in it, appeared to be no less than martyrdom itself.
>
> And they took the bodies of the saints in their open hands and in their arms, and closed their eyes, and shut their mouths. And carrying them in company, and laying them out decently, they clung to them, and embraced them, and prepared them properly with washing and with garments. And then pretty soon they had the same services done for themselves, as those who survived were ever following those who departed before them. But among the heathen all was the very opposite. For they thrust aside any who began to be sick, and kept aloof even from their dearest friends, and cast the sufferers out upon the public roads half dead, and left the dead like refuse, unburied. They shunned them with utter contempt when they died, carefully avoiding any kind of communication and participation with death. This was not easy, though, for them to escape totally, in spite of their many precautions.

Eusebius, *The Oration of the Emperor Constantine**

When Eusebius (ca. 260–ca. 340) chronicles the great acts of Constantine (d. 337), he praises both Constantine and his mother,

Helena. The first excerpt tells of Helena's generosity during her tour of the eastern provinces, particularly to the most vulnerable, that is, the poor, the imprisoned, slaves and the oppressed. Eusebius points out her mercy and hospitality through restorative acts to those less fortunate, not a universal characteristic among rulers.

> On the occasion of a tour she made of the eastern provinces, in the splendor of imperial authority, she made abundant gestures of generosity to the people of several cities collectively, as well as on individuals who approached her. At the same time she scattered largess among the soldiers freely. But especially abundant were the gifts she bestowed on the naked and unprotected poor. To some she gave money, to others an ample supply of clothing. She freed some from prison or from the bitter slavery of the mines. Others she delivered from unjust oppression, and others again, she restored from exile.

Eusebius also praises Constantine's generosity in receiving and housing guests for the dedication of the church at Jerusalem. According to Eusebius, Jerusalem became packed with emissaries from every province for this imperial festival full of splendor and largesse. Interesting among the details is that, while the emperor did indeed offer hospitality on a grand scale to those attending the ceremony, he apparently also distributed money and clothing to the needy in the city. Hospitality to one's immediate guests might be expressed through aid to strangers at the gate.

> The director and chief of these officers was a most useful servant of the emperor, a man well known for faith and piety, and thoroughly acquainted with the Divine word. His profession of faith during the time of the persecution was well known, and therefore he was deservedly entrusted with the arrangement of the present proceedings. Accordingly, in faithful obedience to the emperor's commands, he received the assembly with courteous hospitality, and entertained them with feasts and banquets on a scale of great splendor. He also distributed lavish supplies of money and clothing among the naked and destitute, and the multitudes of both sexes who suffered from lack of food and the common necessities of life. Finally, he enriched and beautified the church itself throughout with offerings of imperial magnificence, and thus fully accomplished the service he had been commissioned to perform.

Pachomius, Life

The famous father of desert monasticism, Pachomius (ca. 290–346), received hospitality himself at a crucial moment in his life when he was conscripted into military service and local Christians brought him food. This story opens as he and other recruits who were forced to serve are taken from their village.

As he was led away to the boat with his companions, he raised his eyes to heaven and sighed, saying, "My Lord Jesus, may your will be done!" They got on board and the boat sailed north with them. When they arrived at Ne, capital of the ancient empire, the men were brought into the city and thrown into prison. In the evening, some citizens of that city brought bread and victuals to the prison, and they compelled the recruits to eat, because they saw them sunk in great affliction. When young Pachomius saw them, he asked the men who were with him, "Why are these people so good to us when they do not know us?" They answered, "They are Christians, and they treat us with love for the sake of the God of heaven."

Later, when he settled down, he continued the pattern of hospitality by growing vegetables not only for himself, but for the poor or strangers passing by to share.

Young Pachomius too went south until he arrived at a deserted village called Seneset, scorched by the intensity of the heat. And he began to think about the place, in which there were not many but a few inhabitants. He went down to the river, into a small temple the ancients called Pmampiserapis. There he stood and prayed. The Spirit of God seized him: "Struggle and settle down here." The thing pleased him and he settled down there, growing some vegetables and some palm-trees in order to feed himself or some poor man of the village or again some stranger who should happen to pass by in a boat or on the road.

Ambrose, Three Books on the Holy Spirit, To the Emperor Gratian*

Ambrose (ca. 339–397) was bishop in Milan during a time when Christians were gaining power and prestige in the culture. He was the powerful preacher who captured the imagination of Augustine of Hippo for the Christian message. In this treatise he praises the humility that characterizes the practice of foot-washing, a key symbol of hospitality, giving it almost sacramental status in his treatment of it here. Ambrose points not only to Abraham and Gideon as models, but to Jesus himself who authorizes this act of hospitality.

How great is that excellence! As a servant, You wash the feet of Your disciples. As God, You send dew from heaven. But You don't only wash feet, you also invite us to sit down with You, and by the example of Your dignity exhort us, saying, "You call Me Master and Lord, and that's good, for so I am. If, then, I the Lord and Master have washed your feet, you ought also to wash one another's feet."

I, then, wish also myself to wash the feet of my brothers. I wish to fulfill the commandment of my Lord. I will not be ashamed of myself, nor look down on what He Himself did first. Good is the mystery of humility, because while washing the pollution of others I wash away my own. But all were not able to exhaust this mystery. Abraham was, indeed, willing to wash feet, on account of a feeling of hospitality. Gideon, too, was willing to wash the feet of the Angel of the Lord who appeared to him, but his willingness was confined to one. He was willing as one who would do a service, not as one who would invite fellowship with himself. This is a great mystery which no one knew. Lastly, the Lord said to Peter: "What I do you don't know now, but will know later." This, I say, is a divine mystery that even those who wash will inquire into. It is not, then, the simple water of the heavenly mystery whereby we are made worthy of having part with Christ.

Basil, *Letter 94**

Writing in 372 to Elias, the governor of the province, Basil (330–379) is concerned to clear up any misgivings Elias may have about Basil or his ministry. He describes a developed system of offering hospitality to strangers and the sick, including medical care, training for gainful employment, and transportation. This is a vivid description of the content of hospitality and the practices it can entail. Basil also makes the case for how these practices of hospitality might benefit the government as well.

Now I would like those who are besieging your impartial ears to be asked what harm the government suffers from me? What depreciation is suffered by any public interests, whether small or great, by my administration of the Churches? I suppose it might be argued that I have done damage to the government by building a magnificently appointed church to God, and round it dwellings, one liberally assigned to the bishop, and others underneath, allotted to the officers of the Church in order, the use of both being open to you who are civil servants and your escort. But whom do we harm by building a place of hospitality for strangers, both for those who are on the road and for those who need medical treatment on account of sickness? A way of giving them the comfort they want, the doctors, nurses, transportation and escort? All these people must learn such skills as are necessary to make a living and have been found essential to long-term employment. They must also have buildings suitable for their skills, all of which are an honor to the place, and, as their success is credited to our governor, confer glory on him. . . . But if, before we get a chance to meet, you are driven by the pleadings of some people's slander to give up any of your good will towards me, do as Alexander did. The story is, as you remember, that, when one of his friends was being slandered, he left one ear open to the slanderer, and carefully closed the other with his hand, with the object of showing that the one whose duty is to judge ought not to be easily and wholly given over to the first occupants of his attention, but should keep half his hearing open for the defense of the absent.

Basil, *The Long Rules*

The Long Rules *are instructions for communal life written in a question and response format. Care for orphans often fell to various religious communities. Orphans as a class are identified in early Christian literature as having a special claim to hospitality. Basil offers very thorough instructions regarding details of caring for orphans left in the monks' care. Specific acts of hospitality include taking them in without waiting to be asked, "on our own initiative," housing and feeding them, educating them, and disciplining them wisely.*

Indeed, those children who are bereft of their parents we should take in on our own initiative, so that we may become fathers of the orphans in emulation of Job. . . . They should be reared with all piety as children belonging to the entire community, but meals and quarters for both girls and boys should be separate, to avoid their being too familiar or too self-confident with their elders . . . and to ensure decorous behavior in other respects, the children's quarters should be separate from those of the more advanced in perfection.

Along with other advantages, the quarters inhabited by the monks will not be disturbed by the drilling which is necessary for the young in learning their lessons.

But as regards sleep and rising, the hours, the quantity, and the quality of the meals, specific routines and diets appropriate for children should be arranged. Moreover, one who is advanced in years should be placed in charge of these little ones, a person of more than average experience and who has a reputation for patience. Thus, he will correct the faults of the young with fatherly kindness and give wise instruction, applying remedies proper to each fault, so that, while the penalty for the fault is being exacted, the soul may be exercised in interior tranquility. Has one of them, for example, become angry with a companion? According to the seriousness of his offense, he should be made to care for this comrade and wait on him; for the practice of humility fells, as it were, an angry spirit, while arrogance usually breeds anger within us. Has he partaken of food out of time? Let him fast for most of the day. Has he been accused of eating immoderately or in an unseemly fashion? Let him be deprived of food at meal time and forced to watch the others who know how to eat properly, so that he may be at once punished by abstinence and taught proper decorum. Has he uttered an idle word, or insulted his neighbor, or told a lie, or said anything at all that is forbidden? Let him learn restraint in fasting and silence.

Moreover, to add a point which we had forgotten and which is not out of place here, since certain trades must be practiced even from early childhood, whenever any children appear to have an aptitude for these, we should not oppose their remaining during the day with their instructors in the art. At nightfall, however, we should invariably send them back to their companions, with whom they must also take their meals.

Gregory of Nyssa, Homily Concerning Almsgiving

Gregory of Nyssa (ca. 330–ca. 395) was younger brother to the famous Basil of Caesarea and served the church as monk and bishop in the late fourth century. He is perhaps best known as a theologian of the eastern church who assisted in establishing an orthodox doctrine of the trinity. In this sermon, Gregory offers an amazing plea for Christians to offer hospitality to the poor and sick as he describes a dire situation where people were living on the streets and begging in the markets. He tells of people making holes in the ground to store their meager provisions and putting knees together to form a table. Acts of hospitality here include listening to those in want, offering personal resources and offering a home in the Word of God.

Now is the opportune time to be ungrudging towards the naked and unclothed since a multitude of captives is at our door. There is no lack of strangers and wanderers, and the seeking hand is always extended. For all these people their home includes the open sky, inns, plazas, streets, and deserted market places. They dwell in caves like night ravens and owls (Psa. 102.6), and their clothing is torn rags. The farmer takes notice of them and shows mercy. If any food falls their way, they jump upon it. Springs provide water for animals, and holes in the ground acts as their storehouse from which they do not allow anything to escape but keep close guard over them. Knees held together form a table and the ground is their bed. A river or pool freely bestowed by God forms a bath which does not require construction. A wanderer out in the fields did not live like this from the beginning but only as a result of calamities and necessity. A person who fasts is supplied with life's necessities is sufficient reason why we should be generous towards our unfortunate brethren. Give to the poor anything you greedily consume. Let the just fear of God provide for your compensation. Exercise a healthy self-control by showing discretion between two conflicting affections, your satiety and your brother's hunger. Doctors perform their work in a similar fashion. They drain some patients of fluids and give them to others in order to preserve the health of both by addition and discharge. Pay attention to sound advice. Let reason open wide your gates. Allow advice coming from those in want to affect the wealthy. Do not enrich the impoverished by argumentation. When they hear the eternal Word of God, let it give them a home. Provide the needy from your own abundance.

The needy and sick person is doubly poor. Helpless persons of good health move about from door to door; they carefully approach affluent persons and beseech everyone at cross roads. However, those afflicted by illness are restrained in confining shelters and are put in corners as Daniel was cast into the pit (Dan 14.32). Here they look forward to your tenderness and concern for the poor as awaiting Ambakoum (16) . . .

But you say, "I am poor." Even so, give what you have. God does not seek that which is beyond your strength. Give your bread; to one, give a drink of wine and to another, a garment. In this way the charity of many dissolves the misfortune of one person. Moses did not receive money for the tent of worship from one individual but from everyone (Exod. 35.5). Some brought much gold and others brought silver, while the poor brought skins or goat hair. Do you not see that the offering of the widow surpasses the one from rich man? She gave everything in her possession (Mark 12.42).

John Chrysostom, *Homily 41 on Genesis*

Chrysostom (ca. 347–407) preached many sermons on Genesis. Abraham is a favorite topic and Chrysostom has much to say about the practice of hospitality in his discussion of Abraham at the Oaks of Mamre (Genesis 18). In this sermon, he identifies Abraham's practice of watching at midday for travelers in need of hospitality. He encourages watching for the unfamiliar as well as the familiar face as the condition for welcome.

He was putting hospitality into practice to such a degree as to be unwilling to entrust to anyone else in the household the task of attending to guests. . . . This, you see, was the great extent of the just man's hospitality and the extraordinary degree of his virtue, the fact that he behaved like this at midday. Very properly, too, since he realized that people obliged to travel are in need of much service at that time particularly, accordingly he chose that time as suitable, seated himself and kept an eye out for passers-by without caring whether they were known to him or not. You see, it is not part of hospitality to worry about such things: friendliness involves sharing one's possessions with all comers. Since he cast a wide net of hospitality, he in turn was judged worthy to welcome the Lord of all with his angels. Hence Paul too said, "Do no neglect hospitality, for through it some people have entertained angels all unawares," referring precisely to the patriarch. Hence Christ too said, "Whoever receives one of the least of these in my name, receives me."

John Chrysostom, *Homily 43 on Genesis*

In another sermon on Genesis, Chrysostom discusses Abraham's acts of hospitality, such as offering food and shelter. Beyond the obvious, other acts of hospitality include giving respect and paying attention to the visitors.

Do you see here as well hospitality manifested, not in richness of fare but in generosity of attitude? I mean, when he succeeded in bringing them into his house, at once he gave evidence of the signs of hospitality. He occupied himself in attending on them, providing something to eat and giving evidence of respect and attention to the visitors in his belief that they were only human beings, travelers of some kind.

John Chrysostom, Homily 66 on the Gospel of Matthew*

John Chrysostom, bishop of Constantinople, was a champion of the poor and did not hesitate to use his bully pulpit while still a preacher in Antioch. As he calls upon the laity to consider the distribution of wealth, he reminds them of the duties of hospitality already performed by the church, enumerating an amazing list. Among the practices of the church he lists the care of 3,000 widows and virgins, prisoners, the sick, travelers and strangers, and the maimed, as well as daily provisions to those needing food.

Let us distribute the whole multitude of the city then among the poor, and you will see how great a disgrace it is. For, indeed there are few very rich, but those that come next to them are many. The poor, like the rich, are much fewer than these. Yet, although there are so many people that are able to feed the hungry, still many go to sleep hungry, not because those with means are not able easily to aid them, but because those with means exhibit great barbarity and inhumanity. For if these two groups, the wealthy and those next to them, were to distribute among themselves those who need bread and clothing, there would hardly be one poor person to the care of fifty or even a hundred of those with means. Yet nevertheless, with such a great abundance of people who could help them, still they are wailing every day. Just so you learn the inhumanity of the others, when the church is possessed of a revenue of one of the lowest among the wealthy, and doesn't even rank among the very rich, consider how many widows it takes care of every day, how many virgins! For indeed the list of them has already reached up to three thousand. Together with these, the church takes care of those that dwell in the prison, the sick in the caravans neighborhood, the healthy, those that are away from their home, those that are maimed in their bodies, those that wait upon the altar. On top of that, just in terms of food and clothing the church serves those who come casually every day, and still her substance is in no respect diminished. So that if only ten people were thus willing to spend, there would be no poor.

John Chrysostom, Homily 45 on Acts of the Apostles*

As is often the case, John Chrysostom minces no words in calling his flock to specific acts of mercy and hospitality. In this sermon on the book of Acts he offers practical suggestions of the sort of behaviors Christians are called to practice. At the very least, they should watch for strangers and be curious enough to find out who they are and what they need. He encourages Christians to supply those necessities and consider receiving strangers into their homes. Christians may not avoid the demands of hospitality with the excuse that the Church will take care of these people. Instead, they might consider building a xenon, *a small apartment for strangers, in their own homes. His arguments are stinging and pointed.*

How many of the kindred are strangers? There is a common apartment in the Church, which we call the *"xenon."* Be inquisitive, sit before the doors, personally welcome those who come. Even though you may not wish to take them into your houses, at any rate in some other way receive them, by supplying them with necessities. "Why, doesn't the Church have the means" you will say? Certainly she has. But what difference does that make to you? If they are fed from the common funds of the Church, how can that benefit you? If another person prays, does it follow that you are not bound to pray? Why don't you say, "Don't the priests pray? Then why should I pray?" "But I," you will say, "give to one who cannot be received there." Give, though it be to that one. We just want to be sure that you give at any rate. Hear what Paul says: "That it may relieve them that are widows indeed, and that the Church be not burdened" (1 Timothy 5:16). Do it however you want, only do it. But I put it, not, "that the Church be not burdened," but, "that you be not burdened." For at this rate you will do nothing, leaving all to the Church. This is why there is a common room set apart by the Church, that you may not say these things. "The Church," say you, "has lands, has money, and revenues." And has she not charges? I ask; and has she not a daily expenditure? "No doubt," you will say. Why then do you not lend aid to her moderate means? I am ashamed to have to say these things. However, I will force no one, if any one imagines I am speaking out of mixed motives. Make for yourself a guest-chamber in your own house. Set up a bed there, set up a table there and a candlestick (2 Kings 4:10). For isn't it absurd, that if soldiers happen to come, you have rooms set apart for them, and show much care for them, and furnish them with everything, because they protect you from the visible war of this world? Yet strangers have no place where they might abide? Gain a victory over the Church. Do you want to put us to shame? Then do this. Surpass us in generosity. Have a room, to which Christ may come. Say, "This is Christ's space. This building is set apart for Him." Even if it is just a basement and tiny. He won't refuse it. Christ goes about "naked and a stranger." It is only a shelter He wants. Give it to Him, even if it's not much. Don't be uncompassionate, nor inhuman. Don't be so earnest in worldly matters, yet so cold in spiritual. Let your most faithful servant be the one entrusted with this office, to bring in the maimed, the beggars, and the homeless. These things I say to shame you. For, indeed, you ought to receive them in the upper part of your house. But if you won't do even this, then although it is below, where you keep your mules and your servants, receive Christ there. Maybe you shudder at hearing this? What do you expect, when you don't do even this? Look, I plead with you. Look, I command you. Let this be a matter to be taken up in earnest. But you do not want it this way, perhaps? Do it some other way. There are plenty of poor men and poor women. Set apart some one of these constantly to remain there. Let the poor man live there if only as a guard to your house. Let him be to you like a wall and fence, shield and spear. Where alms are, the devil would not dare approach, nor any other evil thing. We should not overlook so great a gain.

*John Chrysostom, Homily 19 on 2 Corinthians**

Chrysostom here addresses a tricky question asked by each generation of Christians: how much do I give? Chrysostom tries to define what is enough, what is too little and what is too much. Since hospitality entails various acts of giving, this sermon is relevant for understanding this bishop's notion of what early Christians were to do.

"As it is written, He has scattered abroad, he has given to the poor; His righteousness abides for ever." This is the import of "abound," for the words, "he has scattered abroad," signify nothing else but giving plentifully. For though things in themselves do not last, their results do. For this is the thing to be admired, that when they are kept they are lost. But when dispersed abroad they abide, even abide forever. Now by "righteousness," here, he means love towards all. For this makes righteous, consuming sin like a fire when it is plentifully poured out. Let us not therefore neatly keep score, but sow with a generous hand. Don't you see how much others give to actors and harlots? Give at least half to Christ, of what they give to dancers. As much as they give of ostentation to those upon the stage, you should give at least that much to the hungry. . . . But as long as you spend it upon your belly and on drunkenness and waste, you never think of poverty. But when the need is to relieve poverty, you become poorer than anybody. And when feeding hangers-on and flatterers, you are as joyous as though you had fountains to spend from. But if you chance to see a poor man, then the fear of poverty besets you. . . . For I am not leading you to the lofty peak of total poverty but for the present I require you to cut off extras and to desire what is sufficient alone. Now the boundary of what is sufficient entails using those things which it is impossible to live without. No one debars you from these, nor forbids you your daily food. Notice I say food, not feasting. Clothes, not ornament. Yes, if one should inquire accurately, this is in the best sense feasting. For, think about it. Which should we say more truly feasted, the one whose diet was herbs, who was in sound health and suffered no uneasiness or the one who had the table of a Sybarite, and was full of ten thousand disorders? Very plainly the former. Therefore let us seek nothing more than this, if we would at once live luxuriously and healthfully, just set these boundaries to sufficiency. And let those who can be satisfied with grain and can keep in good health, seek for nothing more. But let those who are weaker and require a diet with garden herbs, not be hindered of this. But if any be even weaker than this and require the support of meat in moderation, we will not debar them from this either. For we do not advise these things in order to injure or kill people but to cut off what is superfluous, i.e., anything which is more than we need. For when we are able even without a thing to live healthfully and respectably, certainly the addition of anything else is a superfluity.

So let us think the same way about clothing and the table and a dwelling house and all our other wants. So that in everything ask what is really necessary. For what is superfluous is also useless. Once you have practiced living on what is sufficient, then if you have a mind to imitate that widow, we will lead you on to greater things than these.

Jerome, *Preface to the Commentary on Ezekiel**

Jerome (342–420) gives us insight into the situation at his monastery at Bethlehem during the early decades of the fifth century as refugees flooded to the east after the sack of Rome. In this preface to a commentary, the biblical scholar apologizes for having been remiss in completing it. He explains that the demands of hospitality supersede his study of Scripture. He decries the harassment of refugees by those hoping to find treasure. His own community suspends their quiet discipline to tend to the many unexpected guests. It is hard to determine precisely what relief is offered, but suffice to say Jerome is aware of the hardships of their travel, hunger and sickness.

There is not a single hour, nor a single moment, in which we are not relieving crowds of brothers, and the quiet of the monastery has been changed into the bustle of a guest house. And so much is this the case that we must either close our doors, or abandon the study of the Scriptures on which we depend for keeping the doors open. . . . I am not boasting, as some perhaps suspect, of the welcome given to the brothers, but I am simply confessing the causes of the delay. Who could boast when the flight of the people from the West, and the holy places, crowded as they are with penniless fugitives, naked and wounded, plainly reveal the ravages of the Barbarians? We cannot see what has occurred without tears and moans. Who would have believed that mighty Rome, with its careless security of wealth, would be reduced to such extremities as to need shelter, food, and clothing? And yet, some are so hard-hearted and cruel that, instead of showing compassion, they break up the rags and bundles of the captives, and expect to find gold about those who are nothing more than prisoners. In addition to this hindrance to my dictating, my eyes are growing dim with age and to some extent I share the suffering of the saintly Isaac, that is, I am quite unable to go through the Hebrew books with such light as I have at night, for even in the full light of day they are hidden from my eyes owing to the smallness of the letters. In fact, it is only the voice of the brothers which makes it possible for me to master the commentaries of Greek writers.

*Augustine, Tractate 58**

Well known as a theologian and bishop of Hippo, Augustine (354–430) preached regularly to his congregation seeking to guide them in the faith and educate them in the Christian life. He preaches here on foot washing as an important Christian practice. It can be practiced with the heart, in a spiritual sense, as well as with the hand. Later in the sermon he describes foot washing as a "sacramental sign" of grace, so that the act of forgiving one another becomes an act of hospitality just as does foot washing.

"If I, then," He says, "your Lord and Master, have washed your feet, you also ought to wash one another's feet. For I have given you an example, that you should do as I have done to you." This, blessed Peter, is what you did not know when you were not allowing it to be done. This is what He promised to let you know afterwards, when your Master and your Lord terrified you into submission, and washed your feet. We have learned, brothers, humility from the Highest. Let us, as humble, do to one another what He, the Highest, did in His humility. Great is the commendation we have here of humility. The faithful do this to one another in turn, even in the visible act itself, when they treat one another with hospitality; for the practice of such humility is generally prevalent, and finds expression in the very deed that makes it discernible. And so the apostle, when he would commend the well-deserving widow, says, "If she is hospitable, if she has washed the saints' feet." And wherever such is not the practice among the saints, what they fail to do with the hand, they do with the heart, if they are of the number of those who are addressed in the hymn of the three blessed men, "O you holy and humble of heart, bless you the Lord." But it is far better, and beyond all dispute more in line with the truth, that it should also be done with the hands. Nor should any Christian think it beneath him to do what was done by Christ. For when the body is bent at a brother's feet, the feeling of such humility is either awakened in the heart itself, or is strengthened if already present. For what else does the Lord apparently intimate in the profound significance of this sacramental sign, when He says, "For I have given you an example, that you should do as I have done to you," but what the apostle declares in the plainest terms, "Forgiving one another, if any man have a quarrel against any, even as Christ forgave you, so also do you"? Let us therefore forgive one another's faults, and pray for one another's faults, and thus in a manner be washing one another's feet. It is our part, by His grace, to be supplying the service of love and humility. It is His to hear us, and to cleanse us from all the pollution of our sins through Christ, and in Christ, so that what we forgive even to others, that is, loose on earth, may be loosed in heaven.

Paulinus of Nola, *Letter 24*

Paulinus (353–431) was bishop at Nola where he and his wife founded a home for monks and the poor. In this letter written around 400 Paulinus praises his friend Severus for his use of possessions to offer hospitality to travelers and the poor. He makes an insightful connection between own-

ing things and offering hospitality. If Severus's home were crammed with furniture, there would be no empty space for guests. Further, Severus does not stand upon his aristocratic status, but offers hospitality by living the life of those he serves.

As I have said, you have undertaken two saintly roles, by refusing to own the land you have retained, and by achieving perfection through that which you have sold. So in your apparent role of owner you are perfect, because your mind is free from the ties of possessions; mindful of how short the time is, you fulfill Paul's injunction by possessing without possessing, for you keep possessions not for yourself but for those with nothing. You play host in your house so that your house may be a hospice. You are a traveler from your native land, and an exile in this world that you may dwell in Paradise and be a citizen of your former country. You do not crowd your houses with dining tables, or cram them with masses of furniture or wealth. You measure off a corner for yourself and fill the house with travelers and beggars. You live as a fellow servant with your own slaves. The temporary lodging which is your dwelling you do not possess like the father of a household, but you lodge there like a mercenary or a lodger, paying the Lord a regular rent for the favor of the lodging by serving your neighbors with body and mind.

Paulinus of Nola, Letter 29

Again writing to Severus around 400 Paulinus informs him of Melania's (ca. 383–438) activities offering hospitality to refugees even at great risk to herself. In particular, Melania was willing to stand in solidarity with other orthodox Christians under Arian persecution and welcome five thousand monks, offering them refuge.

Of her many divine virtues I shall recount just one, so that from this you can assess all her achievements. During the notorious reign of Valens, when the rage of the Arians assailed the church of the living God using that king of impiety as their lackey, Melania was the leader or companion of all who stood fast for the faith. She gave refuge to fugitives or accompanied those arrested. But after she had hidden those who were the objects of greater hatred from the heretics because of their notable faith, and those who helped to conceal them had incurred loathing, the torches of the devil fired the serious discord.

She was ordered to be haled forth for holding the state law in contempt and to suffer the fate awaiting her hidden protégés unless she agreed to produce them. She advanced fearlessly, desirous of suffering, and rejoicing at the unjust proclamation. Though she had not anticipated arrest, she flew along before her would-be escort to the judge's tribunal. His respect for the woman before him troubled him, and his surprise at her bold faith caused him to drop his heretical rage.

About the same time she fed five thousand monks, who lay in hiding, for three days with her own bread, so that by her hand the Lord Jesus again fed in the desert the same number as of old. But now His kindness was all the greater as the hidden monks were being accorded less freedom and affection than that former five thousand who had voluntarily assembled before the Lord in freedom and in peace.

Sulpitius Severus, Dialogues*

Sulpitius (ca. 360–420) recounts the travels of his friend Postumianus when his boat was forced to land on the north coast of Africa just short of Alexandria. Postumianus reports that at first he thought the land empty of human inhabitants until he ventured further inland. There Postumianus meets up with a Cyrene presbyter who welcomed him and his companions warmly with kisses and tears, prayed with them, housed them for seven days and fed them. When Postumianus offers the Cyrene gold in return, he refuses. These kind acts encompass the stages of hospitality from welcome to sending forth.

Three years ago, Sulpitius, I said goodbye and set sail from Narbonne, and on the fifth day we entered a port of Africa. The voyage had gone so well, by the will of God, that I had in my mind a great desire to go to Carthage, to visit those localities connected with the saints, and, above all, to worship at the tomb of the martyr Cyprian. On the fifth day we returned to the harbor, and launched back out into the sea. Our destination was Alexandria. But as the south wind was against us, we were almost driven upon the Syrtis. The cautious sailors, however, guarding against this, stopped the ship by casting anchor. The continent of Africa then lay before our eyes, and, landing on it in boats, when we perceived that the whole country round was destitute of human cultivation, I penetrated farther inland, for the purpose of more carefully exploring the locality.

The sea-coast of the Cyrenians is indeed the most remote, bordering on that desert which lies between Egypt and Africa, and through which Cato formerly, when fleeing from Caesar, led an army.

Chapter 4. Then I directed my steps toward the hut that I had beheld from a distance. There I find an old man, in a garment made of skins, turning a mill with his hand. He saluted and received us kindly. We explained to him that we had been forced to land on that coast, and were prevented by the continued raging of the sea from being able at once to pursue our journey. We also explained that, having made our way to shore, we wanted, as is in keeping with ordinary human nature, to become acquainted with the character of the locality, and the manners of the inhabitants. We added that we were Christians, and that the principal object of our inquiry was whether there were any Christians amid these solitudes. Then, indeed, he, weeping for joy, throws himself at our feet, and, kissing us over and over again, invites us to prayer. At the same time, he spreads sheep skins on the ground and makes us sit down upon them. He then serves up a breakfast truly luxurious, consisting of half of a barley cake. Now, we were four, while he himself consti-tuted the fifth. He also brought in a bundle of herbs, of which I for-get the name but they were like mint, were rich in leaves, and yielded a taste like honey. We were delighted with the exceedingly sweet taste of this plant, and our hunger was fully satisfied.

However, on the following day, when some of the natives had come together to visit us, we discovered that this host of ours was a Presbyter—a fact which he had concealed from us with the greatest care. We then went with him to the church, which was about two miles away, and was concealed from our view by an intervening mountain. We found that it was constructed of common and worth-less trees, and was not much more imposing than the hut of our host, in which one could not stand without stooping. On inquiring into the customs of the local people, we found that they were not in the habit of either buying or selling anything. They didn't even know the meaning of either fraud or theft. As to gold and silver, which people generally deem the most desirable of all things, they neither possess them, nor do they desire to possess them. For when I offered that Presbyter ten gold coins, he refused them, declaring, with profound wisdom, that the church was not helped but rather injured by gold. We presented him, however, with some pieces of clothing.

Sulpitius Severus, *The Life of Martin of Tours**

Severus (ca. 360–420) describes the hospitality of Martin of Tours (d. 397), a well-known leader of his day and bishop of Tours. Martin had founded the community at Tours and was influential in the spread of monasticism in Gaul. Specifically, Martin showed kindness and a warm welcome as well as humility. Martin even washes Severus's feet himself, much to Severus's chagrin.

And at this time it is hardly believable with what humility and with what kindness he received me! He warmly wished me joy, and rejoiced in the Lord that he had been held in such high estimation by me that I had bothered to take a trip just out of my desire to see him. Unworthy me! (in fact, I hardly dare acknowledge it), that he should have deigned to admit me to fellowship with him! He went so far as in person to present me with water to wash my hands, and at eventide he himself washed my feet. I was not brave enough to resist or oppose his doing so. In fact, I felt so overcome by the authority he unconsciously exerted, that I thought it a crime to do anything but acquiesce in his arrangements.

John Cassian, *Institutes of the Coenobia**

John Cassian (360–435) was a monk who studied asceticism in Egypt then traveled west to establish monasteries in Marseilles. His Institutes, setting forth basic rules for monastic life, have widely influenced other monastic rules in the west. Sometimes the act of welcome requires suspending rules, such as fasting. Recognizing Christ in his guests, an elder places hospitality above piety, knowing that fasting can be pursued again once the guests are on their way.

When we had come from the region of Syria and had sought the province of Egypt, in our desire to learn the rules of the Elders. We were astonished at the eagerness of heart with which we were received there so that no rule forbidding refreshment until the exact time the fast was over was observed, such as we had been brought up to observe in the monasteries of Palestine. Except in the case of the regular days, Wednesdays and Fridays, wherever we went the daily fast was broken. When we asked why the daily fast was thus ignored by them without scruple one of the elders replied, "The opportunity for fasting is always with me. But as I am going to conduct you on your way, I cannot always keep you with me. And a fast, although it is useful and advisable, is yet a free-will offering. But the exigencies of a command require the fulfillment of a work of charity. And so receiving Christ in you I ought to refresh Him, but when I have sent you on your way I shall be able to balance the hospitality offered for His sake by a stricter fast on my own account. For 'the children of the bridegroom cannot fast while the bridegroom is with them' but when he has departed, then they will rightly fast."

The Lives of the Desert Fathers

The report (ca. 400) tells of the travels of some monks from Palestine into Egypt and the desert fathers they encounter there. Many practices of hospitality are noted throughout. In this story, the act of welcoming a visitor is itself a central act of hospitality. The welcome of this elderly desert father sets forth the basic behaviors of warm welcome, smiling face and expressing interest in the guest.

I.17. One could see the saint already in his ninetieth year with his body so completely worn out by his *ascesis* that even his beard no longer grew on his face. For he ate nothing apart from fruit, and after sunset at that, in spite of his advanced age, having formerly lived a life of great ascetic discipline. And he never ate bread or anything that needed to be cooked.

18. When he invited us to sit down, we thanked God for our meeting with him. He for his part, after welcoming us like his own dear children after a long absence, addressed us with a smiling face in the following words: "Where are you from, my children? Which country have you traveled from to visit a poor man?" 19. We told him where we were from, adding, "We have come to you from Jerusalem for the good of our souls, so that what we have heard with our ears we might perceive with our eyes."

Again a group of monks offers hospitality to a stranger among them. The story is told of an ascetic who, in his old age, falls prey to demons and in distress sets off at night on a journey to civilization. On his way he happens upon a monastery. They receive hospitably this great one who had fallen. Their acts include washing his feet and face, praying, preparing a table and offering him whatever they had.

I.54. When dawn broke, the settled region was still far away, but he toiled on, suffering from the burning heat of the sun. He began to look around him, scanning the horizon on all sides to see if a monastery would appear where he could go and refresh himself. 55. As it happened a monastery did appear. Some pious and faithful brethren received him, and treating him like their true father, washed his face and his feet. Then, after saying a prayer, they prepared a table and invited him with love to partake of whatever they had.

This story is about Abba (Father) Or in the Thebaid of Egypt. He, too, models the acts of warm embrace, prayer, foot washing, and sharing of himself. Further, Abba Or played servant to his disciples, building shelter for them and seeing to their needs.

II. 7. When the father saw us, he was filled with joy, and embraced us, and offered a prayer for us. Then, after washing our feet with his own hands, he turned to spiritual teaching. . . .

11. This man, at any rate, was so renowned among many of the other fathers that when a large number of monks came to him, he called together everybody who lived near him and built cells for them in a single day, one delivering mortar, another bricks, another drawing water, and another cutting wood. And when the cells had been completed, he himself saw to the needs of the newcomers.

The author of this account was impressed with the hospitality of the entire city of Oxyrhynchus that had posted watchmen in order to receive strangers hospitably. Not only clerics, but laity received the guests. Their enthusiasm was so great that, in pulling the visitors to go home with them, the visitors' clothes were torn.

V.5. The chief officials and magistrates of the city [Oxyrhynchus], who distributed largesse to the common people, had watchmen posted at the gates and entrances, so that if some needy stranger should appear, he would be taken to them and receive victuals for his sustenance. And what can one say about the piety of the common people, who when they saw us strangers crossing the agora [marketplace] approached us as if we were angels? How can one convey an adequate idea of the throngs of monks and nuns past counting? 6. However, as far as we could ascertain from the holy bishop of that place, we would say that he had under his jurisdiction ten thousand monks and twenty thousand nuns. It is beyond my power to describe their hospitality and their love for us. In fact each of us had our cloaks rent apart by people pulling us to make us go and stay with them.

When these travelers visited Abba Apollo in the desert, their welcome was similar. The features of foot washing, prayer, and food are present. Admittedly, the author reports that fellow monks were received this way, not necessarily all guests.

VIII. 48. Three of our party were on our way to visit the saint. We were seen and recognized from afar by the brethren, who had already heard about our arrival from him. They came running to meet us, singing psalms. For this is what they generally do with all their visitors. And when they had prostrated before us with their faces to the ground, they kissed us, and pointing us out to each other, said, "See, the brothers have arrived about whom the father spoke to us three days ago, saying that in three days three brothers from Jerusalem will visit us." 49. Some of them went in front of us and others followed behind, singing psalms, until we came near to where the saint was. When Father Apollo heard the sound of singing, he greeted us according to the custom that all the brethren follow. When he saw us, he first prostrated, lying full length on the ground; then getting up he kissed us, and having brought us in, prayed for us; then, after washing our feet with his own hands, he invited us to partake of some refreshment. He does this with all the brethren who come to visit him.

The monks of Nitria were well known for their dedication to discipline and are widely reported in ancient sources. Here the author praises their hospitality as well. Again, the pattern is repeated of warm greeting, foot washing, offering food and drink, and sharing spiritual life.

XX.5. We also put in at Nitria, where we saw many great anchorites. Some of them were natives of that region, others were foreigners. They excelled each other in the virtues and engaged in rivalry over their ascetic practices, giving proof of all the virtues and struggling to surpass each other in their manner of life. 6. Some applied themselves to contemplation, others to the active life. When a group of them saw us approaching from a distance through the desert, some came to meet us with water, others washed our feet, and others laundered our clothes. Some of them invited us to a meal, others to learn about the virtues, and others to contemplation and the knowledge of God. Whatever ability each one had, he hastened to use it for our benefit. Indeed how can one relate all their virtues, since one is totally unable to do them justice?

Additions to the text by Rufinus include these acts of hospitality:

XX.5. Then we came to Nitria, the best-known of all the monasteries of Egypt, about forty miles from Alexandria. . . . Though they are divided by their dwellings they remain bound together and inseparable in faith and love. So as we drew near to that place and they realized that foreign brethren were arriving, they poured out of their cells like a swarm of bees and ran to meet us with delight and alacrity, many of them carrying containers of water and of bread, according to the rebuke of the prophet when he said to some, "ye came not forth to meet the children of Israel with bread and water." When they had welcomed us, first of all they led us with psalms into the church and washed our feet and one by one they dried them with the linen cloth they were girded with, as if to wash away the fatigue of the journey, but in fact to purge away the hardships of worldly life with this traditional mystery.

What can I say that would do justice to their humanity, their courtesy, and their love; each of them wanted to take us to his own cell, not only to fulfil the duties of hospitality, but even more out of humility, in which they are indeed masters, and out of gentleness and similar qualities which are learned among them according to graces that differ but with the one and same teaching, as if they had left the world for this one end. Nowhere have I seen love flourish so greatly, nowhere such quick compassion, such eager hospitality. And nowhere have I seen such meditation upon Holy Scripture, or a better understanding of it, or such discipline of sacred learning. You might well think that each of them was an expert in the wisdom of God.

Maximus of Turin, Sermon 34 On Hospitality in the Gospel

An impressive collection of sermons by Maximus of Turin (d. 408–423) includes several on hospitality. Interestingly, he addresses the duties of the guest in this sermon on hospitality. Referring to Jesus' instructions to the disciples in Matthew 10:11, Maximus concludes that receiving hospitality as well as offering it is a virtuous act and should not be violated by inconstancy.

Your holiness, brethren, has attended to the Gospel reading and to how the Lord set down for His disciples, among the other virtues that they were to pursue, the laws of hospitality as well. For He says: "In whatever city you enter, ask in it who is worthy, and remain there until you leave," and so forth. Clearly these are holy and divine words, which both gave the disciples the privilege of choosing first and also completely did away with any lightmindedness. For in establishing a norm He saw to it that a holy man would neither be quick in making a judgment nor frivolous in changing his host. For just as He conceded to us the ability to make a decision, so He also wished us to remain constant. How reprehensible it is when a man who announces the Gospel and teaches others not to go astray himself begins to wander about in different places, to abandon the house that he had greeted with peace and to sadden the host upon whom he had brought a blessing! For hospitality is a great grace and ought not to be easily violated: it is open to all, ready for all, and both gladly welcomes saints and patiently puts up with sinners.

Maximus of Turin, Sermon 60

In another sermon, this time preaching on the Lord's birthday, Maximus cites acts of hospitality as appropriate ways to celebrate Christmas. He points to gifts that enable hospitality to travelers, widows and the poor.

Therefore, brethren, let us who are about to celebrate the Lord's birthday cleanse ourselves from all the filth of our sins. Let us fill his treasuries with gifts of different kinds so that on the holy day there might be the wherewithal to give to travelers, to refresh widows, and to clothe the poor. For what sort of thing would it be if in one and the same house, among the servants of a single master, one should vaunt himself in silk and another should be completely covered in rags; if one should be warm with food and another should endure hunger and cold; if, out of indigestion, one should be belching what he had drunk yesterday and another should not have compensated for yesterday's dearth of food? And what will be the effect of our praying? We ask to be freed from the enemy, we who are not generous with our brethren. Let us be imitators of our Lord! For if He wished the poor to be sharers with us in heavenly grace, why should they not be sharers with us in earthly goods?

Gerontius, *The Life of Melania the Younger*

Melania the Younger (ca. 383–438), wealthy Roman matron and granddaughter of Melania the Elder, fled Rome with her husband, Pinianus, as it came under hostile attack. They liquidated their considerable assets and set upon a virtuous life, whereupon they weighed the challenges of asceticism. Concluding that the rigors of an ascetic discipline might lead to failure, they instead chose a path of hospitality for the sick, the stranger, the poor, and the imprisoned, an equally virtuous spiritual practice. This biography was written by Gerontius ca. 452.

Thus by God's grace having successfully accomplished this virtue, they turned anew to another one. Together they wisely considered the matter and said, "If we take upon ourselves an ascetic discipline that is beyond our strength, we will not be able to bear it because of the softness of our way of life. Our body will not be able to bear it, will weaken completely, and later we will be likely to surrender ourselves to sensuality." For this reason they chose this righteous practice for themselves. They went around to simply all who were sick, visiting them in order to attend to them. They lodged strangers who were passing through, and cheering them with abundant supplies for their journey, sent them on their way. They lavishly assisted all the poor and needy. They went about to all the prisons, places of exile, and mines, setting free those who were held because of debt and providing them with money. Like Job, the blessed servant of the Lord, their door stood open to any of the helpless.

Palladius, *Dialogue on the Life of John Chrysostom*

Palladius (ca. 363–425) was a monk and churchman who wrote this work on the life of John Chrysostom (ca. 347–407) as a defense of John's ministry. Of particular interest was the attack by Theophilus, bishop of Alexandria, on Chrysostom, bishop of Constantinople, when the latter offered hospitality to the Nitrian monks the former had exiled for doctrinal irregularities.[4] In this case, hospitality means offering spiritual guidance and sanctuary. Although Chrysostom himself does not provide for their physical needs, women in the church do. As a result, Chrysostom was removed from his see, ultimately dying in exile. Palladius likely wrote this apologetic from exile himself in 406–408.

The monks then were forced by necessity to change about from place to place, and they finally reached the capital, where Bishop John had been installed by God's hand for the spiritual guidance of our rulers. They fell down at his knees, imploring him to help souls plundered and abandoned by those more accustomed to this action than to doing good. John arose and beheld fifty sincere men with habits worn gray with their holy labors. Stung to the quick by his feeling of brotherly love as was Joseph, he burst into tears and asked them: "What sort of boar of the wood . . . or singular wild beast has been doing mischief to this fruitful vine?"

Then they said: "Please be seated, father, and bind up the horrible wounds we have suffered because of Pope Theophilus's madness, if indeed you can heal our swollen wounds. For if you cannot speak up for us either out of respect or fear of Theophilus, so is the case with other bishops. Then the only thing left for us to do is to approach the emperor and acquaint him with the man's evil actions, thereby bringing ill fame to the Church. If you have any interest in the well-being of the Church, then, consider our petition and please persuade Theophilus to allow us to go to our home in Egypt. We have done no wrong against the law of the Savior or against him."

John thought he could easily change Theophilus's bad feeling towards the monks and willingly took up the matter. He called them together and instructed them for the love of God they should not reveal the reason for their presence "until I send word to my brother Theophilus." He gave them quarters in the Church of the Resurrection for sleeping, but did not provide for other necessities of life. Some pious women brought their daily sustenance, and they themselves helped to some extent by the labor of their own hands.

Palladius, *Lausiac History*

Palladius (ca. 363–425) wrote this account, named for the imperial chamberlain to whom it was dedicated, Lausus, in 419 of his experiences among spiritual leaders in Syria, Egypt, and Palestine. Reporting his year with the monks of the Nitrian region he tells of some five thousand monks throughout the area with seven bakeries to feed them. Their hospitality to guests took the form of meaningful participation in the life of the community, a way of dwelling together.

7.4. The guesthouse is close to the church. Here the arriving guest is received until such time as he leaves voluntarily. He stays here all the time, even if for a period of two or three years. They allow a guest to remain at leisure for one week; from then on he must help in the garden, bakery, or kitchen. Should he be a noteworthy person, they give him a book, not allowing him to converse with anyone before the sixth hour. On this mountain there are doctors living, and also pastry cooks. They use wine, too, and wine is sold.

In a reversal of roles, this secular businessman carried on practices of hospitality for the monks at Nitria. His hospitality included acts of restoration, caring for the sick. He even designated a successor to continue his ministry.

13. Apollonius

1. There was a business man named Apollonius who had renounced the world and lived on Mount Nitria. As he was too advanced in years to learn a craft or to work as a scribe, he lived on the mountain for twenty years engaged in this business: with his own money and his own efforts he would buy all kinds of medicines and groceries at Alexandria and provide for all the brethren in their sicknesses.

2. He could be seen making his rounds of the monasteries from early morn to the ninth hour, going in door after door to find out if any one was sick. He used to bring grapes, pomegranates, eggs, and cakes such as the sick fancy, and he found this a very profitable livelihood in his old age. When he died he left his wares to one just like himself, and he encouraged him to carry on with this service. For there were five thousand monks living on the mountain, and there was a need for this visiting, since the place was a desert.

Palladius reports the act of courage by Juliana who offered refuge to the famous theologian, Origen, when he was being persecuted. In this case hospitality required opening her home to a known fugitive and sheltering him for two years.

64. Juliana

1. Then there was a maiden, Juliana, in Caesarea of Cappadocia, said to be a most learned and trustworthy woman. She took in Origen the writer when he fled from the insurrection of the pagans, and she kept him at her own expense for two years and looked after him.

This is what I found written in a very old book of verses, and it was written there in Origen's own hand:

2. "I found this book among the things of Juliana the virgin in Caesarea when I was hidden by her. She used to say that she had it from Symmachus himself, the translator of the Jews."

Egeria, *Travels to the Holy Land*

Egeria's travel diary was written ca. 420 as she went on a pilgrimage to the Holy Land.[5] This text has increasingly been recognized as a treasure trove of information on pilgrimage, monasticism and liturgy in the early fifth century. Written to a group of women back home, possibly in Spain, Egeria makes notes on each sacred site of biblical and theological significance. Here she details her visit to the Mount of God, or Mount Sinai, including a vivid description of the monks' hospitality and their role in her ascent up the mountain. Not only do they provide her with shelter and food, they serve as tour guides, escorting her along the trail, showing her the sites and staying with her at the top. Once on top, another set of monks offered hospitality by reading Scripture, conducting Eucharist and offering eulogiae, *or blessings, which were small tokens for guests, often fruit. Later she describes her visit to the spring of Moses. In this context specific acts of hospitality include providing food and lodging, giving one's time and presence, sharing in worship, and offering a small provision for the journey.*

3.1 Late on Saturday, then, we arrived at the mountain and came to some cells. The monks who lived in them received us most hospitably, showing us every kindness. There is a church there with a presbyter; that is where we spent the night, and pretty early on Sunday, we set off with the presbyter and monks who lived there to climb each of the mountains.

They are hard to climb. You don't go round and round them, spiraling up gently, but straight at each one as if you were going up a wall, and then straight down to the foot, till you reach the foot of the central mountain, Sinai itself. Here then, impelled by Christ our God and assisted by the prayers of the holy men who accompanied us, we made the great effort of the climb. It was quite impossible to ride up, but though I had to go on foot I was not conscious of the effort— in fact I hardly noticed it because, by God's will, I was seeing my hopes coming true.

So at ten o'clock we arrived on the summit of Sinai, the Mount of

God where the Law was given, and the place where God's glory came down on the day when the mountain was smoking. The church which is now there is not impressive for its size (there is too little room on the summit), but it has a grace all its own. And when with God's help we had climbed right to the top and reached the door of this church, there was the presbyter, the one who is appointed to the church, coming to meet us from his cell. He was a healthy old man, a monk from his boyhood and an "ascetic" as they call it here—in fact just the man for the place. Several other presbyters met us too, and all the monks who lived near the mountain, or at least all who were not prevented from coming by their age or their health.

All there is on the actual summit of the central mountain is the church and the cave of holy Moses. No one lives there. So when the whole passage had been read to us from the Book of Moses (on the very spot!) we made the Offering [Eucharist] in the usual way and received Communion. As we were coming out of church the presbyters of the place gave us "blessings," some fruits which grow on the mountain itself. For although Sinai, the holy Mount, is too stony even for bushes to grow on it, there is a little soil round the foot of the mountains, the central one and those around it, and in this the holy monks are always busy planting shrubs, and setting out orchards or vegetable-beds round their cells. It may look as if they gather fruit which is growing in the mountain soil, but in fact everything is the result of their own hard work.

We had received Communion and the holy men had given us the "blessings." Now we were outside the church door, and at once I asked them if they would point out to us all the different places. The holy men willingly agreed. They showed us the cave where holy Moses was when for the second time he went up into the Mount of God and a second time received the tables of stone after breaking the first ones when the people sinned. They showed us all the other places we wanted to see, and also the ones they knew about themselves. I want you to be quite clear about these mountains, reverend ladies my sisters, which surrounded us as we stood beside the church looking down from the summit of the mountain in the middle. They had been almost too much for us to climb, and I really do not think I have ever seen any that were higher (apart from the central one which is higher still) even though they looked like little hillocks to us as we stood on the central mountain. From there we were able to see Egypt and Palestine, the Red Sea and the Parthenian

Sea (the part that takes you to Alexandria), as well as the vast lands of the Saracens—all unbelievably far below us. All this was pointed out to us by the holy men. . . .

11.8. Now we had to hurry to carry out our intention of reaching Mount Nebo. As we traveled along, the local presbyter from Livias (we had asked him to leave his home and accompany us because he knew the area so well) asked us, "Would you like to see the water that flows from the rock, which Moses gave to the children of Israel when they were thirsty? You can if you have the energy to turn off the road at about the sixth milestone." At this we were eager to go. We turned off the road at once, the presbyter led the way, and we followed him. It is a place with a tiny church under a mountain—not Nebo, but another one not very far from Nebo but further in. A great many monks lived there, truly holy men of the kind known here as ascetics.

The holy monks were good enough to receive us very hospitably, and welcomed us indoors. Going in with them we joined them in prayer, and they then very kindly gave us the "blessings" which it is normal for them to give to those whom they entertain. Between the church and the cells was a plentiful spring which flowed from the rock, beautifully clear and with an excellent taste, and we asked the holy monks who lived there about this water which tasted so remarkably good. "This," they told us, "is the water which holy Moses gave the children of Israel in this desert." As usual we had there a prayer, a reading from the Books of Moses, and one psalm.

Theodoret of Cyrrhus, *A History of the Monks of Syria*

Theodoret (ca. 393–ca. 466) is a well known figure in the history of Syrian Christianity. He gave away his property and took on the religious life. He was known as a wise and generous person. He compiled this record of the monastics of northern Syria during the fourth and fifth centuries which provides a window into their practices, spirituality and common life. Several practical aspects of hospitality are singled out. In the first selection, attention to detail is recognized. In the next one, Theodoret identifies the monk Abraham's hospitality through his having beds ready for whatever strangers appeared, preparing delicious food for them and sharing fellowship at the table.

X. Theodosius
    4. Not least did he attend to looking after guests, entrusting this

charge to men adorned with gentleness and modesty of spirit and possessing love for their neighbor. He himself examined everything minutely, checking to see if each detail was carried out in accordance with the rules laid down. He became so famous as a result of all this that sailors even more than a thousand stades away invoked in danger the God of Theodosius and by naming Theodosius lulled the surge of the sea.

XVII. Abraham

7. While wearing down his body with such labors, he was inexhaustible in the services he rendered to others. For strangers who came a bed was ready, glistening and select rolls were offered, wine of a fine bouquet, fish and vegetables and all the other things that go with them; he himself at midday sat with the diners, offering to each portions of the fare provided, giving goblets to all and bidding them drink, an imitation of his great namesake—I mean the Patriarch—who served his guests but did not dine with them.

Life together of desert monastics was often called "wrestling school" because of its rigorous and demanding discipline for the ascetic life. This reference makes clear that hospitality to guests and the needy was part of that life.

XXX. Domnina

6. As I have said, numerous are the pious wrestling schools of men and women not only among us but also in all Syria, Palestine, Cilicia, and Mesopotamia. In Egypt, it is said, some retreats have five thousand men each, who work and in-between sing hymns to the Master, not only providing themselves with the necessary food out of their labor, but also supplying guests who come and are needy.

John Rufus, The Life of Holy Peter the Iberian

Peter the Iberian (ca. 409–488), originally from Georgia, was a pilgrim himself to the Holy Land. With other ascetics, he welcomes pilgrims to holy places and feeds them. This was a crucial ministry of hospitality without which many might not have survived.

As they were living by themselves and still had some money left out of what they had brought from Constantinople, they decided to perform good works by welcoming and refreshing the pilgrims and poor folk who came from all sides to pray at the Holy Places. They laid in a supply of provisions, and invited in pilgrims in such numbers that it often happened that they had ten tables in one day, especially on high feasts.

Julianus Pomerius, The Contemplative Life

The balance of spiritual discipline with generous hospitality is echoed in Julianus Pomerius (fl. ca. 500) in his instruction on monastic hospitality penned around 500. Pomerius discusses both the active and contemplative life and the virtues needed for each. Love or charity, a chief characteristic of hospitality, is the primary rule. One can have love without ascetic practice but not ascetic practice without love. Therefore, hospitality may require one to relax the rules ("unbending myself") in order to be in hospitable fellowship.

Chapter 24. It is often beneficial to place hospitality to visitors before fasting or abstinence.

1. We should, however, do our abstaining and fasting in such a manner that we do not put ourselves under the necessity of fasting or abstaining; otherwise, we shall be doing an optional thing under constraint rather than out of piety. If, for instance, interrupting my fast, I give refreshment to some visitors, I do not break my fast, but I fulfill a duty of charity. Again, if by my abstinence I sadden my spiritual brethren, who I know derive enjoyment from my unbending myself, my abstinence should be called not a virtue but a vice because continued abstinence and fasting, unless interrupted when occasion requires, actually makes me vainglorious and saddens my brother, whom charity requires me to serve; and it certainly shows that I have no fraternal charity. For charity alone without abstinence makes any Catholic perfect; and abstinence without the addition of charity either brings about the ruin of all or perishes itself.

Life of the Blessed Bishop Fulgentius

When Fulgentius (ca. 467–532) first entered upon the religious life in the late fifth century, this young African tried to remain anonymous, but his learning and erudition were evident. He was persuaded to stay with Eulalius, bishop of Syracuse, in Sicily. He received ample hospitality, and, as guest, became host, devoting himself to the care of strangers, as a way to learn spiritual discipline. His practices of hospitality included receiving strangers and supplying them with food.

The blessed Fulgentius, heeding the salutary counsel of the bishop and laying aside the fervor of his original intention, let himself be persuaded to stay in Siracusa for a few months, with the holy Eulalius supplying fitting lodging and meals. But, because strong characters cannot remain idle, always carrying on the works of charity, even in the very modest quarters he had accepted, he began to offer hospitality to many who came; still a stranger himself, needing the assistance of others, he took in strangers. The holy Eulalius marveled at the freedom which blossomed in his soul, and, expanding with happiness as he saw Fulgentius, to whom, as one who had nothing, he supplied food for each day, himself giving something to eat to those in need. And, if it may be said, the great are accustomed to grow by comparison with the lesser, although the holy Eulalius was altogether perfect in dealing with the poor, still, watching the activities of the blessed Fulgentius, he became still more merciful and generous.

Joshua the Stylite, Chronicle

The famine and plague of Edessa in 500/501 is well attested in ancient literature. Though little is known of Joshua, this account from ca. 507 gives the vivid details of destitution and lament across the land and some idea of how Christians responded. The courts of the church and the xenodochia *were full of sick and dying. Acts of hospitality included care for the sick, prayers, and removal and burial of the dead.*

The governor blocked up the gates of the colonnades attached to the winter bath and laid down in it straw and mats, and they used to sleep there, but it still wasn't enough room for them all. When the fathers of the city saw this, they too established infirmaries, and many went in and found shelter in them. The Greek soldiers too set up places in which the sick slept, and charged themselves with their expenses. They died by a painful and melancholy death and though many of them were buried every day, the number still went on increasing. For a report had gone forth throughout the province of Edessa, that the Edessenes took good care of those who were in want. As a result, a countless multitude of people entered the city. The bath too that was under the Church of the Apostles, beside the Great Gate, was full of sick people, and many dead bodies were carried forth from it every day. All inhabitants of the city were careful to attend in a body the funeral of those who were carried forth from the *xenodocheion* (guest house), with psalms and hymns and spiritual songs that were full of the hope of the resurrection. The women too were there with bitter weeping and loud cries. And at their head went the diligent shepherd Mar [Father] Peter and with them too was the governor, and all the nobles. When these were buried, then every one came back, and accompanied the funeral of those who had died in his own neighborhood. And when the graves of the *xenodocheion* and the Church were full, the governor went forth and opened the old graves that were beside the church of Mar Kona, which had been constructed by the ancients with great pains, and they filled them. Then they opened others, and even those were not enough for them, and at last they opened any old grave, no matter what, and filled it. For more than a hundred bodies were carried out every day from the *xenodocheion*, and many a day a hundred and twenty, and up to a hundred and thirty from the beginning of the latter Teshri [November] until the end of Adar [March]. During that time nothing could be heard in all the streets of the city except weeping over the dead or the lamentable cries of those in pain. Many too were dying in the courts of the Great Church, and in the courts of the city and in the inns. And they were dying also on the road, as they were coming to enter the city. In the month of Shebat [February] too the shortages were very great, and the pestilence increased. Wheat was sold at the rate of thirteen kabs for a dinar and barley eighteen kabs. A pound of meat was a hundred numia, and a pound of fowl three hundred numia, and an egg forty numia. In short there was a dearth of everything edible.

There were public prayers in the month of Adar [March] on account of the pestilence, that it might be restrained from the strangers [*xenioi*], and the people of the city, while interceding on their behalf, resembled the blessed David when he was saying to the Angel who destroyed his people, "If I have sinned and have done perversely, wherein have these innocent sheep sinned? Let your hand be against me and against my father's house."

Benedict of Nursia, *Rule*

Benedict (ca. 480–ca. 550) is often considered the father of western monasticism, having established a monastery at Monte Cassino ca. 525. While based on earlier rules the **Rule of St. Benedict** *spread throughout the west where it set the monastic ideal. Chapter 53 of the Rule provides an exceptional description of receiving guests in which Benedict offers a step-by-step instruction for the practice of hospitality, from the manner of meeting guests to the prayer and kiss of peace to foot washing and separate lodging.*

Chapter 53. On the Reception of Guests.

Let all guests who arrive be received like Christ, for He is going to say, "I came as a guest, and you received me." And to all let due honor be shown, especially to the domestics of the faith and to pilgrims.

As soon as a guest is announced, therefore, let the Superior or the brethren meet him with all charitable service. And first of all let them pray together, and then exchange the kiss of peace. For the kiss of peace should not be offered until after the prayers have been said, on account of the devil's deceptions.

In the salutation of all guests, whether arriving or departing, let all humility be shown. Let the head be bowed or the whole body prostrated on the ground in adoration of Christ, who indeed is received in their persons.

After the guests have been received and taken to prayer, let the Superior or someone appointed by him sit with them. Let the divine law be read before the guest for his edification, and then let all kindness be shown him. The Superior shall break his fast for the sake of a guest, unless it happens to be a principal fast day which may not be violated. The brethren, however, shall observe the customary feasts. Let the Abbot give the guests water for their hands; and let both Abbot and community wash the feet of all guests. After the washing of the feet let them say this verse: "We have received Your mercy, O God, in the midst of Your temple."

In the reception of the poor and of pilgrims the greatest care and solicitude should be shown, because it is especially in them that Christ is received; for as far as the rich are concerned, the very fear which they inspire wins respect for them.

Let there be a separate kitchen for the Abbot and guests, that the brethren may not be disturbed when guests, who are never lacking in a monastery, arrive at irregular hours. Let two brethren capable of filling the office well be appointed for a year to have charge of this kitchen. Let them be given such help as they need, that they may serve without murmuring. And on the other hand, when they have less to occupy them, let them go out to whatever work is assigned them.

And not only in their case but in all the offices of the monastery let this arrangement be observed, that when help is needed it be supplied, and again when the workers are unoccupied they do whatever they are bidden.

The guest house also shall be assigned to a brother whose soul is possessed by the fear of God. Let there be a sufficient number of beds made up in it; and let the house of God be managed by prudent men and in a prudent manner.

On no account shall anyone who is not so ordered associate or converse with guests. But if he should meet them or see them, let him greet them humbly, as we have said, ask their blessing and pass on, saying that he is not allowed to converse with a guest.

Chapter 36 of the Rule *focuses attention to the physical needs of the sick through restorative acts of hospitality.*

Chapter 36. On the Sick Brethren.

Before all things and above all things, care must be taken of the sick, so that they will be served as if they were Christ in person; for He Himself said, "I was sick, and you visited Me," and, "What you did for one of these least ones, you did for Me." But let the sick on their part consider that they are being served for the honor of God, and let them not annoy their brethren who are serving them by their unnecessary demands. Yet they should be patiently borne with, because from such as these is gained a more abundant reward. Therefore the abbot shall take the greatest care that they suffer no neglect.

For these sick brethren let there be assigned a special room and an attendant who is God-fearing, diligent and solicitous. Let the use of baths be afforded the sick as often as may be expedient; but to the healthy, and especially to the young, let them be granted more rarely. Moreover, let the use of meat be granted to the sick who are very weak, for the restoration of their strength; but when they are convalescent, let all abstain from meat as usual.

The Abbot shall take the greatest care that the sick be not neglected by the cellarer or the attendants; for he also is responsible for what is done wrongly by his disciples.

Procopius, Buildings of Justinian

Justinian, Emperor from 527 to 565, included among his vast building projects hospices and hospitals. We learn of his building program from Procopius's careful documentation (ca. 560). This brief excerpt tells us that beyond the structure itself, the services of medical personnel and medicines were provided as well to the sick poor. These practical acts of mercy offered a place of hospitality to the poor who were not likely to be welcome elsewhere in society.

Book II Mesopotamia

X. Thus did the Emperor Justinian reconstruct the walls of Antiochia. He also rebuilt the entire city, which was burnt by the enemy. . . . Moreover, he made provision for the sick poor in that place, and built dwellings for them, separate for the different sexes, in which they were supplied with attendants, and the means of curing their diseases. At the same time he established hospices for strangers who might be staying for any time in the city.

Gregory the Great, *Epistle 56 to Peter, Subdeacon**

Gregory the Great (ca. 540–604) was a wealthy young Roman who sold all he had and gave the money to the poor. He turned to monastic life, found success in several leadership positions in the church and eventually became Pope. His correspondence gives valuable information on the conduct of church affairs in the sixth century. In this letter, Gregory instructs a subdeacon to distribute money and food to the poor for the dedication of the Oratory of the Blessed Mary. Christian festivals and ceremonies were occasions of hospitality to those who might be left out if not attended to. The consecration of sacred space required acts of inclusion and generosity.

Being exceedingly desirous of observing the festivals of saints, we have thought it needful to address this our letter of direction to your Experience. We want to inform you that we have arranged for the dedication of the Oratory of the Blessed Mary recently built in the cell of brothers where the abbot Marinianus presides, which will be conducted with all solemnity and with the help of the Lord, in the month of August, so that what we have begun may, through the Lord's operation, be completed. But, inasmuch as the poverty of that cell requires that we should assist in that day of festival, we therefore desire you to give for celebrating the dedication, to be distributed to the poor, ten coins in gold, thirty jars of wine, two hundred lambs, two area of oil, twelve sheep, and a hundred hens, which may be afterwards charged in your accounts. Provide, therefore, for this to be done at once without any delay, that our desires, God granting it, may take speedy effect.

Gregory the Great, *Epistle 62, To Januarius,*
*Archbishop of Caralis in Sardinia**

Gregory instructs a leader, this time an archbishop, in the practices of hospitality. He tells Januarius, Archbishop of Caralis, to take up the cause of a widow, Catella, offering her protection and justice. The particular act of hospitality here involves restoring justice in social and economic terms.

If our Lord Himself by the testimony of Holy Scripture declares Himself to be the husband of widows and father of orphans, we also, the members of His body, ought with the soul's supreme affection to set ourselves to imitate the head, and saving justice, to stand by orphans and widows if need be. We have been given to understand that Catella, a religious woman who has a son serving here in the holy Roman Church over which we preside under God, is being troubled by the exactions and molestations of certain persons. Therefore, we think it needful to exhort your Fraternity by this letter not to refuse to afford your protection to this same woman, knowing that by things of this kind you both make the Lord your debtor and bind us to you the more in the bonds of charity. For we wish the causes of the aforesaid woman, whether now or in future, to be taken care of by your judgment, that she may be relieved from the annoyance of legal proceedings, and yet by no means be excused from submitting to a just judgment. Now I pray the Lord to direct your life in a prosperous course towards Himself, and Himself to bring you in His mercy to the kingdom of glory that is to come.

*Gregory the Great, Epistle 33, To Anthemius, Subdeacon**

Particular hospitality is warranted in the case of converted Jews who may find themselves alienated from the Jewish community, yet not fully accepted in the Christian community. Here Gregory designates orphaned Jewish children to receive money from church accounts.

Those whom our Redeemer vouchsafes to convert to himself from Judaism we ought, with reasonable moderation, to help. Otherwise, as God forbid should be the case, they would suffer from lack of food. Accordingly we charge you, under the authority of this order, not to neglect to give money every year to the children of Justa, who is of the Hebrews, namely, to Julianus, Redemptus, and Fortuna, beginning from the coming thirteenth Indiction. Further, know that the payment is by all means to be charged to your accounts.

Gregory the Great, *Epistle 35, To Anthemius, Subdeacon**

To the same subdeacon Gregory writes regarding captives and paying their ransom, a Christian duty and act of hospitality to those in bondage. He tells Anthemius to redeem not only freemen who have been captured, but slaves as well, even if their masters cannot pay for their release. Beyond that, the subdeacon is to learn about each captive, his name, occupation and home, ostensibly for their rehabilitation. Finally, Gregory encourages Anthemius to negotiate a moderate price if he can.

How great is our grief, and how great the affliction of our heart, from what has taken place in the regions of Campania we cannot express. But you can see for yourself from the great scope of the calamity. With regard to this state of things, we send your Experience by the magnificent Stephen, who brings these presents, money for the relief of the captives who have been taken, warning you that you give your whole attention to this business, and vigorously carry it out. In the case of freemen whom you know don't have enough means to ransom themselves, immediately redeem them. But, should there be any slaves, and you find that their masters are so poor that they cannot come forward to redeem them, don't hesitate to recover them, too. Similarly, be sure to redeem the slaves of the Church who have been lost by your neglect. Further, whomsoever you have redeemed, by all means be at pains to make out a list, containing their names, and a statement of where each is staying, and what he is doing, and where he came from. Bring that list with you when you come. Moreover, quickly show yourself so diligent in this business that those who are to be redeemed may incur no risk through your negligence, or else you will come afterwards to be highly culpable before us. But work especially for this also, that, if possible, you may be able to recover those captives at a moderate price. Set down in writing, with all clearness and nicety, the whole sum expended, and give us your written account with speed. The month of May, Indiction 14.

John Moschos, *Spiritual Meadow*

In the Spiritual Meadow *John Moschos (ca. 550–619) chronicles the hospitality of desert fathers and the spiritual wisdom they imparted. In this account, acts of hospitality on the road from Jericho to Jerusalem, an arduous and steep climb, focus on the needs of travelers and strangers.*[6] *This elder carries packs or children, repairs worn shoes, supplies clothing, water and food, and even buries the dead.*

There was an elder living at the Cells of Choziba and the elders there told us that when he was in his home village, this is what he used to do. If ever he saw somebody in his village so poor that he could not sow his own field, then, unknown to the man who worked that land, he would come by night with his own oxen and seed—and sow his neighbor's field. When he went into the wilderness and settled at the Cells of Choziba this elder was equally considerate of his neighbors. He would travel the road from the holy Jordan to the Holy City Jerusalem carrying bread and water. And if he saw a person overcome by fatigue, he would shoulder that person's pack and carry it all the way to the holy Mount of Olives. He would do the same on the return journey if he found others, carrying their packs as far as Jericho. You would see this elder, sometimes sweating under a great load, sometimes carrying a youngster on his shoulders. There was even an occasion when he carried two of them at the same time. Sometimes he would sit down and repair the footwear of men and women if this was needed, for he carried with him what was needed for that task. To some he gave a drink of the water he carried with him and to others he offered bread. If he found anyone naked, he gave him the very garment that he wore. You saw him working all day long. If ever he found a corpse on the road, he said the appointed prayers over it and gave it burial.

Leontius, *Life of St. John the Almsgiver*

John the Almsgiver (fl. ca. 611) was patriarch of Alexandria in the early seventh century. His charity and hospitality were legendary. When refugees from Syria begin pouring into Alexandria, John takes his case to the clergy so that they will be first to offer hospitality. Further, he builds poorhouses and hostels and provides for their maintenance. When Jerusalem itself is pillaged, John sends the resources of his diocese to ransom captives and for war relief so that even his enemies are impressed by his generosity.

At that time the Persian armies invaded and laid waste the whole country of the Syrians, and the inhabitants of all the towns there came in great numbers with bishops and other clergy and governors and sought refuge in Alexandria. In the greatness of his mind and the generosity of his purpose he supported them all liberally, supplying most abundantly each one's necessities.

When he learned that some of the bishops staying in Alexandria were in need, he summoned the richer members among the leading clergy and when he had brought them together he exhorted them with many counsels and then laid down that they all, and he himself first of all, should pay one pound of gold a year to their poverty-stricken colleagues.

He made a similar arrangement for the needy priests and deacons and the rest of the clergy of the Church, freely granting to each in every rank a certain sum of gold yearly corresponding to the particular labor of his own station so that his wants might be satisfied.

In addition to this he built a great many poorhouses and hostels for strangers, and he decreed that all the corn and all the necessary expenditure for the feeding of their inmates should be paid for from the revenues of the Church.

After Rasmoizan the governor, or rather the general-in-chief, of Chosroes, King of the Persians, had demolished all the holy places of Jerusalem, the news of this wickedness came to the ears of the thrice blessed Patriarch. When he heard of this horrible insolence and learned that all the holy things had been committed to the flames, then just as though he had been an inhabitant of the places which had suffered thus he sat down and made lament. . . .

And on receiving this news of this disaster he sent a man, dearly loved of God, Cresippus by name, and at that time in charge of the monasteries of the Ennaton, to view the destruction of the holy places in Jerusalem. And by his hands he sent a large sum of money and an abundance of corn, wine, oil and pulse; also garments for laymen and for monks; and for the sick various kinds of eatables, and finally, a great many beasts of burden for the distribution of these necessaries. He not only took much thought for those who had been captured in the towns but he took measures with great care for those from the monasteries who had suffered a similar fate, and especially for the women from the convents. A number of the latter had been done to death by the Persians and about a thousand of the nuns were captured, so John sent a large sum of money to ransom them and then he restored them all, settling them in convents.

The Persian governors heard of John's surpassing liberality and boundless sympathy—for certainly he was most appropriately named "the Almsgiver"—and therefore they were very eager to see him—for even an enemy respects a man's virtue—and they offered money to Dion, who was governor at that time, if he would make it possible for them to see him.

Besides all this, John sent Theodore, bishop of Amathus, to rescue those who had been taken prisoners by the Medienians, and with him Anastasius, abbot of the mount of the great Antony, and Gregory, bishop of Rhinocoroura; by their help he effected the rescue of very many captives, both men and women, whom he redeemed by paying large sums of gold.

Sometimes the practice of hospitality requires that members of the community be held in check out of concern that they might exert or even abuse their power and thereby undermine hospitality to those seeking justice. The beloved John, bishop of Alexandria, finds that he must restrain his own disciplinary officials in order to welcome the vulnerable.

On another occasion the thrice-blessed found out that some who had been wronged by those who had gone to law with them and wished to appeal to the Patriarch were prevented from so doing through fear of the ushers and the disciplinary officials and the rest of his retinue. So he devised the following plan which was pleasing unto God.

Every Wednesday and Friday he had a seat and two stools placed in the open in front of the church and there he sat in company with a few virtuous men, or with the gospel in his hands and allowed no member of his great retinue to approach him except one disciplinary official. He was anxious to give confidence and ready access to those who wished to consult him, and on their behalf he caused justice to be done immediately by the disciplinary officials, and he used to order the latter not to touch food until they had settled the matter.

Antony of Choziba, *The Life of Saint George of Choziba*

This Life *tells of strict desert spirituality in the early 600s in Judea. The monastery at Choziba sat on the road from Jerusalem to Jericho, attracting pilgrims and other travelers. It is interesting to think about the demands that hospitality might place on a guest. In many religious communities, guests are kept separate from the community for the protection of both. In others, guests are included in daily tasks, trained for jobs and asked to help with the tasks of living. This account from the life of George of Choziba (ca. 570), written by Antony of Choziba ca. 630, gives an example of the latter, as strangers or guests are asked to help cut firewood for the year.*

[T]hey would cut at one time [the firewood] they needed for the whole year and would call together to help both the monks from their cells and, if they could also help out, some others who were not monks [*xenoi*].

Hospitality to visitors included not only baking bread but also the upkeep of cisterns and transport of water, essential to sustaining common life in the Judean monasteries.

The old man used to ask [the] cellarers . . . not to do the baking without him. For he said that it was an especially great reward to do such work in this holy place, for most of the bread was consumed by visitors. He also took on the ministry of the cisterns that were along the road to Jericho . . . and work along with the gardeners too and willingly perform each ministry. He was eagver to show great cooperation concerning the monastery's work on behalf of visitors, not only on account of the reward but also because he was eager and wished to be an example for the brothers.

Visigothic Code

The Visigothic laws are a compilation of the codes of Justinian and Theodosius as well as earlier oral Visigothic laws written in the fifth century. Produced about 650, this incorporates both Roman jurisprudence and emerging ecclesiastical law. Offering hospitality raised sticky legal questions when fugitives were involved. If a fugitive sought sanctuary in a church, what were Christians to do? Was hospitality required under those circumstances? This law provides some protection for those seeking sanctuary and enjoins clerics to ensure them safety from injury at least and to negotiate their pardon at most.

Book IX. IV. A Debtor, or a Criminal, Cannot Be Forcibly Removed from a Church, and Must Pay Such Debts, or Penalties, as Are Due.
  No one shall presume to seize a person who seeks sanctuary in a church, or at its doors. However, he may petition a priest or a deacon to restore said person to him. If a debtor or a criminal takes refuge there, and he should not be liable to the penalty of death, the

ecclesiastic in charge of the church may interpose his good offices, and request that said party be pardoned or discharged. If a debtor should take refuge in a church, the church shall have no right to protect him but the priest or deacon must surrender him, without delay, with the admonition that his creditor shall neither injure nor enslave him who claimed the right of asylum. The creditor must state, in the presence of said priest or deacon, within what time he shall expect the payment of the debt. Just because the intervention of the church may be invoked for purposes of mercy, is not a reason why persons should be deprived of their property.

Bede, *Ecclesiastical History of the English People*

In his account of John, abbot of the monastery at Tours, the church historian Bede (673–735) reports that John went to see Benedict in Britain under the pope's orders to teach the monks there how to chant and read in the Roman manner. Along the way, Bede tells us that offering hospitality could include providing escorts for companionship and safety for traveling guests.

As he was returning to his own land, not long after he had crossed the Ocean, he was attacked by illness and died. Because of his great affection for St. Martin over whose monastery he presided, his body was taken by his friends to Tours and honorably buried there. He had been hospitably entertained by the church in that place on his way to Britain and had been earnestly asked by the brothers to take that road on his return to Rome and to stay at the same church. In fact they provided him with men to accompany him on his journey and to assist him in his appointed task. Though he died on the way, nevertheless the testimony of the English to the catholic faith was carried to Rome and most gladly received by the pope and by all those who heard it or read it.

Bede, *The Life of St. Cuthbert*

Monastic hospitality set the ideal and guests were greeted warmly and attentively. Bede conveys this ideal in the following Celtic scene from the life of Cuthbert (d. 687), describing the practice of washing the feet of guests upon their arrival, usually with warm water in a footbath. This was always an act of hospitality performed by the abbot or a monk, never by a servant. Here the foot washing is reciprocated by guests to host.

Now when this same dwelling-place and these chambers had been built with the help of his brethren, Cuthbert the man of God began to dwell alone. At first, indeed, he used to go forth form his cell to meet the brethren who came to him, and to minister to them. And when he had devoutly washed their feet in warm water, he was sometimes compelled by them to take off his shoes and to allow them to wash his feet.

Boniface, *Correspondence: Bishop Daniel of Winchester Gives Wynfrith a Letter of Introduction (718)*

The letters of Boniface (680–754), who spent his career as a missionary in Germany, and his correspondents, tell of the comings and goings of ecclesiastics in the eighth century. Hospitality was essential, not only to ecclesiastics, but to all travelers. Here is a letter of introduction given by a bishop to one of his priests to remind potential hosts of their duty. Bishop Daniel specifies the importance of receiving travelers with a warm welcome.

To godly and merciful kings, all dukes reverend and beloved bishops, priests and holy abbots and to all the spiritual sons of Christ, Daniel, a servant of the servants of God.

Though the commandments of God should be observed by all the faithful with sincerity and devotion, Holy Scripture lays special stress on the obligation of offering hospitality to travelers and shows how pleasing to God is the fulfilment of this duty. As a reward for his kindly hospitality, Abraham was judged worthy of receiving the blessed angels in person and of enjoying their holy converse. Lot also on account of this same service was snatched from the flames of Sodom.

So it will redound to your eternal welfare if you extend to the bearer of this letter, Wynfrith, a holy priest and servant of almighty God, a warm welcome such as God loves and enjoins. In receiving the servants of God you receive Him whom they serve, for he promised, "He who receives you, receives me."

Pope Gregory II Commends Bishop Boniface to the Christians of Germany (722)

Because Boniface was charged with converting Germany to Catholic Christianity, hospitality was to be extended to him and his work. The Pope here instructs Christians about what that hospitality entails, including providing escorts for Boniface's travel, food and shelter, and whatever else he needs. The Pope reminds them of the identification of the apostles with Christ.

> We exhort you, then, for the love of our Lord Jesus Christ and the reverence you bear to His apostles, to support him by all the means at your disposal and to receive him in the name of Jesus Christ, according to what is written of His disciples: "He who receives you, receives me." See to it that he has all he requires; give him companions to escort him on his journey, provide him with food and drink and anything else he may need, so that with the blessing of God the work of piety and salvation committed to him may proceed without hindrance, and that you yourselves may receive the reward of your labors and through the conversion of sinners may find treasure laid up for you in heaven.

Pope Gregory II Replies to Questions Put by Boniface (726)

This letter suggests that the question of how to welcome those carrying contagion had arisen in Christian communities. Pope Gregory responds matter-of-factly.

> Lepers who belong to the Christian faith should be allowed to partake of the body and blood of the Lord, but they may not attend sacred functions with people in good health. In the case of a contagious disease or plague attacking a church or monastery you ask whether those who have not been infected may escape danger by flight. We declare this to be utterly foolish; no man can escape the hand of God.

Letter to the Archbishop Egbert of York

Finally, this brief sentence from Boniface to the Archbishop of York says worlds about hospitality and the servant leadership of the archbishop.

> I am sending also a cloak, and a towel to dry the feet of the brethren after you have washed them.

Eigil, *The Life of St. Sturm*

Most correspondence traveled by private messenger in the ancient world. Messengers, therefore, became a class of travelers, in a sense, who were both strangers and guests. While one might not know the person bearing the message, the messenger was usually a representative of a personal relation or acquaintance, though not always. When the bishop Boniface corresponded with Sturm (d. 779), the abbot of the monastery at Fulda, Sturm gives instructions to his community for hospitality to the messenger. Such acts include showing kindness, offering food at the table and thanking the messenger for his work. This biography was written by Eigil, a monk at Fulda who had worked with Sturm.

"I give thanks to God that so great a bishop should be mindful of my lowly self and should deign to send his messenger to me in this wilderness." Then calling his brethren to him, he commanded them to show all kindness to the messenger. Carefully carrying out his behest, they set a table before him and offered him such food as they had; and when he had eaten, the brethren asked his leave to withdraw. Then the man of God summoned the messenger, thanked him for his labor and said: "Greet the holy bishop Boniface in the name of his servants and say that I will hasten to him as quickly as I can." Then he blessed him and allowed him to return.

Rudolph, *The Life of Saint Leoba*

Leoba (d. 779) helped Christianize western Europe and was considered a spiritual adept of her age. She was the abbess of Bischofsheim near Mainz and was advisor to bishops and kings. This biography, written by a monk of Fulda in the early 800s and based on written and oral accounts of those who knew her, identifies several acts of hospitality, particularly foot washing and an "open door" policy.

She preserved the virtue of humility with such care that, although she had been appointed to govern others because of her holiness and wisdom, she believed in her heart that she was the least of all. This she showed both in her speech and behavior. She was extremely hospitable. She kept open house for all without exception, and even when she was fasting gave banquets and washed the feet of the guests with her own hands, at once the guardian and the minister of the practice instituted by our Lord.

Willibald, *Instructions*

This guidebook is based on the life and pilgrimage of St. Willibald (700–786) in the eighth century, as recorded by an English woman who had listened to Willibald's own accounts. Pilgrims, like all travelers, were at risk for being taken captive for ransom, or being imprisoned or enslaved. Willibald and his companions, when imprisoned on accusations of spying, were mercifully treated by an unknown merchant, a stranger offering hospitality to strangers. In this case, the acts of hospitality were giving alms for their relief, sending food, taking them for baths and taking them to church.

At that time there were seven companions with Willibald and he made the eighth. . . . But when they arrived there [Jerusalem], the governor said at once that they were spies and ordered them to be thrust into prison until such time as he should hear from the king what was to be done with them. Whilst they were in prison they had an unexpected experience of the wonderful dispensation of Almighty God, who mercifully deigns to protect his servants everywhere, amidst weapons of war and tortures, barbarians, and soldiers, prisons and band of aggressors, preserving and shielding them from all harm. A man was there, a merchant, who wished to redeem them and release them from captivity, so that they should be free to continue their journey as they wished. He did this by way of alms and for the salvation of his own soul. But he was unable to release them. Every day, therefore, he sent them dinner and supper, and on Wednesday and Saturday he sent his son to the prison and took them out for a bath and then took them back again. Every Sunday he took them to church through the market place, so that if they saw anything on sale for which they had a mind he could buy it for them and so give them pleasure.

Habits That Foster the Practice of Hospitality

The virtue and practices of hospitality do not emerge automatically in most communities. They must be cultivated. Might there be spiritual disciplines and communal habits that foster a spirit of hospitality? Early Christian communities that valued the practices of hospitality also valued the practice of spiritual disciplines that oriented them to their identity as Christians, to the recognition of Christ in the stranger, and to the spiritual economy that gave meaning to the institutional forms and practices they developed.

These excerpts demonstrate some of the internal habits that helped communities cultivate hospitality. Early Christians recognized that hospitality could not be extended to those outside the community if it was not practiced within the community. Attention to hospitality in worship, in dealing with the wayward, in receiving persecuted and exiled Christians, and in resolving internal conflicts, set a tone and an atmosphere that promoted the continuity of hospitality in all aspects of communal life.

Pseudo-Clementine, *Epistle of Clement to James**

This letter, composed between 200 and 250, calls Christians to a common table as a way to ensure the rule of love. The tradition of potluck dinners in Christian communities is tied to the experience and expression of hospitality.

Clement to James, the Lord, and the bishop of bishops, who rules Jerusalem, the holy church of the Hebrews, and the churches everywhere excellently surrounded by the providence of God, with the elders and deacons, and the rest of the brethren, peace be always. . . . But I know that you will do these things if you fix love into your minds. There is only one fit way to accomplish this, namely, the common partaking of food. Therefore see to it that you are frequently one another's guests, as often as you can, so that you may not fail to do it. For it is the cause of well-doing, and well-doing is the cause of salvation. Therefore all of you present your provisions in common to all your brothers and sisters in God, knowing that, giving temporal things, you shall receive eternal things. Much more feed the hungry, and give drink to the thirsty, and clothing to the naked. Visit the sick, be there for those who are in prison, help them as you are able, and receive strangers into your houses with all eagerness. However, rather than go on and on, remember that philanthropy will teach you to do everything that is good, as misanthropy suggests ill-doing to those who will not be saved.

Pseudo-Clementine, *Homily 3**

This sermon encourages Christians to gather frequently in community in order to build up the body of Christ so that virtue may be lived. Fellowship is a wellspring for mercy and hospitality.

But if you love your brothers and sisters, take nothing from them, but share with them whatever you have. Feed the hungry, give drink to the thirsty, clothe the naked, visit the sick. So far as you can, help those in prison, receive strangers gladly into your own abodes, hate no one. And how you must be pious, your own mind will teach you, judging rightly. But before all else, if indeed I even need say it to you, come together frequently, if it were every hour, especially on the appointed days of meeting. For if you do this, you are within a wall of safety. For disorderliness is the beginning of ruin.

Cyprian, *Letter 14*

Cyprian (d. 258), bishop of Carthage is in hiding when he writes to the presbyters and deacons ca. 250 to be sure to look after the needs of the confessors, Christians who have confessed Christ even under persecution or torture. Their lives could be virtually ruined by financial loss and social ostracization, so these brothers and sisters in Christ, champions of the faith, warranted special care when released from prison. Much more difficult will be the question of what to do with those who could not hold fast under persecution.

To the glorious confessors likewise you must devote especial care. I know that very many of them have been supported by the devotion and charity of our brethren. Nevertheless there may be some in need of clothing or provisions; they should be supplied with whatever is necessary, as I also wrote to you previously when they were still in prison.

Cyprian, *Letter 21*

This letter in Cyprian's correspondence is from Celerinus in which he, too, addresses special care for confessors. In this case, the confessors have been forced to flee their homes and are refugees newly arrived in Carthage. We learn here that some Christian women have met them, taken them home, and given them refuge and hospitality on behalf of the Christian community in Carthage.

I must tell you that I am not the only one to put this request on their behalf, but Statius and Severianus do so as well, and indeed all the confessors who have come here from where you are. To meet them my sisters have gone down to the harbor in person and have escorted them up to the city, they have seen to the needs of sixty-five and have looked after them in every way right up to the present time. All of them are in their care.

But there is no need for me to burden further that holy heart of yours, for I know how eager you are to do works of charity.

Cyprian, *Letter 57*

During a time of systematic persecution of Christians in North Africa, the church struggled mightily with what to do with the "lapsed," those Christians who succumbed to pressure and performed the acts of sacrifice required by the state. After some discussion and prayer, a group of bishops writes the letter below in 252, to report a change in policy. Whereas before these penitents were only admitted to communion on their deathbed, the lapsed may now be admitted to communion as long as they have been serious and consistent penitents. As the bishops anticipate another round of persecution, they want to gather in every soldier for the coming battle.

Some time ago, dearly beloved brother, we had determined, after sharing mutual counsel together, that those who had been tripped up by the Enemy during the hostilities of the persecution, had fallen and defiled themselves with forbidden sacrifices, should continue to do full penitence for a long time; but should they be seized by a dangerous illness, they might receive reconciliation at the very point of death. For neither was it right nor did the compassion and clemency of God our Father allow us to shut the Church against those who knocked or to deny the support which comes with the hope of salvation to those who sorrowed and supplicated; as they departed from this world they should not, therefore, be sent on to the Lord deprived of reconciliation and communion.

But as things are now, we can see that the day is once again beginning to draw near bringing in a second outbreak of hostilities; we have been receiving repeated warnings and frequent signs that we should be armed and be prepared ourselves for the warfare which the Enemy is declaring upon us, that by our exhortations we should be preparing also the people God has deigned to entrust to our care, and that we should be gathering inside the Lord's encampment every soldier of Christ, without exception, all who are eager for arms and cry out for battle.

Given no choice by this crisis, we have decreed the reconciliation is to be granted to those who have never forsaken the Church of the Lord but who have continued to do penitence, mourning and entreating the Lord, without ceasing, right from the very first day of their fall, and that they ought to be armed and equipped for the now imminent battle.

Basil, *The Long Rules*

Basil (330–379) is concerned in this instruction to ensure the community deals with internal conflicts and corrections of one another. It is important to Basil that fair and clear mechanisms are in place so that problems are addressed and not ignored. This allows the community to turn its attentions outward rather than being preoccupied with the inevitable wrangling that can sap a community of its life.

Q. 49. Of controversies in the community.

R. Now, with regard to disputes which arise among the brethren: Whenever certain individuals are in disagreement on any matter, they should not contend with one another in a wrangling spirit, but refer the settlement to those who are more competent than they. Nevertheless, so that good order may not be disturbed by everyone constantly submitting his problems and so that there may arise no occasion for levity or foolishness, some one approved person should be empowered either to refer the disputed point to the community for general consideration or to bring it to the attention of the superior. In this way, the investigation of the question will be more fittingly and more intelligently carried on, for knowledge and experience are nowhere more essential than in matters of this kind. If no workman would entrust the use of his tools to unskilled persons, it is far more important to restrict the use of words to those who will be able to discern competently the proper time, place, and method of questioning, and who, by disputing reasonably and without rancor and by listening intelligently can make accurate contributions toward solving the problem unto general edification.

Basil, *Liturgy*

One way Christians keep the virtue of hospitality present in a community is through the discipline of prayer. The liturgy of St. Basil used in the Orthodox tradition includes intercession for the sick, the traveler, the widow, and the poor. Intercessory prayer is itself one way of offering hospitality to the other as one spiritually welcomes the needs of the other and lifts them up. This liturgy shows a keen awareness of the vulnerability of those traveling and those in need.

The Intercession for the Sickness of the Body and the Malady of the Soul

Priest: Again let us pray to God Almighty, the Father of our Lord and Savior Jesus Christ. We entreat and implore Thy Goodness, O Thou Lover of mankind, to be mindful of those who are sick among Thy people.

Deacon: Pray for our fathers and brethren who are sick, whether they are here or there, that our God, Jesus Christ, may grant them and us the blessing of recovery, and forgive our sins.

People: Lord have mercy.

Priest: Extend, O Lord, Thy mercy and compassion to them and heal them.

Take away, O Lord, from them and from us too all traces of sickness and infirmity.

Those who are still sick, O Lord, grant them recovery. Those who are afflicted by evil spirits, O Lord, do Thou release them.

Those who are in prison, dungeon, exile or captivity, O Lord, do Thou set them free and have mercy upon them.

For Thou untiest the manacled and upliftest the fallen.

Thou art the Hope of the dejected and the Support of the helpless, the Comforter of the weak-hearted and the Harbor of the storm-tossed.

Grant, O Lord, Thy mercy unto the oppressed souls, grant them peace, coolness, grace, support, and salvation. Forgive their sins and their pitfalls.

As for us, O Lord, cure the malady of our souls and the sickness of our bodies.

Thou the eternal and true Physician of our souls and bodies, the Prelate of all flesh, accord us Thy salvation.

People: Lord have mercy.

The Intercession for Travelers

Priest: We beseech Thee, O Lord, Thou great Lover of mankind, to be mindful of our fathers and brethren the travelers.

Deacon: Pray for our fathers and brethren the travelers at any part of the world. Make their passage easy, O Lord, whether by sea, river, lake, land or any other means that our Lord Jesus Christ may bring them home safely and forgive our sins.

People: Lord have mercy.

Priest: Those who intend to travel, O Lord, make their passage also easy whether by sea or land. Bring them back to the haven of peace—the haven of safety.

Accompany them on embarkation and all the way. Bring them

back home with rejoicing and good health. Share the work of thy servants in every good deed.

As for us, O Lord, keep us upright through the period of this estrangement without harm, without stormy violence and without worry unto the end.

People: Lord have mercy.

Serapion, *Prayer Book*

This collection of prayers from Egypt date around 350 C.E., compiled by Serapion who was bishop in the area. This excerpt, like the one from the liturgy of St. Basil, reflects the discipline of intercessory prayer that keeps before the community the most vulnerable people and their needs by lifting them up to God.

We pray thee, O God of compassion, for freemen and slaves, males and women, old men and children, poor and rich; display to all thine own special good, and stretch forth on all thine own special loving-kindness; have compassion on all and grant to all to turn to thee. We beseech thee for those who are traveling from home, grant them an angel of peace as their fellow-traveler, that they may receive no hurt from any one, that they may finish their voyage and their travels in much cheerfulness.

We beseech thee for those who are afflicted and in bonds and in poverty; give rest to each, free them from bonds, bringing them out of poverty; comfort all, thou who art the comforter and consoler.

We pray for the sick, grant them health and raise them up from their sickness, and make them to have perfect health of body and soul; for thou art the Savior and benefactor, thou art the Lord and King of all.

We have besought thee on behalf of all through thy only-begotten son Jesus Christ, through whom to thee is the glory and the strength in the Holy Spirit both now and to all the ages of the ages. Amen.

Macarius, *Homily 3*

Macarius's Fifty Spiritual Homilies *convey what some call his "intoxication with God." This homily addresses the difficulties faced when perceptions of status and power differ among community members. Macarius (300s) encourages the monks in his community to deal with each other in love and respect the work of each brother, regardless of its nature. A spirit of humility and appreciation for each other lends itself to cultivating practices of hospitality.*

The brethren should conduct themselves toward one another with the greatest love, whether in praying or reading Scripture or doing any kind of work so that they may have the foundation of charity toward others. And thus their various tasks or undertakings may find approval with those who pray and those who read and those who work, all can conduct themselves toward each other in sincerity and simplicity to their mutual profit. . . .

The brethren, therefore, regardless of what work they are doing, ought to conduct themselves toward each other in love and cheerfulness. And the one who works should say of him who is praying: "I also possess the treasure which my brother possesses since it is common." And let him who prays say of him who reads: "What he gains from reading redounds also to my advantage." And he who works let him thus say: "The work which I am doing is for the common good." For as the members of the body, being many, are one body and help each other while each still performs its own function, as the eye sees for the whole body and the hand labors for all the members and the foot walks, sustaining all the members and another member suffers with all the others, so also the brethren should be among themselves.

Thus he who prays should not judge the one working because he is not praying. Neither should he who works condemn the one praying because he is resting while he himself is at work. But let each one do whatever he is doing for the glory of God.

John Chrysostom, Homily 66 on John*

John Chrysostom (ca. 347–407) was bishop in Constantinople and a great theologian of his day. He challenged Christians to lead a rigorously moral life. As he closes this sermon on the Gospel of John, he reminds the community that internal disputes can distract from the real work of the gospel. He refers to ongoing debates and "a labyrinth of words," turning attention instead to the practices of hospitality.

Therefore, so that we may not delay you, nor wind together a labyrinth of words, leaving these things we will bid you to hold fast to listening to the Holy Scriptures, and don't fight with words to no purpose. As also Paul exhorts Timothy, filled though he was with much wisdom, and possessing the power of miracles. Let us now obey him, let go of trivial things and hold fast to real works. By that I mean hold fast to brotherly kindness and hospitality; and let us make much account of alms-giving, that we may obtain the promised good things, through the grace and loving-kindness of our Lord Jesus Christ, to whom be glory for endless ages. Amen.

The Lives of the Desert Fathers

Known as the Historia Monachorum *(ca. 400) this is a remarkable account of the spiritual practices of the desert fathers and mothers in the fourth and fifth centuries. The practice of hospitality extended both inside and outside their communities. Early Christians pointed out this correspondence, identifying patterns of internal hospitality that form notions of hospitality beyond the community. The monks at Nitria went so far as to build the cells, or living quarters, of new members, as the following recounts.*

XX. The Monks of Nitria

10. If there were many who came to him wishing to be saved, he called together the whole community, and giving bricks to one, and water to another, completed the new cells in a single day. 11. Those who intended to live in the cells were invited to the church for a feast. And while they were still enjoying themselves, each brother filled his cloak or his basket with loaves or other suitable things from his own cell and brought them to the new ones, so that no one should know which gifts had been brought by which brother. When those who were to live in the cells returned to them in the evening, they were surprised to find everything that they needed.

The story is also told of Macarius sharing grapes with a brother he thought more needful of them than himself, only to receive the grapes after they had made the rounds of the entire community, each monk considering another more needful.

XXIII. Macarius of Alexandria

One day someone gave Saint Macarius a bunch of grapes, and he, thinking not of himself but others, sent them to another brother whom he thought was more delicate than himself. Then the recipient gave thanks to God for his brother's gift, but he likewise did not think of himself but of others and sent them to someone else, and this one to the next, and thus they passed through all the cells which are scattered about in the desert far from each other, each recipient ignorant of the original sender; at last they were returned to him who had first sent them away, Saint Macarius marveled to see in the brethren such self-control and such brotherly love and he continued with more vigor his own attempts at the life of the spirit.

Benedict, Rule

In this well-known rule (ca. 540) for common life, instructions for receiving a stranger monk are set out. The patterns of hospitality to associates set a tone and pattern for the practice of hospitality to outside groups.

Chapter 61. How Pilgrim Monks Are to Be Received.

If a pilgrim monk coming from a distant region wants to live as a guest of the monastery, let him be received for as long a time as he desires, provided he is content with the customs of the place as he finds them and does not disturb the monastery by superfluous demands, but is simply content with what he finds. If, however, he censures or points out anything reasonably and with the humility of charity, let the Abbot consider prudently whether perhaps it was for that very purpose that the Lord sent him.

If afterwards he should want to bind himself to stability, his wish should not be denied him, especially since there has been opportunity during his stay as a guest to discover his character.

But if as a guest he was found exacting or prone to vice, not only should he be denied membership in the community, but he should even be politely requested to leave, lest others be corrupted by his evil life.

If, however, he has not proved to be the kind who deserves to be put out, he should not only on his own application be received as a member of the community, but he should even be persuaded to stay, that the others may be instructed by his example, and because in every place it is the same Lord who is served, the same King for whom the battle is fought. . . .

Let the Abbot take care, however, never to receive a monk from another known monastery as a member of his community without the consent of his Abbot, or a letter of recommendation; for it is written, "Do not to another what you would not want done to yourself."

Leontius, Life of St. John the Almsgiver

John (fl. ca. 611), known as the Almsgiver for his extraordinary generosity, was highly regarded during his time as bishop of Alexandria.

Champion of the poor, advocate for justice, John would not tolerate church officials bullying parishioners or bureaucrats abusing power. Neither would he tolerate gossip among his associates. Here we learn that John tried to promote the discipline of holy conversation that requires the practice of self-control. Gossip and slanderous conversation work against the creation and maintenance of a hospitable environment wherein people are neither ridiculed nor slandered. Conversely, godly conversation can promote a spirit of hospitality and welcome.

18. This saintly man had also a good knowledge of the holy Scriptures, not so much an accurate knowledge of the words through learning them by heart (which is but for vainglory), but by actually practicing their precepts and keeping their commandments. If you looked in at his council-room any day, there was no idle word spoken—unless he was engaged in the settlement of some civic matter—but only stories of the holy fathers, or scriptural questions or dogmatic problems due to the multitude of unmentionable heretics who swarmed in the country. If perchance someone began slanderous gossip, the Patriarch, like a wise man, would courteously turn him of it by starting another subject, but, if the gossiper persisted, he said nothing more at the time but would point him out to the doorkeeper and tell him never again to admit him with those that came to consult the Patriarch; in this way the others were taught through him to practice self-control.

John's life also teaches that virtue, in this case, generosity to others, cannot be coerced. A community can lift up the virtue of hospitality, but if acts of virtue are coerced then they are not authentic and therefore, not virtuous.

27. One day this blessed Patriarch went to visit the poor in the quarter called Caesareum—for there he had had some very long vaulted buildings erected; the floor was covered with wooden boards and mats and rough rugs were provided. Here the poor could sleep during the winter months. Accompanying the Patriarch was a certain bishop, a lover of money and of a most unsympathetic disposition. To him the blessed Patriarch said: "Give Christ's brethren a little present, brother Troilus," for that was his name, for somebody had whispered to the Patriarch that the bishop's attendant was carrying thirty pounds of gold at that moment in order to buy a set of

engraved silver for the bishop's table. The bishop, reverencing the Patriarch's word and more probably momentarily quickened in soul thereby, ordered the man carrying the thirty pounds of gold to give a nomisma to each of the brethren sitting there. In this way the large quantity of gold was quickly spent.

After the Patriarch and the bishop Troilus had both returned to their own residences, the latter, who had performed this act of charity, so to speak, against his will, was seized by unreasoning and soul-destroying anxiety over the money which had been distributed, and as an outcome of his miserliness and pitilessness and change of mind a fit of shivers came over him accompanied by an unnatural feverishness. In consequence of this unexpected illness he straightway took to his bed. When the servant came from the most holy Patriarch inviting him to lunch, he excused himself saying that from some cause or other he had an attack of ague. On receipt of this message the Patriarch at once recognized that it was owing to his having given away those thirty pounds that the involuntary giver was ill, for we have already said Troilus was extremely avaricious and unsympathetic.

John could not bear that he himself should be waited on at table while the other lay in torments in his bed, so in his utter want of arrogance he quickly went to him and with a smile on his face said to him: "You must forgive me, brother Troilus, for you imagine that I was serious when I asked you to give that large amount to our poor brethren, but let me tell you, I only said it in jest. For I wanted to give each of them a nomisma for the holy feast and as my purse-bearer had not a sufficient sum with him, I borrowed it from you, and now see, here are your thirty pounds!"

Hardly had the bishop seen the money in the venerable hand of this true physician and shepherd before the fever suddenly disappeared and the shivering ceased, and his ordinary strength and color returned so that there was no concealing the fact that the money was the cause of his sudden indisposition.

Notes

1. Julianus Pomerius, *The Contemplative Life*, trans. by Sister Mary Josephine Suelzer, *Ancient Christian Writers: The Works of the Fathers in Translation*, no. 4 (New York: Newman Press, 1947), paragraph 24.

2. Welcome is a central theme in the gospel of Luke-Acts and, according to John Koenig, is fundamentally tied to the mission of the church. See pp. 110-120.

3. For treatment of the pivotal image of feast and feeding in New Testament, see Koenig, pp. 15-57.

4. Chrysostom had become entangled in political and theological disputes during his time as bishop of Constantinople, enduring exile when the Empress Eudoxia and his opponent Theophilus, bishop of Alexandria, prevailed in their efforts to discredit him. Palladius reports the fierce conflict that ensued when Theophilus expelled a group of Nitrian monks in 402 from his see on the grounds that they held Origenist doctrine which Theophilus himself had condemned at the Council of Alexandria in 400. The monks sought refuge under Chrysostom's protection in Constantinople and he offered them hospitality as the episcopal office required. Theophilus denounced Chrysostom's reception of the exiled monks, successfully bringing charges against Chrysostom at the Synod of Oaks (403). For an insightful analysis of this controversy see Susanna Elm, "The Dog That Did Not Bark: Doctrine and Patriarchal Authority in the Conflict Between Theophilus of Alexandria and John Chrysostom of Constantinople" in *Christian Origins: Theology, Rhetoric, and Community*, ed. by Lewis Ayres and Gareth Jones (London and New York: Routledge, 1998).

5. For further information on Egeria and her diary see Hagith Sivan, "Holy Land Pilgrimage and Western Audiences: Some Reflections on Egeria and Her Circle," *Classical Quarterly* 38 (ii) 528-535 (1988); Hagith Sivan, "Who Was Egeria? Piety and Pilgrimage in the Age of Gratian," *Harvard Theological Review*, vol. 81, Jan 88, pp. 59-72; Egeria, *Travels to the Holy Land*, trans. John Wilkinson, rev. ed. (Jerusalem: Ariel Publishing House, 1981).

6. The road from Jericho to Jerusalem was some fifteen miles and makes a dramatic ascent from the lowest land on the earth's surface, four hundred feet below sea level, near the Dead Sea, to mountains eight hundred feet above sea level.

Bibliography

Ambrose. "Three Books on the Holy Spirit, To the Emperor Gratian." In *Selected Works and Letters,* translated by the Rev. H. De Romestin, the Rev. E. De Romestin and the Rev. H. T. F. Duckworth. *Nicene and Post-Nicene Fathers of the Christian Church.* Edited by Philip Schaff and Henry Wace. 2nd ser. New York: Christian Literature Company, 1893, X:95.

Antony of Choziba. *The Life of Saint George of Choziba and the Miracles of the Most Holy Mother of God at Choziba.* Translated by Tim Vivan and Apostolos N. Athanassakis. San Francisco: International Scholars Publications, 1994, 46, 56-57.

Augustine. "Tractate 58." In *Tractates on John,* translated by the Rev. John Gibb and the Rev. James Innes. *Nicene and Post-Nicene Fathers of the Christian Church.* Edited by Philip Schaff. 1st ser. New York: The Christian Literature Company, 1888, VII:306-07.

Basil. "Letter 94." In *Letters and Select Works,* translated by the Rev. Blomfield Jackson. *Nicene and Post-Nicene Fathers of the Christian Church.* Edited by Philip Schaff and Henry Wace. 2nd ser. New York: The Christian Literature Company, 1895, VIII:178-80.

_____. *The Liturgy of St. Basil.* Translated by Fayek M. Ishak. Toronto: Coptic Orthodox Church, 1973, 30-32.

_____. *The Long Rules.* Translated by Sister M. Monica Wagner. The Fathers of the Church. Volume 9. Reprint by Daughters of St. Paul. Boston, Massachusetts, 1963, 1:50-54, 2:55-56, 57.

Bede's Ecclesiastical History of the English People. Translated by Bertram Colgrave and R.A.B. Mynors. Oxford: Clarendon Press, 1969, 391.

_____. "The Life of St. Cuthbert." In *Two Lives of Saint Cuthbert: A Life by an Anonymous Monk of Lindisfarne and Bede's Prose Life,* translated by Bertram Colgrave. New York: Greenwood Press, 1969, 219.

Benedict of Nursia. *The Rule of Saint Benedict.* Translated by Leonard J. Doyle. Collegeville, Minn: Liturgical Press, 1948, 54-55, 72-75, 84-85.

Boniface. *The Correspondence of St. Boniface.* In *The Anglo-Saxon Missionaries in Germany,* edited and translated by C.H. Talbot. New York: Sheed and Ward, 1954, 67, 71, 82, 127.

Commodianus. *The Instructions of Commodianus in Favor of Christian Discipline, Against the God of the Heathens.* Translated by the Rev. Robert Ernest Wallis. *Ante-Nicene Fathers: The Writings of the Fathers Down to A.D. 325.* Edited by Alexander Roberts and James Donaldson. New York: The Christian Literature Company, 1885, IV:217.

Cyprian. "Letter 7." In *The Letters of St. Cyprian of Carthage,* translated and annotated by G. W. Clarke. *Ancient Christian Writers: The Works of the Fathers in Translation,* ed. Johannes Quasten, Walter J. Burghardt, Thomas Comerford Lawler, no. 43. New York: Newman Press, 1967, I:67
_____. "Letter 14," I:88.
_____. "Letter 21," I:105-06.
_____. "Letter 57," III:55-56.
Didache. Translated by Cyril Richardson. The Library of Christian Classics, Vol. 1. New York: MacMillan Publishing, 1970, 176-77.
Dionysius. "Epistle 12 to the Alexandrians." In *Epistles,* translated by the Rev. S. D. F. Salmond. *Ante-Nicene Fathers: The Writings of the Fathers Down to A.D. 325.* Edited by Alexander Roberts and James Donaldson. New York: The Christian Literature Company, 1885, VI:108-09.
Egeria. *Travels to the Holy Land.* Translated by John Wilkinson. Rev. ed. Jerusalem: Ariel Publishing House, 1981, 93-95, 106.
Eigil. *The Life of St. Sturm.* In *The Anglo-Saxon Missionaries in Germany,* edited and translated by C.H. Talbot. New York: Sheed and Ward, 1954, 184-85.
Eusebius. *The Oration of the Emperor Constantine.* Translated by Arthur C. McGiffert and Ernest C. Richardson. *Nicene and Post-Nicene Fathers of the Christian Church.* Edited by Philip Schaff and Henry Wace. 2nd ser. New York: The Christian Literature Company, 1890, I:531, 551-52.
Fulgentius. "Life of the Blessed Bishop Fulgentius." In *Fulgentius: Selected Works,* translated by Robert B. Eno. *The Fathers of the Church: A New Translation.* Vol. 95. Washington, D.C.: The Catholic University of America Press, 1997, 23-24.
Gerontius. *The Life of Melania the Younger.* Translated by Elizabeth A. Clark. *Studies in Women and Religion.* Volume 14. New York: The Edwin Mellen Press, 1984, 32-33.
Gregory the Great. "Epistle 1.56." In *Pastoral Rule and Selected Epistles,* translated with Introduction, Notes and Indices by the Rev. James Barmby, D.D. *Nicene and Post-Nicene Fathers of the Christian Church.* Edited by Philip Schaff and Henry Wace. 2nd ser. New York: The Christian Literature Company, 1894, XII:95.
_____. "Epistle 1.62," XII:96.
_____. "Epistle 4.33," XII:157.
_____. "Epistle 6.35," XII:200.
Gregory of Nyssa. "Homily Concerning Almsgiving." In *The Collected Works of Gregory of Nyssa,* translated by Richard McCambly. *Gregory of Nyssa Homepage.* bhsu.edu/dsa-lomon/nyssa/home.html. Greenwich, Conn.: Great American Publishing Society, 1999.
Jerome. "Preface to the Commentary on Ezekiel." In *Principal Works,* translated by W. H. Fremantle. *Nicene and Post-Nicene Fathers of the Christian Church.* Edited by Philip Schaff and Henry Wace. 2nd ser., vol. VI. New York: The Christian Literature Company, 1893, VI:500.
John Cassian. *Institutes of the Coenobia.* Translated by the Rev. Edgar C. S. Gibson. *Nicene and Post-Nicene Fathers of the Christian Church.* Edited by Philip Schaff and Henry Wace. 2nd ser. New York: The Christian Literature Company, 1894, XI:242-43.
John Chrysostom. "Homily 19 on 2 Corinthians." In *Homilies on 1st and 2nd Corinthians,* translated by the Rev. Hubert Kestell Cornish, the Rev. John Medley and the Rev. J. Ashworth. *Nicene and Post-Nicene Fathers of the Christian Church.* 1st ser. New York: The Christian Literature Company, 1889, XII:369-70.
_____. "Homily 41 on Genesis." In *Homilies on Genesis: Saint John Chrysostom,* Volume 2:18-45, translated by Robert C. Hill. *The Fathers of the Church: A New Translation.* Vol. 82. Washington, D.C.: The Catholic University of America Press, 1988, 406-07.
_____. "Homily 43 on Genesis." *Homilies on Genesis: Saint John Chrysostom,* Volume 2:18-45, translated by Robert C. Hill. *The Fathers of the Church: A New Translation.* Vol. 82. Washington, D.C.: The Catholic University of America Press, 1988, 442.
_____. "Homily 66 on John." In *Homilies on John and Hebrews,* translated by the Rev. G. T.

Stupart. *Nicene and Post-Nicene Fathers of the Christian Church.* 1st ser. New York: The Christian Literature Company, 1890, XIV:247.

_____. "Homily 66 on the Gospel of Matthew." In *Homilies on Matthew,* translated by the Rev. George Provost. *Nicene and Post-Nicene Fathers of the Christian Church.* 1st ser. New York: The Christian Literature Company, 1888, X:407.

_____. "Homily 45 on the Acts of the Apostles." In *Homilies on Acts of the Apostles and the Epistle to the Romans,* translated by the Rev. J. Walker and the Rev. J. Sheppard. *Nicene and Post-Nicene Fathers of the Christian Church.* 1st ser. New York: The Christian Literature Company, 1889, XI:276-77.

John Moschos. *Spiritual Meadow.* Translated by John Wortley. Kalamazoo, Michigan: Cistercian Publications, 1992, 16.

Joshua the Stylite. *The Chronicle of Joshua the Stylite.* Translated by W. Wright. Cambridge: University Press, 1882, 32-34.

Julianus Pomerius. *The Contemplative Life.* Translated by Sr. Mary Josephine Suelzer. *Ancient Christian Writers: The Works of the Fathers in Translation.* Edited by Johannes Quasten and Joseph C. Plumpe, no. 4. New York: Newman Press, 1947, 98.

Leontius. *St. John the Almsgiver.* In *Three Byzantine Saints: Contemporary Biographies Translated from the Greek,* edited by Elizabeth Dawes and Norman H. Baynes. Oxford: Blackwell, 1948, pp. 202-04, 212, 228, 237-38.

The Life of Saint Pachomius and His Disciples. Translated by Armand Veilleus. *Pachomian Koinonia,* Volume 1. Cistercan Studies Series, no. 45. Kalamazoo, Mich.: Cistercian Publications, 1980, pp. 27-28.

The Lives of the Desert Fathers: The Historia Monachorum in Aegypto. Translated by Norman Russell. Kalamazoo, Michigan: Cistercian Publications, 1980, 54-55, 61, 64, 67, 77, 105, 106, 148, 153.

Macarius. "Homily 15." In *Intoxicated with God: The Fifty Spiritual Homilies of Macarius,* translated by George A. Maloney, S.J. Denville, N.J.: Dimension Books, 1978, 37.

Maximus of Turin. "Sermon 34." In *The Sermons of St. Maximus of Turin,* translated by Boniface Ramsey. *Ancient Christian Writers: The Works of the Fathers in Translation.* Edited by Walter J. Burghardt and Thomas Comerford Lawler, no. 50. New York: Newman Press, 1989, 82.

_____. "Sermon 60." In *The Sermons of St. Maximus of Turin,* translated by Boniface Ramsey. *Ancient Christian Writers: The Works of the Fathers in Translation.* Edited by Walter J. Burghardt and Thomas Comerford Lawler, no. 50. New York: Newman Press, 1989, 146.

Palladius. *Dialogue on the Life of St. John Chrysostom.* Translated by Robert T. Meyer. *Ancient Christian Writers: The Works of the Fathers in Translation.* Edited by Johannes Quasten, Walter J. Burghardt and Thomas Comerford Lawler, no. 45. New York: Newman Press, 1985, 46-47.

_____. *Palladius: The Lausiac History.* Translated by Robert T. Meyer. *Ancient Christian Writers: The Works of the Fathers in Translation.* Edited by Johannes Quasten, Walter J. Burghardt and Thomas Comerford Lawler, no. 34. New York: Newman Press, 1964, 40-41, 48-49, 145-46.

Paulinus of Nola. "Letter 24." In *Letters of St. Paulinus of Nola,* translated by P. G. Walsh. *Ancient Christian Writers: The Works of the Fathers in Translation.* Edited by Johannes Quasten, Walter J. Burghardt and Thomas Comerford Lawler, nos. 35-36. New York: Newman Press, 1967, II:53.

_____. "Letter 29." In *Letters of St. Paulinus of Nola,* translated by P. G. Walsh. *Ancient Christian Writers: The Works of the Fathers in Translation.* Edited by Johannes Quasten, Walter J. Burghardt and Thomas Comerford Lawler, nos. 35-36. New York: Newman Press, 1967, II:113.

Procopius. *Buildings of Justinian.* Translated by Aubrey Stewart. *The Library of the Palestine*

Pilgrims' Text Society. Vol. II. London: Committee of the Palestine Exploration Fund, 1897, 70-71.

Pseudo-Clementine. "Epistle to James." In *Epistles and Writings*, translated by the Rev. B. P. Pratten. *Ante-Nicene Fathers: The Writings of the Fathers Down to A.D. 325*. Edited by Alexander Roberts and James Donaldson. New York: The Christian Literature Company, 1885, VIII:218, 220.

_____. "First Epistle Concerning Virginity." In *Epistles and Writings*, translated by the Rev. B. P. Pratten. *Ante-Nicene Fathers: The Writings of the Fathers Down to A.D. 325*. Edited by Alexander Roberts and James Donaldson. New York: The Christian Literature Company, 1885, VIII:59-60.

_____. "Homily 3.69." In *Epistles and Writings*, translated by the Rev. B. P. Pratten. *Ante-Nicene Fathers: The Writings of the Fathers Down to A.D. 325*. Edited by Alexander Roberts and James Donaldson. New York: The Christian Literature Company, 1885, VIII:251.

Rudolph. *The Life of Saint Leoba*. In *The Anglo-Saxon Missionaries in Germany*, translated by C. H. Talbot. New York: Sheed and Ward, 1954, p. 216.

Rufus, John. *The Life of the Holy Peter the Iberian*, in *Lives and Legends of the Georgian Saints*, translated by David Marshall Lang. 2d ed. London: Mowbrays, 1976, 66-67.

Serapion. *Prayer Book*. Translated by John Wordsworth. Rev. ed. London: Society for Promoting Christian Knowledge, 1923, 91.

Sulpitius Severus. *Dialogues of Sulpitius Severus*. Translated by the Rev. Alexander Roberts. *Nicene and Post-Nicene Fathers of the Christian Church*. Edited by Philip Schaff and Henry Wace. 2nd ser. New York: The Christian Literature Company, 1894, XI:25-26.

_____. *The Life of Saint Martin*. Translated by the Rev. Alexander Roberts. *Nicene and Post-Nicene Fathers of the Christian Church*. Edited by Philip Schaff and Henry Wace. 2nd ser. New York: The Christian Literature Company, 1894, XI:16.

Tertullian. "To His Wife." Translated by the Rev. S. Thelwall. *Ante-Nicene Fathers: The Writings of the Fathers Down to A.D. 325*. Edited by Alexander Roberts and James Donaldson. New York: The Christian Literature Company, 1885, IV:46, 48.

Theodoret of Cyrrhus. *A History of the Monks of Syria*, translated by R. M. Price. Kalamazoo: Cistercian Publications, 1985, 90, 122-23, 188.

Visigothic Code. Translated by S. P. Scott. Boston: The Boston Book Company, 1910, p. 332.

Willibald. *Instructions*. In *The Anglo-Saxon Missionaries in Germany*, translated by C. H. Talbot. New York: Sheed and Ward, 1954, 162.

CHAPTER SIX

BUILDING A PLACE OF HOSPITALITY: FORMS OF INSTITUTIONALIZATION

Practices of hospitality, whether performed by individuals or groups, were embedded in Christian community. As Christianity became even more structured in the fourth century we see the rise of Christian institutions under the authority of the state. Basilicas were built throughout the empire, the church increasingly owned property and participated in civil governance. Early Christian sources show that many practices of hospitality became institutionalized, that is, Christians enacted the virtue of hospitality through establishing institutions to care for the stranger, the poor, the sick. Some practices of hospitality were regularized through sets of guidelines. Other practices were assigned to particular officers to ensure they were performed. A close look at the fourth century in particular demonstrates the movement from informal to formal practices of hospitality. Institutions, such as hospices, hospitals, and almshouses, whose missions focused on hospitality, emerge as dominant forces by the early fifth century.[1] Early Christianity devoted substantial resources to these institutions, their leadership and their maintenance. Three sets of excerpts that offer a window into the rise of institutional forms of hospitality are included here.

The first section focuses on references to physical buildings or spaces intended for needs of vulnerable populations. The rise of the *xenon*, a building for lodging travelers and strangers, can be seen in the fourth century. We will also find references to poorhouses, orphanages, hospitals, and old-age homes. The second section looks at references to various offices associated with these institutions. These sources offer descriptions of characteristics of office holders as well as duties related to hospitality both in its institutional forms and its less formal expressions. Concerns about proper administration of offices, such as the *xenodochos* or guest master, the guardian of the poor, and the orphanage director, give evidence that these institutions had standing within the church and required the attention of ecclesiastical leaders.

Third, evidence of the institutionalization of practices of hospitality can be found in sets of rules and codes related to those practices. In the second century, the *Didache* sets out guidelines about how many days to lodge traveling evangelists. Later, instructions and codes develop regarding how to receive guests, how to treat the poor, and when hospitality should not be extended. Rules related to practices of hospitality are frequently found within monastic life. These three sorts of evidence, then, buildings, offices, and rules, document the institutional forms that served to codify hospitality within Christianity.

Buildings

Indicative of the central place of hospitality in early Christianity are the many reports of institutions which emerged to address the needs of the stranger, the poor, and the sick. We will look at specific references from early Christian sources regarding buildings used for practices of hospitality. Of course, the first locus of hospitality within the earliest Christian communities was the house church. The New Testament model of the *ecclesia* centered on the house church that gathered for worship and fellowship. It provided the axis for Christian life well into the third century. Paul praises the leaders in whose homes early Christians met. Hospitality, then, was built into the very earliest institutional experiences of Christian life.[2]

Within a generation of Constantine, hospices built and run by Christians began to dot the landscape of the empire. A place for housing strangers, the *xenon*, could be found in many major cities, particularly in the east. The rise of poorhouses, orphanages, old age homes, *xenones*, and hospices can be traced from the mid-300s to the mid-500s when some began to complain that these hospitable institutions were in disrepair and required renovations.

The Emperor Justinian (483–565) spent state revenues on extensive rebuilding for *xenones* and hospitals, as well as for churches and their peripheral buildings, municipal works, and improved roads to ensure travelers' safety.

An explanation is necessary here about vocabulary.[3] The word for stranger or guest is *xenos*, from which the words *xenon* and *xenodocheion* are derived. *Xenon* can be translated variously as home for strangers, hospital, hospice, hostel, or guest house. This can be confusing as a *xenon* can refer to a home for travelers or to a home for the sick. In Constantinople, for instance, Procopius tells us that Justinian and Theodora built several *xenones* for visitors to the city who had no place to stay or could not afford lodging.[4] By the fifth century it was customary in the ancient world for monasteries and churches, particularly those in cities, to have some sort of *xenon* or place for visitors, rich or poor, attached to the building or nearby.

Moreover, in the Byzantine world, a hospital that offered treatment of all sorts of illnesses as well as surgery was usually called a *xenon*.[5] *Xenones* were often staffed with physicians and nurses and could be a place of convalescence. A *xenodocheion*, on the other hand, refers to a guesthouse for guests, strangers, and pilgrims. Because travelers were likely to have ailments or contract disease, a *xenodocheion* could easily include medical care.[6]

Other institutions incorporating practices of hospitality included homes for the aged, for lepers, and for the poor. A *gerocomeion* was a home for the elderly who may or may not be destitute. A *nosocomeion* was a home for the sick or a hospital. A *leprocomion* or leprosarium was a hospital for lepers. A *ptocheion* or *ptochotropheion* was a home for the poor and destitute. Sometimes the *ptochotropheion* was particularly for the poor who could not work due to illness or disability. By the fourth century, porticoes or courts of churches were commonly used by the sick, the dying, and the destitute for refuge. See Palladius's account below of Ephraem using church porticoes to care for the starving and the sick.

It was not uncommon for a *xenon* to accommodate more than one vulnerable population. Just as there was certainly overlap in the populations that were poor, sick, foreigners, or travelers, so the institutions that served them often blended several functions. An institution that housed the sick was likely to house many of the poor and an institution that housed strangers was very likely to house some of the sick.

Two other institutions in early Christianity became locations for the expression of hospitality. A *laura* or *lavra* was a type of monastic community formed by a collection of solitary hermits who live in separate cells and gather only for liturgy. The *cenobium* or community was a monastery with a common life, shared meals, work and religious practice. A desert ascetic would generally begin spiritual training in a *cenobium* before moving to the more austere and difficult life in a *laura*.[7] Both the *laura* and the *cenobium* were sites of hospitality. Excerpts are in approximate chronological order.

Basil, *Letter 94**

Basil (330–379), writing to the governor of the province, Elias, is concerned to clear up any misgivings Elias may have about Basil or his ministry. Dated around 372 C.E. this letter describes a developed system of offering hospitality to strangers and the sick. The hospitality offered here is institutionalized through a building for strangers, medical treatment by doctors and nurses, training for gainful employment, and even escorts and transportation for those needing it.

Now I would like those who are besieging your impartial ears to be asked what harm the government suffers from me? What depreciation is suffered by any public interests, whether small or great, by my administration of the Churches? I suppose it might be argued that I have done damage to the government by building a magnificently appointed church to God, and round it dwellings, one liberally assigned to the bishop, and others underneath, allotted to the officers of the Church in order, the use of both being open to you who are civil servants and your escort. But whom do we harm by building a place of hospitality for strangers, both for those who are on the road and for those who need medical treatment on account of sickness? A way of giving them the comfort they want, the doctors, nurses, transportation and escort? All these people must learn such skills as are necessary to make a living and have been found essential to long-term employment. They must also have buildings suitable for their skills, all of which are an honor to the place, and, as their success is credited to our governor, confer glory on him. . . .

But if, before we get a chance to meet, you are driven by the pleadings of some people's slander to give up any of your good will towards me, do as Alexander did. The story is, as you remember, that, when one of his friends was being slandered, he left one ear open to the slanderer, and carefully closed the other with his hand, with the object of showing that the one whose duty is to judge ought not to be easily and wholly given over to the first occupants of his attention, but should keep half his hearing open for the defense of the absent.

Basil, Letters 142, 143*

In these two letters to accountants, Basil (330–379) refers to hospitals and the administration of funds for the poor. In the first letter, Basil reports a hospital for the poor that he encourages the accountant to exempt from taxation. In the second letter to another accountant, Basil refers to at least two different hospitals, one specifically for the poor. Chorepiscopi *were rural bishops appointed to help the urban bishop carry out the duties of a large diocese. The canons of Nicea in 325 were signed by fifteen* chorepiscopi.[8]

Letter 142

I assembled all my brethren the *chorepiscopi* at the synod of the blessed martyr Eupsychius to introduce them to your excellency. Because you did not attend, they must be brought before you by letter. Know, therefore, this brother as being worthy to be trusted by your intelligence, because he fears the Lord. As to the matters on behalf of the poor, which he refers to your good-will, deign to believe him as one worthy of credit, and to give the afflicted all the aid in your power. I am sure you will consent to look favorably upon the hospital of the poor which is in his district, and exempt it altogether from taxation. It has already seemed good to your colleague to make the little property of the poor not liable to be rated for taxes.

Letter 143

Had it been possible for me to meet your excellency I would have in person brought before you the points about which I am anxious, and would have pleaded the cause of the afflicted, but I am prevented by illness and by press of business. I have therefore sent to you in my stead this *chorepiscopus,* my brother, begging you to give him your aid and use him and to take him into counsel, for his truthfulness and wisdom qualify him to advise in such matters. If you are so good as to inspect the hospital for the poor, which is managed by him, (I am sure you will not pass it without a visit, experienced as you are in the work, for I have been told that you support one of the hospitals at Amasea out of the substance wherewith the Lord has blessed you), I am confident that, after seeing it, you will give him all he asks. Your colleague has already promised me some help towards the hospitals. I tell you this, not that you may imitate him, for you are likely to be a leader of others in good works, but that you may know that others have shown regard for me in this matter.

Gregory of Nazianzus, *Oration 43, Panegyric on Saint Basil**

Thanks to Gregory (329–389), we have another description of the "new city," a hospice for lepers established by Basil of Caesarea in the mid 300s. This panegyric, written ca. 380, gives us not only the fact of an establishment that extended hospitality to the sickest of the sick, but a description of its services and the people who sought them.

What more? A noble thing is philanthropy, and the support of the poor, and the assistance of human weakness. Go forth a little way from the city, and behold the new city, the storehouse of piety, the common treasury of the wealthy, in which the overabundance of their wealth, yes, and even their necessities, are stored. Due to his encouragements, their donations are freed from the power of the moth, no longer gladdening the eyes of the thief, and escaping both the ambition of envy, and the corruption of time. There is no longer before our eyes that terrible and piteous spectacle of men who are living corpses, the greater part of whose limbs have decayed, driven away from their cities and homes and public places and fountains, indeed, and from their own dearest ones, recognizable by their names rather than by their features. They are no longer brought before us at our gatherings and meetings, in our common interaction and union, no longer the objects of hatred, instead of pity on account of their disease, composers of piteous songs, if any of them have their voice still left to them. Why should I try to express in tragic style all our experiences, when words cannot express their hard lot? However he [Basil] took the lead in pressing upon those who had humanity, that they should not despise their fellow human beings, nor dishonor Christ, the one Head of all, by their inhuman treatment of them. Rather, they should use the misfortunes of others as an opportunity of firmly establishing their own lot, and to lend to God that mercy of which they stand in need at His hands. He did not disdain to honor with his lips this disease, even though he had a brilliant reputation and was of noble ancestry himself. He saluted them as kindred, not, as some might assume, from self-righteousness (for who was so far removed from this feeling?). No, he took the lead in going to tend them on account of his beliefs, and so gave instruction not only by his words but also by his actions. The effect produced is to be seen not only in the city, but in the country and beyond, and even the leaders of society have vied with one another in their philanthropy and magnanimity towards them. Others have had their cooks, and splendid tables, and the devices and dainties of confectioners, and exquisite carriages, and soft, flowing robes. Basil's care was for the sick, and the relief of their wounds, and the imitation of Christ, by cleansing leprosy, not by a word, but in deed.

Epiphanius, Panarion

Epiphanius was chosen bishop of Salamis in Cyprus in 366. This panarion, *or medicine chest, written ca. 374, is intended as a remedy for the many unhealthy sects and ideas current in his day. While Epiphanius is intent on showing Aerius as a heretic, an "Arian to the hilt," in the process he also explains to us the place and function of the* ptochotropheion *or almshouse as an established and recognizable institution for the sick and the disabled in fourth century Christianity.*

Aerius is still alive in the flesh and remains in the world, an Arian to the hilt. His doctrines do not differ from those of Arius, and he has pushed his speculations even further than Arius did, sharpened his tongue, and armed his lips with a view to drawing to himself an army of people deceived and a crowd of those whose ears are always itching and whose intellect is slack. 4. For indeed he gave to the world a great, fabulous inanity of a doctrine, a cause of laughter to those with sense, although through it he deceived and drew apart many. 5. He was a fellow student of Eustathius of Sebaste, a place in Pontus or Armenia Minor. For Eustathius and Aerius led the ascetical life together. 6. But when Eustathius was promoted to the episcopacy, Aerius desired it even more, but did not attain it. Hence jealousy arose, but Eustathius apparently remained devoted to Aerius, 7. for immediately afterward he ordained him a presbyter and entrusted to him the hospice, which in Pontus is called a *ptochotropheion*. For the heads of the churches provide such places out of hospitality, and there they give lodging to the injured and infirm and provide for their needs as far as they can.

Jerome, *Letter 66**

Among Jerome's (ca. 342–420) vast correspondence is this letter written in 397 to Pammachius, a Roman senator who had renounced his rank and privilege to become a monk. In addition, Pammachius established a hospice for strangers at Portus which Jerome highlights. He takes the opportunity to comment on his own attempts in this regard as well. Jerome sold holdings in Italy in order to provide hospitality to strangers in Bethlehem. The pattern of building xenodocheia *suggests that not only emperors and empresses established institutions of hospitality.*

I hear that you have erected a hospice for strangers at Portus and that you have planted a twig from the tree of Abraham upon the Ausonian shore. Like Aeneas you are tracing the outlines of a new encampment. Except that he, when he reached the waters of the Tiber, under pressure of hunger had to eat the square flat cakes which formed the tables spoken of by the oracle, while you are able to build a house of bread to rival this little village of Bethlehem wherein I am staying. You propose to satisfy travelers with sudden plenty here after their long privations. Well done.

For my part I am building in this province a monastery and a hospice close by. This way, if Joseph and Mary chance to come to Bethlehem, they will not fail to find shelter and welcome. Indeed, the number of monks who flock here from all quarters of the world is so overwhelming that I can neither stop my enterprise nor bear so great a burden. The warning of the gospel has been all but fulfilled in me, for I did not sufficiently count the cost of the tower I was about to build. Accordingly, I have been constrained to send my brother Paulinian to Italy to sell some old villas which have escaped the hands of the barbarians, and also the property inherited from our common parents. For I am loath, now that I have begun it, to give up ministering to the saints, lest I incur the ridicule of griping and envious people.

Palladius, *Dialogue on the Life of St. John Chrysostom*

Palladius (ca. 363–425), an ascetic and later a bishop, wrote this work on the life of John Chrysostom sometime during 406–408. Its form follows the pattern of the Phaedo *of Plato, offering a platform for the explication of Chrysostom's life, ministry and controversies. Upon Chrysostom's installation as bishop of Constantinople, he set to reforming the see and its administration. This excerpt tells of his establishment of hospitals, especially for strangers, and the good stewardship of funds for them.*

Next he examined closely the accounts of the steward, and he found expenditures that were of no benefit to the church. He ordered all unnecessary spending to be stopped at once. Then he also questioned certain expenses of the episcopal household. Here again he found an over abundance of funds and he ordered the larger portion of them to be shared with the hospital. He built more hospitals and over these he delegated two devout priests in addition to doctors, cooks, and other workers from the unmarried state to look after them. In this way strangers coming from afar to the city and becoming ill could receive proper medical care. This hospital was not only a good venture, but it served for the glory of God as well.

Palladius, Lausiac History

Composed around 419, this record of early monasticism in Egypt is based on firsthand accounts of Palladius's (ca. 363–425) experiences in Egypt, Palestine, Syria, and Asia Minor and is considered by historians to be relatively reliable. It offers stories of the various holy men and women he encountered. Palladius tells of a wealthy virgin who inadvertently offered her resources to help a hospital for the poor, an establishment that had an upper floor for women and a ground floor for men.

Now they say that the blessed Macarius wished to tap a vein of this virgin to alleviate her greed. This Macarius, priest and superior of the poorhouse for cripples, devised the following ruse. In his younger days he had been a worker in stones, what they call a gem engraver. He went to her and said: "Some precious stones, emeralds and hyacinths, have come into my possession; whether they are simply a find or stolen property, I cannot say. Their value has not been ascertained, since they are priceless, but they can be had by anyone who has five hundred coins."

"If you take them, you will get your five hundred coins back from one stone; the rest you can use to pretty up your niece."

Intent on his every word, the maiden took the bait and fell at his feet. "I beseech you," she exclaimed, "do not let anyone else have them." Then he invited her: "Come to my house and see them." She was not willing to wait, however, but threw down the five hundred coins for him, saying: "Take them as you wish, for I do not want to see the man who puts them up for sale."

He took the five hundred coins and gave them for the needs of the hospital. Some time elapsed, and since the man seemed to have a very great reputation in Alexandria, and a love of God, and was charitable (he was active until he was a hundred; we spent some time with him ourselves), well, she was discreet about reminding him. Eventually she found him in the church and asked him: "I beg you, what did you decide about those stones for which I gave you the five hundred coins?"

He said in reply: "Just as soon as you gave me the money I put it down for the price of the stones. If you wish, come and see them in the hospital, for they are there. Come and see if they please you; if they do not, take your money back."

Now the hospital had the women on the upper floor and the men on the ground floor. And leading her he brought her up to the entrance and asked: "What do you want to see first, the hyacinths or the emeralds?"

She replied: "As you please."

He took her to the upper floor, pointed out the crippled and inflamed women, and said: "Look, here are your hyacinths!" And he led her back down again and showed her the men: "Behold your emeralds! If they do not please you, take your money back!"

Turning about then, she left, and going back she became ill from much grief, because she had not done this in God's way.

Palladius also reports that Ephraem the Syrian (306–373) established a hospice for the sick and hungry at Edessa during a famine. Ephraem used the resources of the wealthy to set up an institution of hospitality for the needy.

When a great famine befell the city of Edessa he [Ephraem] had compassion for the whole countryside which was being ravaged, and he went to those who were well-to-do and spoke to them: "Why do you not have pity on the people who are perishing, instead of letting your wealth rot for the condemnation of your own souls?"

They looked about and said: "We have no one whom we should trust to care for those suffering from famine, for all of them make it into a business."

He asked: "How do I seem to you?" For he had a great reputation among them, not for evil, but for good.

They said: "We know that you are a man of God." "Why do you not trust me?" he asked. "Look, I will appoint myself your guest-master."

And he took money and divided up the porticoes, and he put up about three hundred beds and cared for the famished ones. The dead he buried, and he took care of those who had hope of life, and, as a matter of fact, he daily provided refreshment and help to all those who came to him each day because of the famine; and this he did with the money allotted to him.

When the year was over and prosperity followed and they had all gone back home, he had no more to do. He went back to his cell and died within the month. God had given him the chance for a crown at the very end. He left some writings, too, most of which are worthy of attention.

In this brief description of Magna, a devout woman, Palladius refers to hospitals already in existence in Ancyra.

In this same town of Ancyra lived many other virgins, probably two thousand or more. They practiced chastity and were remarkable women indeed. One of them, Magna, was a most revered woman and takes an eminent place among them. She lived a most ascetic and chaste life, keeping her conversation such that even bishops honored her for her excellent piety. She gave money for hospitals, for the poor, and for bishops on pilgrimages, never ceasing from work. She did this in secret through her most trusted servants, and at night she never left the church.

In another story, Palladius cites the hospital as an institution for Christian service. The function of the church porch as a makeshift hospital is evident here when a compassionate monk helps to deliver a baby there.

Also in this very same city we found a monk. So great was his mercy and so kind was he that he went about at night and had mercy on the needy.

He neglected neither the prison nor the hospital, neither the poor nor the rich, but he helped all. To some he gave words of good cheer, being himself stout of heart. Some he encouraged, others he reconciled; to some he gave bodily necessities, to others, clothing. What is wont to happen in all great cities occurred here, too; for on the church porch there was gathered a crowd of people, some unmarried, others married, lying there for their daily food.

It happened one time in winter that a woman was lying in labor on the church porch at midnight. He heard her crying out in pain. Leaving his customary prayers, he went out and looked at her. He found no midwife, but instead took the midwife's place, not at all squeamish about the unpleasant aspects of childbirth, for the mercy which worked in him had rendered him insensible to such things.

The Lives of the Desert Fathers

Not only cities and prominent areas boasted institutions of hospitality. The desert ascetics prized their tradition of hospitality and records show the central place of guests both sacred and secular. A fourth century visitor to the desert recorded (ca. 400) what he heard and saw of these spiritual fathers of the desert, including a report of the guesthouse at a monastery in Thebaid in Egypt. Perhaps especially because rules of enclosure were so strict this community developed a guest house, a specific place to offer hospitality to those who could not enter.

1. In the Thebaid we also visited a monastery belonging to one Isidore, which was fortified with a high brick wall and housed a thousand monks. Within the walls were wells and gardens and all that was necessary to supply the needs of the monks, for none of them ever went out. The gatekeeper was an elder, and he never allowed anyone to go out or to come in unless he wished to stay there for the rest of his life without ever leaving the enclosure. 2. This gate-keeper had a small guest house near the gate where he put up visitors for the night. In the morning he would give them gifts and send them on their way in peace.

Joshua the Stylite, *Chronicle*

In 507 C.E. Joshua chronicled, among other things, the famine and plague of Edessa that had occurred in 500/501. He describes throngs of people wandering the streets, picking at trash and sleeping in doorways. As people began to die of disease, others wasted away from hunger and children were left orphans. In the midst of this tragedy, Joshua tells of the institutions and remarkable ministry of hospitality provided to those sick, starving or dead, including an infirmary attached to the church. His chronicle records the existence of a xenodocheion *and its administrator, the* xenodochos.

XLII. Dead bodies were lying exposed in every street, and the citizens were not able to bury them, because, while they were carrying out the first that had died, the moment that they returned, they found others. By the care of Mar [Father] Nonnus, the *xenodochos*, the brothers used afterwards to go about the city and to collect these dead bodies. And all the people of the city used to assemble at the gate of the *xenodocheion* and go forth and bury them, from morning to morning. The stewards of the Church, the priest Mar Tewath-il and Mar Stratonicus (who some time afterwards was deemed worthy of the office of bishop in the city of Harran), established a hospital among the buildings attached to the Church of Edessa. Those who were very ill used to go in and lie down there; and many dead bodies were found in the infirmary, which they buried along with those at the *xenodocheion*.

XLIII. The governor blocked up the gates of the colonnades attached to the winter bath and laid down in it straw and mats, and they used to sleep there, but it still wasn't enough room for them all. When the fathers of the city saw this, they too established infirmaries, and many went in and found shelter in them. The Greek soldiers too set up places in which the sick slept, and charged themselves with their expenses. They died by a painful and melancholy death and though many of them were buried every day, the number still went on increasing. For a report had gone forth throughout the province of Edessa, that the Edessenes took good care of those who were in want. As a result, a countless multitude of people entered the city. The bath too that was under the Church of the Apostles, beside the Great Gate, was full of sick people, and many dead bodies were carried forth from it every day. All inhabitants of the city were careful to attend in a body the funeral of those who were carried forth from the *xenodocheion*, with psalms and hymns and spiritual songs that were full of the hope of the resurrection. The women too were there with bitter weeping and loud cries. And at their head went the diligent shepherd Mar Peter and with them too was the governor, and all the nobles. When these were buried, then every one came back, and accompanied the funeral of those who had died in his own neighborhood. And when the graves of the *xenodocheion* and the Church were full, the governor went forth and opened the old graves that were beside the church of Mar Kona, which had been constructed by the ancients with great pains, and they filled them. Then they opened others, and even those were not enough for them, and at last they opened any old grave, no matter what, and filled it. For more than a hundred bodies were carried out every day from the *xenonodocheion*, and many a day a hundred and twenty, and up to a hundred and thirty.

XLIV. There were public prayers in the month of Adar [March] on account of the pestilence, that it might be restrained from the strangers *[xenoi]*, and the people of the city, while interceding on their behalf, resembled the blessed David when he was saying to the Angel who destroyed his people, "If I have sinned and have done perversely, wherein have these innocent sheep sinned? Let your hand be against me and against my father's house."

*Sozomen, Ecclesiastical History**

When, in the middle of the fourth century, Julian the Apostate (332–363) became emperor of Rome, he attempted to reinstate traditional pagan religion. In his efforts, Julian encourages his pagan priests to follow the lead of the "Atheists," that is, Christians or Galileans. Julian points to Christians' success in their caring for others, noting hospitals for strangers and the poor. Certainly this was the reputation of many Christians and some institutionalization of practices of hospitality had occurred by Julian's time. Sozomen (fl. ca. 440), the church historian, quotes Julian's letter in this regard.

The emperor was deeply grieved at finding that all his efforts to secure the predominance of paganism were utterly ineffectual, and seeing Christianity excelling in repute. He was particularly chagrined on discovering that the wives, children, and servants of many of the pagan priests had been converted to Christianity. On reflecting that one main support of the Christian religion was the life and behavior of those who professed it, he determined to introduce into the pagan temples the order and discipline of Christianity, to institute various orders and degrees of ministry. He moreover resolved to found monasteries for the accommodation of men and women who desired to live in philosophical retirement, as likewise hospitals for the relief of strangers and of the poor and for other philanthropical purposes. He wished to introduce among the pagans the Christian system of penance for voluntary and involuntary transgressions. But the point of ecclesiastical discipline which he chiefly admired, and desired to establish among the pagans, was the custom among the bishops to give letters of recommendation to those who traveled to foreign lands, wherein they commended them to the hospitality and kindness of other bishops, in all places, and under all circumstances. In this way did Julian strive to ingraft the customs of Christianity upon paganism . . . for I can produce a letter written by the emperor himself on the subject. He writes as follows:

"To Arsacius, High-Priest of Galatia. Paganism has not yet reached the degree of prosperity that might be desired, owing to the conduct of its principal practitioners. The worship of the gods, however, is conducted on the grandest and most magnificent scale, so far exceeding our very prayer and hope. Let our Adrastea be propitious to these words, for no one could have dared to look for so extensive and so surprising a change as that which we have witnessed within a very short space of time. But are we to rest satisfied with what has been already effected? Ought we not rather to consider that the progress of Atheism has been principally owing to the humanity evinced by Christians towards strangers, to the reverence they have manifested towards the dead, and to the misleading seriousness which they have assumed in their life? It is requisite that each of us should be diligent in the discharge of duty. I do not refer to you alone, as that would not suffice, but to all the priests of Galatia.

"You must either put them [pagan priests] to shame, or try the power of persuasion, or else deprive them of their sacred offices, if they do not with their wives, their children, and their servants join in the service of the gods, or if they support the servants, children, or wives of the Galileans in treating the gods impiously and in preferring Atheism to piety. Then exhort the priests not to frequent theaters, not to drink at taverns, and not to engage in any trade, or practice any nefarious art.

"Honor those who yield to your correction, and expel those who disregard it. Establish hospitals in every city, so that strangers from neighboring and foreign countries may reap the benefit of our philanthropy, according to their respective need."

Theophanes Confessor, Chronicle

The Chronicle *represents an ambitious attempt to offer systematic annals not only of the Roman and Byzantine empires but also of Arab domination of the Christian east. This work relies on many other chronologies and histories. It is especially useful here for a careful record of institutions built or refurbished that carry out the practices of hospitality during the fifth and sixth centuries. The pattern of imperial support for such institutions is clear as some are destroyed and rebuilt only to be destroyed again by fire.*

A. D. 452/3. In this year the blessed and pious Pulcheria died in the Lord. She had done many good deeds and left all her possessions to the poor. Marcian [Roman emperor] readily distributed these large amounts. She herself had founded numerous houses of prayer, poor-houses, hostels for travelers, and burial-places for strangers, among which was the church of the holy martyr Laurentius.

A. D. 518/19. With the impious Severus out of the way, Paul, the *xenodochos* of the hospice of Euboulos, was appointed bishop of Antioch. The emperor gave as largesse a thousand pounds of gold to the city of Antioch and provided law and order to the other cities by curbing disturbances among the people.

A. D. 531/2. The porticoes from the arch of the Forum to the Chalke were burned, and also the shops of the silversmiths and the whole palace of Lausos were destroyed by fire. They killed unsparingly the soldiers who attacked them. Then they broke into houses and began to loot their contents. They set fire to the entrance of the palace (the one with the bronze roof), the portico of the *Protectores*, and the senate-house by the Augustaion. The partisan went down to the Julian harbor (I mean that of Sophia), to the palace of Probus in search of weapons, crying "Another emperor for the city!" They set fire to the palace of Probus which was gutted. Next they went and burned the baths of Alexander, the great hospice of Sampson (where the patients perished), and the Great Church along with all its columns. It collapsed entirely on all four sides.

A. D. 563/4. In December, a great fire broke out, and the hospice of Sampson was completely gutted as too were the buildings in front of the quarter of Rufus and also the middle court, near the Great Church.

It is not clear whether Theophanes's reference to "the Orphanage" is to an area of the city named because of the orphanage there or to a previously existing orphanage which became the site of the new church.

A. D. 571/2. In this year [Roman emperor] Justin began to build the church of the holy apostles Peter and Paul in the Orphanage, and the church of the Holy Apostles in the Triconch (the one that had been burned during the reign of Zeno).

A.D. 580/1. In the same year [Roman emperor] Tiberius began to build the public bath at Blachernai and restored many churches, hostels, and houses for the aged. He directed his name be written into the official documents as Tiberius Constantine.

Procopius, Buildings of Justinian

Procopius (ca. 500–565) came from Caesarea in Palestine and had accompanied the general Belisarius on campaigns, eventually being made Prefect of Constantinople in 562. Among his writings, Procopius chronicles the many building projects Justinian (483–565) undertook during his reign (527–565) as emperor. Part of his purpose was to illustrate the good a leader with foresight and wisdom can do and indeed, Justinian fits the bill. In fact, the detail of Procopius's account places Justinian's building campaign as a marker in the history of Byzantine architecture. The pattern of building hospices along with churches is evidenced in this report. Several institutions committed to hospitality are cited here, including hospices, poor-houses, hospitals with free medical care and a refuge for former prostitutes.

Book I Constantinople.

II. The Church of Irene, which was next to the great church, and was burnt down together with it, was rebuilt on a large scale by the Emperor Justinian—a church scarcely second to any in Byzantium except that of Sophia. There was between these two churches a hospice for the relief of destitute persons and those in the last extremity of disease, suffering in body as well as in fortune, which was built in former times by a God-fearing man named Sampson. This hospice of Sampson did not remain unscathed by the insurgents, but perished in the fire, together with the two neighboring churches. The Emperor Justinian rebuilt it in a more magnificent fashion, and with a much greater number of rooms. In addition, he endowed it with a great annual revenue, in order that the sufferings of the more unfortunate may be relieved in it for the future. Inexhaustible as he was in his love for God, he built two other hospices opposite to this, in what are called the houses of Isidorus and Arcadius, being assisted in these pious works by the Empress Theodora.

IX. Upon this shore there stood from ancient times a beautiful palace, the entirety of which the Emperor Justinian dedicated to God, exchanging present enjoyment for the reward of his piety hereafter, in the following manner. There were at Byzantium a number of women who were prostituted in a brothel, not willingly, but compelled to exercise their profession. For under pressure of poverty they were compelled by the procurer who kept them to act in this manner, and to offer themselves to unknown and casual passers-by. There was here from ancient times a guild of brothel-keepers, who not only carried on their profession in this building, but publicly bought their victims in the market, and forced them into an unchaste life. However, the Emperor Justinian and the Empress Theodora, who performed all their works of piety in common, devised the following scheme. They cleansed the State from the pollution of these brothels, drove out the procurers, and set free these women who had been driven to evil ways by their poverty, providing them with a sufficient maintenance, and enabling them to live chaste as well as free. This was arranged in the following manner: they changed the palace, which stood on the right hand as one sails into the Euxine Sea, into a magnificent convent, to serve as a refuge for women who had changed from their former life, in order that there spending their lives in devotion to God, and in continual works of piety, they might wash away the sins of their former life of shame. On this account, this dwelling of these women is called from their work by the name of the Penitentiary.

As one sails from this place towards the Euxine Sea, there is a lofty promontory jutting out from the shore of the strait, upon which stood a Church of the Martyr St. Panteleemon. Beyond this church, in a place which is called Argyronium, there was, in old times, a hospital for poor people afflicted with incurable diseases, which having in the course of time fallen into the last stage of decay, he most zealously restored, to serve as a refuge for those who were thus afflicted.

XI. The above are, described as briefly as possible, the works of the Emperor Justinian in the imperial city. I will now describe the only thing which remains. Since the Emperor dwells here, a multitude of humanity of all nations comes into the city from all the world, due to the vast extent of the empire, each one of them led here either by business, by hope, or by chance. Many of these people's affairs at home have fallen into disorder, so they come with the intention of offering some petition to the Emperor. These persons, forced to dwell in the city on account of some present or threatened misfortune, in addition to their other trouble are also in need of lodging, being unable to pay for a dwelling place during their stay in the city. This source of misery was removed from them by the Emperor Justinian and the Empress Theodora, who built very large hospices as places of refuge in time of need for such unfortunate persons as these, close to the sea, in the place which is called the Stadium, I suppose because in former times it was used for public games.

Book II Mesopotamia

X. Thus did the Emperor Justinian reconstruct the walls of Antiochia. He also rebuilt the entire city, which was burnt by the enemy. Moreover, he made provision for the sick poor in that place, and built dwellings for them, separate for the different sexes, in which they were supplied with attendants, and the means of curing their diseases. At the same time he established hospices for strangers who might be staying for any time in the city.

Book IV Palestine

VI. These were the works of the Emperor Justinian in Cilicia. At Jerusalem he built a church in honor of the Virgin, to which no other can be compared. The inhabitants call it the "new church." Proceeding further, there stand two semicircles, opposite to one another, on each side of the way to the church; while on either side of the other road are two hospices (the work of the Emperor Justinian) one of which is destined for the reception of strangers, while the other is a hospital for the sick poor. The Emperor Justinian also endowed this Church of the Virgin with large revenues. Such were the works of the Emperor Justinian in Jerusalem . . . .

IX. He built cisterns and reservoirs as follows: the poor-house at Bostra in Phoenicia; He rebuilt the bath and poor-house of the city of Cyricum; the poor-house of St. Conon, and the aqueduct of the same saint in Cyprus; the house of SS. Cosmas and Damianus in Pamphylia; and the poor-house of St. Michael in the seaport which is called the naval arsenal of the city of Perga, in Pamphylia.

Cyril of Scythopolis, Lives of the Monks of Palestine

In his extensive description (ca. 555) of the lives and ministries of the many desert monastics, Cyril (ca. 525–558) remarks upon various houses built for the poor, the elderly, and travelers. These excerpts suggest that certainly by the early fifth century building programs that institutionalized practices of hospitality were considered part of the legacy of Christian leaders.

Life of Our Father Saint Euthymius

35. Blessed Eudocia built a huge number of churches to Christ, and more monasteries and homes for the poor and elderly than I am able to count. One of the churches founded by her, named after St. Peter, lies opposite the monastery of the great Euthymius, at a distance of about twenty stades.

Cyril recounts the teachings of St. Euthymius upon the building of a cenobium, *the purpose of which was to welcome whoever comes to the door.*

39. When all were assembled round him [Euthymius] said, "Just as it is not done to eat bread without salt, so it is impossible to achieve virtue without love. For each virtue is made secure through love and humility, with the aid of experience, time and grace. While humility exalts to a height, love prevents falling from this height, since 'he who humbles himself will be exalted' and 'love never fails.' Love is greater than humility, for it was on account of love for us that God the Word humbled himself to become life for us. So attend to yourself and to all your flock, and first of all know this, that it had pleased God to make this laura a *cenobium* and that this change will soon take place." He gave them directions as to the place where the *cenobium* was to be built, and about its constitution, reception of guests and zeal in the office of psalmody, and that they should not neglect brethren in distress, specially those oppressed by evil thoughts, but encourage and admonish them always. This he said to the monk appointed superior. To all of them he made this declaration: "My beloved brethren, do not shut to anyone the door of the *cenobium* you are about to build, and God will then grant you his blessing."

St. Sabas is perhaps one of the most famous of desert saints. Cyril gives a vivid picture of his life and activities. The institutionalization of hospitality is illustrated in the following account when St. Sabas uses his inheritance first for a guest-house. Sabas plans beyond the building for its long term maintenance and needs of water supply. This focus on hospices continued in Sabas's life as the community grew and foreign monastics and guests came to visit them.

The Life of St. Sabas

25. When a short time later [St. Sabas's mother] died, he conducted her burial and laid her to rest in a holy tomb. Her wealth he

secured for his own laura. It was with this wealth that he acquired the guest-house [*xenodocheion*] at Jericho with the gardens there, also buying a water-supply for them, and built the guest-house in the laura to serve the fathers, and achieved much else besides. 31. After occupying the throne of Jerusalem for eight years and three months, Archbishop Sallustius died in Christ on 23 July of the second indiction, and Elias, often mentioned in my account of the holy Euthymius, succeeded to the patriarchate, in the fifty-sixth year of the life of blessed Sabas. Patriarch Elias built a monastery near the episcopal palace and brought together in it those ascetics of the holy church of the Resurrection who had been scattered in the district around the Tower of David, assigning to each of them a cell with every bodily comfort. When they had been gathered together, as has been said, our father Sabas purchased various cells from them and made them into a hospice for the laura. To the north of the cells he purchased were other cells, which he wished to purchase on behalf of foreign monks. . . . The blessed one gave the price of the cells and founded a second hospice for the relief of monks coming from abroad. He also acquired two hospices for Castellium, one in the holy city not far from the Tower of David and the other in Jericho in one of the gardens he had bought.

In addition Sabas petitions the Emperor for a hospital in Jerusalem.

LXXII. Some days after this, the Emperor sent for St. Saba, and said to him, "Father, I hear that you have founded many monasteries in the wilderness, but wherever you wish for it, ask for a revenue for the needs of the inmates, and we will provide one, that they may pray for us and for the commonwealth committed to our charge." He answered: "They who pray for your Holiness need no revenues of this sort, for the Lord is their portion and revenue, who in the wilderness rained bread from heaven upon a stiff-necked and rebellious people. But, most holy Emperor, we beg of you for the restoration of the holy churches throughout Palestine. We ask you for a grant from the public funds, for the rebuilding of the holy houses which have been burned by the Samaritans, a subsidy to the Christians of Palestine, who have been made few and robbed. Moreover we beg you to establish a hospital in the Holy City for the nursing of sick strangers." LXXIII. Now those things which Father Saba asked our most holy Emperor without delay were carried out Moreover, in accordance with the holy old man's third request, he founded a hospital in the midst of Jerusalem. It contained at first one hundred beds, and he set apart for it a clear annual revenue of eighteen hundred and fifty pieces of gold. Afterwards he ordered that the hospital should contain two hundred beds, and added that much more sure and inalienable revenue to it.

Cyril tells also of St. Theodosius who set out to build a cenobium, *but first built a hospice to receive guests.*

Life of Saint Theodosius

3. The great Theodosius, on the day after the departure of the *illustris*, found the said money hidden in the safe. With it he first of all founded a hospice above the cave, where he welcomed everyone who visited him; he also bought two little asses, and would go on his own to fetch what was needed for the body. Then he commenced the building of his *cenobium*. From this time many began to hasten to him, asking to live with him; and he accepted them and guided them in following the perfect will of God. God helped him in everything, and "he was a successful man," as we hear of Joseph.

Antoninus Martyr, *Pilgrim Account*

Pilgrimage to the holy land has a rich tradition in early Christianity.[9] By the middle of the fifth century, pilgrims to Palestine could count on way stations, sacred shrines marking biblical events and figures, and a network of hostels and monastic communities associated with those shrines. While all we know of this pilgrim is that he was a native of Placentia, from his account (ca. 560) we can deduce that he was of hardy stock and determination. His travels extended not only to Palestine but to Sinai, Egypt and Mesopotamia. Like most pilgrims of his day, he appears to accept holy sites at face value as straightforwardly historical locations of biblical events. Particularly helpful for us here are his references to hospices established in various places, often associated with churches. In addition, this pilgrim tells us of baths associated with churches which provided not only sanitation for the poor and the traveler, but blessing from holy waters as well.

VII. We came to the place where the Jordan leaves the sea, and at that place we crossed the Jordan, and came to a city named Gadara, which is also called Gabaon. In that quarter, three miles from the city, are warm springs which are called the Baths of Helias, in which lepers are cleansed. There is also a hospice.

IX. Then we came to the place where our Lord, with five loaves and two fishes, fed five thousand men, not counting women and children, which lies in a wide plain on which are olive and palm groves. Then we came to the place where the Lord was baptized. There, too, is the little hill of Hermon, which is mentioned in the psalm. At the foot of the mountain itself, a cloud rises from the river at the first hour after sunrise, and comes to Jerusalem over the basilica which is in Sion, and over the basilica of the Sepulchre of our Lord, and over the basilica of the Blessed Mary and St. Sophia, which was the Praetorium where our Lord was tried. Over these places the dew from the cloud falls like rain. Physicians collect it, and in it they cook all food for the hospices, for many diseases are healed where the dew falls, of which the prophet David sings, "Like as the dew of Hermon which fell upon the Mount Sion."

XXIII. From Sion we came to the Basilica of the Blessed Mary, where there is a large congregation of monks and also hospices for strangers, both for men and women. There I was received as a pilgrim. There were countless tables, and more than three thousand beds for sick persons.

XXIV. [A church at the Pool of Siloam] has two baths made by human hands out of marble. Between the two baths runs a partition. In one men, and in the other, women, bathe for a blessing. In these waters many cures are effected, and even lepers are cleansed.

XXVII. Also when we came out of the greater gate [of the Basilica of the Blessed Mary], we came to the tomb of St. Isitius, whose body lies there. Here also loaves are given to the poor and to pilgrims, according to the directions of the blessed Helena.

Gregory the Great, *Epistle 2 to Vitalis, Guardian of Sardin**

In this letter to Vitalis, Gregory (ca. 540–604) relays the deteriorated state of guest-houses or xenodocheia, *and the need for upkeep. Because this letter is dated roughly in the late sixth century we can conclude the* xenodocheia *that had been built earlier had begun to fall into disarray. Gregory holds various officers in charge accountable for such upkeep which suggests that hostels and hospitals were a part of the ecclesiastical bureaucracy in the sixth century.*

From the information given us by your Experience we find that the hospitals [or guest-houses, *xenodocheia*] all around Sardinia are suffering from grievous neglect. As a result, our most reverend brother and fellow-bishop Januarius would have had to be most strongly reprimanded, if it weren't for his old age and simplicity, and the sickness which you have told us about besides. Seeing, then, that he is in no condition to order anything done, you warn the steward of that Church, and Epiphanius, the archpresbyter, under our strict authority, that they themselves at their own peril carefully and profitably work to set those same hospitals in order. For, if there should be any neglect there after this, let them know that they won't be able to excuse themselves before us in any manner, or to any extent.

Gregory the Great, *Epistle 6, to Brunichild, Queen of the Franks**

This letter from Gregory to Brunichild, Queen of the Franks, also indicates the degree to which institutions of hospitality had become embedded in Christian culture. When a Christian monarch builds a church, it is not uncommon to follow suit with a monastery and hospital.

On learning from the information contained in your letters that you have built the Church of Saint Martin in the suburbs of Augustodunum, and a monastery for hand-maidens of God, and also a hospital in the same city, we rejoiced greatly, and returned thanks to Almighty God, who stimulates the sincerity of your heart to the doing of these things.

Radegund, *Life*

Radegund (525–587), a queen and abbess in western Europe, was praised for her hospitality and generosity. This excerpt from her life story tells of a house she built in Athies. A hospice dedicated to her still exists at Athies.

Turning her mind to further works of mercy, she built a house at Athies where beds were elegantly made up for needy women gathered there. She would wash them herself in warm baths, tending to the putrescence of their diseases.

John Moschos, *The Spiritual Meadow*

In this collection of spiritual stories from around 600, John tells of a woman whose faithfulness led to the conversion of her husband. She encourages him to "lend money to the God of the Christians." When her husband asks to see this God, she takes him to the poor lying on the porches of the church at Nisbis. The porches of great churches were per-haps the last place the poor and sick might be welcome. Happily, the story ends with a miracle returning his investment and his conversion (see p. 127).

On the island of Samos, Mary, the friend of both God and the poor, the mother of Master Paul, the military official attached to the court, told us that there was a Christian woman in Nisbis whose husband was a pagan. They possessed fifty *miliarisia*. One day, the husband said to his wife: "Let us lend out that money and get some advan-tage from it, for in drawing on it a little at a time, we are going to spend it all." The wife answered: "If you insist on lending this money, come, lend it to the God of the Christians." He said to her: "Well, where is this God of the Christians, so we can lend it to him?" She said: "I will show you. Not only shall you not lose your money, but it shall even earn interest for you and the capital shall be dou-bled." He said to her: "Come on, then; show me him and we will lend to him." She took her husband and led him to the most holy church. Now the church at Nisbis has five large doorways. As she brought him to the entrance, there where the great porches are, she showed him the poor and said: "If you give to these persons, the God of the Christians receives it, for these are all his." Immediately, and with gladness, he gave the fifty *miliarisia* to the poor, and went back to his house.

In this brief reference John Moschos also reports the existence of a hos-tel or guest-house between two churches.

There is a hostel here, near the lighthouse, between the Church of Saint Sophia and the Church of Saint Faustus, with a guest-master in charge. One day this man invited me to go up to the hostel to replace him for a few days.

Leontius, *Life of St. John the Almsgiver*

In setting down the life of John the Almsgiver in the 600s Leontius wanted to encourage Christians of his own day by the inspirational char-acter of John's life without the sort of pretentious writing so common in Byzantine hagiography. Here is a plain-spoken yet vivid picture of the life of John, bishop of Alexandria, called the Almsgiver, in seventh-century Egypt with all his difficulties and frustrations. The maze of ecclesiastical officials often hampers John's ability to act on his commitment to the poor and oppressed though his passion radiates from every page. These excerpts show his concern for refugees and the starving during a widespread famine. For our purposes here, we note the many institutions founded, including a maternity hospital, to deal with these problems.

At that time the Persian armies invaded and laid waste the whole country of the Syrians, and the inhabitants of all the towns there came in great numbers with bishops and other clergy and governors and sought refuge in Alexandria. In the greatness of his mind and the generosity of his purpose he supported them all liberally, supplying most abundantly each one's necessities.

In addition to this he built a great many poorhouses and hostels for strangers, and he decreed that all the corn and all the necessary expenditure for the feeding of their inmates should be paid for from the revenues of the Church.

Once when a severe famine was oppressing the city and the holy man's stewards were, as usual, ceaselessly distributing money or some small gift to the needy, some destitute women overcome with hunger and but lately risen from child-bed were obliged to hasten to receive help from the distributors while they were still in the grip of abdominal pain, deadly pale, and suffering grievously; when the wondrous man was told of this, he built seven lying-in hospitals in different parts of the city, ordered forty beds to be kept ready in each and arranged that every woman should rest quietly in these for seven full days after her confinement and then receive the third of a nomisma and go home.

[Regarding refugees from Syria in Alexandria] He accordingly gave immediate orders that the wounded and sick should be put to bed in hostels and hospitals which he himself founded, and that they should receive care and medical treatment without payment and that then they should be free to leave as each of them should choose. To those who were well but destitute and came to the daily distribution he gave sixpence apiece to the men and one shilling apiece to the women and children as being weaker members.

One day this blessed Patriarch went to visit the poor in the quarter called Caesareum—for there he had had some very long vaulted buildings erected; the floor was covered with wooden boards and mats and rough rugs were provided. Here the poor could sleep during the winter months.

Again this glorious man could not bear the thought that righteous and commendable achievements should come to an end with his brief life, so what did he do? He built from the foundations up hostels for strangers, asylums for the old, and monasteries, and he gathered together companies of holy monks and thus through the good works which are done therein he has won a memorial of his righteousness which shall never pass away.

Offices

Another revealing source of information about practices of hospitality in early Christianity is the apparent development of offices to administer institutions of hospitality. Many of these hospitable institutions had significant land holdings and financial resources. Their proper stewardship became increasingly important. By the fifth century there are warnings against exploiting such offices for financial gain and encouraging the appointment of leaders of good character to administer funds for the poor, hospices, and hospitals.[10]

Several excerpts highlight the duties of the clergy with regard to hospitality. Bishops in particular were responsible for offering hospitality within their jurisdiction. Church revenues were allotted for the bishop's expenditures on the poor, the widowed, the orphaned, the sick, and strangers.

In addition to the clergy who generally carried responsibilities for hospitality, there were officers who administered institutions of hospitality or whose function required specific practices of hospitality. *Xenones* and *xenodocheion* were administered by *xenodochoi*, usually appointed by the local bishop and under ecclesiastical authority. Even when the administrator was appointed by someone else, in this case usually the founder or patron of the *xenon*, the *xenodochos* was still accountable to the laws of church and state regulating such institutions, especially the proper administration of their funds and properties. The office of *xenodochos* carried weighty financial responsibilities as well as prestige as *xenodochoi* frequently became bishops. The *xenodochos* could mortgage or even sell institutional estates. Regulations of just how much involvement a *xenodochos* could have in the *xenon*'s finances emerge in both church and civil law in the fifth century. Penalties for poor administration and prohibition of simony were enacted.

The *orphanotrophoi* were administrators of orphanages who carried not only the responsibility of administering the orphanage, but also of serving as primary trustee for the estates of minors under their care.

Houses for the poor were administered by *ptochotrophos* who were also important in church affairs and accountable for the disbursement of funds. The *ptochotrophos* was sometimes considered the guardian of the poor.

All of these officers were to be strictly accountable to the bishop whose jurisdiction included their institution.[11] Ultimately, the bishop held fiduciary responsibility for the administration of institutions of hospitality within his see, so the rise of administrators for those institutions was tied to the increase of resources available to run them. There is considerable textual evidence that early Christians put great consideration into the use and distribution of the material resources at their command. Church officers, in particular, had to ensure proper use of church funds through sound administration and just distribution. Several of the excerpts below reflect that concern.

Within monastic communities, those assigned duties of hospitality such as the gatekeeper, infirmarian, and guest-master, receive specific job descriptions that reflect the value placed on the virtue of hospitality. Moreover, office holders were to be of esteemed character. The office of guest-master was in touch with the outside world so the person chosen for this job was someone "of tact and virtue."[12] The keeper of the cellar, the porter at the door, the one caring for the special needs of the sick, all carried duties of hospitality.[13] The excerpts below include descriptions of various monastic offices related to institutionalized practices of hospitality.

Polycarp, *Epistle to the Philippians**

Polycarp (ca. 69–155), bishop of Smyrna, is an early witness to the development of Christianity in the late first and early second centuries. This letter to the Christian community at Philippi lays out the duties of the presbyter, specifying that this office holder extend care to vulnerable groups. This is an instance in which hospitality is extended through visiting rather than receiving.

Chapter 6 The Duties of Presbyters and Others

And let the presbyters be compassionate and merciful to all, bringing back those that wander, visiting all the sick, and not neglecting the widow, the orphan, or the poor, but always "providing for that which is becoming in the sight of God and people." Let them abstain from all wrath, preferential treatment of persons, and unjust judgment, keeping far off from all covetousness, not quickly crediting slander against any one, not severe in judgment, as knowing that we are all under a debt of sin.

Hermas, *The Shepherd**

This very early Christian text was written in the second century by Hermas whom we know that was a Christian slave sold at Rome and set free by his owner, Rhoda. It offers many visions of Christian community, its virtues and practices. As the church of the second century began to organize, the role of the bishop became increasingly important. In Hermas's vision, those bishops who fulfill their particular responsibility for hospitality are promised reward.

And from the tenth mountain, where were trees which overshadowed certain sheep, they who believed were the following: bishops given to hospitality, who always gladly received into their houses the servants of God, without pretending. And the bishops never failed to protect, by their service, the widows, and those who were in need, and always maintained holy conversation. All these, accordingly, shall be protected by the Lord for ever. They who do these things are honorable before God, and their place is already with the angels, if they remain to the end serving God.

*Justin Martyr, First Apology**

One of the earliest reports of Christian worship comes from Justin Martyr (ca. 100–ca. 165), a highly educated Christian who wrote this apology ca. 155 at Rome to explain Christian practice and teaching. This account describes not only general worship practices but also the office of president whose duties include hospitality to widows, orphans, sick, and strangers. This suggests a very early date for the institutionalizing of practices of hospitality within the Christian community.

Chapter 67 Weekly Worship of the Christians

And we afterwards continually remind each other of these things. And the wealthy among us help the needy; and we always keep together. For all things with which we are supplied, we bless the Maker of all through His Son Jesus Christ and through the Holy Ghost. And on the day called Sunday, all who live in cities or in the country gather together to one place. The memoirs of the apostles or the writings of the prophets are read, as long as time permits. Then, when the reader has stopped, the president verbally instructs and exhorts everyone to the imitation of these good things. Then we all rise together and pray. When our prayer is ended, bread and wine and water are brought, and the president in like manner offers prayers and thanksgivings, according to his ability, and the people assent, saying Amen. There is a distribution to each, and a participation of that over which thanks have been given, and to those who are absent a portion is sent by the deacons. And they who are well to do and willing, give what each thinks fit. What is collected is deposited with the president, who cares for the orphans and widows and those who, through sickness or any other cause, are in need, and those who are in bonds and the strangers sojourning among us. In other words, the president takes care of all who are in need.

Ambrose, *On Duties of the Clergy**

Ambrose (ca. 339–397), the bishop of Milan, warns clergy against the dangers of extravagant hospitality. While he expects them to entertain strangers and travelers by virtue of their office, they are not to give way to banquets and feasting.

For this reason I think that what you wisely do is befitting to the duties of clerics, and especially to those of the priesthood—namely, that you avoid the banquets of strangers, but do so in a way that you are still hospitable to travelers and give no occasion for reproach by reason of your great care in the matter. Banquets with strangers engross one's attention, and soon produce a love for feasting. Tales, also, of the world and its pleasures often creep in. One cannot shut one's ears and to forbid them is looked on as a sign of haughtiness. One's glass, too, even against one's will, is filled time after time. It is better surely to excuse oneself once for all at one's own home, than often at another's. When one rises sober, at any rate one's presence need not be condemned by the insolence of another.

244

Nevertheless, says Ambrose, clergy must always be ready to offer hospitality.

Hospitality also serves to recommend many. For it is a kind of open display of kindly feelings, so that the stranger may not lack hospitality, but be courteously received, and the door may be open to him when he comes. It is especially important in the eyes of the whole world that the stranger should be received with honor, that the spirit of hospitality should not fail at our table. We should meet a guest with ready and free service, and look out for his arrival.

Ambrose also advises on the proper use of resources in acts of hospitality. He argues for a liberality that is not extravagant. Liberality in being hospitable should not be confused with expensive entertainments which use resources belonging legitimately to the poor in order to gain the approval of the rich.

There are two kinds of free-giving, one arising from liberality, the other from wasteful extravagance. It is a mark of liberality to receive the stranger, to clothe the naked, to redeem the captives, to help the needy. It is wasteful to spend money on expensive banquets and a lot of wine. Therefore one reads: "Wine is wasteful, drunkenness is abusive." It is wasteful to spend one's own wealth merely for the sake of gaining the favor of the people. People do this when they spend their inheritance on the games of the circus, or on theatrical pieces and gladiatorial shows, or even a combat of wild beasts, just to surpass the fame of their forefathers for these things. All this that they do is just foolish, for it is not right to be extravagant in spending money even on good works.

But it befits the priest especially to adorn the temple of God with fitting splendor, so that the court of the Lord may be made glorious by his endeavors. He ought always to spend money as mercy demands. It behooves him to give to strangers what is right. This must not be too much, but enough. Not more than, but as much as, kindly feeling demands, so that he may never seek another's favor at the expense of the poor, nor show himself as either too stingy or too free to the clergy. The one act is unkind, the other wasteful. It is unkind if money should be lacking for the necessities of those whom one ought to win back from their wretched employments. It is wasteful if there should be too much over for pleasure.

Basil, *Letter 142**

As a church leader, Basil (330–379) offers this letter of commendation regarding the character of the person in charge of administering funds for the poor, an officer responsible for practices of hospitality. Basil's tone of irritation sounds through as he notes that the accountant's failure to show up at the prescribed meeting has necessitated Basil's introducing various chorepiscopi *by letter.*

I assembled all my brethren the *chorepiscopi* at the synod of the blessed martyr Eupsychius to introduce them to your excellency. On account of your absence they must be brought before you by letter. Know, therefore, this brother as being worthy to be trusted by your intelligence, because he fears the Lord. As to the matters on behalf of the poor, which he refers to your good-will, deign to believe him as one worthy of credit, and to give the afflicted all the aid in your power. I am sure you will consent to look favorably upon the hospital of the poor which is in his district, and exempt it altogether from taxation. It has already seemed good to your colleague to make the little property of the poor not liable to be rated for taxes.

John Chrysostom, *Treatise Concerning the Priesthood**

John Chrysostom (ca. 347–407) wrote this treatise to instruct clergy in their duties and responsibilities. Of particular interest in Book 3 are the duties of clergy who care for widows, a protected class within the church. Chrysostom is concerned about the material resources spent on widows as well as the spiritual direction given to them. While he appears exasperated at points with the demands of widows, he nevertheless conveys a sensitivity to not only their social station but to the place of the sick and strangers as well. He reminds officers in charge of caring for widows of the complex psychological dynamics of poverty. His instruction reflects a keen awareness of the difference hospitality can make.

For widows are a class who, on account of their poverty, their age and natural disposition, indulge in unlimited freedom of speech (so I had best call it). They make an unseasonable clamor and idle complaints and lamentations about matters for which they ought to be grateful, and bring accusations concerning things which they ought to accept contentedly. Now the superintendent should endure all these things in a generous spirit, and not be provoked either by their annoyance or their unreasonable complaints. For this class of persons deserve to be pitied for their misfortunes, not to be insulted or have their hardships trampled on, for it would only add insult to the injury poverty brings and would be an act of extreme brutality. One of the wisest of men offers advice to superintendents so they will not be irritated when accosted nor be provoked by continual harassment to become an enemy where he ought to bring aid. Aware of greed and pride of human nature, and considering the nature of poverty and its terrible power to depress even the noblest character and induce people often to act in these same respects without shame, he instructs such a person to be affable and accessible to the supplicant, telling them, "Incline your ear to the poor and give a friendly answer with meekness." And passing by the case of one who succeeds in exasperating (for what can one say to someone who is overcome?), he addresses the man who is able to bear the other's infirmity, advising him before he bestows his gift to correct the supplicant by the gentleness of his countenance and the mildness of his words.

But if any one, although he does not take the property of these widows, nevertheless loads them with innumerable reproaches, and insults them, and is exasperated against them, he not only fails through his gift to alleviate the despondency produced by poverty, but aggravates the distress by his abuse. For although they may be compelled to act very shamelessly through the necessity of hunger, they are nevertheless distressed at having to do it. So when, due to the dread of famine, they are constrained to beg, and due to their begging are constrained to act shamelessly, and then again on account of their shamelessness are insulted, the power of despondency becomes very complex, and accompanied by much gloom, and settles deep within the soul. One who has the charge of these persons ought to be so long-suffering, as not only not to increase their despondency by his fits of anger, but also to remove the greater part of it by his exhortation . . .

But the superintendent of these persons ought not only to be gentle and forbearing, but also skillful in the management of property. For if this qualification is lacking, the affairs of the poor are again involved in the same distress. One who was entrusted not long ago with this ministry, got together a large hoard of money, but neither consumed it himself, nor expended it with a few exceptions upon those who needed it. Instead he kept the greater part of it buried in the earth until a season of distress occurred, when it was all surrendered into the hands of the enemy. Much fore-thought, therefore, is needed, so that the resources of the Church should be neither over abundant, nor deficient, but that all the supplies which are provided should be quickly distributed among those who need them, and the treasures of the Church stored up in the hearts of those who are under her rule.

Moreover, in the reception of strangers, and the care of the sick, consider how great an expenditure of money is needed, for much exactness and discernment is required on the part of those who preside over these matters. For it is often necessary that this expenditure should be even larger than that of which I spoke just now. In that case, he who presides over it should combine prudence and wisdom with skill in the art of supply, so as to dispose the affluent to be competitive and ungrudging in their gifts, so that, in the process of providing for the relief of the sick, he does not vex the souls of those who supply their wants. But earnestness and zeal need to be displayed here in a far higher degree, for the sick are difficult creatures to please, and prone to weakness. Unless great accuracy and care are used, even a slight oversight is enough to do the patient great harm.

John Chrysostom, *Homily 85 on the Gospel of Matthew**

In a sermon on the Gospel of Matthew Chrysostom both highlights and laments the duties of those who offer hospitality when their energies are sapped in administrative tasks. He chastises the people for not taking these duties on themselves more often. He complains that the clergy carry the entire burden and their daily affairs appear more like those of secular magistrates, bargaining over the price of corn and haggling with those who should give willingly to the needs of strangers, widows, and the poor.

These things I do not mention just to complain, but in order that there may be some reform and change, in order that we may be pitied for spending our time in grievous servitude, in order that you may become a revenue and store for the church.

But if you are not willing, behold the poor before your eyes. As many as it is possible for us to satisfy, we will not cease to feed. But those whom it is not possible, we will leave to you, that you may not hear those words on the awful day, which shall be spoken to the unmerciful and cruel. "You saw me hungry and did not feed me."

For together with you this inhumanity makes us laughing-stocks, because leaving our prayers, and our teaching, and the other parts of holiness, we are fighting all the time, some with wine merchants, some with corn-factors, others with retailers of provisions.

Hence come battles, and strife, and daily humiliations and reproaches and jeers, and on each of the priests are imposed names more suitable for houses of secular men. It would have been fit to take our names from other places instead, and to be named from those things which also the apostles ordained. To take our name from the feeding of the hungry, from the protection of the injured, from the care of strangers, from succoring them that are despitefully used, from providing for the orphans, from taking part with the widows, from presiding over the virgins. These ministries, not the care of lands and houses, should be distributed among us.

These are the stores of the church, these the treasures that become her, and that afford in great degree both ease to us and profit to you or, rather, to you ease with the profit. For I suppose that by the grace of God they that assemble themselves here amount to the number of one hundred thousand. If each bestowed one loaf to one of the poor, all would be in plenty. Even further, if each bestowed just one dollar, no one would be poor and we would not undergo so many humiliations and jeers, because of our care about money. For indeed the saying, "Sell your goods, and give to the poor, and come and follow me," might be appropriately addressed to the leaders of the church with respect to the property of the church. For in any other way it is not possible to follow Him as we ought, not being freed from all grosser and more worldly care.

Palladius, *Dialogue on the Life of St. John Chrysostom*

In the process of explaining why Chrysostom usually ate alone, Palladius (ca. 363–425) tells us something of Chrysostom's (ca. 347–407) views regarding the office of bishop as it related to hospitality. Apparently Chrysostom held he would not regularly offer grand meals which, as bishop of Constantinople, he was likely expected to do. Chrysostom also gives advice to the priests to weigh carefully their duties of hospitality against their duties to teach and edify, for, in a busy city like Constantinople, a priest can find himself constantly the guest-master.

But I think the whole and more truthful explanation was this: he [Chrysostom] was excessively thrifty in dealing with men of dainty life and he considered it a sacrilege to expend money on such. At the same time, he removed the incentive for stealth among the stewards so they could not multiply by ten the expenses of the food, thereby getting for themselves what belonged to the poor. In addition to these reasons, he considered the multitude in the city with due deliberation and thought that as a steward of Christ he should look upon everyone, no matter what his rank, as worthy to eat along with him or else he should grant that honor to no one.

He had observed the bad behavior at table and the amount of the outlay on the poor and he shuddered at the whole business, bidding great farewell to such abuses.

Bishop: Now the host must have the cunning of a serpent, but the guilelessness of a dove, and he must pay attention to both precepts: "Give to every one who begs from you" and "Do not bring every man into your home," lest he receive a wolf instead of a sheep, or a bear instead of an ox, selling off his gain for a loss. First of all, it would be helpful for him to examine the place where a man has been placed, whether it be a deserted place or a populous one. Then he should consider how he is situated to act as host; is he the sort who can put up with strange customs? And he should use judgment in regard to the one who claims his service—be he rich or poor, well or sick, in need of food or clothing. It is in these very things that effective charity operates.

Now the blessed Abraham did not give hospitality to governors or generals or men of power in the world about him, those who boasted of horses glittering with their halters and bits, or of Persian trousers with bronze bells attached to noise far and wide the clamor of high conceit. And Abraham inhabited a desert place and he received those who came there. They came to their patriarch across the desert, drawn there by the fame of his virtue or by their own poverty.

Now Lot lived in a city worse than a desert and he befriended strangers passing through because of the inhospitable inhabitants. But if one lives in a well-regulated city, as, for example, Constantinople, in which all are in a sense guest-masters, it is quite possible that some priests neglect the ministry of the Word and busy themselves with food accounts. Such persons forget themselves and become hotel-keepers instead of teachers by watering down their doctrine, and pure knowledge vanishes.

Canons of Chalcedon

The Council of Chalcedon met in 451 to address heresy. The 500–600 bishops meeting there formulated the Chalcedonian Definition, a doctri-

nal statement on the human and divine natures of Christ. In addition, they were interested in ecclesiastical affairs as the canons below show. The clergy who administered poor-houses and hostels were to be clearly under the authority of their local bishops, not free agents. Neither were they to neglect their duties in order to take a more prestigious position elsewhere. These offices had fiduciary responsibilities.

Canon 8. Let the clergy of the poor-houses, monasteries, and martyries remain under the authority of the bishops in every city according to the tradition of the holy Fathers; and let no one arrogantly cast off the rule of his own bishop. Further, if any shall contravene this canon in any way whatever, and will not be subject to their own bishop, if they be clergy, let them be subjected to canonical censure, and if they be monks or laymen, let them be excommunicated.

Canon 10. It shall not be lawful for a clergyman to be at the same time enrolled in the churches of two cities. That is, he cannot be in the church in which he was at first ordained, and in another to which, because it is greater, he has moved from lust for superficial honor. And those who do so shall be returned to their own church in which they were originally ordained, and they shall minister only there. But if any one has already moved from one church to another, he shall not meddle in the affairs of his former church, nor with the martyries, almshouses, and hostels belonging to it. And if, after the decree of this great and ecumenical Synod, any shall dare to do any of these things now forbidden, the synod decrees that he shall be degraded from his rank.

Julianus Pomerius, The Contemplative Life

Pomerius (fl. ca. 500) was an African Christian who migrated to Arles and became the teacher of the famous bishop and saint of Arles, Caesarius, in the fifth century. He was well known in his life time as a leader and teacher. His only surviving work is this treatise on pastoral theology from around 500 which is likely based on his experiences as abbot for a community in Gaul. Pomerius explains that officers who administer the funds for the poor must distribute them properly, including providing for themselves.

The case of those who even with profit to their soul are supported by resources of the Church: Accordingly, the priest to whom the office of administration has been entrusted will receive from the people, not only without cupidity but also with a reputation for conscientiousness, things to be distributed; and he will dispense them faithfully—he who has either left that which was his own to his kinsfolk or distributed it to the poor or added it to the property of the Church, and placed himself for the love of poverty in the number of the poor, so that he himself lives as one voluntarily poor on what he administers to the poor. Clerics, too, poor either by choice or by birth, whether living in homes of their own or in community houses, can receive with fullness of virtue the necessities of life because greed of possessing does not lead them to accept them, but the necessity of living forces them.

John Malalas, *Chronicle*

Justinian's building projects are well known. Malalas (ca. 490–570) reports that Justinian also established officers and regulations to administer these institutions of hospitality. This suggests not only that such offices were well defined by the sixth century but also that concerns had arisen over officers benefitting financially from these appointments. By declaring wealth upon appointment to the office, no officer could later claim rights to ecclesiastical property.

In that year [A. D. 527/8] the emperor promulgated a sacred decree concerning bishops, heads of orphanages, *oikonomoi* and wardens of hospices, that each of those mentioned above should have power of bequest only over those things held as property before entering office, and that immediately upon appointment his wealth was to be declared.

Caesarius of Arles, *The Rule for Nuns*

The final version of this rule of life for nuns was set down by Caesarius (ca. 470–542), bishop of Arles, in 534. Much of his work promoted monasticism for both men and women, but with special interest in nuns, their communities and practices. He takes some pains here to specify duties of various offices related to hospitality, including the cellarer, infirmarian and portress, or keeper of the entrance.

30. Because it often happens that the cellar of a monastery does not contain good wine, it will be the concern of the abbess to provide

the kind of wine out of which the sick and those of more delicate upbringing may be ministered to.

31. By no means let baths be denied those whose infirmity demands it, and let them be taken without murmuring on the advice of the doctor, so that even if she who is ill does not wish to bathe, at the command of an elder religious that is to be done which is necessary for her health. If, however, bathing is not required because of some infirmity, assent should not be given to an eager desire.

32. The care of the sick or of those suffering from some disability ought to be enjoined on one quite faithful and full of compunction, who will seek from the cellarer whatever she should see to be necessary. Such a one should be chosen who will preserve monastic austerity and serve the sick with devoted love. If the needs of the sick should demand it, and it should seem right to the mother of the monastery, the sick shall also have their own storeroom and kitchen in common. Those who are put in charge of the storerooms, either of the wine-cellar or of clothing and books, and those in charge of the entrance and of the wool work, shall receive the keys upon a copy of the Gospels, and they shall serve the others without murmuring. If any of the sisters think that the clothing, shoes, or household goods can be used or treated negligently, they should be severely corrected as defrauders of the goods of the monastery.

Cyril of Scythopolis, *Lives of the Monks of Palestine*

Cyril (fl. ca. 543) chronicles the lives of monks in Palestine from 405 to 558. In this account he highlights the role John played as guest-master, describing it as a ministry that John took on with "eagerness and joy." In this case at least, guest-master included hospitable tasks of cooking and serving meals not only for guests but also for workers at the monastery.

6. On the occasion of the change of offices in the first indiction, the monk appointed steward made this great luminary [John] guest-master and cook. He accepted this ministry with eagerness and joy, and performed tasks for all the fathers, serving each one with all humility and meekness. During this ministry occurred the building of the cenobium outside the laura and to the north, in order that those renouncing this life should first be educated in strict monasticism there in the cenobium, and then live in the laura, once they had been strictly trained in the cenobitic rule; blessed Sabas used to affirm and maintain that, just as the flower precedes the fruit, so the

cenobitic life precedes the anchoritic. While this cenobium was being built, this righteous man was compelled as guest-master, in addition to the other tasks of his office, to cook for the workmen and twice a day to lift and carry the cooked dishes and other provisions and convey them to the laborers ten stades away from the guest-house.

Cyril tells this amusing story of one guest-master, James, who had to learn from an elder that hospitality and frugality are compatible.

40. James and the Dish of Beans

When some time had passed, the above-mentioned James was charged with looking after the guest-house of the great Laura and had to cook for those who went out to the desert to collect faggots. Once when he had cooked a quantity of beans, which we call *pisarion*, and had prepared too much on two successive days, he later threw the left-overs through a window down into the gorge. The elder, on seeing this from his tower, went down secretly, neatly collected the discarded *pisarion*, and spread it out to dry. Later in the year he invited James, on finishing his period of service, to a meal on his own; he cooked the dry *pisarion*, dressed it well and served it. While they were eating, the elder said, "Forgive me, brother, I do not know how to dress food well, and perhaps you did not enjoy the dish." The other replied, "I enjoyed it immensely, venerable father. I have not tasted so delicious a dish for a long time." The old man answered, "Believe me, my child, this is the *pisarion* you threw from the guest-house into the gorge. Know this, that he who is unable to dispense a pot of vegetables so as to satisfy the needs of those in his charge without ever wasting any of the vegetables is not able to govern a community. As the Apostle says, 'If a man does not know how to run his own household, how can he take care of God's Church?' " At these words James went off to his cell much benefitted.

Dorotheos of Gaza, *Dialogue with the Cellarer*

Dorotheos, born just after the turn of the sixth century, was himself a great spiritual leader and Christians sought his advice. He served as both guest-master and infirmarian, offices of hospitality, at different times in his life. In this collection he offers reflections and advice on the spiritual life. Here Dorotheos uses the dialogue form to lay out the duties of the cellarer, especially in relation to the sick.

Abbot. You do not want to fall into anger and to remember injuries, do you? Do not have an all-in attachment to material things and do not lay claim for yourself to anything whatever, or despise even the least thing. But whatever is asked of you, give it gladly. If through negligence or levity anything is broken or lost, don't get upset about it. You ought to act in this way not from contempt for the monastery and its goods—for you have a debt to take care of them with all your ability and zeal—but because you want to be undisturbed and tranquil in mind, always referring what has happened to God as much as possible. This you should be able to do if you manage things not as if they belonged to yourself, but as things dedicated to God and only entrusted to you. This is the way, as I said, not to be too attached to things and not to be led to despise them. If you do not have this as your aim, you will get angry and never be at peace. Being upset yourself, you will upset others.

Cellarer. My mind delights in what you say and I want to act this way, but how is it that whenever I am attending to these affairs I do not find myself capable of doing so?

Reply. Because you do not have these things clearly in your mind all the time. If you want to have these ideas before you at the moment you need to use them, go over them in your mind all the time and set your heart on them, and I am convinced that, by God's grace, you will make progress. Combine prayer with your good intentions. Take great care of the sick, in the first place to gain an understanding sympathy with the sick, but also so that, should you fall sick, God will raise up someone to look after you. "For with what measure you mete, it shall be meted out to you again."

Benedict of Nursia, *Rule*

This influential rule from the pattern of life set by Benedict (480–550) gives careful attention to the offices of those who offer hospitality. Specific chapters address the offices of cellarer, cook and kitchen workers, the porter or keeper of the entrance, and the abbot's duties toward guests at table.

Chapter 31. What Kind of Man the Cellarer of the Monastery Should Be.

As cellarer of the monastery let there be chosen from the community one who is wise, of mature character, sober, not a great eater, not haughty, not excitable, not offensive, not slow, not wasteful, but a God-fearing man who may be like a father to the whole community.

Let him have charge of everything. He shall do nothing without the

Abbot's orders, but keep to his instructions. Let him not vex the brethren. If any brother happens to make some unreasonable demand of him, instead of vexing the brother with a contemptuous refusal he should humbly give the reason for denying the improper request.

Let him keep guard over his own soul, mindful always of the Apostle's saying that "he who has ministered well acquires for himself a good standing."

Let him take the greatest care of the sick, of children, of guests and of the poor, knowing without doubt that he will have to render an account for all these on the Day of Judgment.

Let him regard all the utensils of the monastery and its whole property as if they were the sacred vessels of the altar. Let him not think that he may neglect anything. He should be neither a miser nor a prodigal and squanderer of the monastery's substance, but should do all things with measure and in accordance with the Abbot's instructions.

Above all things let him have humility; and if he has nothing else to give let him give a good word in answer, for it is written, "A good word is above the best gift."

Let him have under his care all that the Abbot has assigned to him, but not presume to deal with what he has forbidden him.

Let him give the brethren their appointed allowance of food without any arrogance or delay, that they may not be scandalized, mindful of the Word of God as to what he deserves "who shall scandalize one of the little ones."

If the community is a large one, let helpers be given him, that by their assistance he may fulfil with a quiet mind the office committed to him. The proper times should be observed in giving the things that have to be given and asking for the things that have to be asked for, that no one may be troubled or vexed in the house of God.

Chapter 35. On the Weekly Servers in the Kitchen

Let the brethren serve one another, and let no one be excused from the kitchen service except by reason of sickness or occupation in some important work. For this service brings increase of reward and of charity. But let helpers be provided for the weak ones, that they may not be distressed by this work; and indeed let everyone have help, as required by the size of the community or the circumstances of the locality. If the community is a large one, the cellarer shall be excused from the kitchen service; and so also those whose occupations are of greater utility, as we said above. Let the rest serve one another in charity.

The one who is ending his week of service shall do the cleaning on Saturday. He shall wash the towels with which the brethren wipe their hands and feet; and this server who is ending his week, aided by the one who is about to begin, shall wash the feet of all the brethren. He shall return the utensils of his office to the cellarer clean and in good condition, and the cellarer in turn shall consign them to the incoming server, in order that he may know what he gives out and what he receives back.

An hour before the meal let the weekly servers each receive a drink and some bread, over and above the appointed allowance, in order that at the meal time they may serve their brethren without murmuring and without excessive fatigue.

Chapter 56. On the Abbot's Table.

Let the Abbot's table always be with the guests and the pilgrims. But when there are no guests, let it be in his power to invite whom he will of the brethren. Yet one or two seniors must always be left with the brethren for the sake of discipline.

Chapter 66. On the Porters of the Monastery.

At the gate of the monastery let there be placed a wise old man, who knows how to receive and to give a message, and whose maturity will prevent him from straying about. This porter should have a room near the gate, so that those who come may always find someone at hand to attend to their business. And as soon as anyone knocks or a poor man hails him, let him answer "Thanks be to God" or "A blessing!" Then let him attend to them promptly, with all the meekness inspired by the fear of God and with the warmth of charity.

Should the porter need help, let him have one of the younger brethren.

If it can be done, the monastery should be so established that all the necessary things, such as water, mill, garden and various workshops, may be within the enclosure, so that there is no necessity for the monks to go about outside of it, since that is not at all profitable for their souls.

We desire that this Rule be read often in the community, so that none of the brethren may excuse himself on the ground of ignorance.

*Gregory the Great, Epistles to Peter, Subdeacon**

Gregory of Caesarea, also known as Gregory the Great (ca. 540–604), wrote many letters during his career as a church leader and Pope. He offers guidance here to a subdeacon whose duties included ensuring the poor were included in festivals and dedications. The first letter directs subdeacon Peter to distribute money and goods to the poor. In the second letter to Peter, Gregory reports that he has disciplined an officer of a xenodocheion *or guest-house for not properly carrying out his duties.*

Epistle 56

Being exceedingly desirous of observing the festivals of saints, we have thought it needful to address this our letter of direction to your Experience, informing you that we have arranged for the dedication with all solemnity, with the help of the Lord, in the month of August, of the Oratory of the Blessed Mary lately built in the cell of brethren where the abbot Marinianus is known to preside, to the end that what we have begun may through the Lord's operation be completed. But, inasmuch as the poverty of that cell requires that we should assist in that day of festival, we therefore desire you to give for celebrating the dedication, to be distributed to the poor, ten coins in gold, thirty jars of wine, two hundred lambs, two area of oil, twelve rams, and a hundred hens, which may be afterwards charged in your accounts. Provide therefore for this being done at once without any delay, that our desires, God granting it, may take speedy effect.

Epistle 32

I have strongly rebuked Romanus for his levity, because in the guest-house *(xenodocheion)* which he kept, as I have now discovered, he has been taken up more with his own profits than with [heavenly] rewards. Him, therefore, if it should seem good to you, leave in your place. See how you can best fortify him, by alarming and admonishing him, that he may act kindly and carefully towards the peasants; and show himself towards strangers and townspeople changed and active. In saying this, however, I am not selecting any person, but leave this to your judgment.

Gregory the Great, *Epistle 8, To Senator, Abbot**

The following letter from Gregory to Senator, abbot (xenodochos) of guest-house, clarifies regulations about directors of such houses taking other positions. In this case, Gregory is concerned about an abbot of a guest-house being promoted to the office of bishop for fear the abbot will take the property of the guest house with him into his new office and use it to benefit his own ends rather than to benefit the poor and strangers. Accordingly, a bishop may not remove a religious worker in a guest-house without consent of the abbot for fear the ministry of hospitality would be damaged.

By a similar definition, according to the desire of the founders, we decree that none of those who may in future have been ordained as abbot or presbyter to the same guest-house and monastery shall dare by any secret scheming whatever to take the office of the Episcopate, unless he has been first deprived of the office of abbot, and another has been substituted in his place; lest, by consuming the property of the guest-house or monastery in unfair expenditure, he should cause most serious pressure of want to the poor and strangers, or to others who live from its resources. Moreover, we forbid that the bishop have license, without the consent of the abbot and presbyter, to remove from the same place any monk for promotion to an ecclesiastical order, or for any cause whatever, lest usurpation in this regard should be carried to such an extent that places which have to be built up by the acquisition of men be destroyed by their removal.

Gregory the Great, *Epistle 44, To Peter, Subdeacon**

Four letters from Gregory address the responsibilities of church officers in using the church's resources for various ministries of hospitality. The first one sets forth instructions, responding to apparent questions raised by church leaders in Sicily. Gregory offers guidelines regarding many financial practices the church had undertaken primarily with regard to property and produce. Resources at the church's disposal, including grain stores, leased farm land and marriage fees were to be administered fairly, with the needs of the peasant and farmer in mind. The church was to host their labor and be hospitable to the people it serves.

With regard to our having so long delayed sending off your messenger, we have been so occupied with the engagements of the Easter festival that we have been unable to let him go sooner. But, with regard to the questions on which you have desired instruction, you will learn below how, after fully considering them all, we have determined them.

We have ascertained that the peasants of the Church are exceedingly aggrieved over the prices of corn, in that the sum appointed them to pay is not kept in due proportion in times of plenty. And it is our will that in all times, whether the crops of corn be more or less abundant, the measure of proportion be according to the market price. It is our will also that corn which is lost by shipwreck be fully accounted for, as long as such loss is not due to neglect on your part in transmitting it. If you allow the proper time for transporting it to pass by, any loss that ensues is your fault. Moreover, we have seen it to be exceedingly wrong and unjust that anything should be received from the peasants of the Church in the way of corn meas-urements, or that they should be compelled to give a larger modius than is used in the granaries of the Church. Therefore, we enjoin by this present warning that corn may never be received from the peas-ants of the Church in modii of more than eighteen sextarii [sixteen sextarii constituted a modius]. . . .

Above all we want you carefully to attend to this, namely, that no unjust weights be used in exacting payments. If you should find any, break them and cause true ones to be made. . . . Further, we have learned that the first charge of burdatio exceedingly cripples our peasants, in that before they can sell the produce of their labor they are compelled to pay taxes; and, not having of their own to pay with, they borrow from public pawnbrokers, and pay a heavy interest for the loan. As a result, they are crippled by heavy expenses. Therefore, we enjoin you by this present admonition to advance to them from the public fund all that they might have borrowed from strangers, and that it be repaid by the peasants of the Church by degrees as they may have wherewith to pay. Otherwise, while the time they are in tight circumstances, they will sell at too cheap a rate what might afterwards have been enough for the payment due, and even so not have enough.

It has come to our knowledge also that immoderate fees are received on the marriages of peasants. Concerning this, we order that no marriage fees shall exceed the sum of one solidus. If any are poor, they should give even less. But if any are rich, let them by no means exceed the aforesaid sum of a solidus. . . .

We have also learned that when some farmers die their relatives are not allowed to succeed them, but that their goods are withdrawn to the uses of the Church. With regard to this, we decree that the rel-atives of the deceased who live on the property of the Church shall succeed them as their heirs, and that nothing shall be withdrawn from the substance of the deceased.

Gregory the Great, *Epistle 30 To Emperor Mauricius**

In another letter Gregory reviews the use of government funds intended for distribution, clarifying that they may be given to needy strangers as well as to natives. Hospitality required the husbanding of resources and Gregory's letter gives evidence of this concern.

The Piety of my Lords, which has always mercifully sustained your servants, has shone forth here so plentifully that the need of all the feeble has been relieved by your bounty. On this account we with prayers and tears beseech Almighty God, who has moved the heart of your Clemency to do this thing, that He would preserve the empire of our Lords safe in His unfailing love, and by the aid of His own majesty extend their victories in all nations. The thirty pounds of gold which my fellow-servant Busa brought, Scribo has distributed faithfully to priests, persons in need, and others. Furthermore, certain females devoted to a religious life *(sanctimoniales foeminae)* have come to this city from several provinces, having fled here after captivity, of whom some, so far as there was room for them, have been placed in monasteries, but others, who could not be taken in, lead a life of singular destitution. On account of them, it has been thought good that what could be spared from the relief of the blind, maimed, and feeble should be distributed to them, so that not only needy natives, but also strangers who arrive here, might receive of the compassion of our Lords.

Gregory the Great, *Epistle 64, To Augustine, Bishop of the Angli**

Gregory responds to Augustine, his fellow bishop of the Angli, on what to do with offerings received by the church there. We see the pattern that would become standard for allocating the church's resources, namely, dividing revenues into quarters with one quarter designated for the poor and another quarter for the bishop's hospitality.

Augustine's First Question: I ask, most blessed father, concerning bishops, how they should live with their clergy: And concerning the offerings of the faithful which are received at the altars, both into what portions they should be divided, and how the bishop ought to deal with them in the Church.

Answer of Saint Gregory, Pope of the City of Rome: Holy Scripture, which no doubt you know well, bears witness, and especially the epistles of the blessed Paul to Timothy, in which he studied to instruct him how he ought to behave himself in the house of God. Now it is the custom of the Apostolic See to deliver an injunction to bishops when ordained, that of all emoluments that come in, four divisions should be made: to wit, one for the bishop and his household on account of hospitality and entertainment; another for the clergy; a third for the poor; and a fourth for the reparation of Churches. But, inasmuch as your Fraternity, having been trained in the rules of a monastery, ought not to live apart from your clergy in the Church of the Angli, which by the guidance of God has lately been brought to the faith, it will be right to institute that manner of life which in the beginning of the infant Church was that of our Fathers, among whom none said that any of the things which he possessed was his own, but they had all things common (Acts 4).

Boniface, *Correspondence: Gregory Invests Boniface with Episcopal Authority (722)*

The division of revenue into four parts with the appropriation of each quarter specified is repeated in this letter from Gregory the Great to Boniface (680–754), as bishop. One full fourth of the church's revenue is clearly set aside to provide hospitality for the poor and for pilgrims.

Gregory, the servant of the servants of God, to the clergy and people [of Thuringia], greeting in the Lord.

He is to divide the revenue and the offerings of the faithful into four parts: one for himself, another to the clergy for their ministrations, a third to the poor and pilgrims, and a fourth for the fabric of the churches, for all of which he must render an account at the judgment seat of God.

Visigothic Code

Compiled around 650 this code reflects developing laws from both civil and ecclesiastical traditions. By the time it was compiled, it was unlawful for a bishop to benefit financially from church properties, including hospitals or poor-houses or from the donations intended for such. The officer in charge was to protect, not exploit, the resources for hospitable use. Particular concern about misuse of donations is noted, suggesting that fiduciary responsibilities were being violated.

Book V. Ecclesiastical Affairs. Chapter VI. Concerning the Arbitrary Conduct of Bishops.

For many rash bishops, prompted by avarice, are in the habit of bestowing upon their cathedral churches, or upon various individuals, or paying out as wages for labor performed, the donations that have been given to their dioceses by the faithful, and, in this way, they not only break the vows of the donors, but are also guilty of sacrilege, in that they thereby defraud the Church of God. We hereby decree that it shall not be lawful for a bishop to appropriate any property belonging to the churches of his diocese.

The Life of St. Cuthbert

In this anonymous life of Cuthbert (d. 687) written about 700, the duties of the guest master are recounted in this story. Cuthbert is the guest master, charged with offering hospitality to whoever stops by. He fulfills this office conscientiously, receiving his guest warmly, washing and warming his feet and offering food.

Chapter II. How He Ministered to an Angel

Now this was another miracle in which Cuthbert the holy man of God was first glorified by the Lord, after he had by the Lord's help taken upon him the yoke of bondservice to Christ and the Petrine tonsure after the shape of the crown of thorns that bound the head of Christ, in the monastery which is called Ripon. This miracle our most trustworthy witnesses who are still alive have testified to. For while a neophyte, he was at once elected by the community to minister to guests on their arrival. Among these, on the morning of a certain day when the weather was wintry and snowy, an angel of the Lord appeared to him in the form of a well-built man in the flower of his age, just as angels appeared to the patriarch Abraham in the valley of Mamre in the form of men. Then having received him kindly in accordance with his wont, still thinking him to be a man and not an angel, he washed his hands and feet and wiped them with towels, and, having in his humility rubbed his guest's feet with his own hands to warm them on account of the cold, he invited him most urgently to wait until the third hour of the day to take food; but he was unwilling and refused on account of his journey. Finally Cuthbert adjured him in the name of our Lord Jesus Christ and so won his consent. When the signal was given at the third hour of the day and prayer was over, he at once set out a table and spread thereon such food as he had.

Rules

References to buildings and offices reveal the development of institutionalized forms of hospitality in early Christianity. In addition, the rules of monastic communities and other written codes of conduct offer evidence of the way hospitality was enacted in early Christian communities. Some of these excerpts give rules that must be followed within a community while others offer encouragement and exhortation to meet vigorous standards of Christian hospitality. These regulations show what sorts of behaviors were expected regarding hospitality and how those behaviors were codified. The rise of rules and codes of conduct, including exceptions to rules, suggests that hospitality was an important virtue that communities valued enough to ensure through regulation.

Apostolic Constitutions

Based on several earlier collections of church law, the Apostolic Constitutions *were compiled between 350 and 400 to help Christians practice their faith. Already in the third century Christians are struggling with how to welcome those one may find offensive or undeserving of help. Scriptural warrants are given for helping "every one who asks." All of these injunctions serve to codify practices of hospitality.*

Book 2.5, On Those Who Have Offended

But yet do not, O bishop, presently abhor any person who has fallen into one or two offenses, nor shall you exclude him from the word of the Lord, nor reject him from common interactions, since neither did the Lord refuse to eat with publicans and sinners. In fact, when He was accused by the Pharisees on this account, He said, "They that are well have no need of the physician, but they that are sick." Therefore, live and dwell with those who are separated from you for their sins, and take care of them, comforting them, and confirming them, and saying to them, "Be strengthened, you weak hands and feeble knees." For we ought to comfort those who mourn, and give encouragement to the fainthearted, lest by deep sorrow they degenerate into distraction, since "he that is fainthearted is exceedingly distracted."

Book 3.4, On Charity to All Sorts of Persons in Want

For what if some are neither widows nor widowers, but stand in need of assistance, either through poverty or some disease, or the maintenance of a great number of children? It is your duty to oversee all people, and to take care of them all. For those who give gifts do not of their own hand give them to widows, but barely bring them in, calling them free-will offerings, so you as a good steward can distribute the gift to those you know are in need. For God knows the giver, though you distribute it to those in need when he is absent. And he has the reward of well-doing, but you the blessedness of having dispensed it with a good conscience. But tell them who was the giver, that they may pray for the person by name. For it is our duty to do good to all, not fondly preferring one or another, whoever they be. For the Lord says: "Give to every one that asks of you." It is evident that it is meant of every one that is really in need, whether the person is a friend or foe, a kinsman or a stranger, single or married.

In this instruction, the Constitutions *again highlight the role of the bishop in ensuring the care and protection of widows, strangers, the hungry, the sick, prisoners, and especially orphans. This concern for orphans should lead to their achieving a self-sufficient and productive adult life.*

Book 4.1, How the Bishop Ought to Provide for the Orphans

Therefore, O bishops, be solicitous about their maintenance, being in nothing wanting to them, exhibiting to the orphans the care of parents, to the widows the care of husbands, to those of suitable age, marriage, to the craftsman, work, to the unable, commiseration, to the strangers, a house, to the hungry, food, to the thirsty, drink, to the naked, clothing, to the sick, visitation, to the prisoners, assistance. Besides these, have a greater care of the orphans, that nothing may be lacking to them. Take care of the maiden, till she arrives at the age of marriage, and you give her in marriage to a brother in the faith. To the young man, give assistance, that he may learn a trade, and may be maintained by the advantage arising from it. Then, when he is skilled in the management of it, he may thereby be enabled to buy himself the tools of his trade, so he may no longer burden any of the brethren, or their sincere love to him, but may support himself. For certainly he is a happy man who is able to support himself, and does not take up the place of the orphan, the stranger, and the widow.

Finally, the regulations instruct the faithful to receive those who are persecuted for their faith. By offering hospitality in the form of sanctuary to these refugees, one participates in their persecution and blessing.

Book 5.1. On Those That Are Persecuted

Receive also those that are persecuted on account of the faith, and who "fly from city to city" on account of the Lord's commandment; and assist them as martyrs, rejoicing that you are made partakers of their persecution, as knowing that they are esteemed blessed by the Lord .

Basil, *The Long Rules*

These rules were written for the benefit of monastic communities of the fourth century. Monasteries in particular were likely places of lodging for travelers and guests. The tradition of monastic hospitality was strong, so much so that Basil (330–379) needed to warn against extravagance. Hospitality is not measured by excess nor should monks think they must keep a guest in the manner to which he or she is accustomed. Rather, hospitality lies in giving to each according to need and sharing one's home authentically not pretentiously. An exception to regular fare may be made for relief of the sick as long as it does not create a disturbance.

. . . we should choose whatever is easy to obtain in each region, cheap, and available for general consumption, and use only those imported foods that are necessary to sustain life, like olive oil and similar products. In addition, if something would be useful for the necessary relief of the sick, this, too, is permitted, if it can be procured without difficulty, disturbance, or distraction.

Q. 20. The rule to be followed in serving meals to guests.
R. Vainglory, the desire to please men, and acting for display are strictly forbidden to Christians under all circumstances, because even a man who observes the precept but does it for the purpose of being seen and glorified by men loses the reward for that observance. All manner of vainglory, consequently, is especially to be avoided by those who have embraced every kind of humiliation for the sake of the Lord's command. But, inasmuch as we see men of the world ashamed of the lowliness of poverty and at pains when they entertain guests to have every article of food both abundant and expensive, I fear that, unwittingly, we are being infected by the same vice and that we are ashamed to be found guilty of the poverty called blessed by Christ. Just as it is not proper to provide ourselves with worldly trappings like a silver vessel, or a curtain edged with purple, or a downy couch, or transparent draperies, so we act unfittingly in contriving menus which deviate in any important way

from our usual diet. That we should run about searching for any-thing not demanded by real necessity, but calculated to provide a wretched delight and ruinous vainglory, is not only shameful and out of keeping with our avowed purpose, but it also causes harm of no mean gravity when they who spend their lives in sensual gratifi-cation and measure happiness in terms of pleasure for the appetite see us also taken up with the same preoccupations which keep them enthralled. What, then, have we to do with costly appointments? Has a guest arrived? If he is a brother and follows a way of life aim-ing at the same objective as ours, he will recognize the fare we pro-vide as properly his own. What he has left at home, he will find with us. Suppose he is weary after his journey. We then provide as much extra nourishment as is required to relieve his weariness.

Is it a secular person who has arrived? Let him learn through actual experience whatever things verbal instruction has not con-vinced him of, and let him be given a model and pattern of frugal sufficiency in matters of food. Let memories of Christian fare linger in his mind and of a poverty which, because of Christ, gives no cause for shame.

If you also change your daily fare, then, for rare quality or abun-dance in food to please a brother's palate, you imply that he takes delight in sensual pleasure and you heap reproaches upon him for his gluttony by the very preparations you make, since you thus accuse him of finding pleasure in such things. In fact, have we not often guessed who or what sort of guest was expected, upon seeing the appearance and quality of the preparations? Sufficiency varies, however, according to physical condition and present need. One, because of his work, requires more substantial food and a larger amount. Another needs a lighter and more digestible diet and suited in other ways to his weakness, but for all alike it should be cheap and easily procured. In every case, care must be taken for a good table, yet without overstepping the limits of the actual need. This should be our aim in giving hospitality—that the individual require-ments of our guests may be cared for. The Apostle says: "as if using this world and not misusing it"; unnecessary expenditure, however, is misuse. Have we no money? So be it. Are not our granaries filled? What of it! We live from day to day. Our livelihood is the work of our hands. Why, then, do we waste food given by God for the poor to gratify the voluptuary, sinning thereby in two ways: by intensifying the former the sufferings of their poverty and increasing the harm-ful results of satiety for the latter.

John Cassian, *Institutes of the Coenobia**

John Cassian (360–435) sets out monastic rules of hospitality when visitors arrive. This approach to hospitality instructs the monks to suspend their regular rules of fasting and abstinence in order to care for guests not accustomed to austerity. Focus on the guest.

5.23 On the Spirit of Gluttony

But when any of the brethren arrive they rule that we ought to show the virtues of kindness and charity instead of observing a severe abstinence and our strict daily rule. Nor should we consider what our own wishes and profit or the ardor of our desires may require, but set before us and gladly fulfill whatever the refreshment of the guest, or his weakness may demand from us.

Palladius, *The Lausiac History*

Palladius (ca. 363–425) includes this account of the famous Pachomius who founded the great cenobium at Tabennisi and set out the Pachomian rule for the common life. This account, written ca. 419, attributes Pachomius's teachings to a tablet given by an angel. The rule regarding visiting monks addresses the problem of gyrovagi, *wandering monks who went from monastery to monastery. Pachomius was concerned that hospitality be offered to those truly on a journey. Further, he specifies a three year trial period before receiving a visitor into full investiture of habit.*

32. Pachomius and the Tabennesiotes

1. The so-called Tabennisi is a place in the Thebaid where lived a certain Pachomius, a man of the kind who live rightly, so that he was deemed worthy of prophecies and angelic visions. He became exceedingly kind and brotherly. One time when he was sitting in his cave an angel appeared to him and told him: "So far as you are concerned, you conduct your life perfectly. It is vain for you to continue sitting in your cave! Come now, leave this place and go out and call the young monks together and dwell with them. Rule them by the model which I am now giving you."

And the angel gave him a bronze tablet on which this was engraved: "A strange monk of another monastery may not eat or drink or stay with them unless he is really on a journey. And one who has come to stay they do not receive into the sanctuary for a period of three years. When such a one has performed the more laborious works, however, he is received, but only after a three-year period."

Sozomen, Ecclesiastical History

Sozomen (fl. ca. 430), like Palladius above, also reports Pachomius's rule delivered by an angel, a rule that specifies hospitality. Sozomen, a lawyer in Constantinople, wrote his church history in the early fifth century as a continuation of Eusebius's church history to 425.

Pachomius, the founder of the monks called the Tabennesians, flourished at the same place and period. The attire and government of this sect differed in some respects from those of other monks. Its members were, however, devoted to virtue . . . . Pachomius at first practiced philosophy alone in a cave, but then a holy angel appeared to him, and commanded him to call together some young monks and live with them. Because he had succeeded well in pursuing philosophy by himself, he was to train them by the laws which were about to be delivered to him, so that he would benefit many as a leader of communities. A tablet was then given to him, which is still carefully preserved. Upon this tablet were inscribed injunctions by which he was bound to permit every one to eat, to drink, to work, and to fast. . . . They were not to admit strangers to eat with them, with the exception of travelers, to whom they were to show hospitality. Those who desired to live with them, were first to undergo a probation of three years, during which time the most laborious tasks were to be done, and, by this method they could share in their community.

Theodoret of Cyrrhus, The History of the Monks of Syria

In Theodoret's (ca. 393–ca. 466) account of desert monastic life in Syria from the fourth and fifth century we find this delightful story of the wise desert father, Marcianus, who knew that the charity of hospitality sometimes requires the suspending of fasting and austere disciplines. This instructive story may raise the question of whether monastic hospitality was flagging in the face of ascetic excess. Theodoret, like John Cassian, gives Christians an exhortation to hospitality in this story.

III. Marcianus

12. I wish to add to this another story to make known his divine understanding. A certain Avitus was the first to set up his ascetic

cell in another desert, more northerly than this one and lying a little to the east, under the north wind that is near to the east wind. He was older than Marcianus in both age and labor, a philosopher nurtured in the austere life. Learning that the man's virtue was common talk everywhere and thinking such a sight more advantageous than protracted solitude, he hurried apace to see what he longed for. Learning of his arrival, the great Marcianus opened the door and received him into his presence. He bade the wonderful Eusebius cook pulses and greens if he had any. When they had had their fill of mutual conversation and had learnt of each other's virtue, they performed together the liturgy of the ninth hour; and Eusebius came bearing the table and bringing loaves. The great Marcianus said to the inspired Avitus, "Come over here, my best of friends, and let us share this table." But he said, "I do not know that I have ever taken food before the evening, and I often continue without food for two or three days together." The great Marcianus replied, "Change your habit today, at least for my sake. Being in a weak bodily state I cannot wait till the evening." When these words did not persuade the wondrous Avitus, he is related to have sighed and said, "I am utterly discouraged and cut to the heart at this: after undergoing such labor in order to see a laborious man and philosopher, you have been disappointed of your hope, and have seen instead of a philosopher at tavern-keeper and profligate." This distressed the most divine Avitus, who said that, rather than hear such words, he would be glad to take meat. The great Marcianus continued, "We too, my friend, lead the same life as you and embrace the same profession, honor labors before repose and prefer fasting to nourishment, and take it only after nightfall. But we know that charity is a thing more to be prized than fasting, since the one is a work laid down by divine law, while the other depends on our own authority. It is right to count the divine laws as far more to be prized than our own." After conversing with each other in this way and partaking of slight nourishment, singing hymns to God and spending three days with each other, they parted, seeing each other again only in spirit.

13. Who then would not wonder at this man's wisdom, governed by which he knew the time for fasting and the time for brotherly love, and knew the distinction between the parts of virtue, and which ought to yield to which, and which be given the victory at the proper time?

Julianus Pomerius, *The Contemplative Life*

The balance of spiritual discipline with generous hospitality is echoed in Julianus Pomerius (fl. ca. 500) in his instruction on monastic hospitality penned around 500. Pomerius discusses both the active and contemplative life and the virtues needed for each. Love or charity, a chief characteristic of hospitality, is the primary rule. One can have love without ascetic practice but not ascetic practice without love. Therefore, hospitality may require one to relax the rules, "unbending myself," in order to be in hospitable fellowship.

Chapter 24. It is often beneficial to place hospitality to visitors before fasting or abstinence.

1. We should, however, do our abstaining and fasting in such a manner that we do not put ourselves under the necessity of fasting or abstaining; otherwise, we shall be doing an optional thing under constraint rather than out of piety. If, for instance, interrupting my fast, I give refreshment to some visitors, I do not break my fast, but I fulfill a duty of charity. Again, if by my abstinence I sadden my spiritual brethren, who I know derive enjoyment from my unbending myself, my abstinence should be called not a virtue but a vice because continued abstinence and fasting, unless interrupted when occasion requires, actually makes me vainglorious and saddens my brother, whom charity requires me to serve; and it certainly shows that I have no fraternal charity. For charity alone without abstinence makes any Catholic perfect; and abstinence without the addition of charity either brings about the ruin of all or perishes itself.

John Malalas, *Chronicle*

This remarkable report from the chronicler Malalas (ca. 490–570) of Empress Theodora's intervention in the sale of girls into prostitution signals the desperate situation of many families in the Byzantine empire. The socially and economically vulnerable had few options and were easily exploited by those with means. Theodora goes so far as to outlaw brothelkeeping. While the decree itself does not give evidence of a particular institution associated with hospitality we know from Procopius that she and Justinian built a sanctuary for women sold into prostitution. By Byzantine standards these women were unfit, once abused, for normal domestic life. This law, then, represents a profound act of hospitality by providing protection and shelter to a vulnerable group.

At that time [ca. 532/3] the pious Theodora added the following to her other good works. Those known as brothel-keepers used to go about in every district on the look-out for poor men who had daughters and giving them, it is said, their oath and a few *nomismata*, they used to take the girls as though under a contract; they used to make them into public prostitutes, dressing them up as their wretched lot required and, receiving from them the miserable price of their bodies, they forced them into prostitution. She ordered that all such brothel-keepers should be arrested as a matter of urgency. When they had been brought in with the girls, she ordered each of them to declare on oath what they had paid the girls' parents. They said they had given them five *nomismata* each. When they had all given information on oath, the pious empress returned the money and freed the girls from the yoke of their wretched slavery, ordering that henceforward there should be no brothel-keepers. She presented the girls with a set of clothes and dismissed them with one *nomisma* each.

St. Caesarius of Arles, The Rule for Nuns

Written in 534 this rule for nuns lays out several regulations related to hospitality. The first notes the propriety required when receiving visitors. Other regulations identify under what conditions meals should be served to guests, enjoin sick sisters to comply with the cellarer, and prohibit assiduous begging at the gates.

38. The abbess must take care that she does not go to guests in the reception room without the honor due her, that is, without two or three sisters. Bishops, abbots, or other religious whose position in life recommends them, ought to be allowed to go into the oratory to pray if they should ask. Care must also be taken that the door of the monastery be open to visitors at convenient hours.

39. You shall never provide meals either in the monastery or out of it for these persons, that is: bishops, abbots, monks, clerics, laymen, women in lay attire, nor the relatives of the abbess or of any of the nuns; nor let a repast be made for the bishop of this city, nor even for the provisor himself of the monastery; nor for women religious of the city unless perchance they are of great holiness of life and such as will maintain sufficiently the reputation of the monastery; but let this be done very rarely.

40. If a woman from another city should come to the monastery to see her daughter or to visit the monastery, if she is a religious and it

seems proper to the abbess, she ought to be invited to dinner, but others never at all; because holy virgins dedicated to God ought rather to pray for all people, leaving all for Christ, than to provide feasts for the body. If a man should wish to see his sister, or daughter, or any relative or a sister-in-law, the visit shall not be denied him, provided the novice mistress or one of the elder religious is present.

42. Of this especially I admonish you, and with this I charge you, holy mother, and esteemed prioress whoever you may be, and also you to whom the care for the sick is committed, choir mistress, and also novice mistress, that you see to it with utmost vigilance that, in the case of any of the sisters who, by reason of the fact that they were brought up with more delicate care, or that they perhaps suffer from some stomach trouble, and cannot abstain as the others, and certainly fast with great effort, if on account of diffidence they do not presume to ask, do you order them to be supplied by the cellarers, and do you order that they take what is given them. Let them most surely trust that whatever they should receive by the dispensation and command of an elder religious at any hour whatever, they receive Christ in that refreshment. The cellarer and she who is to serve the sick shall be called to witness, before God and His angels, about their zeal in care and solicitude for the sick.

I warn you of this also, that because of too much disturbance at the entrance to the monastery, there should not be daily and assiduous begging; but what God should give, as it can be set aside from the needs of the monastery, the abbess shall order to be given to the poor through the provisor.

Benedict, *Rule*

Benedict (480–550) sets out that the distribution of goods must take into account the needs of the sick or weak. Community rules regarding the sick or weak are grounded in hospitality. In this way a community deals with its own members hospitably.

Chapter 34. Whether All Should Receive in Equal Measure What Is Necessary

Let us follow the Scripture, "Distribution was made to everyone according as anyone had need." By this we do not mean that there should be respecting of persons (which God forbid), but consideration for infirmities. He who needs less should thank God and not be discontented; but he who needs more should be humbled by the thought of his infirmity rather than feeling important on account of the kindness shown him. Thus all the members will be at peace.

Above all, let not the evil of murmuring appear for any reason whatsoever in the least word or sign. If anyone is caught at it, let him be placed under very severe discipline.

Chapter 36. On the Sick Brethren

Before all things and above all things, care must be taken of the sick, so that they will be served as if they were Christ in person; for He Himself said, "I was sick, and you visited Me," and, "What you did for one of these least ones, you did for Me." But let the sick on their part consider that they are being served for the honor of God, and let them not annoy their brethren who are serving them by their unnecessary demands. Yet they should be patiently borne with, because from such as these is gained a more abundant reward. Therefore the abbot shall take the greatest care that they suffer no neglect.

For these sick brethren let there be assigned a special room and an attendant who is God-fearing, diligent, and solicitous. Let the use of baths be afforded the sick as often as may be expedient; but to the healthy, and especially to the young, let them be granted more rarely. Moreover, let the use of meat be granted to the sick who are very weak, for the restoration of their strength; but when they are convalescent, let all abstain from meat as usual.

The Abbot shall take the greatest care that the sick be not neglected by the cellarer or the attendants; for he also is responsible for what is done wrongly by his disciples.

Chapter 37. Of the Aged and Children

Although human nature itself is drawn to special kindness towards these times of life, that is, towards old men and children, still the authority of the Rule should also provide for them. Let their weakness be always taken into account, and let them by no means be held to the rigor of the Rule with regard to food. On the contrary, let a kind consideration be shown to them, and let them eat before the regular hours.

Eddius Stephanus, *The Life of Bishop Wilfrid*

Bishop Wilfrid was a central figure in seventh century English church history. The conversion of Northumbria to Roman Christianity and his insistence on the church's authority before secular leaders meant a life marked by exile. *In this excerpt from his biography, Wilfrid offers directions at the end of his life for the distribution of his wealth. The division into four parts reflects a pattern in medieval Christianity which usually regulated that one-fourth of an ecclesiastical estate go to the poor and one-fourth to the demands of hospitality within a diocese. Here Wilfrid designates the last fourth for other Christians who had suffered exile. Hospitality to the poor and the exiled, then, appears regularized in Wilfrid's will.*

Chapter LXIII. [708?]

A short time before his ever-memorable and blessed death, he ordered his treasurer to open his treasury at Ripon in the presence of two abbots and some very faithful brethren, eight in number altogether, whom he had invited, and to put out in their sight all the gold, silver and precious stones; and he bade the treasurer divide it into four parts, according to his direction . . . .

Our holy bishop then said to these faithful witnesses: "Dearest brethren, know this thought of mine which I have long since had in mind, that I should again visit the see of the holy Apostle Peter where I have so often been delivered from trouble and should there end my life, God willing. I intended to take with me the best of the four portions of this treasure to offer gifts in the churches of the Saints; to carry presents to the church dedicated to St Mary the Mother of the Lord; and to offer gifts to St Paul the Apostle for the welfare of my soul. But since God has provided for me otherwise, as often happens to old men, and the day of my death has overtaken me, I bid you, my faithful brethren, in the name of Jesus Christ, to send messengers to carry my gifts to the churches I have named. Of the other three parts, divide one among the poor of my people for the redemption of my soul: the second part let the heads of the two oft-mentioned abbeys divide among themselves so that they may be able to purchase the friendship of kings and bishops. The third part you are to share among those who have labored and suffered long exile with me and to whom I have given no lands and estates; distribute it according to the needs of each man so that they may have the means to maintain themselves after I have departed."

Notes

1. For the institutionalization of hospitality see Bernard P. Prusak, "Hospitality Extended or Denied: *Koinonia* Incarnate From Jesus to Augustine," in *The Church as Communion*, ed.

James H. Provost (Washington, D.C.: Canon Law Society of America, 1984), pp. 89-126. He argues that, among other things, the institutionalization of hospitality shifted the emphasis "from a communion of communities to a communion of bishops" (p. 90).

2. For more on the house church see Carolyn Osiek and David L. Balch, *Families in the New Testament World: Households and House Churches* (Louisville: Westminster John Knox Press, 1997); Vincent P. Branick, *The House Church in the Writings of Paul* (Wilmington, Delaware: M. Glazier, 1989); John Koenig, *New Testament Hospitality: Partnership with Strangers as Mission and Promise* (Philadelphia: Fortress Press, 1985), pp. 61-66; Elizabeth Schussler Fiorenza, *In Memory of Her: A Feminist Theological Reconstruction of Christian Origins* (New York: Crossroad, 1983); Robert Banks, *Paul's Idea of Community* rev. ed. (Peabody, Mass.: Hendrickson Publishers, 1994); Hans-Josef Klauck, *Hausgemeinde und Hauskirche im frühen Christentum* (Stuttgart, Germany: Verlag Katholisches Bibelwerk 1981); Lloyd Michael White, "Domus Ecclesaie: Domus Dei" (Ph.D. Dissertation, Yale University, 1982).

3. For a discussion of charitable institutions in the Byzantine Empire and the terminology used, see J. P. Thomas, *Private Religious Foundations in the Byzantine Empire* (Washington, D.C,: Dumbarton Oaks, 1987); Demetrios J. Constantelos, *Byzantine Philanthropy and Social Welfare* (New Brunswick: Rutgers University Press, 1968); Frances Niederer, "Early Medieval Charity," *Church History* 21 (1952), pp. 285-95; A. R. Hands, *Charities and Social Aid in Greece and Rome* (Ithaca, N.Y.: Cornell University Press, 1968).

4. Procopius, *The Buildings of Justinian,* I. xi. trans. Aubrey Stewart, The Library of the Palestine Pilgrims' Text Society. Vol. II (London: 1896), pp. 39-40.

5. On the history of medicine and the rise of hospitals in the ancient world see Timothy S. Miller, *The Birth of the Hospital in the Byzantine Empire* (Baltimore: Johns Hopkins University Press, 1985); Demetrios Constantelos, *Byzantine Philanthropy and Social Welfare* (New Brunswick: Rutgers University Press, 1968); Peter Van Minnen, "Medical Care in Late Antiquity" *Clio Medica,* Vol. 1: *Ancient Medicine in Its Socio-Cultural Context* ed. by Ph.J. van der Eijk, H. F. J. Horstmanshoff, P.H. Schrijvers (Amsterdam, Atlanta: Rodopi, 1995), pp. 153-69; Lindsay Granshaw and Roy Porter, *The Hospital in History* (London and New York: Routledge, 1989); Ralph Jackson, *Doctors and Diseases in the Roman Empire* (Norman: University of Oklahoma Press, 1988); J. Longrigg, *Greek Rational Medicine: Philosophy and Medicine from Alcmaeon to the Alexandrians* (London: Routledge, 1993); Vivian Nutton, "Healers in the Medical Market Place: Towards a Social History of Graeco-Roman Medicine," in *Medicine in Society: Historical Essays,* ed. Andrew Wear (Cambridge: Cambridge University Press, 1992), pp. 15-58; Timothy Miller, "Byzantine Hospitals," *Dumbarton Oaks Papers* 38 (1984), pp. 53-63; Nigel Allan, "Hospice to Hospital in the Near East: An Instance of Continuity and Change in Late Antiquity," *Bulletin of the History of Medicine* 64 (1990), no. 3:446-62; W. Schubart, "Parabalani," *Journal of Egyptian Archaeology* 40 (1954), 97-101; Peregrine Horden, "Saint and Doctors in the Early Byzantine Empire: The Case of Theodore of Sykeon," *The Church and Healing,* ed. W. J. Sheils (Oxford, Basil Blackwell, 1982), pp. 1-13; Guido Manjo, *The Healing Hand: Man and Wound in the Ancient World* (Cambridge, Mass.: Harvard University Press, 1975).

6. Constantelos, p. 153. Many historians note the overlap of functions as well as the overlap of the terms *xenones* and *xenodocheia.* See Allen, pp. 447-48.

7. See Eric P. Wheeler, *Dorotheos of Gaza: Discourses and Sayings* (Kalamazoo, Mich.: Cistercian Publications, 1977), p. 60; Cf. Yizhar Hirschfeld, *The Judean Desert Monasteries in the Byzantine Period* (New Haven: Yale University Press, 1992); Peregrine Horden, "The Death of Ascetics: Sickness and Monasticism in the Early Byzantine Middle East," in *Monks, Hermit and the Ascetic Tradition: Papers Read at the 1984 and 1985 Meetings of the Ecclesiastical History Society,* ed. W. J. Sheils (Oxford: Basil Blackwell, 1985), pp. 41-52; Philip Rousseau, *Pachomius: The Making of a Community in Fourth Century Egypt* (Berkeley: University of California Press, 1990).

8. Ibid., Price, p. 87.

9. While Christians journeyed to Jerusalem in the second and third centuries, it was Constantine's mother, Empress Helena, who began the popularization of pilgrimage in the early 300s with her purported discovery of several sacred sites, including the cross on which

Jesus was crucified. See Jan Willem Drijvers, *Helena Augusta: The Mother of Constantine the Great and the Legend of her Finding of the True Cross* (Leiden: E. J. Brill, 1992); John Wilkinson, "Jewish Holy Places and the Origins of Christian Pilgrimage," in *The Blessings of Pilgrimage*, ed. Richard Ousterhout, (Chicago: University of Illinois Press, 1990), pp. 41-53; John Wilkinson, "Christian Pilgrims in Jerusalem during the Byzantine Period," *Palestine Exploration Quarterly* 108 (1976), pp. 75-101; E. D. Hunt, *Holy Land Pilgrimage in the Later Roman Empire A. D. 312–460* (Oxford: Clarendon Press, 1982); Matthew Dillon, *Pilgrims and Pilgrimage in Ancient Greece* (London: Routledge, 1997).

10. See John Philip Thomas, "The Regulation of Private Religious Foundations under Justinian and His Immediate Predecessors," chapter 2 of *Private Religious Foundations in the Byzantine Empire* (Washington, D.C.: Dumbarton Oaks Research Library and Collection, 1987), pp. 37-58; Constantelos, pp. 216-21.

11. Existing legislation which was reaffirmed by emperors in the ninth century required: "The *oeconomoi* and *xenodochoi*, the *nosocomoi* and *ptochotrophoi*, and the administrators of all other philanthropic houses and besides, all clergymen whatsoever shall be responsible to their bishop to whose jurisdiction they belong and to whom their administration is entrusted." *Epanagoge*, Title Nine, paragraph 19 quoted in Demetrios J. Constantelos, *Byzantine Philanthropy and Social Welfare* (New Brunswick: Rutgers University Press, 1968), p. 218. However, not all philanthropic office holders were clergy. Egypt in particular had a tradition of lay administrators. See Thomas, pp. 63-69.

12. Ibid., Colgrave, *Life of Cuthbert*, p. 317.

13. For description of offices within monasticism see John Ryan, *Irish Monasticism: Origins and Early Development* (1931; reprint Dublin: Irish Academic Press, 1986), pp. 274-75; Yizhar Hirschfeld, *The Judean Desert Monasteries in the Byzantine Period* (New Haven: Yale University Press, 1992), p. 74.; C. H. Lawrence, *Medieval Monasticism: Forms of Religious Life in Western Europe in the Middle Ages,* 2nd ed. (New York: Longman, 1984).

Bibliography

Ambrose. *Selected Works and Letters.* Translated by the Rev. H. De Romestin, the Rev. E. De Romestin and the Rev. H. T. F. Duckworth. *Nicene and Post-Nicene Fathers of the Christian Church.* Edited by Philip Schaff and Henry Wace. 2nd ser. New York: Christian Literature Company, 1893, X:15, 59, 60.

Antoninus Martyr. "Pilgrim Account." In *Of the Holy Places Visited by Antoninus Martyr*, translated by Aubrey Stewart. *The Library of the Palestine Pilgrims' Text Society.* London: Committee of the Palestine Exploration Fund, 1896, II:6-9, 19-22.

Apostolic Constitutions. Ante-Nicene Fathers: The Writings of the Fathers Down to A. D. 325. Edited by Alexander Roberts and James Donaldson. New York: The Christian Literature Company, 1889, VII:414, 427, 433.

Basil. "Letter 94." In *Letters and Select Works*, translated by the Rev. Blomfield Jackson. *Nicene and Post-Nicene Fathers of the Christian Church.* Edited by Philip Schaff and Henry Wace. 2nd ser. New York: The Christian Literature Company, 1895, VIII:179-80.

_____. "Letter 142." In *Letters and Select Works*, translated by the Rev. Blomfield Jackson. *Nicene and Post-Nicene Fathers of the Christian Church.* Edited by Philip Schaff and Henry Wace. 2nd ser. New York: The Christian Literature Company, 1895, VIII:205.

_____. *The Long Rules.* Translated by Sister M. Monica Wagner. The Fathers of the Church. Volume 9. Reprint by Daughters of St. Paul. Boston, Massachusetts, 1963, I:62-66.

Bede. "The Life of St. Cuthbert." In *Two Lives of Saint Cuthbert: A Life by an Anonymous Monk of Lindisfarne and Bede's Prose Life*, translated by Bertram Colgrave. New York: Greenwood Press, 1969, 77-79.

Benedict of Nursia. *The Rule of Saint Benedict.* Translated by Leonard J. Doyle. Collegeville, Minn: Liturgical Press, 1948, 48-50, 52-5, 77-78, 94-5.

Boniface. *The Correspondence of St. Boniface.* In *The Anglo-Saxon Missionaries in Germany*, edited and translated by C. H. Talbot. New York: Sheed and Ward, 1954, 72-73.

Caesarius of Arles. *The Rule for Nuns of St. Caesarius of Arles*. Translated by Sr. Maria Caritas McCarthy. Washington, D.C., Catholic University of America Press, 1960, 180-81, 183-84.

Canons of Chalcedon (451). Edited by Henry R. Percival. *Nicene and Post-Nicene Fathers of the Christian Church*. Edited by Philip Schaff and Henry Wace. 2nd ser. New York: The Christian Literature Company, 1899, XIV:273, 275.

Cyril of Scythopolis. *Lives of the Monks of Palestine*. Translated by R. M. Price. Kalamazoo, Michigan: Cistercian Publications, 1991, 18-19, 140, 225.

Dorotheos of Gaza. *Discourses and Sayings*. Translated by Eric P. Wheeler. Kalamazoo, Michigan: Cistercian Publications, 1977, 241-42.

Eddius Stephanus. *The Life of Bishop Wilfrid by Eddius Stephanus*. Translated by Bertram Colgrave. New York: Cambridge University Press, 1985, 137.

Epiphanius, Bishop of Salamis. *The Panarion of St. Epiphanius: Selected Passages*. Translated by Philip R. Amidon. New York: Oxford University Press, 1990, 326.

Gregory of Nazianzus. "Oration 43." In *Select Orations*, translated by Charles Gordon Browne and James Edward Swallow. *Nicene and Post-Nicene Fathers of the Christian Church*. Edited by Philip Schaff and Henry Wace. 2nd ser. New York: The Christian Literature Company, 1894, VII:416.

Gregory the Great. "Epistles 1 and 2." In *Pastoral Rule and Selected Epistles*, translated with Introduction, Notes, and Indices by the Rev. James Barmby, D.D. *Nicene and Post-Nicene Fathers of the Christian Church*. Edited by Philip Schaff and Henry Wace. 2nd ser. New York: The Christian Literature Company, 1894, XII:88-90, 95, 108.

_____. "Epistle 2." In *Selected Epistles*. XIII:103.

_____. "Epistle 5." XII:174.

_____. "Epistle 6." XIII:93.

_____. "Epistle 11." XIII:74-75.

_____. "Epistle 13." XIII:95.

Hermas. *Shepherd*. Translated by the Rev. F. Crombie. *Ante-Nicene Fathers: The Writings of the Fathers Down to A. D. 325*. Edited by Alexander Roberts and James Donaldson. New York: The Christian Literature Company, 1885, II:52.

Jerome. "Letter 66." In *Principal Works*, translated by W. H. Fremantle. *Nicene and Post-Nicene Fathers of the Christian Church*. Edited by Philip Schaff and Henry Wace. 2nd ser. New York: The Christian Literature Company, 1893, VI:138-40.

John Cassian. *Institutes of the Coenobia*. Translated by the Rev. Edgar C. S. Gibson. *Nicene and Post-Nicene Fathers of the Christian Church*. Edited by Philip Schaff and Henry Wace. 2nd ser. New York: The Christian Literature Company, 1894, XI:242.

John Chrysostom. "Homily 85 on the Gospel of Matthew." In *Homilies on Matthew*, translated by the Rev. George Provost. *Nicene and Post-Nicene Fathers of the Christian Church*. 1st ser. New York: The Christian Literature Company, 1888, X:510.

_____. *Treatise Concerning Priesthood*. Translated by the Rev. W. R. W. Stephens. *Nicene and Post-Nicene Fathers of the Christian Church*. 1st ser. New York: The Christian Literature Company, 1889, IX:55-56.

John Moschos. *Spiritual Meadow*. Translated by John Wortley. Kalamazoo, Michigan: Cistercian Publications, 1992, 85, 155-56.

Joshua the Stylite. *The Chronicle of Joshua the Stylite*. Translated by W. Wright. Cambridge: University Press, 1882, 32-34.

Julianus Pomerius. *The Contemplative Life*. Translated by Sr. Mary Josephine Suelzer. *Ancient Christian Writers: The Works of the Fathers in Translation*. Edited by Johannes Quasten and Joseph C. Plumpe, no. 4. New York: Newman Press, 1947, 76, 98.

Justin Martyr. *First Apology*. Translated by Alexander Roberts and James Donaldson. *Ante-Nicene Fathers: The Writings of the Fathers Down to A. D. 325*. Edited by Alexander Roberts and James Donaldson. New York: The Christian Literature Company, 1885, I:185-86.

Leontius. *St. John the Almsgiver*. In *Three Byzantine Saints*, edited by Elizabeth Dawes and Norman H. Baynes. Oxford: Blackwell, 1948, 202-3, 214, 237, 256-57.

The Lives of the Desert Fathers: The Historia Monachorum in Aegypto. Translated by Norman Russell. Kalamazoo, Michigan: Cistercian Publications, 1980, 101.

Malalas, John. *The Chronicle of John Malalas.* Translated by Elizabeth Jeffreys, Michael Jeffreys and Roger Scott. Melbourne: Australian Association for Byzantine Studies, University of Sydney, 1986, 249, 255-56.

Palladius. *Dialogue on the Life of St. John Chrysostom.* Translated by Robert T. Meyer. *Ancient Christian Writers: The Works of the Fathers in Translation.* Edited by Johannes Quasten, Walter J. Burghardt and Thomas Comerford Lawler, no. 45. New York: Newman Press, 1985, 39, 75-77.

_____. *Palladius: The Lausiac History.* Translated by Robert T. Meyer. *Ancient Christian Writers: The Works of the Fathers in Translation.* Edited by Johannes Quasten, Walter J. Burghardt and Thomas Comerford Lawler, no. 34. New York: Newman Press, 1964, 38-39, 92-93, 116-117, 148-149.

Polycarp. *Epistle to the Philippians.* Translated by Alexander Roberts and James Donaldson. *Ante-Nicene Fathers: The Writings of the Fathers Down to A.D. 325.* Edited by Alexander Roberts and James Donaldson. New York: The Christian Literature Company, 1885, I:34.

Procopius. *Buildings of Justinian.* Translated by Aubrey Stewart. *The Library of the Palestine Pilgrims' Text Society.* London: Committee of the Palestine Exploration Fund, 1897, II:14-15, 31-33, 39-40, 70-71, 138, 142-43, 148-50.

"Radegund, Queen of the Franks and Abbess of Poitiers (ca. 525–87)." In *Sainted Women of the Dark Ages*, translated by JoAnn McNamara and John Halborg. Durham: Duke University Press, 1992, 72.

Sozomen. *Ecclesiastical History.* Translated by Chester D. Hartranft. *Nicene and Post-Nicene Fathers of the Christian Church.* Edited by Philip Schaff and Henry Wace. 2nd ser. New York: The Christian Literature Company, 1890, II: 291-92, 337-38.

Theodoret of Cyrrhus. *A History of the Monks of Syria.* Translated by R. M. Price. Kalamazoo: Cistercian Publications, 1985, 42-43.

Theophanes Confessor. *The Chronicle of Theophanes Confessor: Byzantine and Near Eastern History A.D. 284–813.* Translated by Cyril Mango and Roger Scott. Oxford: Clarendon Press, 1997, 164, 250, 279, 353, 361, 372.

Visigothic Code. Translated by S. P. Scott. Boston: The Boston Book Company, 1910, 147-48.

CHAPTER SEVEN

THE COMMUNION OF SAINTS: MODELS OF HOSPITALITY

This chapter comprises excerpts from texts that offer models of hospitality. It may be that the best way to convey the place of hospitality in early Christianity isn't to talk *about* it, but to tell stories of its practice. There are easily as many narratives of hospitality as there are expositions, if not more. That's why the previous chapters of this book are full of stories of early Christian practice of hospitality. It is in the actual stories of actual people and the creative ways they sought to be hospitable that the riches of the tradition come through.

One way we form identity and community is by telling family stories. If you grew up going to family reunions you know how much the stories told there year after year formed you as a child, your idea of yourself and your clan, and your sense of the possibilities for your life. In the Christian family, we tell stories, too, and much to the same purpose. The stories of the Christian family tell something not only about who we've been, but also about who we long to be. They offer a vision of a life of grace and love that we can live into. They testify mightily to the power and spaciousness of God's grace to transform lives. They hold us accountable to a tradition that claims us and puts claims on us to be faithful. So, stories about hospitality that lift up individuals as models are not just about those saints and heroes. They are stories about God, and they are stories about us.

Some people are cited again and again as models of hospitality, most notably Abraham under the oaks of Mamre. Others we find sprinkled here and there, such as Rahab and the widow of Zeraphath. Still others are seldom told at all, such as the holy man of Edessa, whose amazing hospitality to strangers ensured that Syrian Christianity would never look at strangers the same way again. And then there is the stork, a model of hospitality from the animal world.

It helps to have a concrete picture of the practice of a virtue. Below are excerpts from texts that offer models.

Clement of Rome, *First Letter to the Church at Corinth**

This is the earliest Christian document we possess outside of the New Testament. Written around 96 C.E. from the church at Rome to the church at Corinth, early on this anonymous letter was attributed to Clement (fl. ca. 96), bishop of Rome at the turn of the first century. In this portion, the letter praises the virtue of hospitality, offering Abraham, Lot, and Rahab as models.

And again [Scripture] says, "God led Abram out, and said unto him, 'Look up now to heaven, and count the stars if you can even number them. So many will your seed be.' And Abram believed God, and it was counted to him for righteousness." On account of his faith and hospitality, a son was given him in his old age, and to show obedience, he offered him as a sacrifice to God on one of the mountains which He showed him.

On account of his hospitality and godliness, Lot was saved out of Sodom when all the country round was punished by means of fire and brimstone.

On account of her faith and hospitality, Rahab the harlot was saved. For when spies were sent by Joshua, the son of Nun, to Jericho, the king of the country found out that they had come to spy on their land. He sent men to seize them, in order that, when taken, they might be put to death. But the hospitable Rahab took them in and concealed them on the roof of her house under some stalks of flax. So when the king's men arrived and said "Some men who are spying on our land came in here. On the king's command, bring them out," she answered them, "The two men you're looking for came to me, but quickly left again and are gone." She did not give away the spies to them. Then she said to the men, "I know for certain that the Lord your God has given you this city, for the fear and dread of you have fallen on its inhabitants. When you do take it, keep me and my family in safety." And they said to her, "It shall be just as you have spoken to us. As soon as you know that we are coming, gather all your family under your roof, and they shall be saved. Anyone found outside of the house will perish." Moreover, they gave her a sign that she should hang scarlet fabric from her house. This symbol showed that redemption would come through the blood of the Lord to all who believe and hope in God. You see, beloved, that there was not only faith, but prophecy, in this woman.

Basil, Homily 8 on Genesis*

Basil of Caesarea (ca. 330–379) wrote nine sermons on the creation stories in the opening chapters of Genesis. Here he considers the creation of birds and their virtues. Both storks and crows offer models because of their solidarity and the hospitality they offer the aged and injured among their own ranks. Basil describes how storks help their aged parents, snuggling close to keep them warm and using their own wings to help them fly.

The conduct of storks comes very near intelligent reason. In these regions the same season sees them all migrate. They all start at one given signal. And it seems to me that our crows, serving them as escort, go to bring them back, and to help them against the attacks of hostile birds. The proof is that in this season not a single crow appears, and that they return with wounds, evident marks of the help and of the assistance that they have lent. Who has explained to them the laws of hospitality? Who has threatened them with the penalties of desertion? For not one is missing from the company. Listen, all you with inhospitable hearts, you who shut your doors, whose house is never open either in the winter or in the night to travelers. The tender care of storks for their old would be enough to make our children love their parents, if they would just reflect upon it. There is no one so failing in common sense as not to think that it's a shame to be surpassed in virtue by birds devoid of reason. The storks surround their father, when old age makes his feathers drop off, warm him with their wings, and provide abundantly for his support. Even in their flight they help him as much as they can, raising him gently on each side upon their wings, a conduct so notorious that it has given to gratitude the name of "antipelargosis."

Gregory of Nyssa, Homily: As You Did It to One of These, You Did It to Me

Gregory of Nyssa (ca. 330–395), younger brother to Bail, was a great preacher and theologian of the fourth century. Well known for his defense of the Nicean faith, he also called Christians to a faithful witness to their

faith. Gregory set forth the final judgment as the context for his reflec-
tions on Jesus' commandment to care for "the least of these." After using
the priest and Levite from the parable of the Good Samaritan as negative
examples, Gregory turns to an unlikely source for positive examples. He
offers as models the sick and maimed themselves. They offer hospitality to
one another. Those most afflicted become those most merciful.

What a dreadful fate! Neither flowing streams nor rivers can wash
away the defilement of their illness. If dogs greedy for blood lick up
water, beasts do not consider this revolting. If a sick person
approaches water, men immediately want no share of it. They speak
of such incidents in detail and deplore them while the wretched
throw themselves at the feet of other persons out of necessity
because they have become suppliants to everyone they encounter.
Often this depressing sight has saddened me; I despair at their condition and their memory troubles me. I have seen their pitiful
dilemma, a sight which moves me to tears. They resemble dead men
by the wayside; rather, they are no longer men but are left in this
wretched condition because they have lost recognizable characteristics. They hate themselves, curse the day of their birth, and despise
that day on which their lives began. They are ashamed of calling
themselves human and thus do not insult [human] nature; they
always live in misery and send up a continuous lament. When looking at themselves, they always have an occasion for sorrow; they are
at a loss, rather, they think that they no longer have bodies because
sickness, the only thing left to them, wastes them away. Such unfortunate persons consider these afflictions and do not have the
strength to see because their vision is impaired. They seek to
describe their condition and cannot because disease hinders their
ability to speak. They wish to eat food and cannot because their
mouths have ulcers. Unfortunately, they lack sensation like the dead
because their senses have been destroyed. How do such persons see,
smell, or touch? What about the other senses which gradually lose
their power or become completely corrupt? In all these conditions
they wander like animals and exchange their [human] nature in
search for verdant pasture. They endure hazards to obtain food by
barter and show their distress to everyone through supplication.
Affliction leads them, and they sustain each other in difficulty. Each
person supports the other by using their limbs for those more unfortunate. This does not apply for just one individual, but all wisely
employ hardship as anyone can see when they are gathered

together. Each one shows mercy and demonstrates sympathy. Their distress in an occasion for assistance which they reveal by mutual service. One person has mutilated hands, another has a swollen stomach, while yet another's face is mutilated; still another person has a withered limb. Anyone with such a deprivation exhibits severe disability.

Gregory of Nyssa, *On the Making of Man**

Here Gregory reflects on why humans were the last of creation to be made. His argument is that God, the model host, wanted to have every-thing prepared for humanity, the guest. The model host, then, is God, who thought of everything in creation of the world and only desires that we take enjoyment in the banquet prepared.

2. Why Humans Appeared Last, After Creation

For not as yet had that great and precious thing, humanity, come into the world of being. It was not to be expected that the ruler should appear before the subjects of his rule. But once the dominion was prepared, the next step was that the ruler should be manifested. When, then, the Maker of all had prepared beforehand, as it were, a royal lodging for the future king (meaning the land, islands, sea, and the heaven arching like a roof over them), and when all kinds of wealth had been stored in this palace (and by wealth I mean the whole creation, all that is in plants and trees, and all that has sense, and breath, and life; and—if we are to account materials also as wealth—all that for their beauty are reckoned precious in human terms, as gold and silver, and the substances of your jewels which all delight in—having concealed, I say, abundance of all these also in the bosom of the earth as in a royal treasure-house), he thus mani-fests humans in the world, to be the beholder of some of the won-ders therein, and the Lord of others. By enjoyment humans might have knowledge of the Giver, and by the beauty and majesty of the things seen, might trace out that power of the Maker that is beyond speech and language.

For this reason humanity was brought into the world last after the creation, not being rejected to the last as worthless, but as one whom it behooved to be king over his subjects at his very birth. We all know that a good host does not bring a guest to his house before the prepa-ration of the feast, but, when he has made all due preparation, and decked with their proper adornments his house, his couches, his table, brings his guest home when things suitable for his refreshment are in readiness. In the same manner the rich and generous Host of our nature, when He had decked the habitation with beauties of every kind, and prepared this great and varied banquet, then introduced humans, assigning to them as their task not the acquiring of what was not there, but the enjoyment of the things which were there. For this reason He gives to humanity as foundations the instincts of a twofold organization, blending the Divine with the earthy, that by means of both humans may be naturally and properly disposed to each enjoyment, enjoying God by means of a more divine nature, and the good things of earth by the sense that is akin to them.

*Ambrose, On the Duties of the Clergy**

Ambrose (ca. 339–397), a Roman lawyer and governor who became bishop of Milan, was a renowned preacher in the middle of the fourth century. In this treatise on the duties of the clergy, Ambrose conducts an extended discussion of hospitality and its responsibilities. Again we see Abraham as well as Lot offered as examples of hospitality.

Hospitality also serves to recommend many. For it is a kind of open display of kindly feelings, so that the stranger may not lack hospitality, but be courteously received, and the door may be open to him when he comes. It is especially important in the eyes of the whole world that the stranger should be received with honor, that the spirit of hospitality should not fail at our table. We should meet a guest with ready and free service, and look out for his arrival.

This especially was Abraham's praise, for he watched at the door of his tent, so that no stranger by any chance might slip by. He carefully kept a lookout, so as to meet the stranger, and anticipate him, and ask him not to pass by, saying: "My Lord, if I have found favor in your sight, don't pass by your servant." Therefore, as a reward for his hospitality, he received the gift of posterity

Lot also, his nephew, who was close not only in relationship but also in virtue, on account of his readiness to show hospitality, turned aside the punishment of Sodom from himself and his family. People ought therefore to be hospitable, kind, upright, not wanting whatever belongs to another, willing to give up some of their own rights if assailed, rather than to take away another's. They ought to avoid disputes, to hate quarrels. They ought to restore unity and the grace of quietness.

Ambrose, *Concerning Widows**

Finally, Ambrose turns his attention to the order of widows and finds there a model of hospitality, particularly in the widow of Zarephath who offered hospitality to Elijah (1 Kings 17:1-16).

We are not bound by any prescribed limit of hospitality. Why do you think that what is of this world is private property when we hold this world in common? . . . It is good for us to attend to the principle of hospitality, to be ready to give to strangers, for we, too, are strangers in the world.

But how holy was that widow, who, when pinched by extreme hunger, observed the reverence due to God, and was not using the food for herself alone, but was dividing it with her son, so she might not outlive her dear offspring! Great is the duty of affection, but that of religion brings more return. For just as she should put no one else before her son, so she should put the prophet of God before her son and even before her survival. For she is believed to have given to him not just a little food, but the whole support of her life, who left nothing for herself. She was so hospitable that she gave the whole, so full of faith that she believed at once.

John Chrysostom, *Homily 41 on Genesis*

John Chrysostom (ca. 347–407), patriarch of Constantinople and famous preacher, gave many sermons on the book of Genesis. He returns again and again to Abraham as the model of hospitality. While we might think of Abraham as the father of the covenant, John figures him primarily as one who is obedient in his hospitality. Here Abraham is the "just man" to whom he refers.

He was putting hospitality into practice to such a degree as to be unwilling to entrust to anyone sense in the household the task of attending to guests. Other people, by contrast, in many cases not only do not show such concern but just the opposite, trying to avoid meeting visitors as if they were forced to receive them against their will.

The just man, on the other hand, was not like that: he was sitting at the door of his tent at midday. This, you see, was the great extent of the just man's hospitality and the extraordinary degree of his virtue, the fact that he behaved like this at midday. Very properly, too, since he realized that people obliged to travel are in need of much service at that time particularly, accordingly he chose that time as suitable, seated himself and kept an eye out for passers-by without caring whether they were known to him or not. You see, it is not part of hospitality to worry about such things: friendliness involves sharing one's possessions with all comers. Since he cast a wide net of hospitality, he in turn was judged worthy to welcome the Lord of all with his angels. Hence Paul too said, "Do no neglect hospitality, for through it some people have entertained angels all unawares," referring precisely to the patriarch. Hence Christ too said, "Whoever receives one of the least of these in my name, receives me."

John Chrysostom, Homily 21 on Roman*

Again Chrysostom offers Abraham as an example, emphasizing his willingness to offer hospitality even though he didn't know who the visitors were. In his own day, complains John, people are too hard-hearted and self-satisfied even when they should know the true identity of their guest as Christ. The biblical examples of Abraham, the widow who received Elijah, and the Shunamite, by contrast, are eager to welcome those who pass by.

For he spent the whole day upon it [hospitality], waiting for this welcome prey, and when he saw it, leaped upon it, and ran to meet them, and worshiped upon the ground, and said, "My Lord, if now I have found favor in Your sight, do not pass by Your servant" (Genesis 18:3). Not as we do, if we happen to see a stranger or someone poor, knitting our brows, and not deigning even to speak to them. And if after thousands of entreaties we are softened, and tell our servant to give them a little something, we think we have quite done our duty. But he [Abraham] didn't do that. He assumed the role of a supplicant and a servant, though he did not know who he was going to take under his roof. But we, who have clear information that it is Christ Whom we take in, do not grow gentle even for this. But he both beseeches, and entreats, and falls on his knees to them, yet we insult those that come to us. And he indeed did it all by himself and his wife, whereas we don't do it even through our assistants. But if you have a mind to see the table that he set before them, there too you will see great bounteousness, but the bounteousness came not from excess of wealth, but of the riches of an eager will. Yet weren't there many rich people then? Still none did anything of the kind. How many widows were there in Israel? Yet none showed hospitality to Elijah. How many wealthy people again were there not in Elijah's day? But the Shunamite alone gathered in the fruits of hospitality. Abraham did, also, whom beside his generosity and ready mind it is right to also admire the fact that when he had no knowledge who the visitors were, yet he acted hospitably.

John Chrysostom, Homily 30 on Romans*

Chrysostom here highlights the women of the New Testament who are credited by Paul as key in the establishment of the early church. Commenting here on Acts *as well as* Romans, *Chrysostom cites the hospitality offered by these women who presided over churches in their homes.*

"Unto whom not only I give thanks, but also all the Churches of the Gentiles" (Romans 16:4).

Here he hints at their hospitality, and financial assistance, holding them in admiration because they had both poured forth their blood, and had made their whole property open to all. You see these were noble women, hindered no way by their sex in practicing virtue. And this is as might be expected. "For in Christ Jesus there is neither male nor female" (Galatians 3:28). And what he had said of the former, that he said also of this. For he had also said about her, "she has been a comforter of many, and of myself also." So, too, of this woman "not only I give thanks, but also all the Churches of the Gentiles." Now that he might not seem to be a flatterer, he also adduces a good many more witnesses to these women. Romans 16:5. "Likewise greet the Church that is in their house."

For she had been so estimable as even to make their house a Church, both by making everyone in it believers, and because they opened it to all strangers. For he was not in the habit of calling any houses Churches, except where there was much piety, and much fear of God deeply rooted in them.

John Chrysostom, Homily 34 on 1 Corinthians*

Here Abraham is the model of hospitality because of his understanding of wealth and liberality. Job, too, is set forth as an example of hospitality on this count.

But again the discourse reverts to our former question, namely, "if the rich are no way useful to us, why are they made rich?" What must we answer? That they are not useful who so make themselves rich, whereas those surely who are made rich by God are in the highest degree useful. You can learn this from the very things done by those whom we just now mentioned. So Abraham possessed wealth for all strangers, and for all in need. For he, who on the approach of three men (or so he thought), sacrificed a calf and kneaded three measures of fine flour and did all that while sitting in his door in the heat of the day. Consider with what generosity and readiness he used to spend his resources on all, along with his goods giving also the service of his body, and this at such an advanced age! Being a harbor to strangers, to all who had come to any kind of need, and possessing nothing as his own, not even his son, since at God's command he actually delivered up even him. Along with his son he gave up also himself and all his house, when he hastened to snatch his brother's son out of danger. He did this not for money's sake, but out of mere humanity.

Such also was the blessed Job. "For my door," he says, "was open to every one who came. I was eyes to the blind, and feet to the lame. I was a father to the needy, the stranger hasn't lodged in the street, and the helpless, whatever need they had, were satisfied, neither have I allowed one helpless man to go out of my door empty-handed" (Job 29:15, 31:32). And much more, too, than this, more than we can now recount, he continued to do, spending all his wealth on the needy.

John Chrysostom, *Homily 19 on 2 Corinthians**

In this sermon Chrysostom addresses the question: How much does one truly need? How much is ever enough? In this context, he appeals to the generosity and the hospitality of the widow of Zarephath (1 Kings 17:1-16) as a model of faithfulness over against the miserliness of his own age.

So let us think also about clothing and about the table and about a place to live and about all our other needs. In every thing ask about what is necessary. For what is superfluous is also useless. Once you have practiced living on what is sufficient, then, if you have a mind to imitate that widow, we will lead you on to greater things than these. For you have not yet attained her level if you are still anxious about what is sufficient. For she soared higher even than this. What she truly needed, she gave away, all of it. Will you then still distress yourself about such things that are necessary? Don't you blush to be shown up by a woman, to not only not imitate her, but to be left even far behind her? For she did not say the things we say, "But what will happen to me if I spend all and have to beg from others?" She, in her great generosity, stripped herself of all she had. What shall we say about the widow in the Old Testament in the time of the prophet Elijah? For the risk she ran was not of poverty, but even of death and extinction, and not hers only, but her children's, too. . . . You see the Lord of the prophets asking for help, and yet not even then do you become humane. Instead, even though you have coffers overflowing, you do not share from your overabundance. . . . For how was it she did not say, as it would have been likely that a barbarian woman and a foreigner would have reasoned, "If he were truly a prophet, he would not have begged of me. If he were a friend of God, He would not have neglected him. Is it because of sins the Jews suffer this punishment? But why and from what source does this man suffer?" But she entertained none of these thoughts. She opened her house to him, and before her house, she opened her heart. She set before him all she had, and putting natural instinct aside and disregarding her children, she preferred the stranger to all. Consider then how great a punishment will be laid up for us, if we shall do less and are weaker than a woman, a widow, poor, a foreigner, a barbarian, a mother of children, knowing nothing of these things which we know! . . . For what could be more manly than that woman who both against the tyranny of nature, and against the force of hunger, and against the threat of death, stood nobly fast, and proved stronger than all? Hear at least how Christ proclaims her. For, He says, "there were many widows in the days of Elijah, and to none of them was the prophet sent but to her" (Luke 4:25, 26). Shall I say something great and startling? This woman gave more hospitality than our father Abraham. For she did not "run to get a calf from the herd" as he did (Genesis 18:7), but by only a "handful" (1 Kings 17:12) outstripped all that have been renowned for hospitality. For in this was his excellence that he set himself to perform that service. But hers was in the fact that for the sake of the stranger she spared not even her children, and also that she didn't look for the things to come. But we, though a heaven exists, though a hell is threatened, though (which is greater than all) God has done such great things for us and is made glad and rejoices over such things, sink back lazily. Don't do it, I beg you. Let us "scatter abroad," let us "give to the poor" as we ought to give. For what is much and what little, God defines, not by the measure of what is given, but by the extent of the resources of the one who gives.

Palladius, Dialogue on the Life of St. John Chrysostom

Palladius (363–425) offers Isidore up as a model of the use of the church's resources in the practice of hospitality. This treatise was intended as an apology for John Chrysostom and his fierce controversy with the bishop of Alexandria, Theophilus, who Palladius is at pains to show here in his true colors. With Theophilus the villain and Isidore the hero, the guest-master of the hospice is the winner of resources for poor and widowed women.

Now there was a certain Isidore who had been ordained by the blessed Athanasius the Great who was still alive in this eightieth year of age. (Most of the people at Rome knew him since he came there often on ecclesiastical matters, being the guest-master of the church of Alexandria . . . .)

Now a widow of one of the nobles of the city gave Isidore one thousand gold pieces, and she bound him by oath on the table of the Savior that he would purchase clothes for the poorer women of Alexandria and that he must not share this knowledge with Theophilus lest he take the money and squander it on stones. Now Theophilus like Pharaoh has a mania for stones for building, but the Church does not need them—let that for another time; listen to what I have to say about Isidore. Well, he took the money and spent it on the poor and widowed women, and somehow Theophilus found out. Nothing escapes him, whatever is done or said, as he has everywhere spies and listening-posts—not to call them anything else. He called Isidore in and asked as mercifully as you please if that was true. Isidore confessed and did not deny the account of the whole matter. When he heard this, Theophilus shed his patience, and he who was a moment before most kind and courteous became swollen in body in his anger. His whole appearance changed entirely when he heard this from Isidore. He kept quiet for a short while like a dog that bites you when you least expect it, but after two months he produced a document [charging Isidore] when the clergy were convened.

Palladius, The Lausiac History

Christians have long weighed the relative merits of the active and contemplative life. In this story, two brothers choose different paths, yet each excels in the path chosen. After their deaths, the community tries to determine which lived the better life. Not surprisingly, the virtue of each brother is appreciated. Even an ascetic community of early Christians valued the practical activities of receiving the stranger and feeding the hungry. Both Isaias and Paesius are lifted up as models of perfection.

14. Paesius and Isaias.

1. Also there were Paesius and Isaias, sons of a Spanish merchant. . . . They each had in mind to please God, but by taking different ways of life.

3. Now the one shared everything among the monasteries, churches, and prisons; he learned a trade so that he might provide bread for himself and he spent his time at ascetic practices and prayer. The other, however, made no distribution of his share, but built a monastery for himself and took in a few brethren. Then he took in every poor one as well, setting up three or four tables every Saturday and Sunday. In this way he spent his money.

4. After they both were dead, various pronouncements were made about them as though they had both been perfect. Some preferred one, some the other. Then rivalry developed among the brethren in regard to the eulogies. They went to the blessed Pambo and entrusted the judgment to him, thinking to learn from him which was the better way of life. He told them: "Both were perfect. One showed the work of Abraham; the other, that of Elias."

5. One faction said: "By your feet, we implore you, how can they be equal?" And this group considered the ascetic the greater, and insisted that he did what the Gospel commended, selling all and giving to the poor, and every hour both day and night carried the cross and followed the Savior even in his prayers. But the others argued heatedly, saying that Isaias had shared everything with the needy and even used to sit on the highways and gather together the oppressed. Not only did he relieve his own soul, but many others as well by tending the sick and helping them.

6. Pambo told them: "Again I say to you, they are both equal. I firmly insist to each of you that the one, if he had not lived so ascetically, would not be worthy to be compared with the goodness of the other. As for the other, he refreshed strangers, and thereby himself as well, and even if he appeared to carry the load of toil, he had also it relief thereafter. Wait until I have a revelation from God, and then come back and learn it."

They returned some days later and he told them: "I saw both of them standing in paradise in the presence of God."

Palladius also identifies as a model Melania the Elder (ca. 342–410) and her hospitality.

1. I have told above in an offhand way of the wondrous and holy Melania. Nevertheless I shall weave into this account some remaining features. So much wealth did she spend in holy zeal, consumed in a fire as it were, that not I but those rather who inhabit Persia should give the account. No one failed to benefit by her good works, neither in the east nor in the west, neither in the north nor in the south.

2. For thirty-seven years she practices hospitality; from her own treasury she made donations to churches, monasteries, guests, and prisons. Her own family and son and stewards provided the funds for this. She persisted in her hospitality to such an extent that she had not even a span of earth for herself, nor did she permit yearning for her son to separate her from love toward Christ, although she had but one son.

John Rufus, *The Life of Holy Peter the Iberian*

His biographer tells the story of how Peter (ca. 409–488) and his companion, John, left their Georgian home land and traveled in great danger to Jerusalem. Needing safe hosts, they were providentially led to Melania the Younger (ca. 383–438), from the same Roman Christian family as Melania the Elder, her grandmother. Melania the Younger is recognized as a model of hospitality.

Seeing that they were strangers in the Holy Places, God Himself led them to good hosts, guides and helpers in their holy purpose, namely the blessed Melania, a Roman lady residing there with her husband Pinianus and her mother Albina. Among the senatorial families of Rome, they had occupied the first place, possessing lineage, riches and honor, but since they loved Christ dearly and despised all these things, they had renounced the world and departed to live in prayer at the Holy City. When they had arrived there they built two large monasteries on the Mount of Olives, near the holy church of the Ascension, one for men and one for women, and endowed them for the glory of God.

Life of Fulgentius

Even on his deathbed Fulgentius (ca. 467–532) continued the hospitality to the widow, orphan, and stranger that had marked his life. Though troubled by schism and exile, his life witnessed to the grace of

*hospitality to those most vulnerable. For the author of Fulgentius's life
story, this continuity is a sign of his integrity.*

> But not many days had passed, and behold the good Lord called his
> faithful servant home. Then, ordering silence, he rested a while. A
> little later, continuing his care for the poor, when a sum of money
> was brought from which, as a most faithful steward, he gave to the
> needy each day, he ordered all of it to be given away. He recalled the
> names of each widow, orphan, stranger and all the others in need,
> and with careful reflection determined what should be given to each
> one; having no heirs in this world he left to the poor the heritage of
> his charitable solicitude. Nor did he deprive his clergy of their due
> blessing; mercifully taking into account their poverty, in secret he
> carefully took care of everything in advance. He continued in
> prayer, giving a blessing to all who came in to see him. He remained
> lucid until his final hour.

The Holy Man of Edessa

*This poignant and powerful legend from early Syriac Christianity (ca.
480) tells of a noble young man who sought to live his life in solidarity
with the poor and the stranger. When his bishop, Rabbula (d. 435), dis-
covers his identity and his deep love for strangers, the bishop is transformed and carries on the ministry. This story offers not only a model of
hospitality but also a new way of looking at strangers.*

> We will speak of the life of an extraordinary man—if indeed it be the
> story of a man. We prefer not to term him as such, but rather to call
> him an angel who despised all the pleasures of the world. Here then
> is his story.
>   This man was reared in great wealth. But he himself chose to be at
> enmity with wealth and substituted in its place a love for poverty.
> But this was not ordinary poverty, but one of extreme shame and
> reproach. . . .
>   This then is the blessed's manner of life in Edessa. Every day he
> came regularly to the church and to the *martyrium*, accepting noth-
> ing from anyone. He also did not want to be in need for food during
> the day, so that he might keep his fast until evening. Then when
> evening came, he stood at the door of the church with his hand
> extended and received alms from those entering the church.... In
> the evening when all the poor—of which he was one—slept, he

arose, extending his arms in the form of a cross towards a wall or a column, and prayed. . . . All his days were spent in this way.

[Upon the holy man's death the bishop] immediately decided to go to where they had borne the saint for burial. While they were on the way, behold, they met the porters who interred him, as they were returning from where they had buried the heroic one. "Where have you buried him?" They said: "With the strangers, his companions." Then the bishop and his entourage took the porters with them, so that they might show them the grave. When they arrived at the grave, the bishop ordered that it be reopened. He and his entourage, together with the porters, entered so that they might see the corpse and begin to honor it. They then looked and saw in the place where the holy man had been set only his rags. His body, however, was not there. Astonished, these then searched for the corpse in every grave. They found not it, but only his rags. Amazement and profound apprehension seized them for a long period of time.

When the bishop regained his composure, he said, "Let us pray!" Then after he prayed, the holy Rabbula wept and said, "Henceforth far be it from me, my Lord, that there be any other work for me, but only a diligent care of strangers! For who knows how many others there are similar to this holy man who delight in humility and other works pleasing in themselves to God, but not known to us humans because of their humble nature." From then on, the holy Mar Rabbula engaged in and ordered many things to be done for strangers. He continuously poured out his gifts with tremendous zeal upon the poor and strangers and exhorted others by his word to a love for strangers. He ceased his mighty building projects and turned away from a burdensome care for things that are transitory. He attended only to orphans and widows and was solicitous for the misfortunate and strangers. Likewise he was no longer concerned about and provident for only his city, but also cared responsibly for strangers of remote cities and distant countries by supporting them with his gifts, in order that he might be near to God by his sharing in the beatitude promised to the merciful. This is how the blessed Rabbula began and how he brought to fulfillment his love for strangers.

Anstrude, Life

Anstrude (ca. 645–ca. 708) was a nun and abbess at Laon in the late seventh century. Her hagiographer, like so many of medieval saints, focuses on her good works. Of all her works listed, acts of hospitality feature centrally.

> She proved to be humble and pious to her subjects and hospitable to guests. Her doors were open to the needy and to pilgrims. She took care of those who were confined to prison or held in chains. She was untiring in her mercy for widows and orphans, wards and paupers, expending offerings of food to the hungry, drink to the thirsty, consolation to the bereaved, cheer to the sorrowful, visiting the sick, calming the angry, restoring disputants to peace, and finally burying the dead. And her good works spread her fame among the kings of Francia and the great ones of the land and her name was great with honor for love of God.

Bibliography

Ambrose. "Concerning Widows." In *Selected Works and Letters,* translated by the Rev. H. De Romestin, the Rev. E. De Romestin and the Rev. H. T. F. Duckworth. *Nicene and Post-Nicene Fathers of the Christian Church.* Edited by Philip Schaff and Henry Wace. 2nd ser. New York: Christian Literature Company, 1893, X:391-92.

_____. "On Duties of the Clergy." In *Selected Works and Letters,* translated by the Rev. H. De Romestin, the Rev. E. De Romestin and the Rev. H. T. F. Duckworth. *Nicene and Post-Nicene Fathers of the Christian Church.* Edited by Philip Schaff and Henry Wace. 2nd ser. New York: Christian Literature Company, 1893, X:59-60.

"Anstrude, Abbess of Laon (ca. 645, d. before 709)." In *Sainted Women of the Dark Ages,* translated by JoAnn McNamara and John Halborg. Durham: Duke University Press, 1992, 293.

Basil. "Homily 8 on Genesis." In *Letters and Select Works,* translated by the Rev. Blomfield Jackson. *Nicene and Post-Nicene Fathers of the Christian Church.* Edited by Philip Schaff and Henry Wace. 2nd ser. New York: The Christian Literature Company, 1895, VIII:98.

Clement of Rome. *First Letter to the Church at Corinth.* Translated by Alexander Roberts and James Donaldson. *Ante-Nicene Fathers: The Writings of the Fathers Down to A.D. 325.* Edited by Alexander Roberts and James Donaldson. New York: The Christian Literature Company, 1885, I:7-8.

Fulgentius. "Life of the Blessed Bishop Fulgentius." In *Fulgentius: Selected Works,* translated by Robert B. Eno. *The Fathers of the Church: A New Translation.* Vol. 95. Washington, D.C.: The Catholic University of America Press, 1997, 53-54.

Gregory of Nyssa. "Homily: As You Did It To One of These, You Did It To Me." In *The Collected Works of Gregory of Nyssa,* translated by Richard McCambly. *Gregory of Nyssa Homepage.* bhsu.edu/dsalomon/nyssa/home.html. Greenwich, Conn.: Great American Publishing Society, 1999.

_____. "On the Making of Man." In *Select Writings and Letters,* translated by William Moore and Henry Austin Wilson. *Nicene and Post-Nicene Fathers of the Christian Church.* Edited by Philip Schaff and Henry Wace. 2nd ser. New York: The Christian Literature Company, 1893, V:390.

The Holy Man of Edessa. In *Christianity and the Stranger: Historical Essays,* translated by Frederick G. McLeod, edited by Francis W. Nichols. Atlanta: Scholars Press, 1995, 56-63.

John Chrysostom. "Homily 19 on 2 Corinthians." In *Homilies on 1st and 2nd Corinthians,* translated by the Rev. Hubert Kestell Cornish, the Rev. John Medley, and the Rev. J. Ashworth. *Nicene and Post-Nicene Fathers of the Christian Church.* 1st ser. New York: The Christian Literature Company, 1889, XII:370-71.

_____. "Homily 21 on Romans." In *Homilies on Acts of the Apostles and the Epistle to the Romans*, translated by the Rev. J. Walker and the Rev. J. Sheppard. *Nicene and Post-Nicene Fathers of the Christian Church*. 1st ser. New York: The Christian Literature Company, 1889, XI: 504.

_____. "Homily 41 on Genesis." In *Homilies on Genesis: Saint John Chrysostom*, Volume 2:18-45, translated by Robert C. Hill. *The Fathers of the Church: A New Translation*. Vol. 82. Washington, D.C.: The Catholic University of America Press, 1988, 406-7.

_____. "Homily 30 on Romans." In *Homilies on Acts of the Apostles and the Epistle to the Romans*, translated by the Rev. J. Walker and the Rev. J. Sheppard. *Nicene and Post-Nicene Fathers of the Christian Church*. 1st ser. New York: The Christian Literature Company, 1889, XI: 550.

_____. "Homily 34 on 1 Corinthians." In *Homilies on 1st and 2nd Corinthians*, translated by the Rev. Hubert Kestell Cornish, the Rev. John Medley, and the Rev. J. Ashworth. *Nicene and Post-Nicene Fathers of the Christian Church*. 1st ser. New York: The Christian Literature Company, 1889, XII:207-8.

Palladius. *Dialogue on the Life of St. John Chrysostom*. Translated by Robert T. Meyer. *Ancient Christian Writers: The Works of the Fathers in Translation*. Edited by Johannes Quasten, Walter J. Burghardt, and Thomas Comerford Lawler, no. 45. New York: Newman Press, 1985, 42.

_____. *Palladius: The Lausiac History*. Translated by Robert T. Meyer. *Ancient Christian Writers: The Works of the Fathers in Translation*. Edited by Johannes Quasten, Walter J. Burghardt, and Thomas Comerford Lawler, no. 34. New York: Newman Press, 1964, 49-51, 124-25, 134.

Rufus, John. *The Life of the Holy Peter the Iberian* in *Lives and Legends of the Georgian Saints*, 2d ed., translated by David Marshall Lang. London: Mowbrays, 1976, 64-65.

APPENDIX

CONVERSATIONS FOR COMMUNITIES

Hospitality as a Means of Grace

It is with gratitude for the insights and questions of our predecessors that we continue the conversation about hospitality with these early Christian texts.[1]

For me, the central insight is that hospitality is a means of grace. It is an avenue, path, or opening to God's grace in the world in which we both receive grace and pass it on to others. Means of grace are often very simple acts: eating together, praying together, listening to God's word, or simply being together in fellowship. Such concrete experiences become doors that open to the grace that infuses the universe. Hospitality is a way of life infused with grace, a participation in the grace of God all around us, not a set of particular actions or behaviors. Hospitality is more à matter of becoming attuned to grace, and participating in its movement, than it is trying to create a particular atmosphere or situation.

Put this way, hospitality can start to sound ethereal and vague. For hospitality is indeed less than discreet deeds and more of an orientation embedded in the Christian life, a way of being in the world that entails acts of welcome and sustenance, yet is more than those particular acts. This way of being includes mercy, justice, and recognition. All of these characteristics speak of communities and individuals with a mature spiritual awareness of God's grace and presence. It may be that the best way to cultivate hospitality is to cultivate a deep awareness of God's grace and the means that open to it. Only out of that awareness and gratitude can hospitality be genuinely practiced.

Hospitality is a rich spiritual resource that Christianity has to offer. As a witness to God's grace and love, hospitality both welcomes and empowers people. Hospitality is a door to a grace-filled life and an expression of it. It is a form of proclamation of the good news of God's love. It dwells at the heart of the gospel, where Jesus feeds and is fed.

For Reflection and Discussion

Thinking of hospitality as a means of grace is one way to begin the conversation with these texts. The questions that follow suggest other entry points. Some focus on the ancient texts themselves, others on our own lives and experiences of hospitality. Pick questions as jumping off points that are the most useful to your group or situation.

Chapter 1: Hospitality and the Early Christian World

1. Describe a time in your life when you experienced hospitality.
2. Can hospitality be viewed in moral terms? Why or why not?
3. How has God offered you hospitality?
4. Does the recovery of hospitality make any difference in your life? In your community's life?

Chapter 2: For You Were Strangers in Egypt

About the texts:

1. Do you agree with Gregory of Nyssa that we must become strangers to the world in order to prepare our souls for God's work?
2. From his Letter 24 to Sulpitus Severus what does Paulinus of Nola seem to value about Christian life?
3. What images of stranger status do you find in these excerpts?
4. What are some discoveries you made reading these excerpts?
5. What excerpts in this chapter reminded you of your own experience of stranger status?

About our lives:

1. If Sulpitius Severus were your friend, what letter would you write to him?
2. In what ways do you experience stranger status as a Christian in this culture?

3. Does thinking about yourself or your religious community as alien make any difference to how you understand yourself as a Christian?
4. How do you think our larger culture views Christians?

Chapter 3: Having Eyes to See

About the texts:

1. Which, if any, of the arguments about seeing the stranger as Christ were convincing to you?
2. What do you think about the claim many of these excerpts make that hospitality to the stranger is hospitality to Christ?
3. What are some discoveries you made reading these excerpts?
4. What excerpts in this chapter reminded you of your own experience of seeing the stranger as Christ?

About our lives:

1. Does knowing strangers help us know Jesus any better? Can you give examples from your own experience?
2. What have guests in your religious community had to say about hospitality? What can you learn from them?
3. When you look at the ongoing life of your own religious community, who is not here? Why?
4. What language or images does your religious community use for practices of hospitality? Are you givers? Hosts? Guests? Stewards?

Chapter 4: And We Shall All Be Changed

About the texts:

1. What motivations for hospitality did you find in these texts? Are these motivations compelling to you?
2. What do you make of the stories of miraculous abundance?
3. How much risk do these texts about hospitality call for?
4. What are some ways early Christians talk about God in these excerpts?
5. What are some discoveries you made reading these excerpts?
6. What excerpts in this chapter reminded you of your own experience of transformation?

About our lives:

1. What gifts of the spirit already exist in your religious community?
2. In what ways might hospitality transform lives in your religious community?
3. What boundaries must your religious community safeguard when practicing hospitality? Are there parts of the common life that cannot be lost in order to gain life?
4. Can you live with the idea that the dynamics of hospitality are not fair, that is, that reciprocity is not proportional? Does that matter to you?
5. In what ways are members of your religious community present to one another? To strangers?
6. What experiences of miraculous abundance can you attest to?
7. Is the practice of hospitality distinctive with the Christian life, that is, does it warrant special tending? Or is the practice of hospitality basically identical with practices of mercy, kindness, and fruits of the spirit?

Chapter 5: Unbending Oneself

About the texts:

1. Which acts of welcome, restoration, dwelling with, and sending forth that you read about in these excerpts would make you feel welcome?
2. Is the rule in the *Didache* too harsh? Why or why not?
3. What do you think of the demand in some texts for material support to strangers and the sick?
4. Dionysius's letter tells the dramatic story of Christians who died caring for the sick. Does this fall within the sphere of hospitality? Did they go too far?
5. What are some discoveries you made reading these excerpts?
6. What excerpts in this chapter reminded you of your own experiences of offering or receiving hospitality?

About our lives:

1. What practices of hospitality fit your religious community? What dangers might be present in hospitable practices?
2. What rules of your religious community might be helpful to

strangers? What rules might have to be suspended for strangers?

3. What rituals do you practice that cultivate a spirit of hospitality in your life or religious community?
4. How much of hospitality is simply a matter of being and how much is a matter of doing?

Chapter 6: Building a Place of Hospitality

About the texts:

1. Do the accounts of buildings, offices, and rules seem to you consistent with the spirit of hospitality?
2. Significant resources of the state were given to these institutions of hospitality. What do you think about that?
3. What are some discoveries you made reading these excerpts?
4. What excerpts in this chapter reminded you of contemporary forms of institutionalized hospitality?

About our lives:

1. Does your religious community put anyone in charge of hospitality? Would that make any difference?
2. Do strangers need special places or people?
3. Do some in your religious community have particular gifts for particular hospitable practices? What are they?

Chapter 7: The Communion of Saints

1. What testimonies can you offer about models of hospitality in your own life or in the life of your religious community?

General Questions About Hospitality

1. Are there resources in these ancient voices for the internal conflicts Christianity faces among divergent perspectives and witnesses? How might hospitality be useful to seeking Christian unity while honoring distinctive witnesses?
2. Are there resources in these ancient voices for contemporary pilgrimage models, such as Cursillo and Walk to Emmaus?
3. Who and where are the vulnerable populations in our society today? What do these early Christian voices have to offer to

those in ministry to such vulnerable groups? What do those in ministry to vulnerable groups have to teach the rest of us about hospitality?

4. Are there people within the secular culture who see themselves as spiritual seekers, but as strangers to Christianity? How might we host and welcome them? Can Christians offer welcome and restoration to the larger, secular culture? In what ways can or can't they?

Note

1. Many recent authors have begun the conversation on hospitality in contemporary Christian life. Most notable among them is Christine D. Pohl, *Making Room: Recovering Hospitality as a Christian Tradition* (Grand Rapids, Michigan: William B. Eerdmans, 1999). For hospitality in congregational life, see James Appleby, "Helping Guests Feel at Home: Five Churches' Bright Ideas for a Warmer Welcome," *Leadership* (Summer 1998), pp. 53-54; Rosemary Luling Haughton, "Sharing the Household of God," *The Other Side* 35, no 1 (1999), pp. 26-30; "Hospitality Houses Care for Inmates' Families," *Family Ministry* 12 (Winter 1998), pp. 59-61; John Perkins, "The Authentic Church," *The Other Side* 29 (1993), pp. 44-47; Christine D. Pohl, "Welcoming the Stranger: What Hospitality Teaches Us About Justice," *Sojourners* 28 (1999), p. 14; Kimberly C Richter, "Protagonist Corner: Welcoming Everyone into the Church Building," *Journal for Preachers* 22, no. 4 (1999), pp. 57-58; Archie Smith, Jr., "Hospitality: A Scriptural Resource for Building Community," *The Journal of the Interdenominational Theological Center* 25 (Spring 1998), pp. 139-51; Edward P. Wimberly, "Methods of Cross-Cultural Pastoral Care: Hospitality and Incarnation," *The Journal of the Interdenominational Theological Center* 25 (Spring 1998), pp. 188-202. For an example of curriculum designed to address hospitality, see Nancy Lanman, "Entertaining Angels Unawares: Where Do Today's Vulnerable People Fit into Jesus' Call for Hospitality? [Heb 13:1-9]," *Christian Social Action* 11 (December 1998), pp. 33-35. For further scholarly treatment of hospitality in contemporary Christian life, see Henri Nouwen, *Reaching Out: The Three Movements of the Spiritual Life* (New York: Image Books, 1975); Thomas W. Ogletree, *Hospitality to the Stranger: Dimensions of Moral Understanding* (Philadelphia: Fortress Press, 1985); Parker Palmer, *The Company of Strangers: Christians and the Renewal of America's Public Life* (New York: Crossroad, 1981).

PRIMARY SOURCES

Alcuin. *The Life of St. Willibrord.* In *The Anglo-Saxon Missionaries in Germany,* edited and translated by C. H. Talbot. New York: Sheed and Ward, 1954.

"Aldegund, Abbess of Maubeuge (d. 684) and Waldetrude, Abbess of Mons (d. ca. 688)." In *Sainted Women of the Dark Ages,* translated by JoAnn McNamara and John Halborg. Durham: Duke University Press, 1992.

Ambrose. *Selected Works and Letters.* Translated by the Rev. H. De Romestin, the Rev. E. De Romestin, and the Rev. H. T. F. Duckworth. *Nicene and Post-Nicene Fathers of the Christian Church.* Edited by Philip Schaff and Henry Wace. 2nd ser., Vol. X. New York: Christian Literature Company, 1893.

"Anstrude, Abbess of Laon (ca. 645, d. before 709)." In *Sainted Women of the Dark Ages,* translated by JoAnn McNamara and John Halborg. Durham: Duke University Press, 1992.

Antoninus Martyr. *Of the Holy Places Visited by Antoninus Martyr.* Translated by Aubrey Stewart. *The Library of the Palestine Pilgrims' Text Society.* Vol. II. London: Committee of the Palestine Exploration Fund, 1897.

Antony of Choziba. *The Life of Saint George of Choziba and the Miracles of the Most Holy Mother of God at Choziba.* Translated by Tim Vivan and Apostolos N. Athanassakis. San Francisco: International Scholars Publications, 1994.

Apostolic Constitutions. Ante-Nicene Fathers: The Writings of the Fathers Down to A.D. 325. Edited by Alexander Roberts and James Donaldson. Vol. VII. New York: The Christian Literature Company, 1889.

Augustine. *Homilies on the Gospels.* Translated by the Rev. R. G. MacMullen. *Nicene and Post-Nicene Fathers of the Christian Church.*

Edited by Philip Schaff. 1st ser., Vol. VI. New York: The Christian Literature Company, 1887.

_____. *Tractates on John.* Translated by the Rev. John Gibb and the Rev. James Innes. *Nicene and Post-Nicene Fathers of the Christian Church.* Edited by Philip Schaff. 1st ser., Vol. VII. New York: The Christian Literature Company, 1888.

"Austreberta, Abbess of Pavilly (650–704)." In *Sainted Women of the Dark Ages,* translated by JoAnn McNamara and John Halborg. Durham: Duke University Press, 1992.

"Balthild, Queen of Neustria (d. ca. 680)." In *Sainted Women of the Dark Ages,* translated by JoAnn McNamara and John Halborg. Durham: Duke University Press, 1992.

Basil the Great. *Letters and Select Works.* Translated by the Rev. Blomfield Jackson. *Nicene and Post-Nicene Fathers of the Christian Church.* Edited by Philip Schaff and Henry Wace. 2nd ser., Vol. VIII. New York: The Christian Literature Company, 1895.

_____. *The Long Rules.* Translated by Sister M. Monica Wagner. *The Fathers of the Church,* Vol. 9. Reprint by Daughters of St. Paul. Boston, Massachusetts, 1963.

_____. *The Liturgy of St. Basil.* Translated by Fayek M. Ishak. Toronto, Canada: Coptic Orthodox Church, 1973.

Bede. *Bede's Ecclesiastical History of the English People.* Translated by Bertram Colgrave and R.A.B. Mynors. Oxford: Clarendon Press, 1969.

_____. *Two Lives of Saint Cuthbert: A Life by an Anonymous Monk of Lindisfarne and Bede's Prose Life.* Translated by Bertram Colgrave. New York: Greenwood Press, 1969.

Benedict of Nursia. *The Rule of Saint Benedict.* Translated by Leonard J. Doyle. Collegeville, Minn: Liturgical Press, 1948.

Bishop Sarapion's Prayer-Book: An Egyptian Sacramentary Date Probably About A.D. 350-356. With introduction, notes, and indices by John Wordsworth. Second edition, revised. London: SPCK, 1923.

Boniface. *The Correspondence of St. Boniface.* In *The Anglo-Saxon Missionaries in Germany,* edited and translated by C.H. Talbot. New York: Sheed and Ward, 1954.

The Book of Pontiffs: The Ancient Biographies. Translated by Raymond Davis. Liverpool: Liverpool University Press, 1989.

Bordeaux Pilgrim. *Itinerary from Bordeaux to Jerusalem*. Translated by Aubrey Stewart. *The Library of the Palestine Pilgrims' Text Society*. Vol. I. London: Committee of the Palestine Exploration Fund, 1897.

Caesarius of Arles. *The Rule for Nuns of St. Caesarius of Arles*. Translated by Sr. Maria Caritas McCarthy. Washington, D.C., Catholic University of America Press, 1960.

Canons of Chalcedon (451). Edited by Henry R. Percival. *Nicene and Post-Nicene Fathers of the Christian Church*. Edited by Philip Schaff and Henry Wace. 2nd ser., Vol. XIV. New York: The Christian Literature Company, 1899.

The Civil Law, Including the Twelve Tables. Translated by S. P. Scott. New York: AMS Press, 1973.

Clement of Alexandria. *Stromata*. *Ante-Nicene Fathers: The Writings of the Fathers Down to A. D. 325*. Edited by Alexander Roberts and James Donaldson. Vol. II. New York: The Christian Literature Company, 1885.

_____. *The Instructor*. *Ante-Nicene Fathers: The Writings of the Fathers Down to A.D. 325*. Edited by Alexander Roberts and James Donaldson. Vol. II. New York: The Christian Literature Company, 1885.

_____. *Who Is the Rich Person that Shall Be Saved?* Translated by the Rev. William Wilson. *Ante-Nicene Fathers: The Writings of the Fathers Down to A.D. 325*. Edited by Alexander Roberts and James Donaldson. Vol. II. New York: The Christian Literature Company, 1885.

Clement of Rome. *First Letter to the Church at Corinth*. Translated by Alexander Roberts and James Donaldson. *Ante-Nicene Fathers: The Writings of the Fathers Down to A. D. 325*. Edited by Alexander Roberts and James Donaldson. Vol. I. New York: The Christian Literature Company, 1885.

Commodianus. *The Instructions of Commodianus in Favor of Christian Discipline, Against the God of the Heathens*. Translated by the Rev. Robert Ernest Wallis. *Ante-Nicene Fathers: The Writings of the Fathers Down to A.D. 325*. Edited by Alexander Roberts and James Donaldson. Vol. IV. New York: The Christian Literature Company, 1885.

Cyprian. *The Letters of St. Cyprian of Carthage*. Translated and annotated by G. W. Clarke. *Ancient Christian Writers: The Works of the Fathers in Translation*, ed. Johannes Quasten, Walter J. Burghardt, Thomas Comerford Lawler, nos. 43-46. New York: Newman Press, 1984–86.

———. *Treatise 8: On Works and Alms*. Translated by the Rev. Ernest Wallis. *Ante-Nicene Fathers: The Writings of the Fathers Down to A. D. 325*. Edited by Alexander Roberts and James Donaldson. Vol. V. New York: The Christian Literature Company, 1884.

Cyril of Scythopolis. *The Life of Saint Saba*. Translated by Aubrey Stewart. *The Library of the Palestine Pilgrims' Text Society*. Vol. XI. London: Committee of the Palestine Exploration Fund, 1895.

———. *Lives of the Monks of Palestine*. Translated by R. M. Price. Kalamazoo, Mich.: Cistercian Publications, 1991.

Didache. Translated by Cyril Richardson. The Library of Christian Classics, Vol. 1. New York: MacMillan Publishing, 1970.

Dionysius. *Epistles*. Translated by the Rev. S. D. F. Salmond. *Ante-Nicene Fathers: The Writings of the Fathers Down to A. D. 325*. Edited by Alexander Roberts and James Donaldson. Vol. VI. New York: The Christian Literature Company, 1885.

Dorotheos of Gaza. *Discourses and Sayings*. Translated by Eric P. Wheeler. Kalamazoo, Mich.: Cistercian Publications, 1977.

The Earliest Life of Gregory the Great, by an Anonymous Monk of Whitby. Translated by Bertram Colgrave. Lawrence, Kan.: University of Kansas, 1968.

Eddius Stephanus. *The Life of Bishop Wilfrid by Eddius Stephanus*. Translated by Bertram Colgrave. New York: Cambridge University Press, 1985.

Egeria. *Travels to the Holy Land*. Translated by John Wilkinson. Rev. ed. Jerusalem: Ariel Publishing House, 1981.

Eigil. *The Life of St. Sturm*. In *The Anglo-Saxon Missionaries in Germany*, edited and translated by C. H. Talbot. New York: Sheed and Ward, 1954.

Epiphanius, Bishop of Salamis. *The Panarion of St. Epiphanius: Selected Passages*. Translated by Philip R. Amidon. New York: Oxford University Press, 1990.

Epistle to Diognetus. Translated by Alexander Roberts and James Donaldson. *Ante-Nicene Fathers: The Writings of the Fathers Down to A. D. 325.* Edited by Alexander Roberts and James Donaldson. Vol. I. New York: The Christian Literature Company, 1884.

Eusebius. *The Oration of the Emperor Constantine.* Translated by Arthur C. McGiffert and Ernest C. Richardson. *Nicene and Post-Nicene Fathers of the Christian Church.* Edited by Philip Schaff and Henry Wace. 2nd ser., Vol. I. New York: The Christian Literature Company, 1890.

"Eustadiola, Widow of Bourges (ca. 594–684)." In *Sainted Women of the Dark Ages*, translated by JoAnn McNamara and John Halborg. Durham: Duke University Press, 1992.

Fulgentius. *Fulgentius: Selected Works.* Translated by Robert B. Eno. *The Fathers of the Church: A New Translation.* Vol. 95. Washington, D.C.: The Catholic University of America Press, 1997.

Gerontius. *The Life of Melania the Younger.* Translated by Elizabeth A. Clark. *Studies in Women and Religion.* Vol. 14. New York: The Edwin Mellen Press, 1984.

"Gertrude, Abbess of Nivelles (628–658)." In *Sainted Women of the Dark Ages*, translated by JoAnn McNamara and John Halborg. Durham: Duke University Press, 1992.

Gregory of Nazianzus. *Select Orations*, translated by Charles Gordon Browne and James Edward Swallow. *Nicene and Post-Nicene Fathers of the Christian Church.* Edited by Philip Schaff and Henry Wace. 2nd ser., Vol. VII. New York: The Christian Literature Company, 1894.

Gregory of Nyssa. *Select Writings and Letters.* Translated by William Moore and Henry Austin Wilson. *Nicene and Post-Nicene Fathers of the Christian Church.* Edited by Philip Schaff and Henry Wace. 2nd ser., Vol. V. New York: The Christian Literature Company, 1893.

_____. *The Collected Works of Gregory of Nyssa.* Translated by Richard McCambly. *Gregory of Nyssa Homepage.* bhsu.edu/dsa-lomon/nyssa/home.html. Greenwich, Conn.: Great American Publishing Society, 1999.

Gregory the Great. *Pastoral Rule and Selected Epistles.* Translated with Introduction, Notes and Indices by the Rev. James Barmby, D.D. *Nicene and Post-Nicene Fathers of the Christian Church.* Edited by Philip Schaff and Henry Wace. 2nd ser., Vol. XII. New York: The Christian Literature Company, 1894.

_____. *Selected Epistles.* Translated with Introduction, Notes and

Indices by the Rev. James Barmby, D.D. *Nicene and Post-Nicene Fathers of the Christian Church.* Edited by Philip Schaff and Henry Wace. 2nd ser., Vol. XIII. New York: The Christian Literature Company, 1898.

Hermas. *Shepherd.* Translated by the Rev. F. Crombie. *Ante-Nicene Fathers: The Writings of the Fathers Down to* A.D. *325.* Edited by Alexander Roberts and James Donaldson. Vol. II. New York: The Christian Literature Company, 1885.

The Holy Man of Edessa. In *Christianity and the Stranger: Historical Essays,* translated by Frederick G. McLeod, edited by Francis W. Nichols. Atlanta: Scholars Press, 1995.

Jerome. *Apology in Answer to Rufinus.* Translated by Ernest Cushman Richardson. *Nicene and Post-Nicene Fathers of the Christian Church.* Edited by Philip Schaff and Henry Wace. 2nd ser., Vol. III. New York: The Christian Literature Company, 1893.

_____. *Principal Works.* Translated by W. H. Fremantle. *Nicene and Post-Nicene Fathers of the Christian Church.* Edited by Philip Schaff and Henry Wace. 2nd ser., Vol. VI. New York: The Christian Literature Company, 1893.

John Cassian. *Institutes of the Coenobia.* Translated by the Rev. Edgar C. S. Gibson. *Nicene and Post-Nicene Fathers of the Christian Church.* Edited by Philip Schaff and Henry Wace. 2nd ser., Vol. XI. New York: The Christian Literature Company, 1894.

John Chrysostom, *Homilies on Acts of the Apostles and the Epistle to the Romans.* Translated by the Rev. J. Walker and the Rev. J. Sheppard. *Nicene and Post-Nicene Fathers of the Christian Church.* 1st ser., Vol. XI. New York: The Christian Literature Company, 1889.

_____. *Homilies on Genesis: Saint John Chrysostom,* Volume 2:18-45. Translated by Robert C. Hill. *The Fathers of the Church: A New Translation.* Vol. 82. Washington, D.C.: The Catholic University of America Press, 1988.

_____. *Homilies on Galatians, Ephesians, Philippians, Colossians, Thessalonians, Timothy, Titus, and Philemon.* Translated by the Rev. James Tweed. *Nicene and Post-Nicene Fathers of the Christian Church.* 1st ser., Vol. XIII. New York: The Christian Literature Company, 1889.

_____. *Homilies on John and Hebrews.* Translated by the Rev. G. T. Stupart. *Nicene and Post-Nicene Fathers of the Christian Church.* 1st ser., Vol. XIV. New York: The Christian Literature Company, 1890.

_____. *Homilies on Matthew*. Translated by the Rev. George Provost. *Nicene and Post-Nicene Fathers of the Christian Church*. 1st ser., Vol. X. New York: The Christian Literature Company, 1888.

_____. *Homilies on 1st and 2nd Corinthians*. Translated by the Rev. Hubert Kestell Cornish, the Rev. John Medley, and the Rev. J. Ashworth. *Nicene and Post-Nicene Fathers of the Christian Church*. 1st ser., Vol. XII. New York: The Christian Literature Company, 1889.

_____. *Treatise Concerning Priesthood*. Translated by the Rev. W. R. W. Stephens. *Nicene and Post-Nicene Fathers of the Christian Church*. 1st ser., Vol. IX. New York: The Christian Literature Company, 1889.

John Moschos. *Spiritual Meadow*. Translated by John Wortley. Kalamazoo, Mich.: Cistercian Publications, 1992.

Joshua the Stylite. *The Chronicle of Joshua the Stylite*. Translated by W. Wright. Cambridge: Cambridge University Press, 1882.

Julianus Pomerius. *The Contemplative Life*. Translated by Sr. Mary Josephine Suelzer. *Ancient Christian Writers: The Works of the Fathers in Translation*. Edited by Johannes Quasten and Joseph C. Plumpe, no. 4. New York: Newman Press, 1947.

Justin Martyr. *First Apology*. Translated by Alexander Roberts and James Donaldson. *Ante-Nicene Fathers: The Writings of the Fathers Down to A.D. 325*. Edited by Alexander Roberts and James Donaldson. Vol. I. New York: The Christian Literature Company, 1885.

Lactantius. *The Divine Institutes*. Translated by the Rev. William Fletcher. *Ante-Nicene Fathers: The Writings of the Fathers Down to A.D. 325*. Edited by Alexander Roberts and James Donaldson. Vol. VII. New York: The Christian Literature Company, 1889.

Leo the Great. *Leo the Great, Letters and Sermons*. Translated with introduction, notes and indices by the Rev. Charles Lett Feltoe, M.A. *Nicene and Post-Nicene Fathers of the Christian Church*. Edited by Philip Schaff and Henry Wace. 2nd ser., Vol. XII. New York: The Christian Literature Company, 1894.

Leontius. *St. John the Almsgiver*. In *Three Byzantine Saints*, edited by Elizabeth Dawes and Norman H. Baynes. Oxford: Blackwell, 1948.

Life of the Blessed Bishop Fulgentius. In *Fulgentius: Selected Works*, translated by Robert B. Eno. *The Fathers of the Church: A New Translation.* Vol. 95. Washington, D. C.: The Catholic University of America Press, 1997.

"The Life of Olympias." In *Jerome, Chrysostom, and Friends: Essays and Translations, t*ranslated by Elizabeth A. Clark. New York: Edwin Mellen Press, 1979.

The Life of St. Andrew the Fool. Edited by Lennart Ryden. *Studia Byzantina Upsaliensia*, 4:1 and 4:2. Acta Universitatis Upsaliensis. Uppsala: Almquist andWiksell, 1995.

The Life of St. Boniface. In *The Anglo-Saxon Missionaries in Germany*, edited and translated by C. H. Talbot. New York: Sheed and Ward, 1954.

The Life of Saint Pachomius and His Disciples. Translated by Armand Veilleus. *Pachomian Koinonia*, Vol. 1. Cisterican Studies Series, no. 45. Kalamazoo, Mich.: Cistercian Publications, 1980.

Lives and Legends of the Georgian Saints. Translated by David Marshall Long. Crestwood, New York: St. Vladimir's Seminary Press, 1976.

The Lives of the Desert Fathers: The Historia Monachorum in Aegypto. Translated by Norman Russell. Kalamazoo, Mich.: Cistercian Publications, 1980.

Macarius. *Intoxicated with God: The Fifty Spiritual Homilies of Macarius.* Translated by George A. Maloney, S.J. Denville, N.J.: Dimension Books, 1978.

Malalas, John. *The Chronicle of John Malalas.* Translated by Elizabeth Jeffreys, Michael Jeffreys and Roger Scott. Melbourne: Australian Association for Byzantine Studies, University of Sydney, 1986.

Matthews, Victor and Don C. Benjamin, eds. *Old Testament Parallels: Laws and Stories from the Ancient Near East.* New York: Paulist Press, 1997.

Maximus the Confessor. *The Ascetic Life and The Four Centuries on Charity.* Translated and annotated by Polycarp Sherwood. *Ancient Christian Writers: The Works of the Fathers in Translation.* Edited by Johannes Quasten and Joseph C. Plumpe, no. 21. New York: Newman Press, 1955.

Maximus of Turin. *The Sermons of St. Maximus of Turin.* Translated by Boniface Ramsey. *Ancient Christian Writers: The Works of the Fathers in Translation.* Edited by Walter J. Burghardt and Thomas

Comerford Lawler, no. 50. New York: Newman Press, 1989.

Palladius. *Dialogue on the Life of St. John Chrysostom.* Translated by Robert T. Meyer. *Ancient Christian Writers: The Works of the Fathers in Translation.* Edited by Johannes Quasten, Walter J. Burghardt, and Thomas Comerford Lawler, no. 45. New York: Newman Press, 1985.

———. *Palladius: The Lausiac History.* Translated by Robert T. Meyer. *Ancient Christian Writers: The Works of the Fathers in Translation.* Edited by Johannes Quasten, Walter J. Burghardt, and Thomas Comerford Lawler, no. 34. New York: Newman Press, 1964.

Patrick. *The Works of St. Patrick.* Translated and annotated by Ludwig Bieler. *Ancient Christian Writers: The Works of the Fathers in Translation.* Edited by Johannes Quasten, Walter J. Burghardt, and Thomas Comerford Lawler, No. 17. New York: Newman Press, 1953.

Paula and Eustochium. *Letter to Marcella About the Holy Places.* Translated by Aubrey Stewart. *The Library of the Palestine Pilgrims' Text Society.* Vol. I. London: Committee of the Palestine Exploration Fund, 1897.

Paulinus of Nola. *Letters of St. Paulinus of Nola.* Translated by P. G. Walsh. *Ancient Christian Writers: The Works of the Fathers in Translation.* Edited by Johannes Quasten, Walter J. Burghardt, and Thomas Comerford Lawler, nos. 35-36. New York: Newman Press, 1967.

Polycarp. *Epistle to the Philippians.* Translated by Alexander Roberts and James Donaldson. *Ante-Nicene Fathers: The Writings of the Fathers Down to A.D. 325.* Edited by Alexander Roberts and James Donaldson. Vol. I. New York: The Christian Literature Company, 1885.

Procopius. *Buildings of Justinian.* Translated by Aubrey Stewart. *The Library of the Palestine Pilgrims' Text Society.* Vol. II. London: Committee of the Palestine Exploration Fund, 1897.

Pseudo-Clementine. *Epistles and Writings.* Translated by the Rev. B. P. Pratten. *Ante-Nicene Fathers: The Writings of the Fathers Down to A.D. 325.* Edited by Alexander Roberts and James Donaldson. Vol. VIII. New York: The Christian Literature Company, 1885.

"Radegund, Queen of the Franks and Abbess of Poitiers (ca. 525–587)."

In *Sainted Women of the Dark Ages*, translated by JoAnn McNamara and John Halborg. Durham: Duke University Press, 1992.

Richardson, Cyril. *Early Christian Fathers*. The Library of Christian Classics, Vol. 1. New York: MacMillan Publishing, 1970.

Rudolph. *The Life of Saint Leoba*. In *The Anglo-Saxon Missionaries in Germany*, translated by C. H. Talbot. New York: Sheed and Ward, 1954.

Rufus, John. *The Life of Holy Peter the Iberian*. In *Lives and Legends of the Georgian Saints*, translated by David Marshall Lang. 2nd ed. London: Mowbrays, 1976.

"Sadalberga, Abbess of Laon (ca. 605–670)." In *Sainted Women of the Dark Ages*, translated by JoAnn McNamara and John Halborg. Durham: Duke University Press, 1992.

Serapion. *Prayer Book*. Translated by John Wordsworth. Rev. ed. London: Society for Promoting Christian Knowledge, 1923.

The Seven Ecumenical Councils of the Undivided Church, Their Canons and Dogmatic Decrees, Together with the Canons of All the Local Synods Which Have Received Ecumenical Acceptance. Edited by Henry Percival, M.A., D.D. *Nicene and Post-Nicene Fathers of the Christian Church*. Edited by Philip Schaff and Henry Wace. 2nd ser., Vol. XIV. New York: The Christian Literature Company, 1896.

Sozomen. *Ecclesiastical History*. Translated by Chester D. Hartranft. *Nicene and Post-Nicene Fathers of the Christian Church*. Edited by Philip Schaff and Henry Wace. 2nd ser., Vol. II. New York: The Christian Literature Company, 1890.

The Statutes of the School of Nisibis. Translated by Arthur Voobus. *Papers of the Estonian Theological Society in Exile*, Vol. 12:15-17. Stockholm: Estonian Theological Society in Exile, 1961.

Sulpitius Severus. *Dialogues of Sulpitius Severus*. Translated by the Rev. Alexander Roberts. *Nicene and Post-Nicene Fathers of the Christian Church*. Edited by Philip Schaff and Henry Wace. 2nd ser., Vol. XI. New York: The Christian Literature Company, 1894.

_____. *The Life of Saint Martin*. Translated by the Rev. Alexander Roberts. *Nicene and Post-Nicene Fathers of the Christian Church*. Edited by Philip Schaff and Henry Wace. 2nd ser., Vol. XI. New York: The Christian Literature Company, 1894.

Tertullian, *To His Wife*. Translated by the Rev. S. Thelwall. *Ante-Nicene Fathers: The Writings of the Fathers Down to A.D. 325*. Edited by Alexander Roberts and James Donaldson. Vol. IV. New York: The Christian Literature Company, 1885.

Theodoret of Cyrrhus. *A History of the Monks of Syria*. Translated by R. M. Price. Kalamazoo, Mich.: Cistercian Publications, 1985.

_____. *Ecclesiastical History*. Translated by the Rev. Blomfield Jackson. *Nicene and Post-Nicene Fathers of the Christian Church*. Edited by Philip Schaff and Henry Wace. 2nd ser., Vol. III. New York: The Christian Literature Company, 1893.

Theophanes Confessor. *The Chronicle of Theophanes Confessor: Byzantine and Near Eastern History A.D. 284–813*. Translated by Cyril Mango and Roger Scott. Oxford: Clarendon Press, 1997.

Visigothic Code. Translated by S. P. Scott. Boston: The Boston Book Company, 1910.

Willibald. *Instructions*. In *The Anglo-Saxon Missionaries in Germany*, translated by C. H. Talbot. New York: Sheed and Ward, 1954.

INDEX OF PRIMARY SOURCES